Industrialisation an

Industrialisation and Society: A social history, 1830–1951 provides an essential introduction to the effects of industrialisation on British society, from Queen Victoria's reign to the birth of the Welfare State in the 1940s.

This book deals with the remarkable social consequences of the Industrial Revolution as Britain changed from an agricultural society to an urban society based on industry. As the first nation to undergo an industrial revolution, Britain was also the first to deal with the unprecedented social problems of rapid urbanisation combined with an unparalleled growth of population.

Industrialisation and Society surveys contemporary ways in which the government and ordinary people tried to cope with these new pressures, including the reflective critical thinking of the age. In particular, this important study considers

- the Victorian inheritance
- mid- and late Victorian social change
- the challenge from the left
- industrial change and the countryside
- Edwardian England and Liberal reforms
- the two world wars and the inter-war years
- the coming of the Welfare State.

Eric Hopkins is Senior Research Fellow in Economic and Social History, Fellow of the Institute for Advanced Research in Arts and Social Sciences at Birmingham University, and Visiting Professor at Wolverhampton University. He has published widely, and his recent books include *Working Class Self-Help in Nineteenth Century England* (1995) and *Charles Masterman (1873–1927), Politician and Journalist: The Splendid Failure* (1999).

Industrialisation and Society
A social history, 1830–1951

Eric Hopkins

London and New York

First published 2000
by Routledge
11 New Fetter Lane, London EC4P 4EE

Simultaneously published in the USA and Canada
by Routledge
29 West 35th Street, New York, NY 10001

Routledge is an imprint of the Taylor & Francis Group

© 2000 Eric Hopkins

Typeset in Baskerville by Helen Skelton, London
Printed and bound in Great Britain by MPG Books Ltd,
Bodmin, Cornwall.

British Library Cataloguing in Publication Data
A catalogue record for this book is available from
the British Library

Library of Congress Cataloging in Publication Data
Hopkins, Eric
        Industrial Britain : a social history, 1830–1951 /
    Eric Hopkins
        p. cm.
    Includes bibliographical references and index
    ISBN 0-415-18777-X. – ISBN 0-415-18778-8 (pbk.)
        1. Industrialization–social aspects–Great Britain
History. 2. Great Britain–Economic conditions–
19th century. 3. Great Britain–Economic conditions–
20th century. 4. Great Britain–Social conditions–
19th century. 5. Great Britain–Social conditions–
20th century. 6. Industries: Social aspects. Great
Britain–History. I. Title.
    HC256.5.H643   2000
    306.3'0941–dc21   99-41908
                                             CIP

ISBN 0-415-18777-X
ISBN 0-415-18778-8 (pbk)

In memory of my late wife, the ever-tolerant Barbara, and for our three children, Ruth, Hedley, and Valerie.

Contents

Tables   viii
Introduction   ix

1   The Victorian inheritance   1

2   The mid-century years   21

3   After equipoise: urban problems, 1870–1900   57

4   Industrial change and the countryside,
    1830–1951   84

5   The challenge from the left   100

6   Edwardian England and the Liberal reforms   127

7   The Great War, 1914–18   159

8   The inter-war years, 1918–39   182

9   War and the coming of the Welfare State   225

    Envoi   258
    Notes   259
    Select bibliography   280
    Index   292

Tables

1.1	Family involvement in the main areas of occupation, 1801–3	2
1.2	Population growth in industrial towns, 1801–51	7
2.1	Official literacy figures, 1841–71	44
3.1	Children over ten working part time in the 1890s	63
3.2	Booth's classification of income levels in London	74
6.1	Causes of primary poverty in York, c.1900	128
6.2	Strikes and working days lost, 1907–14	147
7.1	Trade union membership, 1912–20	167
8.1	Factory sizes, 1937	190
8.2	Secondary school population, 1913–37	192
8.3	Unemployment in major industries, 1932 and 1938	193
8.4	Poverty in York, 1899 and 1936	200
8.5	Families on or below the minimum standard of sufficiency, Kingstanding Estate, Birmingham, 1939	202
8.6	Trade union membership and working days lost, 1925–39	210
9.1	Results of the 1945 general election	242
9.2	New houses completed, 1946–51	248
9.3	Results of the 1951 general election	253

Introduction

The title of this book may require a few words of explanation. It is not an industrial history of Britain, but is an examination of the social results of industrialisation from about 1830 to 1951. These results, combined with the unparalleled growth of population in the nineteenth century, may be said to have transformed the nation from one that was fundamentally rural to one based very largely on industry, the first of its kind in the world. This book is therefore concerned with the consequences of enormous changes in the mode of life of people of all classes, but principally of the working classes, and with the emergence of major social problems, some of which, such as poverty and unemployment, remain unsolved to the present day. In a nutshell, the book is about the social results of the Industrial Revolution and the attempted solutions of the problems as they arose. One simple truth in this connection needs to be emphasised: the Victorians could hardly have anticipated where the tide of innovation would lead them by the end of the century, let alone by 1951. They had simply to react as they thought fit as their world was visibly changing all round them, adapting themselves to new situations and inevitably facing new difficulties. For this reason, this book attempts from time to time to comment on the thinking of the age, and indeed on contemporary criticisms of the way society was developing. The Victorians were surprisingly self-critical, and it remains a tragedy that the Great War of 1914–18 brought to an abrupt end so much that was promising in Victorian and Edwardian thought and action.

A last word or so on the period covered by this book: the starting date, 1830, is a convenient date to begin any discussion of the social results of industrialisation, because it is only from about this date onwards that the major problems such as those relating to urbanisation really begin to loom large. By the mid-nineteenth century, the Victorians were in no doubt that they had real and formidable problems facing them. The concluding date, 1951, really fixed itself. The early post-World War II years saw major efforts to remedy the darker consequences of industrialism, setting new agendas for social reform. The struggle to contain those consequences has continued ever since, with a marked swing to individualism and against collectivism in the 1980s and 1990s, and with outcomes still unpredictable at the present day.

1 The Victorian inheritance

Generations of students studying the subject of the Victorian inheritance have been concerned to assess the significance of the new electoral system brought in by the Reform Act, 1832, the reform of the old poor law in 1834, the evangelical revival, and the increasing controversy over the corn laws which culminated in their repeal in 1846. These are the familiar contours of the political landscape in the years just before and then following Victoria's accession in 1837. One can add other developments such as the influence of Benthamism and the growth of the Chartist movement, which sit rather awkwardly with the other changes, but may all be conveniently assumed to represent aspirations for *reform*. The Victorian inheritance may therefore be simply conceived to be principally about reform in a variety of guises. This, it might be said, is what those in power were all about: this was their real business. They were basically *reformers*. It is to be noted that Volume XIII in the *Oxford History of England* is appropriately entitled *The Age of Reform 1815–1870*.

In fact, though this approach with its emphasis on political matters has much still to recommend it, there is the danger of failing to penetrate to the deeper truths of the social problems inherited by the Victorians. True enough, they had to address the demands for constitutional reform from the Chartists, and to decide whether to repeal the corn laws. Of at least equal importance, however, were the fundamental issues arising from a profound change in the country's economic system. These had begun to manifest themselves originally in the eighteenth century, accompanied by an unparalleled increase in population. These twin forces of industrialisation and population growth were of ever-increasing significance after the beginning of the nineteenth century. By the 1830s, they could no longer be ignored and were demanding positive action. The influence of these great forces may be seen in many aspects of social life: for example,

Table 1.1 Family involvement in the main areas of occupation, 1801–3

Families in commerce	205,800
Families in industry and building	541,026
Families in agriculture	320,000

working conditions, the home environment, the relief of the poor, religious observance, and class relationships. In this introductory chapter, it is proposed to discuss each of these aspects of social conditions in turn, and then to survey some current attitudes and beliefs.

In general terms, industrialisation meant a change from an economy based on agriculture to one based on industry and commerce.[1] This is not to say that there was little or no industry or commerce in Britain before the coming of the Industrial Revolution – of course there was; British industry was perhaps the most active in Europe, and her commerce was already worldwide. But it was all subsidiary to agriculture, and as Professor Mathias has put it, 'the greatest single flywheel of the economy was the land, the greatest source of wealth in rent, profits, and wages, and the greatest single employer'.[2] Moreover, agriculture was closely connected with many subsidiary industries, such as brewing, milling, leatherworking, and the weaving of woollen cloth. The coming of fundamental change in industry was to alter all this. By the beginning of the nineteenth century, it has been calculated by Lindert and Williamson (1983) that the numbers of families engaged in industry and building were already well ahead of those in agriculture. The figures for 1801–3 are given in Table 1.1.[3]

It is not proposed to rehearse here in detail the full extent of technological change which had taken place by 1837 – they are all very well known – but some indication of their impact in the first half of the nineteenth century may help to supply a perspective. Of the staple industries of the time, the textile industry was pre-eminent, being based increasingly on factory production employing steam-driven machinery; the import figures tell their own story. The consumption of raw cotton rose from 52 million pounds (lb) in 1800 to 588 million pounds in 1850, while raw wool imports, which totalled 1,571,000 pounds in 1772, by 1824 had reached 23,849,000 pounds. Cotton exports increased in value from £6.941 million in 1801 to £37.269 million in 1829. As for the other great industry, coal mining, output figures soared from about 5.23 million tons in 1750 to 30.86 million tons in 1830, reaching a five-year average by the mid-nineteenth century of 68.4 million tons. In the iron industry the production of pig iron, which was about 28,000 tons in the mid-eighteenth century, had leapt to 200,000 tons by 1801.[4]

As might be expected, all this expansion of production did not occur in each industry at an even and uniform pace. In the textile industry, for example, the new cotton industry became mechanised faster than the old-established woollen industry; yet even in cotton there still remained some 40,000 handloom weavers in 1850. The steam power that became so extensively used in the cotton industry did not replace water power till the 1820s, and even in such an important industrial centre as Birmingham, steam power was not adopted on any significant scale until after 1830.[5] In the Black Country to the west of Birmingham, the manufacture of iron was carried on in large-scale foundries, but alongside them existed innumerable small-scale coal pits, and myriads of small metalware workshops producing nails, chains, and many kinds of hardware right up to the mid-nineteenth century and beyond. Thus, there were large industrial works side by side with small workshops, many still of a domestic nature, and characteristic of a small master economy.[6] This extraordinary mixture of the old and the new was to be found elsewhere in industrial Britain, and serves as a warning against any assumption that mechanisation had triumphed throughout industry by 1851. In that year, those working in the principal non-mechanised industries (about 5.5 million workers) outnumbered those in the mechanised industries, even when coal is included in the latter (1.75 million), by three to one.[7] Moreover, it has for some time been commonplace to observe that the pace of economic growth during the Industrial Revolution was far slower than had been thought previously.[8] There were no overnight changes, and old production methods died hard even in the revolutionary cotton industry where the pace of change was greater than elsewhere.

Nevertheless, given these qualifications, by the time of Victoria's accession, significant and far-reaching change in industry had taken place, and the lives of the nation's working population had been affected as a result. A simple example of this is provided by the government's increasing awareness of the effect of variations in trade in an economy which was becoming more and more industrialised. In 1830, the Select Committee on Manufacturers' Employment, which had been appointed to investigate this subject, reported that 'fluctuations in employment frequently occur in manufacturing districts [and are] productive of great distress'.[9] Their solution to the problem was remarkably advanced for the time in that they advised the setting up of unemployment fund societies into which all workmen would be made to contribute regularly – a project which only came to fruition ninety years or so later with the enactment of a limited scheme of unemployment insurance in 1911.

It was in the 1830s, of course, that the drive to steam-powered production in the cotton industry was intensified, with the result that the numbers of handloom weavers who were put out of work increased rapidly; their numbers fell from nearly 250,000 in 1820 to the 40,000 in 1850 mentioned earlier. There were hardly any left at all by 1860.[10] Parliamentary commissioners reported on their distressed state in 1839, 1841, and 1845.[11] Meanwhile, the growth of industry in the towns was driving increasing numbers of workers from the countryside into the fast-growing cities and towns of the Midlands and the north. The Boulton & Watt steam engine had made it no longer necessary for heavy industry to go into the countryside in search of water power; the steam engine could be sited anywhere convenient for the supply of coal and available transport facilities. So the towns expanded mightily, but not without a growing middle-class concern for the working conditions of very young children and women in the new textile factories. A succession of poorly enforced factory acts were passed, starting in 1802. In 1833 there was enacted the first effective factory act (effective because it provided for the appointment of government inspectors), but the campaign for a shorter ten-hour day continued until the passing of the Ten Hour Act in 1847.[12]

It is not surprising that the expansion of industry should have led to an increase in labour disputes, and to greater efforts of the industrial working classes to protect their interests at work. In the 1830s these endeavours grew in scale. Combinations in trade (that is, trade unions) were not unknown in the eighteenth century among the skilled working classes; they were disliked by many employers, and always open to prosecution under the law of conspiracy, and in some trades were even prohibited by act of parliament. Following a panic about revolutionary conspiracies at the end of the 1790s, they were declared illegal by the Combination Acts, 1799, 1800, but were made legal again when these acts were repealed in 1824 and 1825. By the 1830s the trade union movement was growing. Its roots were still in the skilled trades, and it was by now especially active in the cotton industry in Lancashire, where the factory system made recruitment easier. John Doherty, a former Irish spinner, was the one permanent official (he was paid £1.13.0 a week) of a Manchester union with over 2,000 members in 1829; in that year, the union called its members out on a strike against wage cuts which lasted six months.

Subsequently that year Doherty attempted to form a national union of cotton spinners (the Grand General Union of Cotton Spinners, 1829) and then, even more ambitiously, tried to set up a national trade union for all trades, the National Association for the Protection of Labour (NAPL), 1829. It lasted about two years before collapsing. As a pioneering effort, its fame has been overshadowed by a much better-known union, the Grand National Consolidated Trade Union (GNCTU). This union of all trades in fact lasted only six months or so, but its greater fame is partly because Robert Owen became associated with it at the end of its short life, and partly because of the case of the Tolpuddle Martyrs, 1834. This notorious incident concerned six Dorsetshire agricultural labourers who tried to set up a branch of the GNCTU. In doing so, they used a simple initiation ceremony designed to impress on new members that they must be resolute against their employers. They were prosecuted for swearing illegal oaths under the half-forgotten Illegal Oaths Acts, 1797, directed originally against revolutionary conspiracies, and they were sentenced to seven years' transportation. After a considerable outcry, and protest marches in London, the six labourers were pardoned in 1836, and brought back home by 1838.[13]

There is another reason why the GNCTU has been given rather greater prominence than perhaps it deserves. This is that the earlier historians of trade unionism, Sidney and Beatrice Webb, greatly overstated the membership of the GNCTU at half a million or so. In reality, the paid-up membership was only 16,000. In fact, both the NAPL and the GNCTU tried to do too much: the problems of national organisation were far too great, especially the difficulties of national communication before the national network of the railways had been built, and before the institution of the penny post.[14] Even today there is no one union including all trades on a national basis. But in the early 1830s, when the nation's constitution was being reformed, culminating in considerable national turmoil in the passing of the Reform Act, 1832, perhaps all things seemed possible; and in 1836 a further reform organisation was established, the London Working Men's Association, which was to lead to the national reform movement known as Chartism.

However, the Tolpuddle Martyr case had only a marginal effect on trade unionism – it was certainly not a major cause of the collapse of the GNCTU – and unionism continued as before in the major towns and cities, especially among the skilled trades. There were large-scale strikes among the Preston spinners in 1836, among the Staffordshire potters in 1834–5, and in 1837 in Glasgow among the cotton spinners.

In this last city, the strike among the cotton spinners resulted in much violence, and five spinners were put on trial for conspiracy, intimidation, and murder. As a result, a select committee on trade unions was appointed in 1838. The evidence given before this committee is remarkable for showing how strong unionism could be among skilled workers, and how much antagonism there could be between workers and employers, with violence on both sides. Nevertheless, the evidence given related mainly to two well-known trouble spots, Glasgow and Dublin. In other parts of the country, hostility to trade unions appears to have been much less, for many employers thought it better to work amicably with unions than (literally) be at daggers drawn. Some certainly regarded unions as something like a necessary evil, a growing product of increased industrialisation. Employers of this way of thinking no doubt thought it better to attempt to work with them on a peaceful basis than to be in a state of constant warfare over wages and working conditions. Few would be likely to dispute that by the 1830s, trade unions had come to stay.

So far, this chapter has concentrated on industrial change and its consequences for working conditions. We turn now to living conditions. Here the scene is dominated by the immense increase in population which began sometime in the eighteenth century and continued throughout the nineteenth century. Roughly speaking, the population of England and Wales increased by about 50 per cent between 1750 and 1801, that is, from about 6 million to 9 million; between 1801 and 1911 it increased again about four times, from 9 million to 36 million. The causes of this vast expansion have been debated at length by historians. Some time ago the most popular theory was that it was caused by a fall in the death rate. More recently, this interpretation has been challenged: there might indeed have been a fall in mortality rates, but the more important cause, it is now argued, is the lowering of the age of marriage which itself led to a rise in the birth rate.[15] This view is still largely accepted, though the alleged cause (a rise in real wages) has been disputed.

The consequences of this explosion in population were extraordinary. If there had been no Industrial Revolution, it is a reasonable assumption that the towns of the nineteenth century in England would have expanded fourfold in line with the national increase in population; but with the growth of industry, many expanded far beyond this. Preston, for example, increased by about six times between 1801 and 1851, and Bradford by eight times between the same dates. Other industrial towns grew as shown in Table 1.2.[16] The results of such expansion were unprecedented for the towns

Table 1.2 Population growth in industrial towns, 1801–51

	1801	*1851*
Birmingham	71,000	233,000
Glasgow	13,000	104,000
Leeds	53,000	172,000
Liverpool	82,000	376,000
Manchester	75,000	303,000
Sheffield	46,000	135,000
Wolverhampton	13,000	50,000

concerned, and will be examined in more detail in the following chapter. For the present, it is sufficient to say that many industrial towns were faced with great problems of housing, water supply, sanitation and drainage, as multitudes of newcomers poured in from the countryside. Yet many towns had only the most rudimentary forms of local government to tackle the new challenges presented by urban growth. At the accession of Victoria, it seems fair to say that the most immediate and pressing problem on the domestic front was the state of the towns. They were fast becoming the place where most of the nation lived, and the standard of life in them was causing increasing concern ('a mean and grovelling mode of existence', one observer called it). Here the most immediate results of industrialisation confronted the visitor, greatly intensified by the sheer press of numbers.

Another aspect of the social problems arising from the new towns was the problem of poor relief, which was made more difficult by fluctuations in trade and the varying amount of employment available.[17] The old poor law dating from Tudor times had essentially been a mode of relieving rural poverty. After the French wars, parliament appointed select committees on the poor law in 1815 and 1824, and passed a minor Poor Law Act (Sturge Bourne's Act) in 1819. The whole system, which was paid for through local rates, was becoming more and more expensive. Further, there was considerable disquiet at the subsidising of low wages in the southern, agricultural parts of the country (the so-called 'Speenhamland system'), which was thought to have the unfortunate consequences of allowing employers to reduce wages to nominal levels, leaving the labourer to seek outdoor relief for the rest. All incentive to work hard was thus removed, and the labourer became demoralised. It is no wonder that the Whig reforming government of the 1830s should first appoint a royal commission on the poor laws in 1832, and then reform the whole system by the

Poor Law Amendment Act, 1834. The new poor law was essentially deterrent in character, designed to frighten off idlers and scroungers by the 'workhouse test' (all applicants for relief were to go into the workhouse); and by the 'less eligibility' rule, whereby conditions in the workhouse were deliberately made harsh, or 'less eligible' than the standard of life of the lowest-paid labourer; the reasoning here was that no-one who could find work, however ill-paid, would prefer to go into the workhouse.

The new poor law provoked great hostility and led to an anti-poor law movement which aimed to prevent the setting up of the new, large union workhouses. In fact, it proved impossible to relieve all paupers within the workhouse, especially in times of local mass unemployment, so it became necessary to allow some measure of outdoor relief as had been the practice before 1834. Such outdoor relief was given only in return for a disagreeable task of work, such as stone-breaking in the workhouse yard. In practice, the workhouse was much feared and disliked, and it became the last refuge for those who literally had nowhere else to go – the aged, the sick, and the very young, especially orphans. It was these categories of paupers who were in effect victimised by the new system in order to keep out the workshy. In the course of time, the problem presented by the workhouse inmates came to be seen as how best to meet the needs of the helpless poor who had no alternative but to submit to the degradation of going into the workhouse. They really needed specialised care, but it took time for this to be realised.

Another aspect of life in the 1830s which is well known, but at first sight cannot be readily linked to industrialism, is the religion of the people. It was once fashionable to see religious activity as springing from a desire to escape the miseries of industrial life. This view was expressed originally by Karl Marx, in his famous dictum that religion was 'the opium of the people', while the French historian, Elie Halévy, argued that religion, especially Methodism, with its emphasis on hard work and self-discipline, emphasised the need for social conformity. Methodism, according to Halévy, saved England from revolution. E.P. Thompson has taken a rather different line, suggesting that the working classes turned to Methodism *after* the failure of political reform after 1815. For them, Methodism was the chiliasm of despair ('chiliasm' meaning belief in the millennium); it was a ritualised form of 'psychic masturbation'. This somewhat bizarre interpretation appears to ignore the fact that Methodism had been an increasingly powerful force from the mid-eighteenth century onwards, and that Methodism was never millenarianist in belief. It is certainly hard to see how Methodism could have been the result of political despair, though it might conceivably have diverted energies away from political activities and into religious practices.

More recent views have emphasised the theme of social conformity, first sounded between the wars by Halévy. Thus, Dr A.G. Gilbert takes a middle of the road approach: he makes the familiar point that Methodism appealed to the skilled worker, giving him status and responsibility in the organisation and running of the chapel. The hard work and discipline of such men could indeed bring a measure of success and social respect. For this reason, according to Gilbert, Methodism was the giver of hope rather than of despair.[18] It gave hope of better things to the working man and woman in their new industrial environment. So it seems that although the connection between the evangelical movement (still strong in the 1830s) and the changing nature of society is complex and open to different interpretations – Harold Perkin has argued, for example, that Methodism gave working people a sense of separate class identity: it was the midwife of class – it seems a reasonable assumption that working-class religious belief did in fact encourage the growth of self-esteem and personal worth. This must have been of great value, given the stresses of industrial life in the towns which must have been horrendous places for newcomers from the countryside to live in (newcomers soon lost the colour in their cheeks, it was observed). On the other hand, there can be little justification for believing that industrialisation in itself somehow gave rise to Methodism, since Methodism had widespread influence long before the social evils of industrialisation became apparent.[19]

Did industrialisation itself lead to class conflict and to working-class radicalism? Was this another consequence of the changes in the system of production of the time? Again, it is very difficult to demonstrate a direct causal relationship. In some of the factory districts undoubtedly there was political unrest. Manchester itself, great Cottonopolis, is a prime example, with the notorious massacre in St Peter's Fields in 1819 (a peaceful political meeting was broken up by hussars; eleven were killed). Peterloo is still seen as the most alarming political disturbance in England in the whole nineteenth century. *The Times* reported that the wretchedness of the Manchester working classes 'seems to madden them against the rich, who they dangerously imagine engross the fruits of their labour without their having any sympathy for their wants'. Twelve years later, a Manchester pamphlet, entitled *The Reformers' Prayer*, roundly declared:[20]

> From all those damnable bishops, lords, and peers, from all those bloody murdering Peterloo butchers, from all those idle drones that live on the earnings of the people, good Lord deliver us ...

On the other hand, industrial areas such as Birmingham and the Black Country, where the factory system as such hardly existed in the 1830s, seem to have been far less class-conscious, and class co-operation and old-fashioned paternalism were much more in evidence in the 1830s. Indeed, the Birmingham Political Union, led by the banker Thomas Attwood, was a powerful element in the reform movement which led to the passing of the Reform Act, 1832, a movement which had substantial working-class support in Birmingham.[21] A fair conclusion in this matter is that whatever political unrest existed when Victoria came to the throne owed more to the traditional radicalism of parts of the skilled working classes in England (itself fostered by notions of equality emanating from France during the Revolution) than to hostile reactions to the progress of industrialisation.[22]

One exception to this, however, was the small-scale but not insignificant co-operative movement of the time. In the early 1830s, there existed numerous small co-operative enterprises, mostly trading in nature, but often aiming ultimately to found communities along Owenite lines.[23] On his return from America in 1829, Owen himself set about establishing so-called equitable labour exchanges first in London in 1832 and then in Birmingham in 1833. In these exchanges, goods were exchanged on the basis of their value judged by the amount of labour which had gone into them. They all failed, as did Owen's last attempt at a co-operative settlement at Queenswood in Hampshire, 1839–46. The early history of the co-operative movement before the national success of the retail movement initiated by the Rochdale Pioneers in 1844 may certainly be construed as a protest against industrial capitalism, but it did not get very far, and was never at any time a threat to the growth of the industrialised economy.[24]

How far were the governments of the day conscious of the need to grapple with the social results of industrialisation? It is interesting to note that even as early as the beginning of the nineteenth century, a factory reform movement was already in existence.[25] Even before this, in 1784 a group of Manchester magistrates were sufficiently concerned at the working conditions of young apprentices in the cotton mills to decide not to allow apprenticeship of any children in mills where they worked more than ten hours a day, or at night. This is perhaps the earliest indication of public concern at the employment of young children in the new factories. Child employment itself was not new, of course, but the length of the working day and its sustained nature were very different from conditions in the average domestic workshop. In 1802 the first Factory Act was passed, introduced by Sir Robert Peel, Senior, who was himself a Bury factory owner. It sought to limit the hours of apprentices to twelve a day, and to forbid all night work. Its weakness lay in the fact that it was to be enforced by locally appointed officials, who were often highly inefficient, if not at times in the pockets of the factory owners. Subsequent acts in 1816, 1825, 1830, and 1831 all suffered from the same weakness, though they did apply to both apprenticed and so-called free children. Eventually, as noted earlier in the chapter, the Factory Act, 1833, was the first really effective factory act since it provided for inspection by government inspectors rather than by local officials. However, the battle for the ten-hour day for women and children continued for a further ten years after Victoria came to the throne.

Thus, opposition to one outstanding aspect of industrialisation – child labour in the new factories – was noticeable from early on, and it received increasing government support. However, it would be quite wrong to suppose that there was general support from the educated public for factory legislation from the very beginning. On the contrary, in spite of the declaration of Richard Oastler, a leading factory reformer, that 'any old washerwoman could tell you that ten hours a day is too long for any child to labour', there were many who disagreed. It was frequently pointed out that shorter hours would reduce wages; sensible employers never overworked their workers because their work would deteriorate in quality; profits were made in the last half-hour, so that a reduction of hours would result in a loss of all profit (an argument put forward by the distinguished economist, Nassau Senior); fixed hours would also mean a loss of trade to overseas competitors. Even working-class reformers such as Francis Place believed that all legislative interference must be pernicious: 'Men must be left to make their own bargains.' Opponents of factory legislation simply rejected all the arguments of the factory reformers as 'the erroneous dictates of the humanity mongers'.[26]

In fact, absurd as some of these arguments of opponents of factory reform appear today, they were not entirely without substance, given the beliefs of the time about factory production. It was well known, of course, that the textile industry was the leading industry in the national economy. It was equally well known that a reduction in children's working hours would very likely lead to a reduction in adult hours, for children's work was essential in keeping the mules and looms working. This conceivably could lead to a reduction in wages, and was in any case a denial of the right of a man to work for as many or as few hours as he pleased. This last point carried considerable weight in an age when increasing emphasis was being placed on economic freedom in economic matters and the need to allow the free operation of market forces; the doctrines preached in Adam Smith's *Wealth of Nations* (1776) had a wide currency, and continued to have throughout much of the century. By the 1860s, free trade had become a principle freely accepted on all sides, together with the associated idea of individualism, or self-help. Both ideas implied a rejection of paternalistic government, which was thought by many not to be the proper business of government. It was one thing for the government to reform the electoral system as they did (after considerable travail) by the Reform Act in 1832, and even to carry out a reform of the old chartered boroughs in 1835; it was quite another thing to embark on any form of welfare legislation of the modern kind. It was the traditional belief that governments were elected primarily to keep the peace at home and defend the country's interests abroad. Any other undertakings were beyond the government's proper functions; they could, and probably would, lead to corruption and increased taxation. Exceptions to this were the occasional great moral issue, such as the abolition of slavery in the British Empire in 1833, or (an issue more of social control than of moral consideration) the first financial grant to the church schools in the same year.

Attempts to regulate working conditions in the textile factories constitute one of the few efforts by the government in the earlier part of the nineteenth century to face the growing problems of industrialism. What about attitudes to the remarkable growth of population? It could hardly be unremarked at the time, and in 1798, the Reverend Thomas Malthus provided a powerful analysis of the phenomenon in his *Essay on Population*. According to Malthus, population and food supply were directly related to each other:[27]

> The power of population is infinitely greater than the power of the earth to produce subsistence for man. Population, when unchecked, increases in a geometrical ratio. Subsistence only in an arithmetical ratio ... by that law of our nature which makes food necessary for the life of man, the effects of these two unequal powers must be kept equal.

The question then arises, how can the two powers be kept in balance? The answer is that in practice it is done through the agency of wars and famines, and by self-restraint in procreation. It follows that efforts to make life easier and more tolerable for the working classes, as for example, by an indulgent poor law system, would only encourage a growth in population, put a greater strain on food supplies, and hence be self-defeating. Malthus actually attacked the poor laws of his time, arguing that if they had never existed, though this might result in a few more cases of severe distress, he had little doubt that 'the aggregate mass of happiness among the common people would have been much greater than it is at present'. As the poor rates continued to rise after the end of the French wars in 1815, these views gained considerable support; though for some, the suggestion that the country might do well to dispense with the poor laws altogether was going too far.

There is no doubt that Malthus had considerable influence over the principles of the new poor law, and his ideas were supported by David Ricardo (1722–1823), who in the same vein argued that wages would always hover around subsistence; if they rose above subsistence, workers would have larger families, and the surplus supply of labourers resulting would depress wages again.[28] These were gloomy conclusions, and reinforced the growing belief that relief to the poor should be kept to a minimum, and they should be encouraged to work. But the thinker who probably had the greatest influence over the shaping of the Poor Law Amendment Act, 1834, was Jeremy Bentham (1748–1832). His theory of utilitarianism was to have great influence not only on this measure, but also on the thought of his follower, James Mill (1773–1836), and on early Victorian thinking generally. Beginning as philosopher, Bentham turned to criticism of the law and legal profession, and also of the workings of government. The psychological basis of his beliefs was remarkably simple (if not naive), and was derived from Hobbes: it was that man's basic motivation is derived from the sensations of pleasure and of pain:[29]

> Nature has placed mankind under the governance of two sovereign masters, *pain* and *pleasure*. It is for them alone to point out what we ought to do, as well as determine what we shall do. On the one hand, the standard of right and wrong, on the other the chain of causes and effects, are fastened to their throne.

Since man is ruled by his emotions in this way, the task of government is to seek to achieve the greatest happiness of the greatest number.

Following the passage just quoted, Bentham goes on to propound further his view that all men are subject to the forces of pain and pleasure:

> In a word, a man may pretend to abjure their empire: but in reality he will remain subject to it all the while. The *principle of utility* recognises this subjection, and assumes it for the foundation of that system, the object of which is to rear the fabric of felicity by the hands of reason and of law.

Bentham and his disciples became known as utilitarians, or philosophical radicals, and were strong critics not only of outmoded forms of central government, such as the pre-1832 electoral system, but also of long-standing institutions such as the old poor law. Indeed, it can be said that his *Poor Laws and Pauper Management* (in *Annals of Agriculture*, 1797) provided some of the fundamental principles of the Poor Law Amendment Act, 1834. Certainly the ruthless logic of the 'workhouse test', and of the 'less eligibility' rule, exemplify the application of the pleasure-pain principle. The whole machinery of the old parish-based poor law system, with all its quirks and variety, was subjected to judgement by the principle of *utility*, and was found wanting. The result was a new system, based on 600 or so unions of parishes, and controlled from London by three poor law commissioners, who sent out a stream of General Orders (applicable to all unions), and Special Orders (applicable to individual unions only). Thus, the Benthamite system of centralised supervision in the interests of uniformity and efficiency was triumphant, just two years after Bentham's death.

There is no doubt that Bentham and Malthus made major contributions to the principles on which the new poor law was constructed. However, it must be admitted that it is evident from the report of the commissioners (one of whom was Edwin Chadwick, a former secretary and follower of Bentham) that they were determined in any case to destroy the old poor law, and they ignored any evidence conflicting with their own preconceptions of its shortcomings. Nevertheless, in this particular and important case of the 1834 act, political philosophers made a significant contribution to its operation. The question then arises, how far did the thinkers of the time shape the attitudes and opinions of the legislators of the 1830s? How far did they legislate on principle, and how far were they driven by expediency or simple empiricism? Were there any signs, for example, that the scope of government legislation was being significantly widened?

In fact, there is little to show that anything of this nature was happening. An examination of the major pieces of legislation does not reveal any marked move towards increased state interference. Electoral reform was long overdue, of course – Pitt had attempted it in the 1780s – but the French Revolution had set it back a generation; while the factory act and the abolition of slavery centred on great moral issues, as we have seen. The Municipal Corporation Act was again an overdue reform of local government, and a corollary of the reform of central government by the great Reform Act. The first government grant to the church school societies was a belated acknowledgement of the need for elementary education, especially of the new urban masses, not so much because education was good in itself, but as a means of disciplining them, teaching them that their reward was in the hereafter, whatever their lowly position in this world. There was not much lofty idealism about the first government grant to education, but simply a recognition of the societies' financial needs. The first annual grant was itself very small – £20,000 to subsidise the building of schools by the two societies, the Church of England National Society, and the much smaller Nonconformist British and Foreign Schools Society. There were still many who thought that the working classes had no need of reading and writing; it would only allow them to acquire dangerous, even revolutionary, ideas. The Bishop of Rochester had expressed this view in an extreme form in 1800 during the French wars in an attack on charity schools and Sunday schools:[30]

> schools of Jacobinical rebellion – schools of atheism and disloyalty abound in this country; schools in the shape and disguise of Charity schools and Sunday schools.

So the Whig reforms of the early 1830s hardly brought about a new wave of collectivist legislation; but neither were the political economists and philosophers universally in favour of *laissez-faire* principles. Although James Mill, Ricardo, and Malthus were all suspicious of state intervention, their beliefs varied in emphasis, from one to another. Malthus, for example, actually accepted the need to protect child workers and to assist the church societies. Senior doubted whether factory legislation should be applied to adult labour, but thought that public money might be properly used to provide parks and museums. Earlier on, Adam Smith had also specifically advocated public works, and certain public institutions when they were beyond the resources of private individuals. Senior criticised the indiscriminate rushing up of housing in the new towns, arguing that with all the reverence due for the principle of non-interference, in this matter it had been pushed too far. Again, much of John Stuart Mill's famous chapter on this subject in his *Principles of Political Economy* (1848) is given up to examples of permissible departures from the principles of *laissez-faire*. Thus, there is really no unanimity among these thinkers on the subject of the limits of state interference.

Similarly, it would be wrong to look for unanimous views among members of the government. Lord Melbourne himself (prime minister in 1835, and again, 1836–41) had an easy-going and indeed, cynical outlook on life. He was really more than half against the humanitarian reformers of the day – they would only worry the poor, he thought – and he disliked their confidence in their ability to do good. 'Try to do no good,' he argued, 'and then you won't get into any scrapes.' As for religion, his remark made after hearing a sermon on the consequences of sin, is famous: 'Things are coming to a pretty pass when religion is allowed to invade private life.'[31] It is true, of course, that Melbourne is more representative of the Georgian than the early Victorian age, but with leadership like this, the Whig governments of the later 1830s were unlikely to be drawn into any foolhardy adventures in state intervention. At the same time it would be clearly unwise to suppose that the sacred principle of *laissez-faire* actually inhibited any major growth of state action. The fact of the matter seems to be that early Victorian governments seemed to have no fixed ideas in either direction. It is also worth remembering that even if there had been general agreement about the need to do more about the social problems arising from industrialism, the government lacked the resources to tackle them, for the civil service was still remarkably small in numbers. It was still recruited by patronage, and the days of recruitment by competitive examinations were still some way in the future.

All in all, the scope of government in early Victorian times was still very limited. Not a great deal had changed since Lord Liverpool had expressed the view that most of the miseries of mankind were beyond the reach of legislation. On the other hand, there were some new developments in the 1830s with the beginnings of the factory inspectorate and the appointment in 1839 of a special committee of the Privy Council to administer the annual grant to the church societies, together with the appointment of the first school inspectors. In effect, this meant that new civil service departments were being created; and it has been argued that this gave rise to a kind of administrative momentum in favour of reform. The inspectors would report on progress, a new body of specialised knowledge would be built up, and all this would have to be taken into account by the government. Future reform would be shaped by past experience, and government officials would have an increasingly important part to play in the process. This is an interesting interpretation of the actual growth of government participation in reform, though it has not been without its critics.[32] At the very least, it makes the point that the creation of government inspectorates increased awareness of the potentialities for further reform. There may well be some significance in Russell's remark in 1840 that when he first entered parliament in 1813, 'it was not usual for governments to undertake generally all subjects of legislation. Since the Reform Bill, it has been thought convenient that the Government should propose changes in the laws.'[33] Legislative attitudes were clearly beginning to change after the triumph of the great Reform Bill.

In the final analysis, the early Victorians stood upon the threshold of great changes in the social fabric, nearly all traceable to the twin forces of industrialisation and the growth of population. Working conditions had been most radically affected by the coming of the factory system, though its impact was much more limited by 1851 than is sometimes supposed. Nevertheless, the regulation of working hours for children and women in 1833 set valuable precedents not only for further reform of factory hours and the working environment, but also for the extension of regulation after the mid-century to workshops and other places of work. Perhaps it is worth mentioning at this point that in spite of all the adverse publicity the factory system received at the time, the factories did provide relatively well-paid work when compared with the wretched wage levels of agricultural labourers; and it was in the factory districts that trade unionism made an effective start on both a regional and a national basis. Agricultural labourers, by way of contrast, were not to achieve any degree of unionisation until the 1870s, and then it was a slow and uncertain start.

As for the home environment, enough has been said already to emphasise the extent of the problem of urban expansion in Victorian times. Indeed, it was in the first ten years of the reign that a succession of reports revealed the parlous condition of the rapidly growing industrial towns (see the next chapter). Of all the consequences of industrialisation, it was this which posed the most urgent and alarming problems for the early Victorians. Curiously enough, the actual movement of immigrants from the countryside into the towns has not received much attention in contemporary literary accounts, though daily hordes must have made their way on foot or by cart into urban areas. The actual towns themselves of course, have been described in the novels of the time, as for example, in Disraeli's *Sybil, or the Two Nations* (1845), in Mrs Gaskell's *Mary Barton* (1848) and *North and South* (1855), and in Dickens' *Hard Times* (1854). There are also graphic descriptions of the worst parts of Manchester in F. Engels' *The Condition of the Working Class in England in 1844* (1845). At the mid-century, the towns presented the ominous threat of widespread epidemics of cholera, typhus, and typhoid.

Associated with the problems of living conditions were problems arising from old age, and also sickness, which frequently resulted in loss of work. It was the task of the new poor law to relieve the poverty arising from all three conditions. Later it was to emerge in the 1880s that as much as a third of the new urban masses were living in poverty. Moreover, unemployment was becoming an increasingly noticeable feature of the industrial economy, and one already recognised in 1830. In the years 1839 to 1842 the Victorians had to face probably the worst depression of the century. It coincided with the political challenge of the Chartist movement. The causes of this movement were varied and complex, but they included a measure of industrial unrest, especially in 1842. Chartism also raised issues of class-consciousness, particularly at the time of the presentation of the 1842 petition when the movement became strongly working class in nature. Chartism will be discussed in more detail in the next chapter.

Lastly, a word or so on the subject of religious observance: its importance in strengthening social conformity among the working classes has already been remarked upon. No drastic changes within this area confronted the Victorians, though there were certain developments within the Church of England which deserve comment, though they are unlikely to have had much effect on working-class believers. The adherents of the Oxford Movement (or the Tractarian Movement) were members of the Anglican church in Oxford who emphasised the essential continuity of Church of England doctrines with those of the Church of Rome.[34] Their views were made known in a number of tracts, the most famous of these being Tract XC, which appeared in February 1841. This tract sought to prove that the Thirty Nine Articles (subscribed to by every Anglican clergyman) contained nothing contrary to traditional Catholic belief. Almost inevitably, this led to some of its supporters, and principally John Newman, finally breaking away and joining the Roman church. Those who remained became known as Anglo-Catholics. It was a highly intellectual movement, and could not have meant a great deal to the average working-class member of the Church of England. Among the Methodists, however, there occurred another schism (the Primitive Methodists had already separated themselves in 1810) when the New Connexion was formed in the 1830s; but this was for internal reasons based on doctrinal and personal differences, and cannot be ascribed to any fresh developments of industrialism.

When Victoria came to the throne, there were probably very few observers who would have surveyed the situation inherited by the Victorians from previous reigns in quite the same manner in which it has been surveyed in this chapter. Yet if the historian has the privilege of hindsight, his view is still necessarily partial, in the simplest sense of the word – he cannot know it all, and may well overlook or ignore aspects which were thought of major importance at the time. For example, in 1837 the future of the monarchy was the subject of some controversy, and it was by no means so well established as it was to appear to be at the end of the century. On the other hand, presumably it would have been difficult to have predicted the enormous boom in railway construction which was to characterise the mid-1840s – railway mania, it was called, following an earlier minor boom in railway building in 1835–7 – which did much to lift the country's economy out of depression. The Victorian period was so full of incident and character that by means of what Professor Burn has called 'selective Victorianism' it is possible to trace almost any pattern which one fancies.[35] So it would be foolish to claim to have singled out in any definitive way all the aspects of economic and social change which were most prominent in the late 1830s. What is certain is that industrialisation was steadily undermining and changing the old social structures, throwing up new characters like George Hudson, the 'Railway King', noticeably in the new industrial towns but at other times almost imperceptibly, as in the more remote rural areas. How far such changes were allowed to go unchecked and unrestrained by the government or its agencies depended on a number of factors. Among them was the traditional belief in the need to keep government interference in check, a belief reinforced by some of the newer economic beliefs of the time; and this has been commented on enough in this chapter.[36] It will be seen operating powerfully against public health reform in the next chapter. Yet even then, some precedents had been established, as in factory reform; and in the mid-century years, some of the more beneficial consequences of industrialisation began to appear in the rise in the standard of living, while some of the darker results of the fundamental changes in the economy were to be subjected to further government legislation. It is sad that the Victorians have so often been depicted as rather dull and stuffy people, often sanctimonious, and indeed, hypocritical. Certainly they had their faults, but willy-nilly they were to become pioneers in the field of social reform, all (as Auden put it) 'to sway forward on the dangerous flood of history, that never sleeps or dies, And, held one moment, burns the hand'.[37]

2 The mid-century years

The mid-century years – the 1840s, 1850s, and 1860s – were really the formative years of the Victorian state. If the social problems which were to become increasingly apparent in this period are to be understood, it should be helpful first of all to sketch in the major economic developments of the time. These were by no means years of uniform prosperity, and this is especially true of the early 1840s.

In fact, the first five years or so of Victoria's reign were actually a period of *Sturm und Drang*, marked by much economic uncertainty and confusion. The earlier prosperity seemed to fade away from 1839 onwards, to be replaced by years of depression, when the process of increasing industrialisation seemed to be grinding to a halt. Trade fell off, unemployment increased. The term 'hungry forties' is certainly appropriate for the early years of the decade. In 1842 there occurred the so-called 'Plug Plot' in the Midlands and the north in which plugs were knocked from boilers by strikers moving from works to works. Large areas of the industrial Midlands and Lancashire were for a time immobilised, and the disturbances were so widespread that more recently historians have termed the whole episode the General Strike of the 1840s.[1] In fact, the strikes were so scattered and the evidence for concerted action between the strikers is too fragile to justify the term 'General Strike'. However, what is abundantly clear is the depth of suffering of those out of work at this time.

This can be graphically illustrated by accounts of distress in the Black Country. In the normally prosperous and expanding town of Stourbridge, employment had hitherto been easy to obtain in the local iron, mining, and glass-making trades. Yet in November 1841, a local newspaper commented that at no former period in the last twenty years had there been such poverty and wretchedness. For example, one underhand puddler had been out of work for thirteen weeks – he had a wife and two children – and thirty pawn tickets; the clothing and bedding of hundreds had gone already – how would they bear the winter?[2] When winter came, by January 1842 it was said that a third of the inhabitants were in distress – indeed, more than half of the entire population of the district were in a state of destitution; there were fifty homes without a bed – 'a pig-sty or a dog-kennel is a luxury compared with the accommodation they enjoy'. Soup was being distributed, 7,800 quarts per week at 1d per quart,[3] but in the following month the soup kitchen closed down for want of funds.[4]

For the rest of 1842, conditions continued to be bad. In June of that year there were still thousands out of work in the area while many of the principal shops in Stourbridge High Street had closed, those remaining open not paying their expenses. Colliers were parading the town in groups of a dozen or so, demanding relief. Sheep stealing had begun in earnest.[5] By August, the Board of Guardians was unable to pay its bills, and by September there was much stealing of potatoes and turnips from the local fields.[6] Distress continued as the next winter approached, and intensified in the early months of 1843. In January 1843 there were 262 in the Stourbridge workhouse, twenty-two more than the guardians regarded as the maximum they could take. The *Worcestershire Chronicle* commented, 'The situation of vast numbers of the labouring class is appalling. Hundreds of the nailers have not half employment. The ruin is extending upwards.'[7] Funds were distributed from the London-based Manufacturers' Relief Fund, and employment offered digging gravel and on road works. Meanwhile, by March 1843 Lord Stamford, at Enville Hall, just outside Stourbridge, was said to be feeding hundreds by his bounty.[8] The depression did not begin to lift until August 1843, when four puddling furnaces in Stourbridge Iron Works were at last relit. By November, nailing was recovering, and the iron trade was much more active.[9] In February 1844 the Stourbridge Manufacturers' Relief Fund closed down. Later in 1844, the numbers in the workhouse reached their lowest for twelve months, and by November, the iron trade was flourishing again, with not an iron works standing (that is, all were in full production).[10]

This little excursion into local history serves to show the reality sometimes concealed behind the generalisations of macroeconomic history. Stourbridge had been a prosperous small town in the 1830s, its population increasing to 17,597 by 1841,[11] and it was obviously hard hit by the prolonged depression, especially in the iron trades. Thus, periodic unemployment, one outstanding characteristic of industrialisation, was only too apparent in Stourbridge, and indeed, nationally. If by this time the process of industrialisation was beginning to result in a slow improvement in real wages (whatever had happened in the hotly disputed earlier decades of the Industrial Revolution),[12] this seemed to have been accompanied by more pronounced variations in trade and greater instability of employment – something of which the government was increasingly aware, as we have seen in Chapter 1.

One popular belief of the time was that trade could be improved if free trade could be allowed in corn – that is, if the protective corn laws of 1815 were abolished. This, it was argued, would stimulate trade by reducing the price of bread; and there was much hostility towards the farming community among industrial employers, leading to the founding of the Anti-Corn Law League by Cobden and Bright. The prime minister, Robert Peel, first modified the duties on imported corn in 1842, and then finally repealed the corn laws in 1846 except for a purely nominal duty. This was a triumph for the industrial and commercial interests of the country at the expense of the agricultural interest who felt betrayed by Peel and his Conservative ministry. Curiously, the repeal of the corn laws did not do much to lower the price of bread (transport costs from the Baltic were still heavy), and repeal was not the principal reason for the return to prosperity in the later 1840s.

The more basic reason for this was perhaps the sudden boom in railway construction of the 1840s, amounting to a kind of railway mania (a term used at the time) as vast sums were invested in the building of trunk lines. This certainly provided a stimulus within the economic system for increased investment, production, and employment. However, it would be unwise to take this argument too far and certainly not to the extent of claiming that the railways saved the emerging system of industrial capitalism.[13] The return to prosperity was so marked that by 1851, on the initiative of Prince Albert, the Great Exhibition was staged in Hyde Park, a magnificent showcase for a revived British industry. The exhibition really came at the beginning of two decades of increasing prosperity, often described as 'the great Victorian boom', or the 'golden era' of Victorian industrial expansion. It was all based on free trade, which had become the economic gospel of the time, seen not only in the repeal of the corn laws, but in Cobden's Free Trade Treaty with France in 1860, and in Gladstone's Crown and Summit Budget of 1860, abolishing all but a few import duties on foreign trade. Free trade had become an unquestioned doctrine, while industry flourished, the metal trades now edging ahead compared with textiles (the percentage of the labour force in textiles dropped from 29 per cent in 1851 to 24 per cent in 1871, while the percentage in metals advanced from 13 per cent in 1851 to 17 per cent in 1871).[14]

This picture of a great period of boom conditions has not gone unchallenged in recent years, principally by Professor Roy Church, who has claimed that although admittedly economic growth was 'extraordinarily great' in 1853–6, 1863–5, and 1871–3, it was severely limited at other times, so that the mid-Victorian years experienced marked, but unspectacular economic growth: 'in most other respects – notably price trends, euphoria, and prosperity – the conception of a distinctive historical unity for 1850–73 is a myth'.[15] Be this as it may (it was once fashionable for historians seeking to revise earlier interpretations to use the word 'myth'), the impression persists of a much more benign economic climate after 1850, with an increase in real wages. As for euphoria and class relationships, the latter would certainly appear to have improved after the decline of the Chartist movement with the failure of the Third Petition in 1848, and indeed, improved economic conditions have always been considered to be one cause of the failure of the movement to revive in the 1850s. Greater confidence in the sober character and reliability of the respectable working man was certainly shown in the efforts made by both Liberals and Tories in the 1850s to introduce a limited measure of electoral reform, conferring the vote on the male householder in the towns, an aim finally achieved by Disraeli as Conservative prime minister in 1867. Although it may be necessary, therefore, to modify earlier views of the reality of the great Victorian boom, in spite of Church's view that it deserves 'only a severely qualified affirmative', there still seems little reason to doubt that on the whole, the 1850s and 1860s were years of comparative prosperity.

Public health and housing

So much for the economic background to the mid-century years: we may now examine the social problems arising from the further advances of industrialisation. In the first place, there were the problems of unemployment and poverty which we have seen loomed large in the 1840s. Then again there were problems relating to working conditions, the length of the working day, and the continued quite unregulated employment of young children in workshops, brick-yards, rope-walks, and elsewhere. But perhaps the most urgent problem of all, requiring the most immediate attention, was the state of the towns and the hazards to health arising from them. Disease was no respecter of person: even though the middle classes had in many cases moved to the more salubrious suburbs of the industrial towns, they might still fall victim to a water-borne disease such as cholera. The medical profession was well aware of this, even though they remained ignorant of the precise ways in which disease was transmitted from one person to another until later in the century. Moreover, there was the question of what kind of person was growing up in the new towns, what kind of creature was being bred in the foul conditions which characterised them. Southwood Smith, a leading public health reformer, set out the problem forcibly enough in his evidence before the Health of Towns Commission appointed by Peel in 1843:[16]

> In the filthy and crowded streets of our large towns and cities you can see human faces retrograding, sinking down to the level of brute tribes, and you find manners appropriate to the degradation. Can anyone wonder that there is among these classes of the people so little intelligence, so slight an approach to humanity, so total an absence of domestic affection, and of moral and religious feeling? ... if from early infancy, you allow human beings to live like brutes, you can degrade them down to their level.

In other words, according to Southwood Smith, without urban reform, there was the danger of breeding a race of degenerates.

Why should such a situation have come about? Towns existed before the Industrial Revolution, of course, and London in particular was one of the largest cities in the world. Urbanisation in itself was nothing new. What was unprecedented, as pointed out in the last chapter, was the four-fold increase in the nation's population in the nineteenth century, so that all towns were likely to expand greatly as a consequence; but much of the additional expansion in the Midlands and the north was due to the Industrial Revolution. As noted earlier, production had been freed from the need for water power, usually on hand in the countryside, by the development of the Boulton & Watt steam engine, thus allowing industrial expansion in the towns. Workers therefore poured in from the surrounding countryside in search of employment which, however arduous, was better paid than agricultural labour. Earlier in this century, the Hammonds argued that parliamentary enclosures deprived many labourers of their customary rights, and drove them into the towns in search of work. This older view was disputed by Professor J.D. Chambers, who placed greater emphasis on rural overpopulation than on enclosure, though his views have been criticised in turn by Professor N.F.R. Crafts and others.[17]

Whatever the underlying causes of immigration from the country-side into the towns, and to what extent it was sheer economic necessity which drew newcomers there, it should also be remembered that there was the lure of higher wages to take into account, and the attractions of a busy town, however hellish the environment. Towns had more pubs, more places of entertainment, more places of worship, more markets and shops than the average small village; and perhaps above all else, they offered a sense of something going on, beyond the supervisory control of squire and parson, and so were attractive to the younger generation. So, for a variety of reasons, a mighty human influx was swallowed up by the towns throughout the nineteenth century, usually as a result of short-distance migration from the surrounding countryside, though long-distance migration seemed more common among the professional middle classes.[18]

How could the immigrant masses be accommodated? Single young men could look for lodgings, of course, but those with families would need rather more living room. To accommodate them, middle-class housing vacated by their former occupants could be split up into tenements, while cellars and attics could be turned into living space. Cellars were often used in this way to house families in Glasgow, Liverpool, and Manchester, though extremely unsanitary because of damp, lack of light, and seepage from underground water or even drains.[19] One other form of accommodation, of course, was the new housing rushed up by speculative or jerry-builders, especially to meet the needs of newcomers to the area. This varied in quality – a point to be returned to later – but much was undoubtedly poorly constructed, and used inferior materials. This was specially so during the long years of war against the French (1793–1815) when timber from abroad was in short supply. Houses were thrown up rapidly not only on the outskirts of town but also on vacant space anywhere; sometimes new rows of houses would be built across the back gardens of existing houses. The main aim was to crowd as many houses onto the building site as possible: often the houses would be built in terraces facing each other across a narrow court, approached by alley-ways between adjacent houses. The simplest pattern was to build on two floors, a ground floor and a first floor, but some houses would have three floors, and attic rooms were common. There was no provision for a tapped water supply, or for gas lighting, nor was the court outside necessarily paved or cobbled. One type of house found in many towns (there seemed to be no regional preference for it) was the back-to-back house. This kind of house was built literally back-to-back with another, which did not permit the houses to be more than one room deep from front to back. Such houses were usually one room down, one room up, and were commonly built in terraces of brick with slate roofs and casement windows. Leeds in particular had vast numbers of such houses, each room measuring the same, that is, 15 feet by 15 feet.[20]

Clearly, housing of this kind, constructed hastily to meet the needs of great numbers of newcomers, could provide little beyond a crude protection against the elements. Moreover, it failed to keep up with the weight of numbers, so that housing was frequently overcrowded (it goes without saying that there were no regulations against this, and very rarely were there any building regulations to comply with). Overcrowding was thus a feature of early Victorian working-class homes. In Preston in 1842 it was stated that in one area examined of about 422 dwellings, there were 2,400 persons sleeping in 852 beds, that is, an average of 5.68 inhabitants to each house, and 2.8 persons to each bed. Further enquiries showed that the sharing of beds (common enough generally at the time) was sometimes taken to extremes – in eighty-four cases, four persons shared a bed, in twenty-eight cases there were five to a bed, and in thirteen cases, six shared a bed. Remarkably, there were actually three cases of seven sharing a bed, and one case of eight in the same bed.[21]

This cramming together of human beings, of both sexes, old and young, was obviously highly unhygienic, but as bad was the complete lack of modern amenities. There was no tapped water; water had to be obtained from a local pump, or purchased by the pail at a penny or twopence a time, or obtained from a nearby stream or river, which was often polluted. There was no deep drainage, though there might be surface open drains to carry off floodwater. Worst of all was the lack of indoor sanitation. What there was took the form of simple earth closets, often provided in the courts in inadequate numbers, and cleaned out at infrequent intervals by night soil men, who would carry the contents in barrows (carts were often unable to get through the narrow alleys) to some convenient dumping ground. There the excrement would be piled up in great heaps (middens) before being sold to farmers as fertiliser. There were also pools of liquid filth known as cesspools. It hardly needs to be added that there was rarely if ever any systematic scavenging, so that rubbish would be left to rot in piles in the court or street.

It is difficult to exaggerate the difficulties of the working-class housewife as she sought to maintain a clean and decent house in such adverse conditions, with mud brought in from the street by visitors, and washing soiled by smuts from local factory chimneys. However, not all new housing was bad, and the size of rooms was not noticeably smaller than in eighteenth-century building. Some houses built in the mid-nineteenth century were of a better quality, some of them surviving today (suitably refurbished, of course) as starter homes. Generally speaking, the higher-paid working classes lived in rather more spacious houses of better quality for which they paid higher rents – this was noticeably so in London.[22] Some houses might share pumps in their backyard – not all housing was built in courts. So there was some variation in quality and even in amenities.

The one outstanding feature of nearly all new urban development was the lack of proper sanitation, and the consequent threat to health from overcrowded privies. It was well known that death rates in the countryside were much lower than in the towns.[23] Earth privies were in use in the villages, too, but could be at a distance from the cottage, and were not so overcrowded. It is worth noting, too, that water closets were not common even in middle- and upper-class homes; it is said that chamber pots were regularly emptied into the cellars at Windsor Castle. Even when water closets had been installed, they did not necessarily drain into underground drainage systems. In Birmingham in the Hagley Road (said to be the finest neighbourhood in the town), they drained into reeking ditches or gutters on either side of the road. There were also cesspits on many premises on this road. Workmen employed to drain one cesspit for a fee of £2 in 1849 found the stench so bad that they demanded another £1, then a further £1 and a pint of brandy for every hour.[24]

Anxiety over the state of the towns began to mount in the 1830s. In 1831 a national outbreak of cholera forced the government to appoint a Central Board of Health, and as many as 1,000 local boards of health were set up by Orders in Council. The first outbreaks of the disease came to the ports on the north-east coast in October 1831, spreading to London by the end of the year. The worst was over by the end of 1832 and the local boards were allowed to lapse. However, local surveys were published by doctors in Leeds, Glasgow, and Manchester, and in 1838 an enquiry was made into the worst areas of London under the direction of the Poor Law Commission. The survey was carried out by three doctors, James Kay (who was the author of the Manchester survey), James Arnott, and Southwood Smith, whose forceful views have already been quoted. Their reports (the Fever Reports) appeared as appendices to the Annual Report of the Commission in 1838.

Then in 1839 the House of Lords authorised an enquiry into the sanitary conditions of the working classes, and the poor law commissioners gave Edwin Chadwick, secretary to the commission, the task of organising the enquiry. Meanwhile, the Health of Towns Select Committee was appointed in 1840, but a bill seeking to put its recommendations into effect was abandoned. In 1842 Chadwick's report was published under the title *Report on the Sanitary Condition of the Labouring Population of Great Britain*. It was extraordinarily wide-ranging, and contained far more information than simple factual description of sanitary conditions: the Birmingham section, for example, gave details of the height of local recruits to the marines, the number of cookshops in the town, and the extent of opium-taking.[25] Finally, in 1844 and 1845 there were published the *First and Second Reports of the Commissioners for inquiring into the State of Large Towns and Populous Districts* (reports of the Health of Towns Commission, appointed in 1843). In addition, Frederick Engels published a graphic description of living conditions in Manchester and elsewhere in his *Condition of the Working Classes in England in 1844* (though this was published in Germany in 1845, the first English edition did not appear in England till 1892).

These reports, together with Engels' investigation, provide a remarkable mass of information, making it obvious that action was urgently required in the towns. Little needs to be added to what has already been said regarding urban conditions, although Engels' famous passage on one of the worst parts of Manchester in 1844 still merits quotation:[26]

> A horde of ragged women and children swarm about, as filthy as the swine that thrive upon the garbage heaps and in the puddles ... The race that lives in these ruinous cottages behind broken windows mended with oilskin, sprung doors and rotten door posts, or in dark wet cellars in measureless filth and stench ... must really have reached the lowest stage of humanity ... In each of these pens, containing at most two rooms, a garret and perhaps a cellar, on the average, twenty persons live ... For each 120 persons, one usually unaccessible privy is provided ...

Such conditions were by no means confined to the larger towns. Among the worst areas in the Stourbridge district, and within two miles of Stourbridge town centre, was a district known as Lye Waste (also known locally as 'Mud City'), where the inhabitants had a tradi-tional right to erect their own cottages, thrown up almost overnight, and made of the local clay. R.A. Slaney, the commissioner for the Health of the Towns Commission for the area, commented:[27]

'Lye – a waste' – an appropriate name. These waste people are almost all nailers: their homes, or rather huts, are of all forms, grouped in two, three, or more together over a wide space. Filthy open ditches, heaps of rubbish and dirt, surround their neglected habitations; disorder and poverty appear on all sides; there are no regulations or attempts at improvement.

In fact, Stourbridge town itself was little better than Lye Waste, though conditions for the whole area were rather better than in most Black Country towns. A prize essay on sanitary reform in the town, dated 1848, makes it clear that Coventry Street, in particular, was in a disgraceful state: 'There are a great number of manure heaps, filthy muck-holes, pig-sties, and the *sock* generally finds its way all over the yards.' Angel Street and Lower Lane were worst of all; the author had never seen worse, in London or elsewhere. There was no drainage, close courts abounded, there were filthy privies, cesspools, open gutters, and many floors were lower than the street, so that drainage ran into them. The floors, however, were actually raised some inches by the accumulation of dirt. The population were lost to all sense of decency and morality, and were frequent victims of disease.[28]

The reader of the reports of the 1840s soon becomes accustomed to descriptions of unsanitary conditions quite appalling by today's standards (but, of course, it must be remembered that it was the business of eye-witnesses to point out the worst conditions they had encountered). Not all was uniformly bad. In some places the inhabitants had procured a private act of parliament which appointed improvement commissioners for their town. They had powers to pave, light, and clean the streets; though this often resulted in only the main thoroughfares being improved. This is true of Birmingham, where a number of Improvement Acts applied.[29] Local businessmen saw to it that shopping areas were reasonably clean and navigable. Thus, in *Sybil, or the Two Nations*, Disraeli describes the main shopping streets of his fictitious town Mowbray as respectable enough, 'with its blazing gaslights and magnificent shops'.[30] Further, there were places where a responsible landlord might exercise a beneficial control, as in Ashton-under-Lyne, where Engels described conditions as much better than in other manufacturing towns thanks to the Earl of Stamford: 'The streets are broader and cleaner, while the new, bright-red cottages give every appearance of comfort' (it seems unlikely that atmospheric pollution allowed the new brickwork to remain bright-red for very long). Then again, even non-industrial towns might have high death rates. Shrewsbury is a good example here, where in 1854 a local enquiry reported that a principal reason for high mortality rates was the practice of the poor of taking drinking water from a place on the banks of the River Severn where the contents of privies were deposited.

By 1844 the Health of Towns Association had been set up under the leadership of Southwood Smith, with branches in numerous towns. Also by this time the acknowledged leader of the public health movement had emerged in the person of Edwin Chadwick, secretary to the Poor Law Commission. Chadwick was not popular with his colleagues: he was opinionated and dictatorial in manner. But undoubtedly he was a powerful advocate of public health reform. His connection with the Poor Law Commission is significant, for he speedily became convinced that sickness among town populations was costing poor law authorities immense sums in care of the sick and in caring for widows and orphans. As he put it very plainly:[31]

> The annual loss of life from filth and bad ventilation is greater than the loss from death or wounds in any wars in which the country has been engaged in modern times.

In other words, it was cheaper in the long run to improve urban conditions by deep drainage, scavenging, and better water supplies than to throw ever-increasing burdens on the poor law authorities. Chadwick agreed with Southwood Smith that the squalid conditions in which the poor lived led to low moral standards, not the other way round. At the same time, he emphasised again and again that although expenditure was inevitable, it would actually save money eventually to install improved sewers and drains.

Another very important aspect of Chadwick's reforming plans was his advocacy of below-ground drainage systems. Of course, surface gutters and open sewers or channels were common enough, but what Chadwick strongly recommended were small, egg-shaped earthenware pipes in which refuse could be flushed away by water. The shape of the pipe, its inclination to the horizontal, and the force of water required, were all important and critical factors. All this was naturally regarded with suspicion by the sceptics, who still thought that disease was somehow spread by smells or miasmas. Chadwick himself believed in miasmas, but was insistent that decaying matter must be removed, for it itself caused disease. As he put it (albeit in a somewhat exaggerated form), 'All smell is, if it be intense, immediate acute disease.'

In spite of what in today's perspectives seems an overwhelming case for public health reform in the 1840s, bills introduced into parliament in 1845 and 1846 were both abandoned, and so was another bill brought forward in 1847 by Lord Morpeth. The central control at the heart of this bill's proposals was bitterly attacked on the grounds that it was 'a general usurpation, behind the backs of the people, of the power which ought to belong to the representatives of the people, and one step more towards the adoption of the continental system of representation ...'[32] One can safely say that 'the people' referred to here meant the middle and upper classes; few male members of the working classes (and no females) had the vote before 1867.

The bill was introduced again in 1848, and again was strongly attacked. The *Leeds Mercury*, for example, which had figured prominently in the factory reform movement, opposed it on the grounds that although all towns should have good sewerage and pure water, these benefits should not be purchased by 'a permanent infringement of the rights of municipal bodies'. *The Economist* also opposed the bill, with a stern warning that it was wrong to try to interfere with the ways of the Almighty in his dealings with mankind:[33]

> Suffering and evil are nature's admonitions: they cannot be got rid of; and the impatient attempts of benevolence to banish them from the world by legislation, before benevolence has learned their object and their end, have always been productive of more evil than good.

What allowed Morpeth to get his bill through at last was the threat of another cholera epidemic (it might be remarked that Morpeth was one of the few who could get on with Chadwick, and in effect was his agent in parliament; he deserves a place of honour in the history of public health). Yet even then the measure was largely permissive, and its operation limited to five years. It set up the Central Board of Health, together with local boards of health, but the latter were to be established only where town councils opted to adopt the act, or where one-tenth of the ratepayers applied for the act to take effect. The setting up of a local board was compulsory only where the death rate was more than 23 per 1,000 – that is, above the national average. London was not included in the act, as it required separate legislation. The new Central Board was not a strong body, and it had little or no money allocated to it.

Nevertheless, it signified the beginning of a national system of public health authorities, unpopular though it was at first. *The Times* is famous for its criticism of the act, declaring that it would rather take its chance of cholera and the rest than be bullied into good health by the new Central Board; and it painted a fanciful picture of Britain suffering 'a perpetual bath night' with master John Bull being 'scrubbed and rubbed, and small-toothcombed until the tears came into his eyes'.[34] In 1853 the board's life was extended by another year to 1854. By then, only 182 local boards had been appointed, and only thirteen had attempted to set up water works or deep drainage schemes. In 1854 the board was reconstituted, and Chadwick was removed from his post as one of the three public health commissioners. The board was finally dissolved in 1858, when its functions were divided between the Home Office and the Privy Council, and this situation continued until the new Local Government Board was established in 1871. Chadwick was pensioned off in 1854, and never again held high office.

Inevitably the question will be asked, why was there so much opposition to the 1848 act? The simplest answer would be to blame the strength of *laissez-faire* beliefs; but there was more to it than this. Drainage schemes cost a good deal of money, and it would be the ratepayers who would have to pay up, even if in the first instance loans could be obtained from the central authorities. Moreover, most ratepayers were middle class and lived well away from the slum areas of their towns, with much less need for sanitary improvements, yet they would have to shoulder the financial burdens resulting from reform. Then again, one of the greatest objections was to the interference with local government and the centralisation of control. There was a long tradition of resentment in the provinces at any form of interference with local self-government. Centralisation was deeply suspected: one correspondent in the *Morning Chronicle* declared that 'Even in Constantinople or in Grand Cairo where plague and cholera are decimating the population, it is doubtful whether such a bill would be desirable.' In the House of Commons, the bill was repeatedly attacked as being 'un-English and unconstitutional, corrupt in its tendency, and an advowal of a determination to destroy local self-government'.[35] Local builders understandably feared that their right to build as and when they liked would be challenged. Members of town improvement commissions disliked the idea of new, rival boards of health. Lastly, not all were convinced by Chadwick's advocacy of small-scale, self-scouring drainpipes, much smaller than the existing nine-inch house drains. The first glazed, earthenware drainpipe in England was actually made at Chadwick's insistence.[36] Many displayed a scepticism on the whole subject, arguing that smells were only natural and had to be tolerated.

To sum up: the most important reasons for opposition to reform were probably interference with local government, and the question of cost. Chadwick was well aware of the latter objection, of course, and this is why he laid such emphasis on the argument that prevention of disease was much cheaper than cure, arguing (for example) that his small-bore drainage system could drain three courts for the cost of draining two under the old system. The cost of public health provision constantly came up in the relevant literature of the time, where there were frequent references to European cities which had a good income from the sale of night soil from privies (Chadwick approved of this). In the Stourbridge Prize Essay, 1848 it was pointed out that Stourbridge could supply nitrogen enough to fertilise 8,000 acres of land from *its urine alone*; all privies should be drained into a tank, the contents pumped up a shaft 60 or 100 feet tall, then distributed to plugs in adjacent fields where it could be squirted over the surface. It seems a remarkable suggestion, though Chadwick himself experimented with a similar idea in 1849.[37]

In the twenty years or so following the passing of the Public Health Act, 1848, a good deal of piecemeal legislation was passed. London acquired its own Board of Works, replacing the old Commissioners for Sewers, by the Metropolitan Local Management Act, 1855. The Common Lodging Acts of 1851 and 1853 were passed to regulate the dirt and overcrowding of workmen's lodgings. Mayhew was told that London's lodging houses accommodated over 80,000 persons per night, and that their living conditions were disgusting beyond belief:[38]

> Nothing could be worse to the health than these places, without ventilation, cleanliness, or decency, and with forty people's breath perhaps mingling together in one foul choking steam of stench.

More nuisance acts were passed in 1848, 1855, 1860, and 1863. The Sewer Utilisation Act, 1865, created a new group of sewer authorities which in effect spread public health legislation into the countryside. Emergency powers to prevent the spread of disease were made available by the Disease Prevention Acts of 1848 and 1855. Finally, the Sanitation Act, 1866, gave additional powers to local authorities, and nuisance removal was made compulsory.

From all this, it is obvious that a great deal was done to extend and amplify the sanitary law in the 1850s and 1860s. Although Chadwick's dismissal was a real blow to public health reform, he was replaced by a much less abrasive and more quietly persuasive personality, Dr John

Simon. Simon was appointed as London's first medical officer of health in 1848, and became medical officer to the General Board of Health in 1855. When the board was dissolved in 1858, its duties were split between the Local Government Act Office and the new medical department of the Privy Council. Simon became the first medical officer of this new department – in effect, the government's chief medical officer. Under Simon's guidance, much administrative progress was made in the following years, though most of the legislation still remained permissive rather than imperative.

In fact, by the 1860s, a bewildering variety of local health authorities existed, each cultivating its own part of a crowded field, and each levying its own local taxation. There were the local boards of health, the poor law guardians, the reformed municipal authorities, improvement commissioners, highway boards, burial boards, select vestries, and so on. A great jungle of authorities had grown up, often conflicting with each other. Yet in spite of this growth of authorities, it was still possible for grossly insanitary conditions to exist. A further brief excursion into Black Country history will make the point.

In 1866, the Stourbridge improvement commissioners secured the passing of an additional Improvement Act. A local newspaper took the opportunity of urging the commissioners to visit anew the worst parts of the town. The paper's own reporter described what he had seen: in one part, a privy used by several families with wet soil oozing upward from the bricks and flowing out into a narrow entry; several pigsties, with pig wash in open barrels, and attached to a privy, an open cesspool; three more privies, dirty and leaky, used by a score of families; close to, a bakehouse in which a batch of bread was observed; there were three tons of night soil and ashes in another part of the court, adjoining two leaky privies, on which barefooted children played; in a corner was a horse in an improvised stable, with a heap of moist manure, over which were two broken windows of sleeping apartments; in Angel Street there were three tons of manure adjoining a pigsty with four pigs, two horses in a stable, and several fowls and chicken. An old woman was asked what she thought of her surroundings. She replied, 'Sure, no choler or faver would ever come nigh them if the Lawd didn't sind it.'[39] Perhaps it paid to be fatalistic when still living in conditions typical of those so often described in Chadwick's report, nearly a quarter of a century before, and apparently still untouched by the efforts of the local improvement commissioners.

By the late 1860s there was still much to be done to repair the ravages of industrialism and its consequences in the industrial towns, but an important start had been made. One last caveat must be made: the reports of the time naturally concentrated on the worst aspects of urban life, but it is necessary to maintain a sense of perspective. Not all the industrial working classes lived in squalor. There was still plenty of respectable working-class housing, and only the very worst housing could properly be called slum property. It is the insanitary horrors in the reports which remain in the memory, for obvious reasons. Professor F.M.L. Thompson has put this point succinctly: 'Victorian slums were nasty, affronts to the wealth and civilisation around them, and it is important to understand what they were like and why they existed; but it is as important to remember that four-fifths or nine-tenths of the people did not live in slum conditions.'[40] This is well said.

Working conditions

It was noted in the previous chapter that among the Whig reforms was the passing of the first effective Factory Act in 1833 – generally regarded as a real step forward in that the first national (as opposed to local) factory inspectors were appointed. At the time, however, it was a disappointment to the reformers in that it failed to reduce the working day for women and children to ten hours (the radical *True Sun* called it 'the infamous White Slavery Bill', and claimed that the Whigs had passed 'a Twelve Hours Humbug'). So the Ten Hours campaign continued. Further factory bills were introduced in 1838, 1839, and 1841, but all failed to pass. Meanwhile, public interest in the issue of child labour led to the appointment of the first Children's Employment Commission in 1840. Among its earliest reports were graphic descriptions of women and children down the mines. The employment of women below ground was limited to certain coal-fields, but the illustrations depicting women at work underground (sometimes half-naked), together with the allegations of sexual immorality down the pits, horrified the Victorian public as much as the drawings of young children chained to coal trucks or carrying heavy loads of coal. Certainly there had been an increase in the employment of both women and children below ground consequent on the great expansion in the production of coal. A bill to stop the employment of all women and girls, and all boys under the age of thirteen, passed the House of Commons at 'railway speed' (as one noble lord put it), but was held up for a while in the Lords, princi-pally by Lord Londonderry, who argued that women were essential for the mining of certain kinds of coal (incredulous voices were raised in the Lords at this astonishing assertion). Ultimately, the Lords passed the bill, though at the cost of lowering the age at which boys might start work below ground from twelve to ten. Inspectors were also appointed by the Mines Act, 1842.

Renewed attempts were made thereafter at factory legislation. Another factory bill was introduced in 1843, only to be dropped because its educational clauses met with opposition; but in 1844 another bill, this time without educational provisions, was successful. The Factory Act, 1844, limited hours for those aged between eight and thirteen to six and a half, and made twelve hours the maximum for women as well as for young people. Moreover, dangerous machinery was also to be fenced (women's hair in particular was liable to be caught up in overhead driving bands). In 1846 yet another factory bill was defeated, but only narrowly; the Ten Hours movement and its supporting short-time committees all over the country at last achieved their ends with the passing of the Factory Act, 1847, which gave the ten-hour day. It had taken sixteen years of campaigning. Unhappily, this was not quite the end of the matter, for children could still be worked in relays, thus permitting a very long working day for adult males. Grey's Factory Act, 1850, made the normal working day from 6 a.m. to 6 p.m., in return for a slight lengthening of women's and young person's hours to ten-and-a-half hours (for which concession Lord Ashley was roundly criticised). Grey's act was amended by a further act in 1853 which settled all doubts, under which the ten-and-a-half hours limitation for young people (to eighteen) and women in effect set the working day for adult men in textile factories as well.

The most famous consequences of industrialisation for working conditions is undoubtedly the development of the factory system, but by 1853 the excessive hours worked by children and young women had at least been curbed, while (as we have just seen), the working day for adult males had also been restricted.[41] Much of this had been achieved by pressure from without, combined with the efforts of Ashley, Fielden, and Saddler within parliament. Yet textile workers in the factories of Lancashire, Yorkshire, and Scotland formed only a small proportion of the nation's labour force, and the regulation of their hours might still be regarded as somewhat exceptional and unnecessary for workers elsewhere. It is true that two further acts were passed in the early 1860s to regulate children's hours of work, but both were to do with the textile industry – the Bleach and Dye Works Act, 1860, and the Lace Act, 1861. It took the appointment of another Children's Employment Commission in 1862, and the seven lengthy reports published by the commission, to advance further the reform of working conditions. Although the commissioners seemed to think that rather less cruelty to children had been revealed than in the 1840s, they were especially concerned at children's working conditions in the brickyards, pottery works, and match factories. The 1864 Factory Act regulated hours and conditions in both pottery and match manufacture, while the 1867 Factory Act redefined factories so as to bring within the scope of the acts large places of work such as ironworks and glassworks, generally allowing only part-time work and no night work for children up to the ages of eleven or twelve. This was a sweeping extension of factory legislation so as to include many workers outside the textile industry.

Of equal and even greater importance was the first Workshop Act, also passed in 1867. It defined a workshop, and excluded all children under eight; children under thirteen could work only part time, while women and other children ('young persons') were restricted to twelve hours. The act is often treated in the textbooks as having little effect, since it was defective in detail and very poorly enforced at first by local inspectors. Matters improved from 1871 onwards, when the factory inspectors took over inspection. Even then, the vast numbers of workshops in areas of domestic industry such as the Black Country made enforcement very difficult, if not actually impossible; one Black Country inspector in 1876 claimed that he had 10,000 workshops on his patch, averaging three and a half persons each – a scarcely believable figure for one area alone. There is no doubt that workshop inspection was a much more difficult problem than factory inspection, and it was notorious that purely domestic workshops, containing only a man and his wife, were rarely inspected – it was not thought proper to prosecute a man for overworking his wife; while in some bigger workshops the school children would troop in to lend a hand after school hours with little fear of interference by inspectors. Nevertheless, 1867 is a key year in the history of the regulation of working conditions. Henceforth, the state was committed to the supervision of working hours and the working environment not only in textile factories but elsewhere as well. It would have been difficult to have predicted this extension of government responsibilities at the beginning of the century.

The trade unions

Meanwhile, trade unionism as a movement made significant progress in the middle years of the nineteenth century, though still confined very largely to skilled workers. It remains unclear how far the movement contributed to Chartism. Many unions forbade participation in political matters, though individual members were free, of course, to take part in Chartist activities. So official union support for Chartism was lacking save in London, where the tailors, shoemakers, cabinet makers, and building craftsmen were all threatened by the employment of unskilled, sweated labour by the employers. Otherwise, the trade unions held aloof. Branches of the Steam Engine Makers Society were actually suspended by the society for placing funds in the Chartist Land Bank. Feargus O'Connor, the Chartist leader, was criticised by the Manchester printers as an unfair employer, while he criticised the craft unions, famously describing them as 'the pompous trades and proud mechanics'. The fact seems to be that although Chartism grew until its supporters included many with sectional aims and interests – for example, there were teetotal Chartists as well as education Chartists – the movement was basically political in its aims. These were set out in the Charter, and aimed to reform parliament, and through universal suffrage, increase working-class political power. This was not the business of the trade unions at this stage of their development, and so they remained apart. Chartism declined, but trade unionism remained, and indeed advanced in the improved trade conditions of the later years of the 1840s.[42]

Even then, the movement as a whole was still very small: the Webbs estimated the membership in 1842 as less than 100,000, that is, about 1.5 per cent of the work force (though it must be remembered that 1842 was a very depressed year). Thus, the trade unionism of the time meant little or nothing to the vast majority of working men and women. When a last, belated effort was made in Sheffield in 1845 to set up a national union of all trades (the National Association of United Trades for the Protection of Labour), it lasted less than three years. Even in mining, where trade unionism was relatively well established, the Miners' Association of Great Britain and Ireland, which was formed in 1842, finally collapsed during the depression in the coal trade in 1847–8. A more encouraging development was the creation of a new amalgamated trade union in 1851, the Amalgamated Society of Engineers (ASE), based principally on the Journeymen Steam Engine and Machine Makers and Millwrights Society, which had been founded in Manchester in 1826.[43]

For the Webbs, the pioneer historians of trade unionism, the setting up of the ASE represented the beginning of a new era, the era of 'model unionism'. They regarded the ASE as a new, model union, setting an example for other unions for the succeeding decades; it was a national union, with high subscription rates, a paid secretary, and conciliatory attitudes towards employers. Modern historians of the trade union movement have rejected nearly all these views, including the Webbs' belief that the earlier period up to 1843 was a revolutionary period, which was succeeded by 'The New Spirit and the New Model' period up to 1860. Briefly, national unions had been tried before (as already noted), paid secretaries were not new, nor were high subscriptions paid by skilled workers (the ASE subscription was 1/- per week); further, the ASE did not become a model for other unions (many remained regional or even local), while it was not always conciliatory in approach. In 1852 it led a large-scale strike of engineers in Lancashire and London. Hence, the Webbs' emphasis on new model unionism was somewhat misplaced, and indeed, one historian has called it 'a piece of historical fiction'; another suggests that what occurred was not the creation of a new model, 'but the strengthening of the old'. Yet when all is said and done, the creation of the ASE remains an important advance. It not only survived, but it prospered; by the mid-1860s, it included up to three-quarters of those employed in engineering, and had a total membership of about 33,000 in 808 branches.

It was undoubtedly the more prosperous conditions of the 1850s and 1860s which encouraged the growth of trade unionism. Overall membership figures have been estimated at about 600,000 in 1859, and 800,000 in 1867 (an estimate by George Potter, editor of the radical journal the *Beehive*): but these figures conceal variations in the size and organisation of unions. Very few were as large or as rich as the ASE, and few offered such a range of benefits. Most concentrated on out-of-work and funeral benefits; for example, the London brickmakers had no sickness fund at all. Union densities varied from trade to trade: in 1867, 90 per cent of cotton spinners were unionised, and 90 per cent of provincial printers, but only 25 per cent of cabinet makers. Sectionalism – the restriction of membership to skilled trades – was still very evident. In the iron industry, for example, the skilled master puddler would be a member of a union, but his young assistant working on the same furnace would not.[44]

One noticeable feature of unionism at this time was the growing respectability of the movement. Increasingly, employers were prepared to negotiate peacefully over wages and working conditions, and this is shown in the development of various local conciliation and arbitration boards. The best-known example of this is the Nottingham Board of Arbitration for the Hosiery Trade, 1860, while the Midlands Iron and Steel Wages Board adopted a system of sliding scales for wages, which were adjusted as iron and steel prices rose and fell. In Birmingham, the alliance system was adopted for a time. By this, wages and conditions were negotiated on the principle of the closed shop (exclusive employment of union members). All this is very different from the savage disputes and sometimes physical violence of the 1830s. Middle-class attitudes to the respectable working classes were certainly changing in the mid-century years. Gladstone is said to have been greatly impressed by the good order and peaceful behaviour of the Lancashire cotton workers thrown out of work during the Cotton Famine which resulted from the American Civil War, 1861–65. The Tories and the Liberals vied with each other in presenting franchise bills, extending the vote to male householders in the boroughs. Disraeli finally succeeded in 1867, when his Reform Act went rather further than he had intended. The bill in its final form was a striking contrast to the Reform Act, 1832, even though still intended by Disraeli as a 'bulwark against democracy'.

However, all was not sweetness and light. Strikes still took place from time to time, one of the most serious being the strike in the London building trades, 1859–60. This arose out of a demand for a nine-hour day in the trades, and led to a general lock-out in London by the building employers. The employers finally broke the strike by the use of the 'document', whereby workers offered employment undertook not to join a union. One result of the strike was the formation of the London Trades Council, a body consisting of leading trade unionists, meeting to discuss political and other matters of interest to the unions, such as factory and mines legislation, the law relating to master and servant, and popular education. After the passing of the 1867 Reform Act, the leaders of the biggest London unions (nicknamed by the Webbs the 'Junta') founded the Labour Representation League, to support the return of working men to parliament. Generally speaking, and in the words of William Allen of the ASE, the purpose of the London Trades Council was 'to look after parliamentary affairs'. Its interests were surprisingly wide, extending even to discussion of foreign policy and its effects on workers abroad.[45]

Thus, the trade unions had reached an interesting stage in their development by the early 1860s. They were to face unexpected setbacks in the late 1860s which will be discussed in the next chapter; but in the early 1860s they were on a new plane of respectability and (on the whole) acceptance by employers when compared with the situation in the earlier years. If, as Adam Smith had observed many years previously, employers were always in conspiracy against their employees, the industrialisation of the first half of the nineteenth century had produced a counteracting force among the skilled trades, at least, by the 1860s. It was ultimately to result in the politicisation of substantial numbers of the working classes thereafter.

Popular education

It seems unlikely that trades unionism could have advanced as it did in the mid-century years without a considerable improvement in popular education. Clearly, working-class leaders needed at least to be literate to take on the responsibility of a branch secretaryship. Following the first annual grant to the church societies in 1833, in 1839 the payment of the grant was placed under the control of a committee of the Privy Council. Government school inspectors were also appointed. In 1846 the secretary to this committee, Dr James Kay (afterwards Sir James Kay-Shuttleworth) introduced a scheme for the training of teachers, first in the schools themselves (the pupil-teacher system, for thirteen-year-olds, lasting five years), then in training colleges. By the 1860s this system was firmly established, and was to continue until the end of the century, and even beyond. In the mid-1860s the annual grant to the societies had reached nearly three-quarters of a million pounds, and had many years previously been extended to include not only the upkeep of the actual buildings, but also the cost of furniture and apparatus. Nevertheless, the church societies were still voluntary bodies, dependent on subscriptions from their supporters. In addition to the church schools, there existed a myriad of private schools, and many Sunday schools. In 1851, it has been estimated that nearly a third of the 2 million at school were in private schools, while 74.5 per cent of working-class children attended Sunday schools.[46]

A number of questions arise from this apparent increase in the numbers of working-class children at school. First, it may be asked, how far was it the direct result of industrialisation itself? Older views on this subject emphasised the need for literacy in the factory, the ability to read notices and instructions and so on, but this is now discounted; child workers in the mills did not really need to be literate, and it seems that literacy actually declined in the late eighteenth and early nineteenth centuries in some industrial areas.[47] In fact, literacy seems to have varied from region to region, dependent on local conditions and attitudes.[48] Overall, it seems likely that the basic motive for change was the increasing acceptance of the importance of social discipline; this is the principal line of argument pursued in this book, qualified by later contemporary perceptions in all probability of the simple usefulness of basic skills of numeracy and literacy.

Another question to be answered is, how far were children actually attending school by the 1860s? In 1833, the *Abstract of Educational Returns* gives a figure of 11 per cent of the population of England and Wales attending school; this figure is repeated in the Census returns for 1851.[49] As the proportion of children between five and twelve was nearly 17 per cent of the total population, this means that about 6 per cent were not in schools at all. Of equal or greater significance was the question of how long children were staying at school: at a conference in 1857, it was stated that of the 2 million on school registers, 42 per cent attended for less than a year, and only 22 per cent for between one and two years.[50] In the mid-1860s, in the industrial county of Staffordshire, only 25 per cent of the school children were aged ten or above.[51] All this is in marked contrast to the seven years of education thought of as an acceptable norm from five to twelve.

From these figures it may be supposed that working-class parents as a whole hardly regarded themselves as deprived of parental rights to education for their children. No doubt many thought that education could be a good thing, but it was not essential for getting on in life. In the Black Country, for instance, it was thought that any boy with gumption should be able to advance himself by his own efforts. They observed that those from their own ranks who had got on could be as well or even better off than middle-class people like solicitors or parsons with books on their shelves. Too much schooling made boys 'rodneys', or cissies. There was a well-known Black Country saying that the father went down the pit and made a fortune; the son went to school and lost it. No doubt much of this hostility was the result of the traditional practice of sending children out to some form of employment as soon as they were physically able to work; even the few pence they earned a week would augment the family income.

It was for this reason that (according to inspectors) parents would urge teachers to 'finish their children off quickly', so that they could start work. Further, it seemed to be more important for some parents to pay the weekly cost of barley and peas for their racing pigeons than to pay the weekly pence (usually two pence or three pence) for school fees.[52]

Yet in spite of problems of this kind in persuading parents to send their children to school, and in spite of low attendances when they did get there, more children appeared to becoming literate in the mid-years of the century. The official literacy figures for these years (Table 2.1) confirm this.[53] Thus, the numbers attending school, for however brief a period, probably increased considerably in this period. No doubt the relative prosperity of the time helps to explain

Table 2.1 Official literacy figures, 1841–71 (%)

	1841	1851	1861	1871
Males	67.3	69.3	75.4	80.6
Females	51.1	54.8	65.3	73.2

this, making it less necessary for parents to send their children out to work early. An interesting attempt by the mines inspector, H.S. Tremenheere, to encourage parents to keep children at school, took the form of a prize scheme in the mining districts which awarded cash prizes to parents keeping their children in attendance, thus compensating them for the loss of children's earnings. About twenty-three of these schemes were instituted by 1859, and cash prizes, accompanied by elaborately designed certificates, were duly awarded.[54]

The increasing size of the school population did not escape the attention of the government. In 1853, Lord Russell introduced a bill to allow larger towns to levy a school rate, but it was rejected. However, in 1858 the Newcastle Commission was appointed to enquire into the state of public education, and to investigate means of extending 'sound and cheap elementary education to all classes of people'. The commission reported in 1861. It estimated that just under one in eight (i.e. about 12 per cent) were attending school in 1858 (so that there was still a shortfall). It also recommended that the cost of schooling should be met by a local county education rate. A further recommendation was that as teachers were spending too much time on frills, and not enough on the three Rs, grants to schools should depend on annual examinations conducted by special inspectors. This was obviously a gesture towards cheapness in education, and the resulting system, put into effect by Robert Lowe, secretary of the Committee of Council for Education, became known as 'payment by results'. The system was based not only on examination results but also on regular attendances. It placed a great strain on pupils and teachers alike, and was heartily disliked by them, and by the school inspectorate, too.

Working-class education made considerable progress by 1870, and the majority of children were attending school by then, though for varying periods, but attendance was still not compulsory, and the education provided was of the most rudimentary kind. Giving evidence before the Newcastle Commission, one inspector, the Reverend James Fraser, suggested that taking into account 'the real interests of the peasant boy ... we must make up our minds to see the last of him, so far as the day school is concerned, at 10 or 11'. He went on to list the basic essentials for such a boy: to spell, read a common narrative, write a letter home, add up a shop bill, have some knowledge of where foreign countries were situated, and above all, understand a plain sermon and know his duty to God and man.[55] Lowe himself underlined this essentially economical approach to working-class education:[56]

> We propose to give no grant for the attendance of children at school unless they can read, write, and cypher; but we do not say that they should not learn more. We do not object to any amount of learning; the only question is, how much of that knowledge we ought to pay for ... We do not propose to give these children an education that will raise them above their station and business in life.

So it was to be a very elementary kind of education which was to be given financial support. Industrialisation had raised the question of extending the education at a very basic level of a working class which was rapidly becoming engaged in industry rather than agriculture. But it was all to be done in a severely utilitarian manner. There was no question of anything approaching what today would be called secondary education, and certainly no intention of raising any child above his 'station or business in life'. Yet even here, the state's financial commitment was becoming increasingly large. Something further simply had to be done to provide wider financial support for working-class education. The church societies were finding it more and more difficult to provide enough school places. The idea of a local education rate, proposed by Russell in 1853, and again by the Newcastle Commission, had always been fiercely contested by the societies, jealous of losing their privileged position, and also by the Nonconformists, who feared an extension of Anglican interest in any new system of elementary schools. As Graham bitterly remarked of the opposition to the 1843 factory bill, 'Religion, the keystone of education, is in this country the bar to progress.'[57] Yet in 1870, as will be seen in the next chapter, the government was forced to remove that bar to progress when they introduced Forster's education bill.

The poor law

One of the most onerous tasks inherited by Victorian governments was the implementing of the Poor Law Amendment Act, 1834, which swept away the old poor law system. That system was replaced by a bureaucratic organisation designed to deter applicants for relief by instituting a harsh regime in the workhouse ('less eligibility') and abolishing all outdoor relief ('the workhouse test'). As noted in the previous chapter, the workhouse after 1834 became a place much feared by the poor, who would do their best to avoid entering it. Hippolyte Taine, the distinguished French observer, commented on this, following a visit to a Manchester workhouse in the 1860s: 'The building is spacious, perfectly clean, well-kept: it has large courts, gardens are attached to it, looks upon fields and stately trees ...' After describing how different categories of paupers were cared for, and the diet provided, he remarked that they were astounded, for the place was 'a palace compared with the kennels in which the poor dwell'. But he went on to say that when offered accommodation in the house, nine out of ten refused:[58]

> I am informed that they prefer their home and freedom at any price, that they cannot bear being shut up and subject to discipline. They prefer to be free and to starve ... The workhouse is regarded as a prison; the poor consider it a point of honour not to go there.

In fact, not all workhouses were as clean and well run as the workhouse visited by Taine. In practice, in the Midlands and the north, it sometimes took years before the new system was implemented, and in some areas the old poor law authorities stubbornly kept to their old traditions. In the south, in the agricultural areas, it proved easier to establish the new poor law, although even here, there could be problems. The Andover workhouse was certainly not as well run as Taine's Manchester workhouse. In 1845 a riot broke out in the Andover house when the paupers, given the job of grinding bones for agricultural fertiliser, fought over the scraps of meat still adhering to the bones. This led to a select committee of enquiry in 1846, and the replacement in 1847 of the poor law commissioners by the new Poor Law Board, with certain *ex-officio* places occupied by senior members of the government. The only other major change in the administration of the new poor law took place in 1871 when the Poor Law Board was absorbed by the new Board of Local Government.

When the history of the new poor law system is surveyed from its inception in 1834 to about 1870, certain features stand out. The first is the lack of uniformity in the system. This is particularly noticeable in the north, where the old poor law had worked reasonably well in helping not only the young, the old, and the sick, but also the unemployed when trade was depressed. Although the central authority made strenuous efforts from time to time to prohibit all outdoor relief, in practice, as already mentioned, it proved impossible to do so in times of industrial depression when the workhouse could not possibly accommodate all applicants for relief; and in any case it was cheaper to give relief outside the workhouse rather than inside. So outdoor relief was widespread during slumps, especially in Lancashire during the Cotton Famine, 1861–5, when it was often administered humanely. Indeed, guardians were urged to be generous, given the circumstances of the time. One eye-witness account of Lancashire guardians illustrates this point very well:[59]

> A clean, old decrepit man presented himself. 'What's brought you here, Joseph?' said the chairman. 'Why; aw've nought to do – nor nought to tak to'. 'What's your daughter, Ellen, doing, Joseph?' 'Hoo's eawt o' wark'. 'An' what's your wife doing?' 'Hoo's bin bed-fast aboon five year'. The old man was relieved at once; but, as he walked away, he looked hard at his ticket, as if it wasn't exactly the kind of thing: and turning round, he said, 'Couldn't yo let me be a sweeper i' the streets, isted, Mr Eccles?'

Second, it is noticeable that in the mid-century years rather more attention was given to separate classes of workhouse inmates. The best example here is that of the children. They always formed a large proportion of workhouse paupers, some staying for only a few weeks, some staying for much longer – bastards, orphans, children deserted by their parents, and so on. A much larger category of pauper child were on outdoor relief: four-fifths of all destitute children were relieved outside the workhouse – on any one day in the period 1834 to 1909 their numbers rarely fell below 200,000, and sometimes were more than 300,000.[60] Inside the workhouse, small children stayed with their mothers, while older children had some sort of teaching, usually of an unsatisfactory nature. By the Poor Law (Schools) Act, 1848, unions were permitted to combine together and set up large boarding schools of up to a thousand children or more. These district schools (often called 'barrack schools') were thought to be a good way of shielding children from the bad influence of adult paupers, and of helping them to get jobs when they grew up. The schools were expensive both to build and to maintain, and were set up mostly in the London area, though many smaller unions continued to provide their own in-house schools. One inspector, E.C. Tufnell, gave enthusiastic support to district schools:[61]

> The main secret for destroying hereditary pauperism … is to well-educate the children away from adult paupers, and then to send them into the world, as far removed as possible from their own miserable relations and parishes, where they have known nothing but vice and misery.

These schools were criticised later in the century for their institutional nature, but some at least provided a better alternative to life in the workhouse itself. Dickens had been an earlier opponent of the new poor law, and his description of life in the workhouse in *Oliver Twist* (1837) is well known, but in 1850 he gave a favourable report of the Manchester Guardians' school at Swinton, describing the scene in the playground where 'some children were enjoying themselves in the sunshine, some were playing at marbles, others were frisking cheerfully'.[62] Although apprenticeship was common under the old poor law, often into husbandry (boys) and domestic service (girls), this practice seems to have declined from the mid-century years onwards, possibly because of the increased emphasis on schooling. In fact, in 1856 the Poor Law Board specifically forbade apprenticeship to domestic service, though apprenticeship to the merchant navy was still permitted by the Merchant Shipping Act, 1835.[63]

Two other categories of workhouse inmates must be mentioned briefly: the physically sick and the mentally ill. In most of the workhouses, very little seems to have been done early on for the sick, while the mentally ill were simply left to their own devices, or locked up if violent. However, a series of articles in the *Lancet* in 1866 on conditions in London workhouses led to reform, and in 1868 the Poor Law Board issued regulations for the provision of sick wards, and the employment of trained nurses. As for the mentally ill, separate wards were established in workhouse infirmaries in 1862, and the Metropolitan Poor Act, 1867 authorised the setting up of separate asylums for the sick or the insane in the London area. During the second half of the century, many workhouse unions in the larger towns built their own separate infirmaries. Unlike the voluntary hospitals of the time, the infirmaries were generally free, and they became the hospitals for the working classes.

The new poor law was to last well into the twentieth century. The major reasons for its existence were the alarming increase in the cost of the old poor law and the belief that the old law was both inefficient and corrupt, the Speenhamland system of supplementing low wages in particular being condemned as encouraging sloth and vice. The principles of the new poor law were harsh and uncompromising. There was no question, of course, of any positive measures either to prevent unemployment, or to help those infirm due to old age, other than the meagre sums given as outdoor relief; and even then, efforts were made from time to time, as in the 1870s, to restrict outdoor relief, and to rely on the deterrent effect of the 'workhouse test'. Thus the new poor law was very different from the old poor law, which, according to William Cobbett, was often viewed as part of an Englishman's birthright.[64] There was nothing shameful about accepting relief in the eighteenth century. Professor Blaug has described the old poor law as a welfare state in miniature, and although this may be to go too far, Professor F.M.L. Thompson has suggested more recently that the popular attitude to the old poor law was one of affectionate attachment.[65]

The working classes clearly did not show any affectionate attachment for the new poor law, and for most, the workhouse and its strict discipline became a symbol of defeat and humiliation. Exceptions to this can be found, as we have seen, especially in the north. Much depended on the Board of Guardians and on the relieving officer; and in times of local distress, outdoor relief became unavoidable, though the allowances given were usually meagre enough. Again, as already noted, more specialised care for different classes of pauper began to develop in the second half of the nineteenth century, and variations in administrative practice were common.[66] Nevertheless, working men and women kept well away from the workhouse as far as possible, relying for support from their friendly society (whenever they could afford the subscriptions), or from local charities, or from relatives.[67] During the Cotton Famine, a special act, the Public Works Act, 1863, actually attempted to provide work, usually on the roads, for unemployed cotton workers, while a 'million pounds fund' was also organised to help them. The Board of Guardians were therefore the last resort for anyone in need of succour, while the workhouses themselves in time contained very few able-bodied inmates. This is well put in a *Report on the Dietaries of Inmates of Workhouses, 1867*:[68]

> At present, those who enjoy the advantages of these institutions are almost solely such as may fittingly receive them, *viz*, the aged and the infirm, the destitute sick, and children. Workhouses are now asylums and infirmaries, and not places where work is necessarily extracted in return for food, clothing, and shelter.

Contemporary attitudes

The early Victorian state had survived the traumas of the early 1840s, and had emerged onto the relatively sunlit plains of the 1850s and 1860s. Professor W.L. Burn has termed these later years the 'age of equipoise'.[69] The Victorians now found themselves to be the most industrialised nation on earth. Moreover, the average Englishman and Englishwoman had become a creature of the towns rather than of the countryside, and this process of urbanisation was to continue for the rest of the century. What, then, did they think of themselves? Up to 1851 they certainly regarded themselves as a Christian people, overwhelmingly Protestant in outlook. This conviction was certainly shaken by the results of the first (and only) national religious census of church and chapel attendance, taken in March 1851 on the same day as the Census of Population. When all allowances were made for non-attendance on account of illness, age, or going to work, it appeared that only one in two in England and Wales actually attended a place of worship on Census Sunday. Moreover, attendance was pitifully low among the working classes in the cities and larger towns, this latter fact leading to much alarm at the apparent loss of faith by working people in urban areas. In fact, this was to ignore the respectable attendance in less industrialised districts, and even in some industrial areas; for example, in industrial Merthyr Tydfil, one of the largest towns in Wales at the time, attendance was 88.5 per cent; but attention was focused very narrowly on the apparently godless state of the urban working masses. Attendance by the middle classes was much higher, as one might expect, and attendance at church or chapel for them had become very much of a social convention; *not* to be seen going to church would certainly give rise to comment. Religious controversy was stirred up further by the publication of Darwin's *The Origin of Species* in 1859. So the great debate on evolution began, in which Thomas Huxley was to emerge as the leading propagandist for Darwinism. In the 1860s, doubt was beginning to creep in, certainly into middle-class thinking. In 1867 Matthew Arnold published his moving poem 'Dover Beach', in which he refers to the Sea of Faith which once was at the full:

> But now I only hear
> Its melancholy, long withdrawing roar,
> Retreating, to the breath
> Of the night-wind, down the vast edges drear
> And naked shingles of the world.

To turn to secular matters: how did contemporaries regard the material progress of the nation in its new role as the workshop of the world? No doubt many of the middle class regarded its achievements with pride, especially after the Great Exhibition, that showcase of British industrial might. At the heart of it all was the nation's great capacity for dedicated work: according to Dickens in *Hard Times*, 'You saw nothing in Coketown but what was severely workful', while Carlyle observed, 'Properly speaking, all work is religion'[70] (a nineteenth-century version of the old tag, '*Laborare est orare*'). In this sense, the Victorians were still highly religious. Moreover, work and its accompanying virtue, thrift, were the product of the highest principle of all, which was self-help.

Indeed, by the 1860s it might appear that *laissez-faire* and individualism had become universally accepted. Certainly in economic matters it had become a truism; many years previously, Bentham had laid it down that in economic matters the government should refrain from interference: '*Be quiet* ought on those occasions to be the motto or watchword of government.'[71] By the 1840s, John Stuart Mill was prepared to admit exceptions to the rule, but of the rule itself, there was no doubt: 'Letting alone should be the general practice, every departure from it unless required by some great good is a certain evil.'[72] This philosophic acceptance of *laissez-faire* was popularised by the famous work entitled *Self-Help*, published by Samuel Smiles in 1859. Its opening passage makes the message very clear:[73]

> 'Heaven helps those who help themselves' is a well-tried maxim, embodying in a small compass the results of vast human experience. The spirit of self-help is the root of all genuine growth in the individual; and, exhibited in the lives of many, it constitutes the true course of national vigour and strength.

It would seem then that by 1860 self-help and the rejection of state interference were hardly controversial – certainly there could be no dispute about this in economic affairs: witness the government's policy of free trade. However, the difficulty again crops up that by that date the state had set up a new, highly centralised poor law system, had regulated the employment of women and children in factories and mines, had financed popular education on an increasing scale, and had even made limited liability available to companies in 1856 and 1862. Further examples are available in the civil registration of births, marriages, and deaths, and in public health matters such as the Public Health Act, 1848, and the removal of nuisances. How can this contradiction between theory and practice be explained?

In the first place, it may be reaffirmed that in economic affairs, free trade held good in practice; as a matter of government policy, it was not finally abandoned till the early 1930s. Second, it was pointed out in the previous chapter that not even Bentham consistently opposed state interference, nor did Malthus. Further, as we have just seen, John Stuart Mill would permit the intervention of the state when it was 'required by some great good'. Third, the simple fact was that industrialisation was transforming society, and as a result, the government was constantly being forced into action as yet another 'great good' came to the fore. No doubt the 'administrative momentum' discussed earlier played a part in all this, though the lead was taken by the dedicated reformers of the time – Shaftesbury, Southwood Smith, Chadwick, Simon, and the rest. So however desirable government non-interference might seem in theory, in practice it became increasingly inevitable, in spite of the attacks on it by opponents such as the philosopher, Herbert Spencer, in his books *The Proper Sphere of Government* (1843) and *Social Statics* (1851). Yet even here, before 1870, its scope was still very limited. Poor relief, it is true, was offered by the state on a national scale, but it was in a severely deterrent form, as we have seen. The working classes kept well away, preferring self-help through friendly societies, or the immense range of Victorian charitable societies, often in the latter case no doubt at the expense of their pride and self-respect. After 1870, however, the proper organisation of charitable aid was seen as more and more of a problem, as will be seen in the next chapter.

Working-class attitudes to industrialisation have already been touched on in the previous chapter, when it was suggested that one manifestation of working-class protest was the co-operative movement. However, this was limited in scope and the movement did not become a major part of working-class life until after 1844, when the success of the Rochdale Pioneers led to a great expansion in co-operative retail trading throughout the country. The Chartist movement was different in nature, of course, and it peaked in the 1840s. How far was Chartism a protest against industrialisation? As noted earlier, it is generally accepted today that Chartism was in its origins a political movement, based on the six points of the Charter, all designed to give better parliamentary representation to the male worker. In essence, Chartism was the product of the traditional radicalism of the British skilled worker, who had been bitterly disappointed at the failure of the 1832 Reform Act to do much for him; but at the same time, many who joined the movement hoped that political reform would bring social reform and a better standard of living.

This is understandable enough, given the depression of the late 1830s and early 1840s. What is difficult to argue is that Chartism was exclusively a revolt against the growth of industry. It is true that some factory workers were Chartists – in his *Sybil, or the Two Nations,* Disraeli has a character called Devilsdust, who is a factory worker who hates the factory bell – but certainly not all factory workers were Chartists protesting against the factory system. There were probably more Chartist supporters among handicraft workers in decaying trades such as the handloom weavers. Thus, protest against industrialisation was an element in Chartism, but only one element. Chartism in fact became something of a bandwagon for protest movements of various kinds, such as teetotal Chartism, and education Chartism. Lastly, it should not be forgotten that Chartism had its middle-class sympathisers. The First Petition in 1839 was actually presented to the House of Commons by Thomas Attwood, the Birmingham banker, and it attracted forty-six votes in that very middle-class assembly.

As for middle-class attitudes in general, very naturally the business and professional classes supported industrialisation as such, and were hostile to the landed classes, sheltered as they appeared to be by the corn laws. However, one dissident group of middle-class critics of industrialism was formed by the Christian Socialists. They sought to bridge the gap between the middle classes and the working classes by the founding of joint industrial enterprises on a fraternal basis, sharing profits and so on.[74] They were led by men such as Charles Kingsley (the famous author of *The Water Babies*), and Frederick Maurice, who had to resign his chair at King's College, London, as a result of his unorthodox doctrinal views. The efforts of the Christian Socialists ultimately came to nothing, in part as a result of personal differences, but they show an awareness that one of the social consequences of industrialisation could be enhanced class differences and indeed class conflict. The 1867 Reform Act was of major significance in this connection since it demonstrated the fact that by the 1860s the House of Commons had decided that the 'respectable' working classes (at least, the male half) could be trusted with the vote, provided the *residuum* were kept out by the household franchise. Thus, one of the early problems of industrial development, the changing relationship between capital and labour, appeared to be reaching a satisfactory conclusion.

This does not mean that criticism of the social results of industrialisation ceased in the mid-century years – far from it – and we may end by referring to four great writers in particular. The first is Karl Marx. His writings and those of his collaborator, Frederick Engels, provide a sustained attack on the development of industrial capitalism which has echoed round the world, and has had a profound effect on the economic and social structure of many countries. However, their two best-known works, *The Communist Manifesto* (1848) and Marx's *Das Kapital* (1861) were not available in English until later in the century, and the influence of Marxism was very limited in this country before the 1880s.

The second writer is Thomas Carlyle (1795–1881), who wrote a book entitled *Chartism* (1839), but who was no supporter of the movement, or indeed of democracy. Increasingly, towards the end of his life, he became obsessed with the notion of leadership (his book *Heroes and Hero Worship* was published in 1840), and with the need for Great Men in history. Yet he had a keen eye for the strains and stresses of contemporary society, and it was Carlyle who first used the phrases, 'the condition of England question' and 'the cash nexus'. His earlier historical works, *The French Revolution* (1837) and *Cromwell's Letters and Speeches* (1845) are still readable, but from 1850 onwards his views become increasingly illiberal and undemocratic (he attacked both the 1867 Reform Act, and the cause of the North in the American Civil War). His last thirty years were years of increasing intellectual isolation. Nevertheless, his earlier views in the 1840s provided a stimulus to debate on the social scene.

The third writer is John Ruskin (1819–1900). Ruskin is best known as an art critic and writer on painting and architecture, but in his later writings he found much to criticise in what he called the universal worship of the Goddess of Getting-On. What he attacked was the materialism of the age, and the basic ideas of classical economics which lay at the root of it. He was no revolutionary, but really a kind of radical Tory, who believed in some sort of hierarchical and paternalistic form of society in which co-operation would be the rule. This entailed the rejection of the principle of *laissez-faire*, of course. Ruskin advocated government 'training schools for youth', government care of the old, and government factories to provide work for the unemployed. He was particularly concerned at the low spiritual and aesthetic life of working people, which he thought was the fault of the rich – 'Alas! It is not meat of which the refusal is cruellest, or to which the claim is validest. The life is more than the meat. The rich not only refuse food to the poor; they refuse wisdom; they refuse virtue; they refuse salvation.'[75] Ruskin was therefore one of the many contemporary observers who expressed concern at the development of what Disraeli had characterised as the two nations of Rich and Poor, and at the spiritual deprivation of the masses.

However, perhaps the best known of all Victorian critics of contemporary society was Matthew Arnold (1822–88), another comfortably off member of the middle classes (he was the son of the great Dr Arnold, headmaster of Rugby). Matthew Arnold was one of the earliest government school inspectors, and hence well placed to observe the schooling of the working classes. In general terms, he was a strong opponent of what he conceived to be the narrowness and parochialism of English society, not so much because of the effect of industrialism, but rather as a result of the dominance of Puritanism ('the prison of Puritanism') since the seventeenth century. In his best-known work, *Culture and Anarchy* (1869), he refers to the main classes of society as Barbarians, Philistines, and Populace. It is the middle classes who are the Philistines, indifferent to the importance of 'culture', which he defines somewhat aloofly as 'the best that has been thought and said' ('anarchy' must be regarded as its opposite). What Arnold really castigated was a low and mean view of civilised life, lacking what the Greeks thought of as the good life, 'invested with a kind of aerial ease, clearness and radiancy ... full of sweetness and light'.[76] Arnold was not really a political animal, though he could express strong views on inequality, as in his essay on *Equality* (1878) in which he attacked the inequality of the distribution of property in the nation – 'Our inequality materialises our upper class, vulgarises our middle class, brutalises our lower.'[77] He characterised himself as a 'Liberal of the Future', which really meant that he had doubts about some major aspects of Liberalism, such as the later campaign for Home Rule. His importance is therefore not so much as a political thinker or theorist – his Liberalism is of a doubtful kind – but as a critic of the materialistic society he saw developing around him. It should be added, of course, that his poetry has also earned him an honoured place among Victorian writers.

This brief sketch of the views of a few of the most distinguished commentators on the mid-Victorian scene should do something at least to dispel any beliefs that all Victorians of the time were unduly complacent and smug about their achievements. Some undoubtedly were, but others did not think that 'getting on' was a spiritually satisfying way of life, and argued that the quality of life of the nation as a whole demanded more serious and indeed urgent consideration. These views were strengthened after 1870 by an increasing concern for the casualties of industrialisation, and this will be examined in the next chapter.

In conclusion, there is one aspect of mid-Victorian life which is sometimes in danger of being overlooked, and this is the development of a national police force, but one under local control. It is part of the unspectacular but very important growth of local government services of the time, and for that reason can be overlooked. In the earlier years of the century, the towns relied upon poorly organised systems of watchmen and parish constables, but in 1829 an important advance was made in London with the establishment of the Metropolitan Police by the home secretary, Sir Robert Peel. Initially, the new policemen were not popular, being regarded by working people as government agents acting as spies and informers. Outside London, the Municipal Corporation Act, 1835, made it necessary for the reformed boroughs to set up police forces supervised by local watch committees composed of town councillors. Progress was slow, and in 1856 there were still thirteen municipalities without forces. Progress was equally slow in the counties: the County Police Act, 1839, was permissive in its wording, and by 1851 forces had been set up in only half of the fifty-six counties of England and Wales. In 1856 all counties were ordered to establish forces, and three national inspectors were appointed to check on standards of efficiency. By 1881 there were still thirty-one borough and county police forces with less than six men each, but national coverage was steadily being achieved, and by the end of the century the 'bobby' on his beat had become a familiar and accepted sight in town and village alike.[78]

In theory, as the towns doubled in size or more in the sixty years after 1851, and as prosperity spread, the crime statistics should have shown a marked increase. In practice, they did not. Civil commotions, when it had always been necessary to call out the troops to restore order, became less frequent. Between 1869 and 1910, troops were brought out to aid the police on only twenty-four occasions. The peak of Victorian crime probably came in the early 1840s (this is not surprising, considering the distress already described), and there was then a fairly steady decline until the end of the century. For example, the annual rate in England and Wales per 100,000 persons for indictable offences against the person fell from 13.4 in 1841–5 to 8.6 in 1896–1900. It is well known that criminal statistics are notoriously difficult to interpret, but it seems very likely that crime actually was reduced in the second half of the nineteenth century, and that the growth of policing must have made its contribution to this.[79] Thus, the establishment of police forces nationwide may be considered one of the more positive consequences of Victorian urbanisation, whatever other problems may be attributed to urban growth.

3 After equipoise
Urban problems, 1870–1900

The first two or three years of the 1870s were years of great prosperity for Great Britain. The American Civil War was over, and so was the great Cotton Famine, so that cotton had regained its place as leader in the industrial economy. Meanwhile, the railway boom of the 1840s had resulted not only in the construction of lines all over Britain, but also in the increasingly profitable construction of railways abroad, the export of locomotives and rolling stock, and the expansion of the international money market to finance railways overseas. Moreover, the iron industry was transformed by the production of cheap steel by the Bessemer converter (1856), and by the Siemens open hearth process which steadily replaced the Bessemer process. Steel became the preferred metal for many purposes, and the iron rails on the railways were changed to steel rails by the 1880s. The coal industry profited by the ever-increasing domestic demand, and also by the further expansion of the metal industries and of steam shipping. Thus, the major staple industries were all booming in the early 1870s, at a time when Prussia (later to become a serious industrial competitor) was engaged in war against first Austria in 1866, and then France in 1870–1, a war followed immediately by the creation of the German Empire in 1871. For a number of reasons, therefore, Britain was on the crest of an economic wave in the early 1870s.

From 1873 onwards, and for just over twenty years, the economic climate changed in such a way that contemporaries themselves used the term 'the Great Depression' and in 1886 a royal commission was appointed to investigate its nature. In its report, the commission described the Depression as exhibiting 'a diminution, and in some cases, an absence of profit, with a corresponding diminution of employment for the labouring classes'. The economist, Alfred Marshall, giving evidence before the commission, referred to 'a depression of prices, a depression of interest, a depression of profits'.[1] So, prices, profits, and interest rates all fell, and there was some increase in unemployment. There were three years of slump in particular – 1879, 1886, and 1894 – and two years of recovery, 1883 and 1890.

There has been great controversy over recent years as to the causes of the Great Depression, but there seems to be general agreement that the root cause was a failure in British industry to innovate and develop, a failure which was widespread in the economy of the time.[2] This in turn raises the difficult question of why this was so, and here the argument has been fierce. A variety of reasons has been examined: they include an alleged shortage of gold on world markets, a switch to home investment from foreign investment, the growth of industry abroad using more modern methods, the failure of second- or third-generation sons to maintain the drive of the industrial pioneers, the lack of adequate technical education, and so on. It is not proposed to examine any of these arguments here, since our main concern is with the social results of industrial change rather than with the changes themselves. In fact, the Great Depression can be a somewhat misleading term when applied to this period, since there was an improvement in the standard of living, due to the fall in prices, and an apparent boom in retailing. However, the main problems of the time continued from the earlier years of industrialisation, that is, problems arising from public health and housing, from working conditions and trade unionism, from poverty and unemployment, and from working-class education. To these we may now turn.

Public health and housing

In 1870 the lack of any national system of public health regulation remained perhaps the most urgent social problem. However, in 1869 a royal sanitary commission had been appointed, and its report in 1871 highlighted not only the multiplicity of local authorities with sanitary duties, but also the often permissive and fragmentary nature of the law. It made the familiar points that proper drainage and water supplies were essential, nuisances must be removed, more burial grounds made available, preventable disease combated, and unfit food inspected and prohibited. Its major recommendation was that the administration of the sanitary law should be made 'uniform, universal, and imperative'. Following the setting up of the Local Government Board in 1871, the principal recommendation of the royal commission was implemented. The Public Health Act, 1872, divided the country into sanitary districts, each to have a single public health authority. In the towns, this would be the municipal authority; in other populous areas, it would be a local board; in rural areas, it would be the district Board of Guardians. Each authority had to appoint a medical officer of health and an inspector of nuisances. Further, the Public Health Act, 1875, codified the existing law, thus spelling out the duties of the new sanitary authorities. Thus, in the space of three years, the country was provided with a national grid of public health agencies, each with its own officers, and with a revised and reorganised body of law to be implemented. The terms of the Public Health Act were indeed so comprehensive that, subject to minor amendments, it remained the basic body of sanitary law for over sixty years, until replaced by the Public Health Act, 1936.[3]

Local authorities were now empowered to get on with the immense task of cleaning up both town and countryside. The major challenge, of course, was to institute deep drainage. This meant the consulting of sanitary engineers, obtaining estimates of cost, the raising of loans, and the calculation of what the result would be for the district rates. Much would depend on the nature of the terrain to be drained, but it would often be necessary to excavate to a depth of nine feet or more in order to drain cellars and low-lying premises. Existing open drains were of no use for sewage, though they might be used for storm water. Even in the smallest town, the whole enterprise was a considerable undertaking, and took time. The Black Country town of Stourbridge was visited by a Local Government Board inspector in June 1886. He reported that the town had recently been sewered, and that house connections were being rapidly made; but there were still over a hundred midden privies 'of the most objectionable type and exceedingly foul'. The cleansing of the midden heaps was 'much neglected', there was no hospital provision, no disinfectant apparatus, and no special provision for cholera. Moreover, the work of the medical officer of health was described as unsatisfactory, and that of the inspector of nuisances was said to be 'Fair. Would be more useful under better direction.'[4] So, some progress was being made, but the pace was slow, and much still depended on local initiative. Nevertheless, the provision of deep drainage nationally was a massive enterprise, though not one receiving much comment in the textbooks, possibly because of its unglamorous nature. Yet it was an example of joint central and local planning, and perhaps the greatest single factor in the improvement of the nation's health in the last quarter of the nineteenth century.

The improvement in working-class housing was another aspect of public health reform after 1870. Even before this date, interest was being shown in better-quality housing for workers – Prince Albert designed a working-class house which was on show at the Great Exhibition, while in London some model dwellings were built by philanthropic bodies such as the Peabody Trust in Shoreditch in 1866, and by Sir Sydney Waterloo's Improved Industrial Dwellings Company, and the Artisans', Labourers', and General Dwellings Company (generally speaking, these dwellings were barrack-like in appearance, the rents were high, and they were not much liked by the working classes). There were also some attempts both by the government and locally to regulate new building and to force landlords to improve their property. The problem here was simply that property rights were regarded as sacred, and any attempt to interfere with them met strong resistance. Torren's Act, 1866, is generally regarded as the first housing act, but its scope was greatly reduced in its passage through parliament. It was intended to compel landlords to carry out improvements, but it had little effect. Two further acts passed by Cross, Disraeli's home secretary, in 1875 and 1879 actually gave local authorities power to demolish slum property, but again the acts were not widely implemented (there was also a further Torren's Act in 1879). Meanwhile, very limited amounts of slum clearance took place in Glasgow, Edinburgh, Liverpool, and Birmingham. In the last city, where Joseph Chamberlain was Lord Mayor from 1873 to 1876, a major demolition of slum property resulted in the building of a new impressive thoroughfare, Corporation Street (unfortunately, very little was done to rehouse the dispossessed tenants).[5]

In London, the situation was much worse than in Birmingham, because in the 1860s there were clearances for the new railway lines and stations, and also for the building of government offices and other office blocks. Where Cross's acts were implemented, they actually made the situation worse. New suburban building was rushed up, but often the rents were relatively high, and travel from the outskirts was expensive. In 1891, 19 per cent of London's accommodation was overcrowded, as compared with 10 per cent in Liverpool, and 16 per cent in Leeds; new slums were being created by this overcrowding. In 1883, Arthur Mearns, a Congregational minister writing under the pen-name of R. Sims, published a widely read pamphlet under the title, *The Bitter Cry of Outcast London*. It contained some strong passages describing the worst slum areas of London:

> Courts reeking with poisonous and malodorous gases arising from accumulations of sewage and refuse scattered in all directions ... dark and filthy passages swarming with vermin ... walls

and ceilings are black with the accretions of filth which have gathered upon them through years of neglect.

In his view, in the very centre of the country's great cities, concealed by the thinnest crust of civilisation and decency, there lurked 'a great mass of moral corruption, of heartbreaking misery and absolute godlessness'.[6]

It is not surprising that publicity of this sort led to increased public concern, and finally to the appointment of a royal commission on housing in 1885. Among its members were the Prince of Wales and Cardinal Newman. The evidence given before the commission amply justified Mearns' description of the London slums. Whole families were often found to be living in a single room. Thus, at 15 St Helena Place, Clerkenwell, the house contained six rooms, occupied by six families, with as many as eight in a room. At 11 Wilmington Place, there were eleven families in eleven rooms, with seven persons in one room. At 30 Noble Street, five families of twenty-six persons in all occupied six rooms, while at 7 New Court, fowls were also kept in the two rooms inhabited by eleven persons.[7] Earth privies were still in use in many parts, and were greatly overused, even in such a fashionable part of London as Westminster:[8]

In a street in Westminster, a witness stated that there was only one [convenience] for all the houses in the street, thirty or forty people inhabiting each house; and that it was open and used by all passers-by ... In some parts of London they are used as sleeping places by the homeless poor who haunt the staircases. In Bristol, privies actually exist in living rooms.

No immediate government action followed, but in 1890 the Housing of the Working Classes Act was passed. This act at first sight might appear to be a breakthrough, since it gave powers to local authorities to provide housing themselves. In fact, few did so. This was partly because of a reluctance to enter into competition with private builders, and the continuing belief that building should be left to private enterprise; and partly because the cost of the housing would put up the rates. In Stourbridge, a public enquiry was held into the need for more housing, and into a plan for building small numbers of working-class homes. When someone queried the lack of finish in the houses – the interior walls were to be of unplastered brick – he was told that if that was good enough for Her Majesty's forces, it was good enough for working-class tenants. In fact, no council houses at all were built in Stourbridge before 1914. When the first ones were erected in the early 1920s, the interior walls were still unplastered.

To sum up: undoubtedly considerable progress in public health measures was made in the years between 1870 and the 1890s. The legislation of the 1870s was a much-needed advance. The concrete proof of this is the installation of deep drainage schemes all over the country, some of them still not completed even in 1914; but a good start had been made. Housing was a different matter. Here the belief in private enterprise building was still a barrier to widespread reform. Nevertheless, local bye-laws laying down standards for new house building became increasingly common, and in 1877 the Local Government Board issued a model set of housing bye-laws and these were adopted in many parts of the country. The result was the building of much so-called bye-law housing – long terraces, each house on a narrow frontage, but built deep from front to back, a style of building much criticised today, but generally of a quality distinctly superior to earlier, jerry-built housing. By 1914, further progress had been made in providing healthier accommodation for the working classes. However, it might be as well to repeat a warning given in the previous chapter, that bad as some housing was without doubt, not all the working classes lived in slums. It was the *residuum* or lumpenproletariat who were the problem.

Working conditions and trade unionism

From 1870 onwards, child labour was prohibited in most places of work, and this ban was reinforced (as will be seen later in the chapter) by compulsory school attendance in 1876 and 1880. Henceforth it was a matter of extending and consolidating the law rather than establishing new principles. Thus, the Factory Act, 1871, put up the age at which girls could start work in brickyards to sixteen, while the starting age for boys underground in the mines was raised to twelve; there was also to be a maximum of fifty-four hours a week for boys under sixteen. In 1876 a commission was appointed to enquire into the working of the separate factories and workshops acts – the regulations were becoming increasingly complicated – and, in 1878, the Factories and Workshops Act attempted to consolidate the law; it was generally considered that the law applied to the workshops was more lenient than the factory laws. By this time, all the major categories of workplaces were covered by legislation (in theory, at least), but there remained the problem of the sweated industries – that is, industries carried on in domestic workshops or actually in the home.

Table 3.1 Children over ten working part time in the 1890s

Lancashire	89,234
Yorkshire	47,775
Cheshire	9,639
Rest of England and Wales	24,038
Total	170,686

Many of these industries were still beyond the reach of the law. Black Country workshops, for example, where man and wife worked together, were still untouched. In 1888 a select committee of the House of Lords reported on the Sweating System (as it was called), with particular reference to such trades as nailing, bootmaking, and tailoring. Another royal commission was appointed in 1892, this time on labour generally. It was followed by a further consolidating act, the Factories and Workshops Act, 1901, but the issue of sweating was not really addressed till the Sweated Industries Act, 1909.

In the last three decades of the nineteenth century, therefore, the regulation of working conditions in industry became widespread, having grown initially from the struggle to restrict the factory hours of children and women. One important consequence of industrialisation was therefore to attempt to keep working hours within civilised limits, and by 1900 the need for this was taken for granted, and largely achieved. Of course, the enforcement of the law was often imperfect, and some employments were still outside the law. This is true not only of the sweated industries, but also of domestic employment, and of work in retail shops, where the hours were still notoriously long. This is especially true of provision shops on Saturdays which remained open until midnight and beyond in order to cater for customers who came in after the pubs closed at twelve.

One exception to the rules regulating the employment of children was provided by the part-timers, that is, children who had reached the required educational standard and who were permitted to start work on a part-time basis at the age of ten, the remainder of the time still being spent in school. In the 1890s, as many as two out of three children over ten in Lancashire were part-timers, and in Yorkshire, Cheshire, and Leicestershire, it was one in every four; in the rest of England, it was only one in thirty-one. The actual figures are as shown in Table 3.1.[9] Obviously enough, small children could be of assistance in the textile mills, where their use over the years had become traditional. However, it has been calculated that in 1891 the part-timers constituted only about 3.5 per cent of the total school population.[10]

Lastly, it is in the second half of the nineteenth century that an important reorganisation of the working week took place. This was the gradual abandonment of St Monday, that is, the practice of not going into work on that day. Employers became increasingly hostile to the custom, especially in Birmingham and the Black Country, and did all they could to enforce attendance on a Monday. By way of compensation, it became the rule to stop work at midday or shortly after on Saturday, and this became the law in 1862 in textile factories. The result was a weekend off work stretching from Saturday afternoon to Monday morning, thus allowing a solid block of leisure time, and the growth of a more extended leisure and entertainment industry as real wages improved in the 1870s and 80s. The most striking manifestation of this was the development of spectator sports such as professional football and cricket.

Trade unionism entered on a new phase of respectability in the 1850s in which the government regulation of working conditions just described was strengthened by trade union action from time to time in defence of their members' interests. Strikes still occurred, of course, but the prosperity of the time allowed both employers and unions to take a more flexible approach in trade disputes. Indeed, the unions themselves were prepared to admit that strikes were not always the best way of resolving labour problems. George Odger, the radical secretary of the London Trades Council, declared roundly that 'Strikes are to the social world what wars are to the political world. They become crimes unless promoted by absolute necessity.'[11] Alexander MacDonald, the leader of the Scottish miners, spoke on the same theme before a select committee of the House of Commons in 1873:[12]

> I look upon strikes as a barbaric relic of a period of unfortunate relations between capital and labour, and the sooner we get rid of it by the more rational means of employer meeting the employed and talking the matter over, the better.

But this is to anticipate events a little, for in the later 1860s, two developments were for a time to set back the progress made by the unions. The first was the Sheffield Outrages of 1866, and the second was the case of *Hornby v. Close* in 1867. The Sheffield Outrages was the name given to a series of violent actions by the Sheffield unions against both union members and employers, these actions being reported in the local press. The Sheffield unions sought to defend themselves, and demanded a government enquiry. They were supported by Robert

Applegarth, who himself suggested a commission of enquiry. This was duly appointed in 1867, and at the same time a separate body of examiners was appointed, with power to enquire into all outrages in Sheffield and elsewhere during the previous ten years; it also had the unusual power of indemnifying all witnesses from prosecution. This was to lead to some extraordinarily frank revelations. The membership of the royal commission was very middle class, as might be expected, but two friends of the trade union movement were included – Thomas Hughes, the Christian Socialist, and Frederic Harrison, the Positivist.

For a time, the report of the examiners, published in August 1867, was very damaging to the trade unions. It stated that 'rattening' was very common in the Sheffield area, and admitted to be so by the unions. This 'rattening' was the intimidation of blacklegs by damaging their workshop tools and equipment. The examiners then went on to claim that of about sixty unions in Sheffield, twelve had been involved in encouraging outrages, some thirty-five incidents in all. The sawgrinders were the worst culprits. They had been party to ten cases where gunpowder had been used and three cases of attempted murder, one of them fatal. Perhaps the most sensational cases were those of the murder of an employer (the murderer had been paid £20 for the shooting by the secretary of the Saw Grinders Union) and the gunpowder attack on the house of a non-union man (the man's wife never recovered from the explosion, while the lodger died from burns; the can of gunpowder had been thrown by a man paid £6 by the union's acting secretary, the payment being concealed in the union's account books).[13] The public was deeply disturbed by these revelations. Frederic Harrison, who had been nominated by the unions as a representative on the commission, wrote privately that unless the unions could justify their practices, they would seem to be 'mere organs of class tyranny'.

Fortunately for the unions, they were skilfully defended by members of the Junta, the Webbs' term for the leaders of the great amalgamated unions. These men, led by Applegarth, met weekly under the title of the Conference of the Amalgamated Trades, and carefully prepared their evidence, stressing their peaceful procedures, extensive membership, and large funds. The employer witnesses understandably voiced their usual grievances, including the opposition of some unions to piecework, to higher pay rates for better workmanship, and to 'chasing' (defined as 'setting too high a pace of work'). A major grievance, as might be expected, was picketing. On this, Applegarth made a measured and indeed remarkable reply:[14]

> I *do* justify picketing … I say that it is perfectly justifiable for men
> to appoint other men to wait at a shop door and say to those who
> come, 'The men were dissatisfied with the terms upon which they
> were working at that place, and if you go in, you will go in and
> undersell us; now we beg you that you will not do that.' This is as
> far as I would justify men in going … If they use threats or coerce
> or intimidate, that is beyond the instructions, and which the laws
> of the society give them; and no-one more than myself would wish
> to bring them under the laws of the country for so doing. If they
> did not do what I have justified, it would be absolute folly to strike
> in many instances …

The commission appeared incredulous at this apparently rose-tinted
claim, so Applegarth referred to a strike in Cardiff where the pickets
had been particularly well behaved. The commission clearly thought
that the conduct of the pickets in Cardiff had been exceptional, and
not the norm: and they asked Applegarth whether he agreed that
their moderation was in fact very unusual. This, of course, he denied.

Nevertheless, on the whole the Junta made an excellent impression,
and their efforts were rewarded by a majority report which recommended that unions should be given a clear legal status, and that
their rules could be registered with the Registrar of Friendly Societies,
provided that they did not permit restrictive practices, such as limiting the number of apprentices. Hughes and Harrison issued their
own minority report, again stressing the peaceful nature of trade
unionism, and claiming that with the exception of recent events in
Sheffield and Manchester, 'attempts on life and limb rarely occur.
The peculiarly atrocious crime of vitriol throwing, with which the
former Reports are full, has not been mentioned here. Nothing has
been heard of either incendiarism or machine-breaking …'[15] All this
is true enough, except that in both Sheffield and Manchester, vitriol
throwing seems to have been replaced by gunpowder attacks. The
minority report also repeated the majority report recommendation
that the legal status of unions should be put beyond doubt, but
without the qualifications set out in the majority report.

While the Sheffield Outrages were being investigated, the case of
Hornby v. Close was also giving the trade unions a good deal of
concern. The Boiler Makers Society had sued their Bradford branch
secretary for the sum of £24 which he refused to pay over to the
society. The society was not a friendly society, but had deposited its
rules with the Registrar of Friendly Societies, acting under the generally held belief that this allowed it to bring a case under the terms of

the Friendly Society Act, 1855. The law regarding the precise legal status of trade unions was still very obscure, and in this case the court ruled that the action must fail. Not only was the society not a friendly society, but the union had no defined legal status, and might still be considered in restraint of trade. The practical result was that union funds could not be protected by bringing such an action – in fact, they could not sue in a corporate capacity. This obviously was a damaging blow, and this is the reason why both the majority and minority reports of the royal commission recommended that the legal status of trade unions should be made clear, once and for all. It was now obviously up to the government to proceed in the matter.

Hitherto the trade unions had steered clear of politics, but in 1868 the Manchester Trades Council held a congress of trade unions to discuss matters affecting trade unions generally. Only twenty-four delegates attended the Manchester meeting, but there were forty delegates at the Birmingham congress the following year, while in 1871, the London congress appointed a Parliamentary Committee, primarily to keep an eye on any new trade union legislation, but also to consider the possibility of electing trade union members to parliament. This actually happened in the 1874 general election, at which the new Parliamentary Committee presented candidates with test questions on their attitude to trade unions. Fourteen Labour candidates stood for election, and two were elected. They were both miners – Alexander MacDonald at Stafford, and Thomas Burt at Morpeth. They were the first working men to become members of parliament.

In 1869 the Gladstone government passed the Trade Unions Funds Protection Act which gave legal protection to trade union funds which had been put at risk as a consequence of *Hornby v. Close*. It then prepared further legislation so as to implement the recommendations of the reports of the royal commission; but the bill introduced in 1871 was unsatisfactory from the unions' point of view, for in addition to putting their legal position beyond doubt, it in effect prohibited picketing, an essential weapon in the trade union armoury. After negotiation, the unions managed to split the two proposals, and to put them into two separate bills. Thus, the Trade Union Act, 1871, allowed the registration of trade unions, while the Criminal Law Amendment Act, 1871, made picketing illegal. This allowed the trade unions to concentrate on getting the second act repealed. The need for this soon became clear: later in 1871, seven women in South Wales were convicted for saying 'Bah, bah' to a blackleg, while in December, 1872 a group of London gas workers went to prison for twelve months under the act, convicted of conspiracy to coerce their employers for merely preparing to strike (their preparation was held to be intimidation).

Another royal commission was appointed in 1874 to report on the labour laws. Burt, the newly elected MP, refused to sit on it, though MacDonald and Thomas Hughes became members. The Parliamentary Committee of the TUC simply boycotted the commission; but although its report was in the Webbs' view 'inconclusive', the new Conservative government led by Disraeli passed the Conspiracy and Protection of Property Act, 1875. This act stated conclusively that trade unions were not conspiracies, and it also legalised peaceful picketing. Another act in 1875, the Employers and Workmen Act, extended previous legislation by abolishing altogether the imprisonment of workmen for breach of contract (employers had been subject only to a fine). Henceforth workmen and employers were to be regarded as equal partners in a contract of employment. Further, in 1876 another Trade Union Act redefined yet again the legal status of unions and attempted to provide additional clarification of the law.

These acts, passed it will be noted by a Conservative government, constituted real gains for the union movement. In fact, the Parliamentary Committee of the TUC announced that the 'work of emancipation' was 'full and complete', and its secretary, George Howell, thought that the committee could be disbanded. The early 1870s were certainly years of advance for the trade unions. Membership grew: by 1874, the TUC claimed to represent 1,191,922 members. Agricultural workers, always difficult to unionise, acquired their own Agricultural Workers' Union, founded by Joseph Arch in 1872. At about the same time, unionism began to spread to the semi-skilled and unskilled trades with the setting up of the Amalgamated Society of Railway Servants in 1871, and the London gas workers' union in 1872. Moreover, hours were reduced in the engineering and building trades by the establishment of a week limited to fifty-four hours – in other words, the nine-hour day, which had been demanded by the Nine Hours League, something which marked the successful conclusion of a five-month strike in the engineering and building industries.

In and after 1873, and for more than the next two decades, prosperity was dimmed by the advent of the Great Depression. It has already been mentioned that in spite of this, the standard of living rose for those in work, the result principally of a fall in the cost of food. Because of this improvement, it is easy to overlook the increase in unemployment which disfigured these years. Indeed, the well-known and standard textbook by Peter Mathias may mislead the casual reader into underestimating the seriousness of unemployment when he reads that on trend the national rate of the out-of-work was '4.6 per cent in the twenty years before 1874, 5.4 per cent from 1875 to 1895'.[16] A rise of less than 1 per cent over twenty years hardly seems very significant. Again, this period is increasingly seen as a period of increased retailing, and of a positive boom in consumer spending,[17] which once more suggests that unemployment was not, perhaps, too serious a threat. On the other hand, it must be remembered that there are really no national figures for unemployment for this period, only figures derived from trade union sources for industrial trades. When these are inspected, a different picture presents itself: in the downswings of the economy, unemployment was marked in a number of trades. For example, the societies of ironfounders and boilermakers has less than 1 per cent of their members unemployed in 1872–3, but more than 20 per cent unemployed in 1879. The great ASE paid out £287,596 in unemployment pay in the years 1878–80, while the Operative Plumbers wrote off nearly a third of their members in the years 1880–2 for non-payment of dues. The National Union of Ironworkers had 35,000 members in 1873; by 1879, membership was down to 1,400. The National Union of Mineworkers also suffered a severe loss of members, while the Agricultural Workers' Union, which claimed to have 100,000 members in 1872, was down to only 4,254 in 1889. Clearly, unemployment was not a historical fiction or myth at this time, and it is no coincidence that the word 'unemployment' itself seems to have come into common use in the 1880s.[18]

However, its incidence certainly varied from year to year, and from place to place. In some areas, unemployment became more persistent and more extensive. This is particularly so in the Black Country, which had hitherto been the second largest producer of finished iron in the country. In the 1870s, local supplies of coal were becoming less accessible, due to the increasing drainage problems in the South Staffs and East Worcestershire coalfield. Here the unplanned workings underground were being likened to waterlogged rabbit warrens. These difficulties also affected the mining of iron ore. Thus, one of the greatest industries of the region began to decline, and emigration from the Black Country to the colonies increased. Stourbridge actually suffered a net loss of population in the 1880s. In the same town, the headmaster of a board school wrote to the local newspaper in 1880 complaining that parents were increasingly unable to pay school fees – a few pence a week – and that children were showing clear signs of hardship: 'the tattered clothes and the attenuated faces of many of the children showing that at their homes there had been a protracted struggle for mere existence.' Another letter later in the year written by a Lye nailer asked why must the children suffer so? Something had to be done, or the condition of the Lye nailers would be worse than the Irish: 'We are half-starved, over head over heels in debt, and with no means of getting out of it.'[19] In the much larger Black Country town of Wolverhampton, the iron industry was similarly in decline, with the largest iron works of all, Thorneycroft's, closing down in 1877 with substantial job losses.[20]

Faced with clear evidence of increased unemployment, the onus was on the government to take action. If the Great Depression was something of a myth, this is not how it seemed at the time in the Black Country, or even in London, where in 1886 there was a march of the unemployed during which windows were broken in Pall Mall, and the police had to intervene. Relief was available for the unemployed in the workhouse, of course, or on outdoor relief, but as has been pointed out more than once, assistance of this kind was detested by the working classes. Not only was it thought humiliating, but it was merely palliative, and did nothing to strike directly at the root of the problem, the shortage of jobs. Moreover, although the governments of the time were well aware of the state of trade, their major preoccupations were with political matters overseas and the issue of Home Rule for Ireland; first Disraeli had to face the problem of the Bulgarian Atrocities in the Balkans, leading to the Congress of Berlin, 1878, then Gladstone became increasingly obsessed with Home Rule when he became prime minister again in 1880. It was not until 1886 that the Liberal government took action to give further help to the unemployed.

Even then, the principle of the Chamberlain Circular, 1886 was not original. We have already noted the passing of the Public Works (Manufacturing Districts) Act, 1863, which allowed local authorities to apply for government loans to finance public works schemes during the Cotton Famine. However, the Chamberlain Circular, sent out to local authorities by Joseph Chamberlain, president of the Local Government Board, did show some awareness of the need for local authorities to provide something other than the usual task of work, usually stone-breaking or oakum picking, in return for assistance. These traditional tasks, the Circular acknowledged, were very hard on the skilled artisan. What was wanted to help artisans temporarily deprived of employment was work which avoided the stigma of pauperism, which all could perform, irrespective of previous occupation, and which did not compete with other labourers still at work. This at least attempted to soften the blow of applying for relief, but, in practice, the employment offered was usually work on the roads, which itself was humiliating enough for the skilled worker. However, the Chamberlain Circular impliedly accepted the fact that not all applicants for poor relief were workshy, and for the most part, they deserved sympathetic consideration; though even then, acceptance of relief still meant the forfeiting of the right to vote. The Chamberlain Circular remained the sole government initiative to relieve unemployment until the early years of the next century.

What of the fortunes of the trade unions after 1876? It has already been mentioned that some suffered loss of members during the Great Depression. On the other hand, and paradoxically enough, unionism actually spread among the less skilled and unskilled. This movement, known as New Unionism, had begun in the early 1870s, was then checked, but revived again in the 1880s. In general terms, the new unions were led by younger men, often socialist in outlook, and critical of the older craft unions. Their greatest success in the 1880s was the famous London Docks strike of 1889 (this strike and others, together with the nature and significance of new unionism, will be discussed at length in Chapter 5). For the present, it will suffice to say that the New Unionism was an important development, but it did not take over unionism as a whole: in 1890, the new unions had a maximum strength of about 350,000, but by 1900 this was reduced to around 204,000, which was less than a tenth of the total trade union membership.

The care of the poor

The subject of the care of the poor has already been glanced at briefly in connection with the unemployed. So far as the poor law system as a whole is concerned, there was little change in the period from the 1870s to the end of the century, the one exception being the attempt after the setting up of the Local Government Board to tighten up the rules and restrict outdoor relief as far as possible – that is, to enforce the workhouse test more rigorously. This was doomed to failure, of course, given the limited accommodation available, and the fact that it was cheaper to give outdoor relief than indoor relief. The process of giving more specialised care to different classes within the workhouse was continued, with particular reference to the children. For example, children were segregated from other inmates in so-called cottage homes; these were separate villas, all on one site, each cottage having fifteen or twenty children with their own house-father and house-mother. In Sheffield in 1893, the 'scattered homes' system was introduced. Such homes were ordinary dwelling houses scattered about the suburbs of Sheffield, and within easy reach of a board school. In 1896, there were nine of these houses in Sheffield, each housing up to twenty children. Both systems must have been an improvement on the large barrack school, though the size of the family units must have precluded the development of anything like the intimate atmosphere of the smaller nuclear family. By the end of the century, small numbers of children were being offered for adoption, while others were being boarded out, and sometimes fostered.[21] Treatment of the children was increasingly more considerate, though Charlie Chaplin alleged that he had witnessed savage Friday morning beatings in the Lambeth workhouse in 1896, while Henry Morton Stanley has described the floggings in the St Asaph workhouse when he was an inmate there.[22]

Although the basic administrative structure of the poor law remained unchanged, there was increasing middle-class discussion of the nature of unemployment in the 1880s, and also of the extent of poverty, especially in the towns. One manifestation of the anxiety over unemployment is to be seen in the growth of the idea of labour colonies. This advocated the establishing of labour settlements for the unemployed in rural areas, where they could be trained in agricultural work and become self-supporting. Their training would also stand them in good stead should they wish to emigrate to the colonies overseas. The outstanding supporter of labour colonies was the Labour leader George Lansbury, who argued that[23]

> all able-bodied men applying for poor law relief should be sent to the colonies or institutes in the country, where the entire work should be reclamatory and in no way penal.
> That it is cheaper to keep men under these conditions than in the workhouse.
> That in this way the men and women may be scattered back again over the country.

Here there was more than an echo of the old cry of 'Back to the Land', a reversal of the way in which industrialisation had lured workers away from the land and into the cities. Another advocate of land colonies was William Booth, founder of the Salvation Army. In his book, *In Darkest England, and the Way Out* (1890), Booth set out a scheme for a labour colony. Although a number of similar projects were put forward, only two gained any prominence – one organised by the Salvation Army in Hadleigh, Essex, and the other set up by the Poplar Board of Guardians (of which Lansbury was a leading member) at Laindon, also in Essex, in 1904. At one time it employed two hundred men, and was run with the financial help of the American business man and philanthropist, Joseph Fels, founder of the Vacant Land Cultivation Society. Needless to say, labour colonies were not to prove the answer to the problem of unemployment.[24]

Another indication of public concern about the state of the poor, but sounding a very different note, was the founding of the Charity Organisation Society (COS) in 1869. The odd title derives from the fact that its members were convinced that much charitable help was being given indiscriminately, to deserving and undeserving alike, and without co-operation between charities. Its immediate aim was to provide help only to the worthy, and after proper investigation; further, the poor should be taught to help themselves in all the usual crises of working-class life (including unemployment and sickness) so that assistance would be necessary only in exceptional circumstances. Charity must aim at moral regeneration; as its secretary, C.S. Loch put it, 'We must use charity to create the power of self-help.' This approach was not necessarily unsympathetic, but was intended to be wholly realistic about the needs of the poor. The COS kept systematic records of its clients, thus laying the foundations of the modern use of casework. It set up its own scheme for training social workers in 1890. According again to Loch, 'Charity works through sympathy [but] it depends on science.' The policy of the COS was obviously not one to make it very popular with the poor, and its doctrines did not make much sense to those on the bottom rung of society, who were hardly able to practise much self-help. Nevertheless, the COS became a highly influential body, and it had six active and leading members on the Royal Commission on the Poor Laws, 1905–9. Their presence there is some indication of the fact that their views had wide general support, and were thought to represent a common-sense, down-to-earth approach.[25]

These developments during the Great Depression, together with the agitation in London over unemployment, encouraged speculation about the amount of poverty in the capital city. The *Pall Mall Gazette* claimed that as many as a quarter of London's inhabitants were living in poverty; and of course, Mearns' *The Bitter Cry of Outcast London* increased the unease. Finally Charles Booth, a member of the well-known shipping family in Liverpool (and no relation to William Booth, the Salvationist) began an enquiry into the lives of the London poor. The result was a massive work in seventeen volumes entitled *Life and Labour of the People in London*, published between 1889 and 1903. Of these volumes, nine were concerned with the

Table 3.2 Booth's classification of income levels in London

	No.	%	
Class A (lowest)	37,610	0.9	In poverty
Class B (very poor)	316,834	7.5	30.7%
Classes C & D (poor)	938,293	22.3	
Classes E & F			
(working class, comfortable)	2,166,503	51.5	In comfort,
Classes G & H			69.3%
(middle class and above)	749,930	17.8	
	4,209,170		
Inmates of institutions	99,830		
	4,309,000		

material conditions of life (four on poverty, five on industry, and all of the rest save the last were on religion).[26] The whole survey was based on visits made in 13,000 streets in London between 1886 and 1891, its information coming from school-board visitors, the police, relieving officers, school divisional committees, and so on.[27] It was the 1892 volume which attracted the most attention and debate, for in it Booth divided the inhabitants of London into eight groups (classes A to H), each group being assessed as being either above or below 'the poverty line', this being set at a minimum income of between 18/– and 21/– a week for a family of man, wife, and three children. The results were as shown in Table 3.2.

In the simplest terms, Booth claimed that 30.7 per cent, or nearly one-third, of the entire population of London were in poverty, in that their income was insufficient to provide minimum standards (and it should be noted that some observers considered that his poverty line was too low, and should have been drawn higher in the income scale, thereby increasing the proportion in poverty). As for Classes A and B, they lived in utter squalor. Booth wrote of Class A:[28]

> Their life is the life of savages, with vicissitudes of extreme hard-ship and occasional excess. Their food is of the coarsest descrip-tion, and their only luxury is drink ... They render no useful service, they create no wealth; more often they destroy it. They degrade whatever they touch, and as individuals are perhaps inca-pable of improvement.

Booth's estimate of 8.4 per cent for classes A and B is quite close to William Booth's figures in his 1890 book of about one-tenth of the total population living in desperate poverty – the 'submerged tenth' as he called them: 'Three million men, women, and children, a vast despairing multitude in a condition nominally free, but really enslaved'. Charles Booth's figure may also be compared with the figure of 25 per cent in extreme poverty contained in a survey conducted a little later by the Marxist founder of the Social Democratic Federation, H.M. Hyndman; and also with another city survey, this time of York, by B.S. Rowntree, published in 1901, which gave a figure of 27.84 per cent in poverty (for Hyndman, see Chapter 5, and for Rowntree's survey, Chapter 6).

As might be expected, Booth's figures caused an immense stir. They were attacked by Professor Bosanquet, who, with his wife Helen, was a prominent member of the COS. Bosanquet argued that London was a special case (and, later, York too); that in all probability Booth's 30 per cent contained many who had a sufficient income but spent it unwisely, resulting in poverty; that 10 per cent was nearer the mark for those in deep poverty; and that Booth had no real, direct evidence for incomes of the heads of households, let alone total family income. However, though it is true that much of Booth's evidence was of a secondary nature, there is no reason to suppose that he manipulated the figures to make them more sensational. He had no particular political axe to grind, unlike Hyndman. In general, it can be said that he was sensitive about the poor, but certainly not sentimental, or sensationalist.[29] His uncompromising remarks quoted above about Class A bear this out.

So what can be said to put Booth's survey into perspective? Back in the 1860s Mayhew's articles on the London working classes had provoked plenty of comment, but Booth's investigation was the first major sociological survey of its subject, and it came at a time of much soul-searching by the Victorian middle classes about the quality of life in the new industrial state. The result of this was the further growth of socialist ideas, and the foundation of such bodies as the Fabian Society in 1884 – developments which will be discussed in more detail in Chapter 5. Given the intellectual climate of the 1890s, it is not surprising that Booth's survey had a major impact on the thinking of the time. However much the COS sought to argue that Booth's figures were exaggerated and misleading, and that much poverty was caused by the working classes' failure to help themselves, the survey came as a great shock to a nation which was beginning to think of itself as a great imperial power, with a new and growing empire in Africa. How could the picture of urban squalor be reconciled with the vision of imperial greatness?

The answer, of course, is that they were both realities, each of which needed to be seen in perspective. Urbanisation certainly owed much to industrialisation, in that whatever were the causes of the national growth of population, industry was undoubtedly the major cause of town growth – that is, industry in the sense of manufacturing industry and the service industries. But what proportion of urban populations had always been poor? If a survey similar to Booth's had been made in say, 1830, how large a part of London's population would have fallen below the poverty line?

There is no way in which this question can be answered, of course, though the Fabians at least attempted to define who the unemployed actually were. For example, in their report of 1886, they described the unemployed as those unemployed due to the trade cycle or to seasonal unemployment, together with the *residuum*, i.e. those either permanently unemployed or casually employed.[30] For the Fabians, of course, as we shall see in Chapter 5, the ultimate answer was socialism. Such a solution was utterly unacceptable to the COS, which was bitterly opposed to any form of collectivism. In *Aspects of the Social Problem* (1895), edited by Professor Bosanquet, Helen Dandy (soon to be Mrs Bosanquet) places great stress on character, and even argues that there is always some reason for a man to be out of work – it is rarely through no fault of his own. In her chapter entitled 'The industrial *residuum*', Dandy says this class is grossly deficient in character, and nothing can be done for them except some help through the poor law. All that can be hoped is that with industrial progress, the *residuum* will gradually disappear. This argument begins to sound like social Darwinism, and of the belief that in the survival of the fittest, the least fittest will gradually die out. Here then are two opposed theories of social development, and in the 1880s the scene was already set for a continuing controversy still raging up to 1914, and even beyond.

It is interesting to speculate just why the 1880s should have been the decade when social concern about unemployment and the poor began to be so widely debated. It may be that the rising standards of living of both the middle classes and the employed working classes are a factor here, and this certainly helps to explain the revival of socialist ideas which will be discussed in Chapter 5. There was certainly a consciousness among the liberal-minded middle class of the contrast between the wealth of the nation as a whole and the amount of urban poverty. In her diaries, Beatrice Webb wrote about the middle-class 'collective or class-consciousness' of sin. Not all of her contemporaries would agree with her, of course, but it still seems that the 1880s constitute a watershed in the history of the social results of industrialisation. The 'Age of Equipoise' had given way to a dawning realisation that much remained to be done to succour the casualties of industrialism in the cities. As it happened, the framework of supportive social services had just begun to be erected, both in the form of local government services and in central legislation. It was to be greatly extended later.

Working-class education

It remains to say something about the provision of elementary education of the working classes. Payment by results may have tightened up teaching in the church schools from 1862 onwards, but there was still the problem of the sheer lack of places for the children whose parents were willing to send them to school, even if it was only for short periods of time. By 1870, the children of most respectable working-class parents were attending school – probably between two-thirds and three-quarters of all children of school age had their names on the registers. In that year, Gladstone's first ministry passed Forster's Education Act. It tackled the problems of the financial difficulties of the church societies by adopting the Newcastle Commission's suggestion that new schools should be financed out of local rates. Where there was a deficiency in school places, a school board was to be elected which would provide additional schooling as required. This was by no means to replace the schools of the societies, but to supplement their work: in Forster's own words, 'to supplement the present voluntary system – that is, ... fill up its gaps at the least cost of public money, with least cost of voluntary co-operation, and with most aid from parents'.[31] The schools could charge fees of up to 9d per week, but were not yet compulsory. However, school boards could pass bye-laws making attendance obligatory between the inclusive ages of five and twelve, with exemptions from the age of ten, dependent on attainment. The knotty problem of what religious instruction should be given in the new board schools – the Nonconformists were determined that it should not be tainted by Anglican doctrines – was solved by the Cowper–Temple clause in the act which required that the teaching of religion should be undenominational, that is, that there should be 'no religious catechism or religious formulary which is distinctive of any particular denomination'.

The 1870 Education Act is still a landmark in social history, introducing for the first time local authority schools to operate alongside the church schools. They soon became known as 'board schools', and after the turn of the century, 'council schools'. Older historians have sought to find more specific reasons for Forster's act other than the shortage of church society funds, such as the success of the Prussian armies against Austria in 1866, and against France in 1870–1, Prussia having a system of popular, state education; but the Newcastle Commission had visited Prussian state schools, and had not thought them superior to the voluntary schools in this country. Again, Lowe's mocking remark made after the passing of the 1867 Reform Act that 'We must educate our masters' seems to have had no effect on the policy of the Gladstone government; many working-class men in 1867 were already literate, and some had the vote even before 1867. There was already middle-class pressure for further educational reform, of course, the National Education League being set up in 1869, demanding free, compulsory, and secular education. So the basic argument seems to hold good that the origins of Forster's act lay in the need to complement the work of the church schools by building new schools where required.

This is not to say that the church societies welcomed the act, and there was a great burst of school building by them in the six months allowed to them to fill existing gaps. Subsequently, new board schools were erected in the cities, the London School Board (LSB) opening its first school in 1873, and by 1875, an additional seventy-eight schools. They were impressive, three-decker buildings, with large windows, playgrounds, and the LSB monogram prominently displayed in the brickwork. They were certainly superior as buildings to the older church schools, and were monuments to the extension of local government powers of the time. They had to face the challenge of teaching some of the roughest children from the worst homes who had hitherto been conveniently ignored by the church societies: the *Schoolmaster* in 1872 referred to the 'younger years of school board life, while the unbroken youth of our country are being raked in from the gutter, the dunghill, and the hedgerow'.[32] In fact, some school boards such as those in London and Birmingham charged higher fees in some of their schools in order to provide places for the children of better-paid parents from more civilised homes.[33]

The greatest problem after the 1870 act was to get the children of unco-operative parents into school, and get them to stay there for at least five years. Inspectors' reports in the mid-1870s show that this was still a problem. In 1876, Lord Sandon's act declared that it was the duty of parents to send their children to school, but by 1880 only 450 out of 2,000 school boards had made attendance obligatory. In

1880, Gladstone's second ministry at last introduced compulsory attendance between five and twelve, with partial or full exemption from the age of ten. This was opposed in some quarters on the grounds that it was an infringement of the personal liberties of the parents; while other opponents pointed out that compulsion was hard on poor parents who had difficulties in finding the school fees. It was true, of course, that fees could be remitted by poor law guardians or by school boards, but the procedure could be humiliating for the parents. In fact, just 10 per cent of school fees were remitted in 1890–1. The answer here, of course, was to make elementary education free in all church and board schools, and this was in effect accomplished by Salisbury's Education Act, 1891, whereby an additional grant was paid to schools which abolished all fees (some church schools actually retained fees in order to keep out children from the roughest homes, and some parents were willing to go on paying on a voluntary basis). From 1891, then, elementary education became both compulsory and free.

There was still a very great deal which remained to be done for working-class education. The school leaving age was raised to eleven in 1893, and to twelve in 1899, but the education provided was still at an elementary level. However, some school boards began to set up higher-grade schools where children could stay on beyond the official leaving age. By 1894 there were sixty higher-grade schools outside London, and by 1900 the LSB had seventy-nine schools of this kind. In such schools, more specialised teaching could earn grants from the Department of Science and Art at South Kensington, and students might take public examinations such as those of the City and Guilds Institute and the Royal Society of Arts. Money was also available from Kensington for evening classes, including some classes in commercial subjects and art and design. One unexpected development was the result of a bill intended to compensate publicans for the loss of their licences when they were withdrawn; the sums of money set aside by the government for this purpose (nicknamed 'whisky money') was then transferred to meet the cost of a small scheme for technical education. The Technical Education Act, 1889, authorised the new county councils (set up in 1888) to raise a penny rate for technical education, and to raise money for new school buildings.

In these various ways, therefore, not only did a national, compulsory, and free system of elementary education come into being, but there were also some tentative steps towards secondary education and what would today be called further education. In fact, evening classes became an important aspect of working-class interest in self-improvement. Meanwhile, the church societies continued to have difficulties in keeping their schools going on a purely voluntary basis, and the Cross Commission on elementary education, 1888, recommended once more that the church schools should receive help from the rates. An education bill was introduced in 1896 to provide this, but was defeated by the combined opposition of the school boards and the Nonconformists, who thought it would be too favourable to the Church of England. In 1894, another royal commission, the Bryce Commission, was appointed, its task to examine the state of secondary education. It recommended that a new central authority should be formed from the Education Department and the Department of Art and Science; and further, that the county councils should take over all local authority secondary education, including the higher-grade schools. In 1899 the new central body came into existence under the title of the Board of Education. It took over the powers of the two departments just mentioned, together with the educational authority of the charity commissioners, hitherto responsible for the old, endowed grammar schools with their middle-class clientele.

Thus, the rudimentary system of voluntary elementary education provided by the church societies had blossomed by 1899 into a large-scale national organisation of schools supervised by a new government ministry. Two other issues had still to be resolved: the first was the future of secondary education, and the second was the old problem of rate-aid to the church societies. As for the first, it was arranged for the London district auditor to disallow spending by the LSB on its higher-grade schools, and when the School Board appealed to the High Court, its appeal was rejected (Cockerton's Judgement, 1899). The High Court held that all expenditure on higher-grade schools and evening classes was illegal and must cease. Finally, Balfour's Education Act, 1902, implemented further the recommendations of the Bryce Commission by abolishing the school boards and transferring their powers to the county councils, who were given authority over both secondary and elementary education. The only exception here was that in the smaller towns and less-populated urban areas, the borough councils and urban district councils created in 1895 could have charge of elementary education. The old board schools continued, of course, but became known as council schools. Further, the church schools were delighted to receive financial assistance from the rates, on condition that the local educational authority could appoint up to one-third of the school managers. With further reference to the provision of secondary education, the county councils were required to survey the need for secondary schools in their counties, and to establish new schools where necessary.

The Balfour Education Act, 1902, was as important in its way as Forster's Education Act, 1870. It is true that is was much disliked by supporters of board schools, who regarded them as democratic institutions, elected directly by the ratepayers. Further, there was much hostility on the part of the Nonconformists to having the Church of England on the rates, and some Welsh ratepayers went to prison on a matter of principle, rather than pay their rates. On the other hand, some school boards, especially in rural areas, were too small to do the job properly, and the new administrative machinery was an improvement, and was much more efficient. Of great importance is the authority given to the county councils to build new county secondary schools. These were usually run on grammar-school lines, and had a proportion of free places filled by scholarships from the elementary schools. Able working-class children might thus pass from elementary school to secondary school and even on to university. Not many did so, of course, for a number of reasons, not least the question of finance, but the opportunity of climbing an educational ladder from council school to university was there, however hard it was to reach the higher rungs.[34]

This chapter has ranged widely over different aspects of social change in the last thirty years of the nineteenth century, but without dwelling on the political challenges which emerged, especially in the 1880s. These challenges will be examined in more detail in Chapter 5. Enough has been said in this chapter, however, to make it clear that during the years of the Great Depression a new kind of England was emerging, and there was a distinct movement towards what might be called modernity. If the earlier period was one of equipoise, there is no doubt of the movement away from equipoise towards the creation of the modern, industrial state. The move towards urbanisation became a settled feature of social life; agriculture was left in the doldrums – few advocated a return to the corn laws. The beginnings of the modern public health system were put in hand, housing needs increasingly acknowledged (though not very effectively as yet), working conditions further regulated, and trade union rights firmly established, with even a first move in the political area with the election of working-class MPs. Working-class education proceeded apace, and at the same time there was more and more concern for the protection of women and children. For example, the age of consent among women was raised from the age of twelve (which seems remarkably low today) to thirteen, and then to sixteen in 1885; and the Married Women's Property Act, 1882, at last allowed married women to retain control of their property after marriage. Children were protected not only by factory and workshop legislation, but by the Prevention of Cruelty to Children Act, 1890, and the Cruelty to Children Act, 1894, by compulsory and free schooling up to the age of twelve (by 1900), and by social services such as county council missioners, the establishment of crèches, and school attendance officers. All these positive changes are indicative of the growth of a modern industrial state which found it increasingly necessary to provide a more civilised mode of existence for its citizens, giving its male members the vote in 1867 in the towns, and then in the countryside in 1884. At a time when the standard of living for the majority was rising, and retailing was booming, industrialisation had clearly come to stay, with all its attendant benefits.

Nevertheless, this was only one side of the picture, as the second half of this chapter has made abundantly clear. If industrial capitalism had brought great advances, even the opening up of a new British empire in Africa, it had also introduced great problems. Unemployment was becoming more and more a feature of the industrial scene, and the unemployed increasingly vocal and inclined to demonstrate. There were still problems arising out of the poor law, and about the growing numbers of old people for whom some sort of old age pension seemed appropriate (this need was disputed by the COS, as might be expected, for they thought self-help and thrift were what was required). The extent of poverty in London had been shockingly revealed by Booth's survey, and later in York by Rowntree. What really could be done about the 'submerged tenth' or the *residuum* in the cities?

It was this darker side of the progress of the nation which led to much anxious speculation. How far was the race actually degenerating in the squalid slums of the metropolis and elsewhere? If Darwin was right about the survival of the fittest, perhaps the corollary was the growth at the base of society of a class of savages who were beyond the reach of civilised influences. Medical opinion of the time, after all, believed that 'feeblemindedness' was inherited and incurable, while the Italian psychologist Lombroso believed in the inheritance of criminal tendencies. There are hints from time to time in the literature of the day of a belief in degeneration, not only in serious novelists such as Hardy and Gissing, but in more popular writers like H.G. Wells, and in liberals like Hobson and Beveridge, and even in socialists like Hyndman and the Webbs.[35] Sometimes one suspects that the observations were made in moments of depression rather than as the expression of deep conviction, and the majority of thinkers by the end of the century seemed to accept that poverty was not necessarily the fault of the individual, thus rejecting the crude social Darwinism mentioned above. Even the COS shifted its ground to some extent by giving up the moral condemnation implied in the terms 'deserving' and 'undeserving', and replacing them by 'helpable' and 'unhelpable', and also by developing the concept of the 'problem family'.[36] However, they clung to the idea of 'character', and the exercise of the will, something believed in by thinkers on both sides of the political divide, by both the Bosanquets and the Webbs, as well as by Hobson, Canon Barnett, and T.H. Green.

This takes us to the point that some thought the adverse social results of industrialisation were curable only by drastic political change. This was directly opposed to Gladstonian liberalism with its great belief in individual freedom, extending even to upholding the individual rights of Afghan tribesmen when faced by invading British armies in 1878–9. Certainly old-style liberalism rejected any political reform involving more state intervention on behalf of the masses – collectivism, something fiercely rejected by Gladstone, who called it 'construction'. But there were those such as the Webbs and the younger breed of new unionists who thought the whole basis of the distribution of wealth under industrial capitalism was wrong, and must be changed. Thus in the 1880s, which was to see the first English translation of Marx's *Das Kapital*, there occurred a distinct revival of socialist thinking in England which was to have a profound effect not only on middle-class intellectuals such as the Webbs, but also on the new breed of trade union leaders who wanted sweeping political change on behalf of the workers. Since these socialist ideas were derived so directly from a deep dissatisfaction with the workings of industrial capitalism, they may be regarded as one of the most remarkable results of industrialisation. They are so important that they deserve a chapter on their own, and together with the changes outlined in this chapter, they provide the essential background to first the Conservative reforms, and then to the much more extensive Liberal reforms of the early twentieth century. In many ways these Liberal reforms provide the climax to the Victorian age. Chapter 5 is therefore given to the subject of the challenge from the left.

4 Industrial change and the countryside, 1830–1951

When Victoria came to the throne in 1837, agriculture still constituted the largest single occupation, and was to remain so for some decades to come.[1] It was still a foundation industry, with many ancillary craft industries associated with it, and with the mainstay of an upper class of wealthy landowners, most of whom leased out much of their estates to a class of tenant farmers, who were the working agriculturalists and employers of the countryside. Its prestige and importance still occupied a significant place in the national consciousness – witness the speed with which the protective corn law of 1815 was passed, prohibiting the import of foreign corn until as a result of a domestic shortage (usually due to poor harvests) the price of corn had risen to 80/– or more a quarter. It was a clumsy and inflexible barrier to the import of foreign corn, and did not work very smoothly, but it is a good indication of the anxiety of parliament to preserve an industry vital to the nation in wartime. It is also a tribute to the influence of the landed classes in that body. In fact, in spite of the corn laws, agriculture was in a somewhat depressed state after the end of the French wars. This was due to a number of reasons. During the wars, agriculture had been very prosperous, and every scrap of the poorest soil went under the plough to grow corn; leases had also been taken out at inflated prices. Peacetime conditions put an end to easy profits; and it took time for farmers to readjust to falling prices and a more competitive situation. The president of the Board of Trade, William Huskisson, attempted to even out the abrupt operation of the 1815 corn law by introducing his sliding scales of duties in 1828 whereby foreign corn could be admitted henceforth at 73/– a quarter, paying a nominal duty of 1/–. Below that figure, duty increased until, at 52/– a quarter, all imports of corn were prohibited. This was an improvement, but it still could be seen as protecting the profits of the landed interest who held political power; and it still tended to keep consumer prices up. (Incidentally, Huskisson was fated to be one of the earliest middle-class victims of industrialisation; a notoriously clumsy man, he rashly stepped into the path of an oncoming locomotive at the opening of the Liverpool to Manchester railway in 1830, and was mortally injured as a result.)

By the opening of the early 1840s, agriculture had recovered from the post-1815 Depression, and was experiencing a mild prosperity; the growing towns needed feeding. But during Peel's Conservative ministry (1841–6), the agricultural interest was struck a severe blow by the industrial and commercial interests which were growing in strength. From their point of view, the corn laws helped to preserve a semi-monopoly in the provision of corn, kept up the price of bread, and therefore led to artificially high wages. As was noted in Chapter 2, the famous Anti-Corn Law League (ACLL), founded by Cobden and Bright in 1839, aimed to abolish the corn laws and may be seen as a part of the growing movement for free trade. The ACLL was backed heavily by the manufacturing interests, and is the first example of a modern political pressure group: it had the financial backing which Chartism had always lacked, and also the benefit of a clearly defined, single aim – repeal of the corn laws. Its message was spread nationwide by extensive propaganda in the form of pamphlets and by paid ACLL lecturers (one of their ploys was to get an emaciated agricultural labourer onto the platform to declare, 'I'm protected, but I be starving!' Agricultural protection did not seem to do much for the average farm labourer).

Peel was in a quandary: his strongest supporters in the Tory party were the wealthy landowners, and to repeal the corn laws was tantamount to committing political suicide. Yet Peel was a free trader, and in his budgets of 1842 and 1845 he completely abolished customs duties on more than 700 articles, mostly raw materials, and he greatly reduced the duties on many imported manufactured goods. He also reduced the duties on the lower end of the sliding scale. The next logical step was to abolish the corn laws altogether. There is the well-known political story of Peel's listening to an ACLL speech in the Commons one day, and then crumpling up his notes, remarking to a colleague on the front bench, 'You must answer this, for I cannot', and stalking from the chamber. There was more to it than the simple principle of free trade, of course. In 1845–6 Ireland was struck by potato blight (potatoes were the principal food of an impoverished population), and the result was the Great Famine in Ireland in which a million died. In order to relieve the suffering, Peel felt compelled to suspend the corn laws and allow free entry of corn into Ireland.

This was followed shortly after by a bill introduced by Peel for the permanent lifting of the corn laws. The landowners were outraged, and considered him to be a traitor: he was soon defeated on a relatively minor matter, and left office. Disraeli, the rising and ambitious young Tory, considered that 'rotten potatoes had put Peel into his damned fright'.[2]

This was to oversimplify, of course. Peel was a man of principle, and he did what he thought was right – in the old-fashioned phrase, he put country before party. But his party was understandably furious. The interesting thing, however, is the strength of the manufacturing and commercial interest of the time, whom Cobden and Bright represented; and this in spite of the fact that landed property was still heavily represented in the Commons, and overwhelmingly so in the Lords. The story might have had a different ending but for the curious fact that agriculture was by no means ruined by the repeal of the corn laws in 1846. This was due to a variety of reasons: when harvests were bad at home, they were often bad also in Europe, so that there was not always a great stock of cheap European corn available to flood British markets. Then again, transport costs from the Baltic wheatlands were still relatively high, and this certainly also applied to the North American cornfields, which became competitive only after transatlantic steam shipping developed in the 1870s. Further, the Crimean War actually stopped all imports of Russian wheat for a time. Lastly, population growth at home and improved real wages helped to keep demand high and domestic production buoyant in the 1850s and 1860s. Repeal probably helped to keep corn prices lower than they would have been, and hence was indeed of benefit to the working classes.

The repeal of the corn laws is among the first signs in Victoria's reign of the growing political power of the manufacturers and commercial interests. The other great example of the influence exerted by industrialisation over the countryside was the steady migration from the country areas to the towns in search of employment. The basic cause of this, of course, was the relative decline of agriculture as a factor of production, a decline which actually accelerated between 1815 and 1831. At the beginning of Victoria's reign, less than a quarter of the national labour force was employed in agriculture, and it supplied less than a quarter of the national income. This decline moderated in pace in the 1830s and 1840s, but after 1851 speeded up again. Agricultural production really failed to increase after the 1870s. Agricultural workers constituted only 15 per cent of the total work force in 1871 – it had been 36 per cent in 1801. By 1911 the figure had shrunk still further to only 8 per cent. By this time the total labour force in agriculture had dwindled from 2.1 million in 1851 to 1.6 million in 1911.[3] It is no wonder that by the turn of the century, the 'flight from the land' had become a familiar and much discussed phenomenon. It is one of the most striking illustrations one could have of the effect of industrialisation on the British nation.

As already noted earlier in this book, most of the movement of population was on a short-distance basis. It was thought earlier on that something like a mass movement took place from the south of England to the Midlands and the north, but this idea has long been discounted.[4] Presumably news of the availability of jobs spread by word of mouth, or after 1840 by the new penny post, or by newspapers circulating in the countryside. Some aspects of this internal migration were touched upon in the report of the 1851 Census, which was the first to require the person's place of birth. Thus, over the period 1841–51, in the heavily industrialised Lancashire and Cheshire, the increase by births was 218,443, while the increase by immigration was nearly as great, 205,375. Similarly, Staffordshire, Yorkshire, Warwickshire, Durham and Northumberland, and South Wales all showed substantial increases due to immigration. In the eastern counties, still a heavily agricultural region, births were 118,574 in the years from 1841 to 1851, but the population rose by only 73,366, so that here there was a net outflow per year (on average) of 4,520 from Norfolk, Suffolk, and Essex. Of course, migration was caused not only by the attraction of industrial vacancies, but also by the availability of jobs locally in agriculture. The coming into operation in the southern counties of the new, strict Poor Law Amendment Act, 1834, with its workhouse test and restrictions on outdoor relief, must also have supplied an additional incentive to move in search of work. All in all, the population was on the move in Victorian times, though the movement into the towns does not seem to have led to any shortage of agricultural labour. As the Census report put it, 'A free circulation of the people is now necessary in Great Britain, to meet the varying requirements of the Public Industry.'[5] This puts it exactly.

Other ways in which industrialisation affected agricultural life may be seen in a number of innovatory techniques in agricultural production, and in the coming of the railways. As for the first, one of the greatest changes in agricultural practices of the eighteenth century was the enclosure movement, but it had largely come to an end by the accession of Victoria to the throne. Whereas about 7 million acres had been enclosed in England between 1760 and 1815, from 1815 to

1845 only 200,000 acres underwent enclosure. By 1820 in England there were only half a dozen counties where open fields still extended to more than 3 per cent of cultivated land.[6] Technical innovations themselves were limited in number in agriculture in the first half of the nineteenth century. One of the earliest was the invention of the threshing machine, but when it was introduced into Kent, its threat to old-fashioned use of the flail led to the Swing Riots in 1830, in which 387 of the machines were destroyed.[7] Perhaps the most important change came in the increasing substitution of iron for wood in the manufacture of farming implements, and also in the replacement of the sickle by the scythe, which was certainly more efficient. Although the steam engine had been in industrial use for draining purposes since the early eighteenth century, it was found difficult to adapt to agricultural use. It was not until the mid-nineteenth century that it was used at all for ploughing, utilising stationary engines and cables, but even then its employment was not widespread. More important advances came in the shape of better drainage systems and an increased use of fertilisers. Thomas Scraggs invented a machine for making cheap drainage pipes in 1842, and from 1848 onwards government loans were made available for drawing off water. Here and there, steam pumps began to replace windmills for drainage. As for fertilisers, their benefits had been known from the seventeenth century or even earlier, but in addition to night soil, there was a greater use at the mid-century of crushed bones and superphosphates, and from abroad, nitrate of soda (from Chile and Peru), mineral potash (from Germany), and guano (from South America). Mechanised farming also began to spread with the use of steam threshing, and also of mechanised reapers and binders.

By the 1850s agriculture had recovered from the scare over the repeal of the corn laws, and entered a period of some prosperity. Thomas Caird, a writer on agricultural matters, had proclaimed that high farming was the best substitute for protection, and the mid-century years were a time of comfortable success for British farming – it has even been called a 'golden era'. The development of the railways certainly contributed to this success. In general terms, it can be said that the railways broke down the isolation of the countryside, making access to the towns with all their services much easier. In more concrete terms, railways permitted a much better delivery of fertiliser, animal foodstuffs, and machinery and implements to the farms, while they made possible a much faster and more extensive delivery of milk and other dairy products to the surrounding districts, and also to cities and towns at a distance. The practice of driving cattle by road to market, which took days if not weeks when the market was London, was superseded by transport by rail. This meant that animals arrived at market with much less loss of weight, in better condition, and able to command a better price. These were all very down-to-earth benefits attributable to the railways, and to them might be added the speedier and wider dissemination of news and ideas with the more efficient distribution of newspapers.

One other result of increasing industrialism must be noted: this is the decline which occurred in some areas of rural industry, especially those based on domestic work such as lacemaking and straw-plaiting. Some of these inevitably lost ground as their processes became mechanised and confined to factories. Thus lacemaking in the south Midland counties and in Devon had declined heavily by the 1890s. So had straw-plaiting in Buckinghamshire, Bedfordshire, Hertfordshire, and Essex: in Bedfordshire, where female plaiters had at one time numbered about 20,700, their number was reduced to only 485 in 1901. Water and wind-driven corn mills also declined in numbers with the spread of steam-driven mills, especially after the advent of roller-milling from 1875 onwards. On the other hand, here and there some rural industries managed to keep going, such as gloving in the Worcester area and in Somerset, while in some places new rural industries were set up, sometimes on a considerable scale. Brickmaking is a good example of this, with new brickworks around Peterborough, in south Bedfordshire, along the Medway valley, together with cement works, and near Rugby. One new enterprise which impressed Rider Haggard early in the twentieth century was the Chivers fruit preservative works at Histon, Cambridgeshire. The factory employed 250 women together with a thousand outworkers. The fruit was prepared in huge, silver-lined boilers, there were tramways and separate packing and printing departments, and all were lit by electricity.[8]

Change in the countryside before the 1870s was slow and unspectacular as compared with changes in industry. Things were very much the same physically as they had been in the 1830s. In industry, public attention had been focused for some time on the issue of child labour, on living conditions in the towns, and on industrial unrest and trade unionism. It was otherwise in agriculture. When the Employment of Children Commission, 1840, carried out a small-scale enquiry into the working conditions of women and children employed in agriculture, they had no great and urgent problems to report. Children were often employed from an early age on simple tasks such as opening and closing gates, and bird-scaring, but a witness pointed out that it was useless to put a child to any physical task before he had the strength to perform it. A young boy, for instance, had to be very strong to undertake ploughing. Hours could be very long in summer, but often there was no work available in December and January when the ground was frozen. Girls were employed in the dairy, but less so in field work, which was more arduous and physically demanding. Generally speaking, there were only two problems raised in connection with the employment of children: one was the system of apprenticeship, which was thought unsatisfactory and inconvenient, and the other was the pernicious practice of employing women and children in gangs, working often at long distances from home, and for very long hours. Otherwise the commissioners considered that agricultural work for both women and children was on the whole a healthy occupation, and the need to regulate hours (as in industrial work) did not arise. There were, however, some references to the very poor state of rural housing.[9]

In 1862 a second Children's Employment Commission was appointed, and this resulted in a further condemnation of ganging, and the Agricultural Gangs Act, 1867, at last laid down regulations for the operation of public agricultural gangs. In the same year, a further commission was appointed into working conditions in agriculture, with the specific task of enquiring 'to what extent the principles of the Factory Acts could be applied in agriculture, especially with a view to the better education of children'. Two separate reports were published as a result, one by H.S. Tremenheere recommending part-time school up to the age of twelve, and the other by E.C. Tufnell, prohibiting all work under nine (Tremenheere was concerned at the loss of children's earnings if any full-time prohibition on work were to be imposed). The Agricultural Children Act, 1873, sought to incorporate both points of view: it forbade all employment in agriculture under eight years of age, while between eight and twelve a certain number of school attendances was required. However, by the 1876 and 1880 education acts, school attendance between five and twelve became compulsory for all children (with certain exemptions).

From the 1870s the fortunes of agriculture took a marked turn for the worse. This was by no means all the result of industrial change. The weather had always been a hazard in the practice of farming, and the 1870s saw an unprecedented run of wet summers, which were followed by droughts in the early 1890s. Between 1884 and 1892 there were only two good harvests. Meanwhile, there were attacks of disease among cattle – foot and mouth disease, liver rot, and swine fever. Most important of all, increasing amounts of corn were now being brought across the Atlantic in steamships. This corn had been grown on the virgin soils of North America, harvested using the latest machinery, and brought to the ports by steam railway. In this country, its competition proved disastrous to home-grown wheat. Wheat prices which had averaged about 51/– a quarter in the 1870s fell in the 1880s to about 37/–, in the 1890s to under 29/–, and in 1894 and 1895 to less on average than 23/–.[10] In addition to this, livestock farming had to face competition from the import of frozen meat arriving in refrigerated ships from as far away as New Zealand. There was so much alarm at these developments that two royal commissions were appointed, the Richmond Commission (1879–82), and the Royal Commission on Agricultural Depression (1893–7).

There is no doubt that the more inefficient wheat farmers suffered badly in the last quarter of the nineteenth century, and a good number went bankrupt and left the land. On the other hand, it is important not to exaggerate the decline of agriculture during these years. Although the acreage under cereals fell noticeably, there were still 7 million acres given up to cereal production in 1913 (it had been 9.6 million acres in 1872).[11] Livestock farmers did comparatively well – there was still a market for home-grown meat as opposed to imported meat; and cheap imported corn reduced the cost of animal foodstuffs. Dairy farming became more profitable (milk production became the largest branch of English agriculture), and market gardening in the neighbourhood of cities and large towns expanded significantly. At the root of these changes was the increase in consumer demand due to the fall in prices and the rise in real wages which led to an increased demand for foodstuffs. After 1900, agriculture was able to adjust to its new circumstances. New farmers emerged with a more commercial outlook, among them a new intake of Scottish farmers with a keen eye on economy and profit. A modest prosperity returned. Agricultural production overall was not greatly reduced in volume, and although cereal production, especially of wheat, had declined, this was compensated for by the increase in livestock farming.[12]

This account of the fortunes of agriculture in Victorian times raises the question of how far the change to an industrial economy had deleterious effects on agriculture after 1837. So far, emphasis has been laid on two aspects of the question: the growing political influence of the industrial and commercial classes, and the movement of population from the countryside to the towns. Is it necessary to add anything further to these changes? In fact, there is still one additional aspect to be considered; for apart from the enactment of the 1815 corn law and its repeal in 1846, government interest was subsequently concentrated far more on industrial and commercial affairs than on agriculture. By and large, the landed interest was left to get on with its own concerns, while industry was subject to a constant stream of commissions, enquiries, and select committees. Not only were industrial working conditions regulated by a succession of factory and workshop acts, but living conditions in industrial towns were also investigated and also regulated in the second half of the century. This is understandable enough, of course, since there was so much in these areas of national life which cried out for action. Agriculture, by way of contrast, had always been there, and agricultural society was left more or less to its own devices. The result was a very noticeable lack of government interest in rural conditions, apart from occasional incidental references to the bad state of rural housing. By the 1870s, the countryside was beginning to be regarded as something of a backwater, and the typical agricultural labourer thought of as Hodge, a dull, rather backward and unenterprising yokel in his old-fashioned smock and heavy boots, much given to leaning over gates, chewing a straw, as seen in a multitude of *Punch* cartoons.

This picture was to change to some extent after 1870, but not to any remarkable degree. Trade unionism among the labourers got off to a faltering start when Joseph Arch founded the Agricultural Workers' Union in 1872 (it had a hard time surviving in the depression in agriculture which followed). The Secret Ballot Act of 1872 gave a much needed element of secrecy in casting a vote, especially in the country, while in 1884 the vote was given to the rural male householder. Schooling in the countryside had always been of intermittent attraction to agricultural parents, owing to the need of families to gain what additional income they could by finding work on the farm for their children; but from 1880 onwards, as we have seen, schooling became compulsory, and educational standards in rural areas slowly improved (though rural schools still had many empty places during harvest time). So Hodge was beginning to improve himself, but given the state of agriculture, especially in the wheat-growing southern counties, his best bet was to get out of the countryside altogether. He voted with his feet, and the result was a remarkable further reduction in his numbers; between 1871 and 1901, the number of male agricultural workers fell by 300,000, nearly a third.[13] The numbers of female workers fell by nearly 46,000, that is, by 79 per cent. Many of these left for domestic services as described in the Flora Thompson classic, *From Lark Rise to Candleford*. This reduction in the size of the workforce had the effect of improving wages, especially in the south; though agricultural workers in the north had always been paid better than in the south, since employers had to compete with the level of local industrial wages. The rise in earnings was quite substantial; in England and Wales the average wage in 1867–70 was 13/9, and this rose to 16/– by 1898, and to 17/11 in 1907. A further benefit here was the fall in food prices in this period which added considerably to the level of real wages.[14]

Although agricultural wages had improved by the end of the century, working conditions were still almost entirely unregulated, and social amenities in the average village were still very limited. In particular, housing conditions remained extremely bad. In the towns, by 1900 new building was regulated by local bye-laws, and a limited amount of slum clearance had begun. In the countryside it was quite otherwise; with the decline in the rural population, little or no new building had been undertaken. Here and there an improving land-lord like the Duke of Bedford built model cottages (two living rooms, a kitchen and scullery, two or three bedrooms, and an outside WC),[15] but these were a rarity. At worst, the typical country cottage might have only one living room, one bedroom, an earthen floor, damp walls, a leaky thatched roof, and an earth privy outside. The effect of bad living conditions on the health of agricultural workers was well known: they were notoriously subject, for example, to rheumatic complaints. In 1900 it was estimated that there was an absolute rural housing shortage of 120,000 houses, with a much larger stock of decaying, insanitary, and overcrowded cottages.[16]

Yet by this time it had begun to sink into middle-class consciences that there were severe social problems in the countryside as well as in the towns, but whereas the urban problems might be thought to be the result of industrialisation, those of the rural areas were really the product of persistent neglect. Further, it was a neglect for which the nation might have to pay dear. For the countryside was still thought of as the principal source of the army's manpower. Recruitment for the Boer War administered a great shock in this respect, with a third of the recruits unable to meet the army's minimum standards. The bogy of national degeneration was there for all to see. The numerous reports on the extent of poverty in the towns sounded further alarms: how could the Empire be maintained without a healthy working class, whether in the city or in the countryside?

When the Liberals came to power in 1906, therefore, there was a certain national awareness not only of the need to alleviate urban poverty but also to improve the living conditions and physical well-being of country dwellers, those who in a sense had been neglected if not forgotten in the race to industrialise. For this reason, the Liberal governments of 1906 and after not only tried to tackle the problems of urban poverty, but also had plans, devised principally by Lloyd George, for attacking what he called the 'land problem'. A speech by Winston Churchill in his radical phase, made at the Drury Lane theatre in April, 1908, brings out this aspect of the New Liberalism very well:[17]

> They saw first of all that this island alone among civilised states presented the melancholy spectacle of a landless peasantry. Side by side with that, and arising as they contended, directly out of that, they saw a blighted and restricted agriculture. The rural population was melting fast into the great cities, and whether they looked at the reports on physical deterioration or at those dealing with the supply of men for the army, no-one could doubt that there was grave reason for alarm in the physical deterioration which was taking place in many of the great cities to which the rural population had been drawn ...

In his account of his investigations into rural conditions in 1901 and 1902, the popular novelist, Rider Haggard, wrote of the attraction of town life for the rural labourer, and of the bad state of his housing:[18]

> The diffusion of newspapers, the system of Board School education, and the restless spirit of our age have changed him, so that nowadays it is his main ambition to escape from the soil where he was bred and try his fortune in the cities. This is not wonderful, for there are high wages, company, and amusement, with shorter hours of work. Moreover, on the land he has no prospects: a labourer he is and in ninety-nine cases out of a hundred, he must remain. Lastly, in many instances his cottage accommodation is very bad; indeed, I have found wretched and insufficient dwellings to be a great factor in the hastening of the rural exodus ...

Undoubtedly, poor rural housing was a major cause of rural dissatisfaction. When the Liberal Party set up its land enquiry committee in 1912, its enquiries confirmed yet again the dreadful state of much village housing, and Volume I of its report, *The Land*, published in 1913, recommended the building of cottages by rural district councils, and cottage lettings to be subject to a minimum notice of six months, together with a number of other measures such as a legal minimum wage and more allotments and smallholdings.[19]

This report really forms a part of Lloyd George's land campaign which will be described in Chapter 6, where it will be noted that the outbreak of war prevented any further progress in land reform. It cannot be said that the Liberal governments got very far in improving rural living and working conditions, but there is the obvious point that earlier on they were preoccupied with the great national issues of old age, sickness, and unemployment, not to mention the constitutional struggle with the House of Lords, and then the looming problems of Home Rule and suffragette violence. However, certain preliminary reforms were undertaken, such as Harcourt's Smallholdings and Allotments Act, 1907, which gave additional powers to local authorities to acquire land compulsorily for resettlement purposes. The allotment movement was certainly helpful, especially to labourers without large cottage gardens, but it hardly went to the root of rural discontents. Again, although the Town and Country Planning Act, 1909, is generally regarded as not achieving very much, in fact it did lead to some 5,000 cottages being closed under its provisions.[20]

In long-term perspective, it is obvious that the agricultural community would play an increasingly minor part in the affairs of the nation as industrialisation increased. For most of Victoria's reign, it still had a massive political presence in the House of Lords, and landed interests were still prominent in the Commons. By the end of the century, however, even this began to change, for to the ranks of the landed proprietors in the Lords there were added new representatives of business interests from the worlds of brewing, publishing, and so on. Business and professional interests also grew in the Commons. By this time, life in the countryside was coming more and more to the attention of the reading public – the flight from the land, poor wages, bad housing conditions, and the spectre of national physical degeneration as a threat to the defence of both the homeland and the Empire. Mixed up with all this was a certain nostalgia for the peaceful country life as compared with the sordid realities of city life – there is a good deal of this in the writings of Charles Masterman (who himself had little or no experience of living in the countryside). It also tinged the popular notions of labour colonies which were essentially agricultural settlements. Not only did they seem to be a possible solution to the problem of unemployment, but they also appeared to offer a more satisfactory way of life, more attuned to nature, than the harsh conditions of life in the towns. The garden city movement of the time was also regarded as an antidote to the soulless existence of much urban life. One way and another, the countryside, albeit at times in an idealised form, remained a matter of national concern.

But that is as far as it went. Agricultural wages were not fixed (unlike miners' wages), housing remained by and large unimproved, agricultural workers were not covered by the unemployment scheme of 1911. The landowning classes had been shaken by the new taxes contained in the 'people's budget', and by the surrender of the House of Lords in 1911, but otherwise they had survived. Indeed, although agricultural rents had fallen, some landowners had profited directly from industrialisation by exploiting mineral rights on their estates, and by the rentals on their extensive urban properties, which could be very lucrative. Socially speaking, the agricultural labourer and his family remained at the bottom of the heap, and the Liberals, however well meaning, had done little to meet his major grievances before war came in 1914.

In concluding this chapter, it is convenient to take the story of agriculture further to the outbreak of World War II in 1939 and then on to 1951. The importance of agriculture in the life of the nation was emphasised in the course of World War I, and particularly so when the adoption of unrestricted U-boat warfare by Germany threatened to starve the country into submission in 1917. By the Corn Production Act, 1917, farmers were guaranteed against losses on wheat and oats for the following five years, while an agricultural wages board was set up to fix minimum wages. During the brief post-war boom, the Agriculture Act, 1920, again guaranteed the cost of production of wheat and oats, and provided for compensation for unexhausted improvements – something of great importance to tenant farmers. With the fall in prices in 1921, however, the government was faced with massive bills, and it therefore repealed the 1920 act. Wages fell heavily – 6,000 labourers came out on strike in Norfolk in 1923 – and the first Labour government in 1924 restored wage-fixing, and at the same time set up county agricultural committees. Protection was finally adopted as a policy by the national government in and after 1932, leading to duties on fruit, flowers, and vegetables, quotas on imported fish, and the establishing of a number of marketing boards designed to improve both production and marketing, for example, the Milk Marketing Board, the Bacon Marketing Board, and boards for potatoes and hops. Subsidies were given to growers of wheat and barley by the Wheat Act, 1932, to livestock farmers by the Livestock Industry Act, 1937, and to the sugar beet industry, for which the British Sugar Corporation was set up in 1935 under government control. Given this massive support, agricultural output expanded by a fifth in the 1930s, land under wheat went up by half a million acres between 1932 and 1937, and pig, poultry, and dairy farming all expanded; but the cost to the government was considerable. It stood at £45 million in 1934, but had increased to £100 million by 1939.[21]

Thus the agricultural industry survived the inter-war years, though it was at a low ebb in the 1920s, and only in the 1930s was it placed on a more secure footing, partly because the long-disputed policy of tariff reform or protection profited both industry and agriculture, and partly because the fear of war made it essential to improve national self-sufficiency in agriculture. It should be added that mechanisation at last began to improve agricultural production between the wars: the number of tractors increased from 16,681 in 1925 to 40,000 in 1937. More combine harvesters were also employed. So after hard times in the 1920s, agriculture underwent a period of convalescence in the 1930s, thanks mainly to government assistance and also to increased consumer demand. It still had an important part to play in the life of the nation, and one that became prominent again during World War II. However, as we have seen, industrialisation had transformed its function from being the fundamental and premier industry at the beginning of the nineteenth century to being the poor relation of manufacturing industry, by the inter-war period. Further, many of the great estates were broken up in the immediate post-war period of the early 1920s as land was sold to pay increased taxation – one-sixth of the land in England changed hands in these years.[22] Agriculture and agricultural society were not what they had been in the early years of Victoria's reign. It is perhaps significant that the two most influential prime ministers of the inter-war years were Stanley Baldwin and Neville Chamberlain. Baldwin was chosen as prime minister because, unlike the more obvious choice, Lord Curzon, he was not a member of the House of Lords. He had a genuine regard for the countryside, but was a small-scale iron manufacturer in Bewdley, Worcestershire (Curzon thought him a person of the utmost insignificance). Chamberlain was a Birmingham businessman, whose family fortunes were based on the manufacture of screws. The days when the government was led by great landowning magnates with seats in the House of Lords like Lord Salisbury were finally over.

Nevertheless, the coming of war again in 1939, and especially Britain's isolated position after 1940, brought a renewed recognition of the importance of agriculture in the life of even a predominantly industrial state. Once more there was the demand for maximum agricultural production, the setting up of war agricultural committees, recruitment to the Women's Land Army, the use of prisoners of war as agricultural labour, and a general swing to arable farming. Mechanisation was speeded up: the numbers of tractors employed increased by over three times to 190,000. Householders were exhorted to 'dig for victory', and suburban flower gardens were dug up and converted to vegetable plots. Overall, agricultural output increased by some 35 per cent during the war.

After the war, and at a time when world agricultural prices were high, and it was necessary to continue rationing (and even increase it), it seemed obvious that support to agriculture should be maintained. Of course, if the economy was to be planned, then agriculture could not be excluded. There was the further point that the agricultural community had a moral claim to be protected as an important part of the nation and a participant in the Welfare State. There was little controversy therefore over the clear need to continue government support for agriculture. The Agriculture Act, 1947, provided for the fixing and guaranteeing of prices by the Ministry of Agriculture. County agricultural committees were given increased powers to evict unsatisfactory farmers, and local authorities were encouraged to provide smallholdings for suitable applicants. Efforts were also made to improve the provision of educational training courses in husbandry. As a result of this, by 1954–5 a 50 per cent increase in agricultural output over pre-war averages was achieved. In particular, wheat acreages rose from a pre-war figure of 1.92 million acres to 2.06 million acres in 1946–7, and then to 2.45 million acres in 1954–5.[23] All this cost money, of course – in 1954–5 the cost to the government was £250 million – and there were some complaints that the government was 'featherbedding' the farmers (a term used at the time). All the same, if the role of agriculture in the economy had been transformed over the previous century or so, it had acquired a new status as an essential and protected part of the life of the nation.

In conclusion, it is clear that after more than a century of industrialisation, agriculture had more than just survived. Inevitably, of course, it had declined in importance in the national economy, and its labour force had been drastically reduced. Throughout most of the nineteenth century after 1830 the agricultural labourer suffered from low wages and inadequate housing. Nevertheless, the adoption of new farming techniques and the greater importance given to livestock farming, dairying, and market gardening allowed farming to adjust to changed circumstances, and the two world wars certainly helped to emphasise the importance of agriculture to the life of the nation. By 1951 the Victorian image of Hodge had virtually disappeared and the agricultural labourer had of necessity become much more of a skilled worker, knowledgeable about petrol and diesel engines, farm machinery, the care of animals, and modern crop practices. Scientific and technological advance, which had had such a profound effect on industry, had also produced great changes in agricultural practice.

5 The challenge from the left

In introducing the subject of left-wing advances during the 1880s, it is customary to refer to the revival of socialist thinking in these years, and references are often made to Robert Owen. However, it has already been pointed out that this could be misleading, for what was considered 'socialist' earlier in the century would not necessarily be thought 'socialist' later on. This is true particularly of the views of Robert Owen who, it has already been suggested, is better regarded as a communitarian than a socialist. The reason for this is that he believed strongly in the creation of small, self-governing communities consisting of both middle-class and working-class men and women, these communities holding property in common. In these settlements, the leadership would be taken in the natural order of things by the educated middle classes who were used to assuming command. Owen had no time for the class struggle, and indeed had little faith in the ability of working men to organise anything; he had a great belief in environmental influences, and as the working classes had little experience of organisation in their daily lives, they had to expect the middle classes to lead (curiously, Owen did not seem to see that he himself was an excellent example of a working man who had become a good manager). So, Owen's socialism was very different from Marxist socialism with its emphasis on class struggle and the final triumph of the working classes. Nevertheless, his ideas were very influential among the early pioneers of co-operative enterprise, most of whom were prepared to engage in retail trading with a view to establishing communities based on Owenite ideas.[1]

It should also be stressed that neither Chartism nor the Christian Socialist movement was 'socialist' in the sense in which the term was beginning to be used in the 1880s. The Chartist movement was many things to many people, as we have seen, and there were some Owenite believers among its followers, but its principal leader in its later days,

Feargus O'Connor, was a strong believer in capitalism and individualism. Although his plans for land settlements were superficially similar to Owen's communities, O'Connor declared roundly that 'My plan has no more to do with socialism than it has with the comet.' As for the Christian Socialists of the early 1850s, their co-operative schemes were based on beliefs in Christian brotherhood, and their paternalistic efforts to promote small-scale tailoring enterprises had all failed by 1854. In fact, the prosperous years of the mid-century were relatively barren years for the spread of modern socialist doctrine in England. The first edition of the *Communist Manifesto* (1848), written by Marx and Engels, was published in German, a first English translation appearing in the *Red Republican* in 1850, but it seems to have had little impact in this country, although this translation appeared in New York in 1871. Over here the English translation in common use was not made till 1888.[2] As for Marx's epic work, *Das Kapital*, the first volume was not published till 1867, again in German, and was in any case an abstruse and difficult read.

However, the 1888 publication date of the English translation of the *Manifesto* is not without significance in that by the late 1880s socialist ideas, with their emphasis on the ultimate breakdown of the capitalist system and the seizure of power by the working classes, were beginning to circulate more widely. The reasons for this are not far to seek: clearly the working classes were increasingly literate, and male householders (and some lodgers) had the vote in both the borough and county constituencies after 1884. Moreover, as we have seen, in spite of the rise in real wages during the Great Depression, the slumps of the period showed that there could be unemployment even among skilled workers, and that material progress would not necessarily continue unchecked for ever. Further, surveys such as Booth's showed the extent of poverty in London, the richest city in the world. For a number of reasons then, criticisms of the capitalist system became more prominent in the 1880s, especially among the younger trade unionists in the so-called 'new unions'. Such criticism was heard less among the older union leaders elected to parliament in and after 1874, who were usually conventional in attitude, and happy to take the Liberal whip – hence the nickname, 'Lib-Labs'. (Joseph Chamberlain referred to them contemptuously in 1894 as 'mere fetchers and carriers of the Gladstonian party', a party from which he had parted company over Home Rule.) In 1894 there were eleven Lib-Labs in the Commons. The programme of the Parliamentary Committee of the TUC – really the parent body of the Lib-Labs – was very limited. It demanded further franchise reforms (this was before the Reform Acts of 1884 and 1885), yet also included old-fashioned proposals such as a return to peasant proprietorship, an impractical and nostalgic harking back to the days of Merrie England.

Younger new unionists such as Tom Mann were openly critical of the policy of the older unions whose policy he condemned as 'half hearted'. According to Mann, all of these unions had large numbers of members out of work even when their own particular trade was busy. They seemed to have no policy other than that of trying to stop wages from falling. In an 1886 pamphlet containing these views, Mann went on to argue:[3]

> The true trade union policy of *aggression* seems entirely lost sight of: in fact, the average unionist of today is a man with a fossilised intellect, either hopelessly apathetic, or supporting a policy which plays into the hands of the capitalist exploiter ...

Note the phrase 'capitalist exploiter'. When in 1891 the royal commission on labour was appointed, Mann was made a member of the commission. It produced a fifth and final report in 1894, but Tom Mann and three other commissioners wrote in addition a minority report. This report contained an indictment of the economic system, under which 5 million working people were 'unable to obtain a subsistence compatible with health or efficiency', about 2 million a day were applying for poor relief, and, in London, 32 per cent were below the poverty line (in some London districts, it was claimed, a half or even two-thirds were below the poverty line). This polemic concluded with a demand for new attitudes in industry:[4]

> To sum up: we regard the unsatisfactory relations between employers and employed as but one inevitable incident of the present industrial anarchy. The only complete solution of the problem is, in our opinion, to be found in the progress of industrial evolution, which will assign to the 'captains of industry' as well as to the manual workers, their proper position as servants of the community.

This is very different from the conciliatory attitudes of the older, craft unions in the late 1860s and early 1870s. Indeed, the forceful approach of the new unionists actually led to a motion being proposed by Keir Hardie at the 1894 TUC, and passed by 219 votes to 61, approving of the nationalisation of the means of production, distribution, and exchange, and of the land. This was scarcely a majority view of the TUC as a whole, but is an indication of the zeal with which the new unionists pursued their objectives.

Meanwhile, two strikes in the late 1880s showed the strength of New Unionism. The first is the famous Bryant & May matchgirls' strike of 1888. There is no doubt that the matchgirls were scandalously exploited by their employers, and this was exposed by the well-known radical Mrs Annie Besant in her socialist paper, the *Link*. She accused the firm of instituting a form of white slavery, and of discharging girls as soon as they were worked out; nobody cared, she claimed, whether they died or went on the streets, as long as the Bryant & May shareholders got their 23 per cent. Mrs Besant helped run the strike, which was successful, and the girls then formed a union of their own.

In the next year, 1889, a new union was formed among the London gasworkers, the National Union of Gas Workers and General Labourers, led by Will Thorne, an intelligent but almost illiterate Irishman from Birmingham, and a member of the Social Democratic Federation (this body will be discussed later in this chapter). The new union's first objective was a reduction in working hours, and this was granted by their employers, the South Metropolitan Gas Company, without the union's having to call their members out on strike. Later in the year, perhaps the most famous strike of the whole period took place in London – the London Docks strike of 1889.

The London dockworkers were a very mixed work force of labourers, some relatively skilled, but the majority less so. Only a minority were already unionised. As was customary at the time, the average labourer was employed on a casual basis, being taken on and paid when a ship came in, and discharged after a few days when the job was finished. Being selected for work involved a desperate struggle to be first in the queue; and after a few hours' heavy labour, a docker might be so hungry that he would discharge himself, take his money, and go off to buy food. According to the manager of the Millwall Docks, who was not unsympathetic to the typical docker: 'They are the most miserable of specimens; there are men who are reduced to the direst poverty, men with every disposition to work well, but without the strength to do it ...'[5]

It was therefore a considerable achievement to bring such an undisciplined work force out on strike, and for the strike to stay solid. This was the achievement of Ben Tillett and his new union (founded 1887) of tea warehousemen. The strike was for an increase in pay from 5d an hour to 6d an hour (the 'docker's tanner'), and was soon joined by many other dockers. Their cause was strengthened by the support of some of London's best-known socialists – Tom Mann, John

Burns, Eleanor Marx (daughter of Karl Marx), Annie Besant, and members of the Social Democratic Federation, whose secretary, H.H. Champion, acted as public relations officer. Public relations were regarded as being of great importance: dockers' marches were organised by John Burns throughout the city, and their orderly behaviour was much remarked upon – there was no unruly behaviour or rioting. Picketing was supervised by Tom Mann, who made sure it was conducted peacefully. The support of Cardinal Manning was obtained – many of the dockers were Roman Catholic. After two weeks, support for the strike began to waver, but a donation of £30,000 to the strike funds from the Australian unions saved the day. After this, a special Mansion House committee of conciliation was set up, and further negotiations led to a final settlement. On 9 September, on Tower Hill, John Burns reminded his audience of how the garrison at Lucknow during the Indian Mutiny watched for the silver shine of the bayonets of the troops coming to their rescue. He continued, 'This lads, is the Lucknow of Labour, and I myself, looking to the horizon, can see a silver gleam – not of the bayonets to be imbued in a brother's blood, but the gleam of the full round orb of the docker's tanner.'[6] The dockers certainly gained their tanner, new working procedures were set up, and Tillett organised a new union for dockers – the Dock, Wharf, Riverside and General Labourers Union. By November, 1889 it had enrolled 30,000 members. It was all a triumph for New Unionism.

However, as mentioned in Chapter 3, it is important to avoid giving the impression that New Unionism dominated the trade union movement as a whole. This is not so, and as already noted, by 1900 the membership of the new unions was still only about a tenth or less of the total trade union membership. Moreover, they were not homogeneous in nature.[7] Some were based on a single industry, some drew their members from several different industries. Not all had a large general element, that is, not all had large numbers of general labourers; some did, some did not. Some were able to afford friendly society benefits, others could not. Not all wanted a 'closed shop', or even were led by socialists. It remains true, however, that on the whole they catered more for unskilled labour than the older craft unions, and they tended to adopt more militant tactics. They did not swing the union movement *en masse* towards socialism, but they did provide a cutting edge in discussion, witness Keir Hardie's motion at the TUC in 1894. Indeed, the older members of the TUC were uncomfortably aware of the political views of their younger brethren, and in 1894 the Parliamentary Committee of the TUC changed the system of voting at congress so as to limit the influence of socialists. Previously, voting had been on an individual basis, and trades councils were represented separately, often by socialists, who could vote additionally as representatives of their unions. In future, trades councils were no longer to be represented, and union delegates were to have one vote per thousand members. Further, every delegate had either to work at his trade, or be a paid union official (this excluded Keir Hardie as a journalist). This therefore reduced socialist influence at the TUC, but certainly did not exclude it to any marked extent, as will be seen later in this chapter.

At this point we may turn from the diffusion of socialist ideas in the trade union movement to the creation of political bodies set up to further the cause of socialism.[8] Two such bodies were established in the 1880s, and became pre-eminent. The first is the Social Democratic Federation (SDF), and the second is the Fabian Society. The SDF began life as the Democratic Federation in 1881, but was reorganised as the SDF in 1884. It became avowedly Marxist in outlook, and its policies were based on the class struggle, and the gaining of political power when capitalism finally collapsed. It was led by H.M. Hyndman, whose social background was indisputably middle class; he was an Old Etonian and had been a student at Cambridge University. As a speaker at political meetings, he stood out among the working men present, with his top hat and frock-coat. He had read *Das Kapital* in a French translation in 1881, which accounted for his Marxist outlook, though in his *England for All* (1881) he admitted that Marx's work would 'mostly be inaccessible to the majority of my countrymen'. In fact, he failed to acknowledge Marx by name, and this seemed to have offended both Marx and Engels, who refused to give the SDF any support. Hyndman went his own autocratic way, one of the eccentric, strong-willed, middle-class Englishmen of the late Victorian period. The SDF never took the name of Communist Party, and such a party was not established in Britain under that name till 1920. Nevertheless, the SDF remained an important political body in spite of its tiny membership in the years up to 1914. One of its most prominent members was William Morris, poet, artist, and designer, but he and other members quarrelled with Hyndman and withdrew from the SDF to form the short-lived Socialist League, afterwards taken over by the anarchists, and henceforth disappearing into obscurity.

The second socialist body, the Fabian Society, is still with us today, as a sort of think-tank for the Labour Party. It was founded by a group of middle-class thinkers and writers whose ranks included Sidney and Beatrice Webb, Graham Wallis, George Bernard Shaw, H.G. Wells, and Annie Besant. The society derived its name from the Roman general Fabius who was supposed to have won his battles by avoiding direct, full-scale attack but by wearing down the enemy by limited but constant pressure. The Fabian Society did not aim at establishing a new socialist political party because they believed that their ideas would gradually permeate the thinking of men and women of all political parties. In this way socialism would be adopted peacefully and democratically over a period of time, and there would be no need for the kind of revolution thought inevitable by Marxists. The essence of Fabian thinking was inevitable, gradual change, away from naked individualism to a sort of refined collectivism, seeking to cure the ills of industrial capitalism, but doing so with due regard for the democratic process, and without resort to any form of violence.

Sidney Webb summed up these beliefs in an oft-quoted passage in his *Fabian Essays*, published in 1889:

> Socialists as well as Individualists realise that important organic changes can only be (1) democratic, and thus acceptable to a majority of the people, and prepared for it in the minds of all; (2) gradual, and thus causing no dislocation, however rapid may be the rate of progress; (3) not regarded as immoral by the mass of the people, and thus not subjectively demoralising to them; and (4) in this country at any rate, constitutional and peaceful.

This seems reasonably clear (rather clearer perhaps than many political pronouncements of the present day). The contrast with the Marxist message is very noticeable; there is no complicated economic argument based on surplus value (Morris admitted he never understood this tenet of Marxism), or upon the inevitability of the collapse of capitalism, or the need for the workers to rise up and seize power. Instead, there is change in society offered on the basis of democratic, gradual, peaceful reform. There is even a reassurance that any change will be 'moral', which presumably implies that moral and/or religious susceptibilities will not be offended, even if secularism appears to be growing. Marxism, of course, by contrast, was a godless creed.

How effective was the Fabian Society in securing converts to socialism? Certainly their views gained a widespread circulation. About three-quarters of a million tracts were sent out between 1887 and 1893. Some thousands of lectures were delivered annually in London and other cities. Its stronghold was in London, of course, where its leading members were well known in London society, and had connections in high places. Sidney and Beatrice Webb were pioneer social historians, and social investigators (Beatrice spent some time helping her kinsman Charles Booth with his survey, even working in a sweat-shop in the East End for a time), while the Webbs had a major role in the founding of the London School of Economics and Social Science in 1895. They were also widely known as opponents of the COS, and of the leaders of the COS, Bernard and Helen Bosanquet.

All this makes it difficult to assess just how influential the Fabian Society was towards the end of the century. Certainly its views had some effect on thinking members of the middle classes, especially those with a conscience who were disturbed at the extent of urban poverty. Writing after World War I about her pre-war experiences, Beatrice Webb commented on the way the conscience of the middle classes was touched:[9]

> The consciousness of sin was a collective or class consciousness: a growing uneasiness, amounting to conviction, that the industrial organisation which had yielded rent, interest and profits on a stupendous scale, had failed to provide a decent livelihood and tolerable conditions for a majority of the inhabitants of Great Britain.

Fabian thinking also had some influence over the Christian Socialist revival. The Christian Socialist Union was set up in 1889, and pledged to apply Christian principles to the social and economic problems of the time. It had a membership of 6,000, including at one time some sixteen bishops. Its issuing of 'white lists' of firms paying trade union rates in 1893, and its support for further factory legislation have caused one historian to call its method 'very Fabian'. But, in practice, most Christian Socialists were more anti-capitalist than pro-socialist; their cautious policy was but a shadow of their critical rhetoric.[10]

So the Fabian Society was a very middle-class body, though not exclusively so. Some leading trade unionists were members, such as Ben Tillett, while Tom Mann was a member of both the Fabian Society and the SDF, though the ideas of the two societies were much opposed to each other. There were ninety independent local Fabian Societies in the provinces, and these included many members of trades councils. It would therefore be unwise to think of the Fabian Society as being too exclusively middle class in nature, though it remained a political propaganda body and never became a political party in itself.

It was in the 1890s that the first move came to provide political representation for the working classes other than that of the handful of Lib-Labs in the House of Commons. Given the dissatisfaction on the left with conformist attitudes of the Lib-Labs, it is not surprising that some fresh move for better representation should be made. However, it might be expected that it would come in London or in one of the other great cities rather than in Bradford. It followed shortly after the election to parliament of Keir Hardie. Together with two other working men, John Burns and Havelock Wilson, Hardie had been elected as an independent in 1892, but whereas Burns and Wilson soon joined the Lib-Labs, he refused to do so, and remained independent; he had already formed a small independent party – the Scottish Labour Party – in 1888. Keir Hardie was one of the most charismatic labour leaders of his time. He had started work in the Lanarkshire pits at the age of ten, had been blacklisted for trade union activities, and had become a journalist and organiser among the Ayrshire miners. He was an avowed socialist, but no Marxist, though like many others, he often used Marxist terms. He was a strong individualist, which was shown by his arrival at the House to take his seat dressed informally with a tweed cap and in a two-horse brake; he was accompanied by a cornet player who obliged with a version of the Marseillaise.[11]

It was Keir Hardie who organised a conference in Bradford in January 1893 – there were already twenty-three labour clubs in the city, so that good local support was assured (between 1882 and 1892, labour representatives on local bodies had shot up from a dozen to 200. In 1895 there were 600 labour councillors on borough councils, and they were to gain a majority in West Ham in 1898, as well as sharing nine seats with the Progressives on the London County Council). Thus, Labour's support was increasing nationally. Hardie's conference was attended by 120 delegates, representing the labour clubs, the Scottish Labour Party, the SDF, the Fabian Society, and a limited number of trade unions. A new political party was set up at the conference, the Independent Labour Party (ILP), to act independently of both the Liberals and the Lib-Labs. Its policy was uncompromisingly socialist, since it aimed at the public owner-ship of the means of production, distribution, and exchange. It had a good deal of local support, and it set up 400 branches inside a year with a membership of about 50,000. The problem was that nationally, it had very little support; and all the candidates who stood for the new party in the general election of 1895 were defeated, including Keir Hardie himself, who lost his seat in West Ham (subse-quently he was returned as member for Merthyr Tydfil in 1900). The new Independent Labour Party had therefore got off to a somewhat unpromising start.

Meanwhile, the trade union movement as a whole continued with its basic policy of collective bargaining, though relations with employers worsened with the handing down of several adverse legal judgements, all critical of trade union practices. Judges were supposed to be completely impartial, of course, but it is remarkable how even at this latter stage of their development, actions by trade unions hitherto thought legal were being challenged successfully in the courts.[12] In *Temperton v. Russell* (1893), a union attempted to boycott a firm of builders which had supplied materials to another firm where the men were on strike. The supplying firm sued the union and it was found guilty of 'maliciously procuring and coercing others to break contracts with the plaintiff', and of conspiring to injure him. In *Trollope v. London Building Trades Federation* (1895), Trollope successfully sued the union for including its name in a blacklist of non-union firms. In *Lyons v. Wilkins* (1897) the plaintiff sued the union secretary over picketing, and obtained a declaration that picketing, even though entirely peaceful, was lawful only to communicate information, and not to persuade to strike. One judge declared, 'You cannot make a strike effective without doing more than what is lawful.' Lastly, in *Charnock v. Court* (1899), a union was found guilty of 'watching and besetting', though their only offence was of trying to persuade two immigrant Irish workers not to break a strike in Halifax, and to return home to Ireland.

As if all these restrictive judgements were not enough, some employers seemed to be mounting an industrial counter-offensive against the unions. For example, the shipowners established the Shipping Federation, which restricted employment to men who were prepared to work with non-union men. They went on to supply black-leg labour in the ports, which led to a violent strike in Hull, where scab labour was employed under army protection. The National Free Labour Association, set up in 1893 by William Collison, actually supplied blackleg labour on demand, mostly to the docks and railways. It was still in existence twenty years later, and Collison declared in his book, *The Apostle of Free Labour* (1913), that his organisation had an average of 80,000 men on his books, covering 150 different trades, all prepared to defy the pickets. Two other disturbing elements must be mentioned: in 1896 the Employers Federation of Engineering Associations had been set up to challenge the ASE, which in 1897 brought its members out on strike for the eight-hour day. They were locked out for six months from July 1897 to January 1898. The ASE was defeated; the strike and lock-out had cost it £489,000. Meanwhile, the employers established their own Employers Parliamentary Council as a rival to the Parliamentary Committee of the TUC. This new council published a book by W.J. Shaxby, *The Case Against Picketing*, explaining how as a result of *Lyons v. Wilkins*, picketing could be challenged in the courts.[13]

The tide seemed to be running against the trade unions by the end of the century. Conscious of this, they founded a new body in January 1899, the General Federation of Trade Unions, the principal aim of which was to build up a general fund for strike purposes; but only forty-four unions agreed to contribute, this number being less than a quarter of the total membership of the TUC. The alternative proposition was to try to increase the representation of the unions in the House of Commons. There was nothing very novel about this; the Lib-Labs were already well established as the parliamentary voice of the union movement, but, as already pointed out, they had not been very successful, and the same could be said of the ILP. Moreover, and it is a vital point, the Liberal Party itself was loath to adopt working-class candidates because, if elected, they had no income to support themselves, or to contribute to party funds. If the Liberal Party was the natural party for the average working man to vote for (though a proportion of such voters still voted Conservative), the failure of the Liberals to appreciate fully this fact was to prove fatal to their future as a party of government, as we shall see.

At the 1899 TUC conference, another attempt was made to require the Parliamentary Committee 'to devise ways and means' for returning more Labour MPs to the next parliament.[14] The committee was asked to invite all the co-operative, socialistic, trade union, and other working-class organisations to co-operate in convening a special congress. The motion incorporating this suggestion was moved by James Holmes, who represented a union with a strong ILP and socialist element, the Amalgamated Society of Railway Servants. It was by no means certain that such a resolution would be passed, and indeed it was debated for three hours. Members of the Parliamentary Committee were not likely to be enthusiastic at the idea of setting up any new and rival body. Others simply disliked the pressure being exerted by the socialists. Still others had further reasons for opposing the motion: the Lancashire textile workers had access to Lancashire MPs through a separate pressure group, the United Factory Textile Workers Association. Many of these Lancashire cotton workers traditionally voted Conservative. The miners, on the other hand, had long-established links with the Lib-Labs. For all these reasons, the proposal to set up a new committee inevitably led to a lengthy debate before being passed by 546,000 votes to 434,000, with abstentions numbering about a sixth. The new unions as a whole were strongly in favour.

The special congress was duly held in London at the Memorial Hall in Farringdon Street on 27 February 1900. It was attended by delegates from the unions (mostly the new unions), though even then the union members represented only half the total membership of the TUC. Other delegates were from the SDF, the Fabian Society, and the ILP. The key resolution was moved by Keir Hardie. Its wording was chosen with care so as to antagonise as few of those present as possible. It proposed the setting up of a new group in parliament:[15]

> a distinct Labour Group in Parliament, who shall have their whips, and agree upon their policy, which must embrace a readiness to cooperate with any party which for the time being may be engaged in promoting legislation in the direct interest of labour...

The last ten words here were the vital ones: there is no reference to socialism or its aims and objectives, and there is a specific undertaking to co-operate with other parties promoting labour legislation. The passing of this motion resulted in the forming of the Labour Representation Committee (LRC), made up of seven members from the unions, two from the SDF, two from the ILP, and one from the Fabian Society (that is, five out of the twelve represented bodies with strongly socialist views). All election expenses were to be paid by the unions (this had not been the case with the ILP, of course). The secretary of the new committee was the impressive ILP leader, James Ramsay MacDonald. In 1906 the LRC took the more appropriate name of the Labour Party, which was later to form two minority governments in 1924 and 1929, and majority governments after World War II, especially after the massive landslide electoral victory in 1945. It seems safe to say that few, if any, in 1900 could have foreseen these remarkable developments.

Indeed, at the time, there seemed little awareness of the momentous nature of the appointment of the LRC: it was regarded as just another pressure group, designed to protect the trade unions against further attacks by their employers or the courts. There was no certainty that it would have sufficient funds to achieve very much. Moreover, the older craft unions were hardly enthusiastic in their support of the new committee. Most of its supporters were members of the new unions, and were socialist in outlook, something which was certainly not true of the typical trade unionist of the time; and as we have seen, Keir Hardie was careful to keep the word 'socialist' out of his resolution. Moreover, the feeling of the meeting was expressed very clearly when the SDF delegates, true to their Marxist convictions, moved a motion for the founding of a new party of a kind they thought necessary:[16]

> A distinct party – separate from the capitalist parties, based upon a recognition of the class war, and having for its ultimate object the socialisation of the means of production, distribution and exchange.

This resolution was defeated by a large majority. There were few hard-line Marxists among the delegates, and though there were a good many socialists among the new unionists, their socialism tended to be of a somewhat utopian nature, certainly opposed to capitalism, but with no very clear ideas about the nature of the socialist state. MacDonald is a not untypical example, full of vague notions of progress 'ever upwards and onwards', but without reference to what Marxists would term the reality of the class struggle and the need to destroy the exploiting capitalist class. Lenin famously remarked rather contemptuously of MacDonald that he was 'a good man, fallen among Fabians'.

Nevertheless, however vague and aspirational the socialism of many of those supporting the creation of the LRC, credit must be given to Keir Hardie and his followers for their achievement. It was his persistence which finally brought its reward in 1900, and his adroit emphasis on the interests of labour rather than on any aims of socialism. His enthusiasm and genuine regard for the working classes (especially at this stage of his life) were not in question. If anyone deserves credit for the creation of the Labour Party, it is he. As we have seen, the trade union movement as a whole was not in favour of any new body, and so is entitled to rather less credit.

The Fabians, of course, had never participated to any marked extent in trade union affairs, and it had always been their belief that Fabian principles should be allowed to permeate the thinking of all political parties, and not become the monopoly of any one party. They pointed to the success of what they considered to be socialist principles in local government – Sidney Webb did this in *Fabian Essays* – that is, in municipal enterprises such as the provision of tramways, drainage schemes, gas and water supplies. Support for such services earned the Fabians the nickname, 'gas and water socialists'. The society really played only a very minor role in the creation of the LRC. It also seems fair to say that in any case their approach to socialism was far more intellectual than that of Keir Hardie and his supporters, and at times harked back to Robert Owen and his belief in the necessity for middle-class leadership. This is certainly true, at least, of Beatrice Webb, who wrote in her diary in 1894 that the ordinary citizen must be made to feel that reforming society was 'no light matter, and must be undertaken by experts specially trained for the purpose'. Shortly after writing this, she spelt out her beliefs in more detail:[17]

> We staked our hopes on the organised working class, served and guided, it is true, by an elite of unassuming experts who would make no claim to superior social status, but would content themselves with exercising the power inherited in superior knowledge and longer administrative experience.

This is Owenite paternalism, of a kind unacceptable to socialists of Hardie's persuasion and Marxists alike.

The last point to be considered in connection with the founding of the Labour Party is the question of how far it was an inevitable consequence of the growth of class-consciousness and the extension of the franchise in 1867 and 1884. At first sight, this might seem a reasonable supposition, except for the fact that the LRC was established not because of the spread of socialist or even radical thinking, but as a defensive measure to safeguard union rights. This is not to say that the desire for better working-class representation might not have expressed itself ultimately in some way or other, but this does not seem to have been the paramount consideration in 1900. The immediate need was to defend the unions against a wave of increasing hostility among employers, whose interests were also being well looked after by the courts. Then again, it must be remembered that for the past half-century or so, it was the Liberal Party which had become the party best able to defend the interests of the working classes, and the party for which most working men voted. But since the 1870s, Gladstone had become obsessed with the issue of Home Rule, which led to a split in the Liberal Party when the first Home Rule bill was introduced in 1886. The party was then gravely weakened, but still committed to Home Rule in the early 1890s (Gladstone unsuccessfully introduced the second Home Rule bill in 1893, and finally retired in 1895). As a result, the Liberals had little time for programmes of social reform;[18] and their failure to adopt working-class candidates (mentioned earlier) told against them. Unfortunately for the Liberals, they continued to be divided over Ireland, and over the Boer War and imperialism. They were out of office from 1895 to the very end of 1905, and by then the damage was done: they had a new and potentially dangerous rival in the new Labour Party. Industrialisation had spawned the towns. The denizens of those towns had acquired a new political party.

As for the trade unions, they were at an interesting stage of development at the end of the nineteenth century. Their membership in 1901 had risen to 2.025 million, spread over 1,322 unions; but by no means were all of these unions members of the TUC – only 198, in fact, were affiliated to that body – a surprisingly low proportion. Further, union membership was less than one-sixth of the occupied population in 1901, and included only about one in four of adult male manual workers. The majority of workers were still to be found in the old staple industries of textiles, mining, engineering, and in railways. In shipbuilding, the union density was about 60 per cent, in mining 56 per cent. There had also been some additional recruitment among white-collar workers – teachers numbered 44,000, postal workers 36,000, shop assistants 19,000, and government civil servants 45,000. Recruitment among women workers was still miniscule. Thus, trade unionism in about 1900 still had far to go before it included even half the occupied population, or had independent representation in parliament; but it was to make remarkable advances by 1914, nearly doubling its membership, as will be seen in the next chapter.[19]

Meanwhile, how did informed opinion view the state of the nation at this stage of industrialisation? In Chapter 2, some reference was made to some of the best-known thinkers and commentators of the mid-century years – Marx and Engels, Carlyle, Ruskin, and Matthew Arnold. By the end of the century the intellectual climate had changed greatly. Whereas the middle years of Victoria's reign were a period of abounding self-confidence and national pride, tempered only by comments (as in Arnold) on the need for improved cultural standards, the 1890s by contrast exhibit an unprecedented amount of self-criticism and concern over social problems. On the one hand there is the recognition that Britain had become the wealthiest and most powerful nation on earth, with the largest empire in the world. On the other hand, the question was asked, what was it all for? Was it right, in particular, for wealth to be so concentrated in the upper and middle ranks of society when a third of the population in the cities was living in desperate poverty? Anxieties were increased by the known fact that attendance at church and chapel was falling towards the end of the century. Intellectual debate was dominated by the evolutionists led by Darwin's earnest disciple, Thomas Huxley, and their opponents. Here was a pioneer industrial state, the first of its kind in the world, now emerging as a democracy, complete with elaborate new systems of local government, public health, police forces, and all the trappings of what today would be called the modern state, yet with its riches so ill-distributed that many of its inhabitants lived in wretched poverty. Of course, historically speaking, the mass of the population had always lived in poverty, but social investigations were now bringing the facts home to the middle classes at a time when the working classes were becoming better educated and increasingly vocal. In her diary for July 1894, Beatrice Webb, who was remarkably unsentimental about the poor, asked herself the question:[20]

> What can we hope from these myriads of deficient minds and deformed bodies that swarm in our great cities – what can we hope from them but brutality, meanness and crime; whether they are struggling for subsistence at the dock gates, or eking out their days in the poor law or penal colony?

The many socialist and reformist writings of the last two decades of the nineteenth century sought to find an answer to this question, as the earlier part of this chapter has tried to show. It is indeed difficult to select thinkers of the time for comment; there are so many. However, of them all, the name of William Morris, also mentioned earlier, remains outstanding as a member of the caring middle classes, troubled (as Beatrice Webb would have it) by their consciousness of sin. He was a person of many talents, of course; in addition to his political activities, he was an author, poet, artist, craftsman, and printer. He himself was said to have wondered 'which of six distinct personalities, he himself really was'.[21]

William Morris was born in 1834 in Walthamstow, North London, into a comfortable middle-class family; his father was a prosperous bill-broker in the City of London. He went to Marlborough, and then Oxford University. After leaving Oxford, he was articled to G.E. Street (architect of the law courts in the Strand), became interested in poetry and painting, and developed a lifelong friendship with Dante Gabriel Rossetti. In 1859 he married, and in 1861, together with friends from the Pre-Raphaelite circle, he formed what was to become a world-famous firm specialising in household design, especially in wall coverings, wood carving, stained glass, metalwork, and furniture. The products of this firm were soon in great demand, and his advice on furnishing became well known: 'Have nothing in your house that you do not know to be useful or believe to be beautiful.' Throughout his life Morris was intensely interested in craftsmanship, and in later years turned to textiles, tapestry, and printing; but from the mid-1870s onwards, he was increasingly involved in politics.

At first he was liberal in his views and a supporter of Gladstone, but by the 1880s he had turned against him, and had become a socialist, bitterly opposed to capitalism. He mounted a famous attack on the system in an article published in 1894, explaining why he had become a socialist:[22]

> Was it all to end in a counting house on the top of a cinder heap, with Podsnap's drawing room in the offing, with a Whig committee dealing out champagne to the rich and margarine to the poor in such convenient proportions as would make all men contented together, though the pleasure of the eyes was gone from the world, and the place of Homer was to be taken by Huxley?

He became a Marxist, and a member of the Social Democratic Federation (he designed their membership card), having read *Das Kapital* in French in 1883; but his Marxism was of an idiosyncratic kind. As mentioned previously, he was somewhat shaky on some of the basic principles. In his own words:[23]

> To speak quite frankly, I do not know what Marx's theory of value is, and I'm damned if I want to know … I have tried to understand Marx's theory, but political economy is not in my line, and much of it appears to me to be dreary rubbish. But I am, I hope, a socialist none the less.

It follows that his views of the future were a strange mixture of conventional Marxist theory and his own beliefs in the importance of arts and crafts ('the pleasure of the eyes'). There would be a revolution of the workers, of course, but though he predicted this would be in the early twentieth century, he later thought the date would be 1952. He had no use for parliament: in his *News From Nowhere* (1891), a utopian view of the future, the Houses of Parliament would be used to store dung. His ideal society of the future would consist of small, self-governing communities, free from central control, with an emphasis on good honest labour and craftsmanship. However, Morris was no mere visionary: in 1883 he broke away from the Social Democratic Federation to form the Socialist League (it had only about 700 members in all, in eighteen branches), but later on the league was taken over by anarchists, and Morris withdrew from it in 1890. What really was the contribution of William Morris to the political thought and attitudes of his day? His part in the arts and craft movement is secure and well known, of course, but it is more difficult to weigh up his services to the socialist movement. His *A Dream of John Ball* (1888) and *News From Nowhere* were both widely read, but they were utopian visions based on a moral rejection of the capitalist system, and as such offer no practical guidance to political action. It is true that Morris did attempt to foster political activity through the Socialist League, but its influence was very limited, and he himself was no great organiser. Like the Christian Socialists, he could see what he considered to be the unacceptable face of capitalism, but like them he was vague on the details of what should replace it, except that it would give due regard to honest labour, craftsmanship, and art. It would certainly be based on the coming to power of the working classes, and on the abolition of property, but much else was unclear. Yet he has been termed 'One of the great inspirers of the Left in England and perhaps the leading second-generation Labour Party father figure'.[24] E.P. Thompson has said that Morris would always occupy a position of unique importance in the British revolutionary tradition; while in the new edition of *Fabian Essays*, published in 1933, George Bernard Shaw called him the greatest socialist of his day.[25] All this may well be so, but in practical politics there were numerous other labour leaders such as Mann, Burns, and above all, Keir Hardie, who could be said to have a greater claim to political fame. Morris' contribution was in the sphere of ideas rather than in political agitation as such.

Among other commentators on the ills of society, the economist and Fabian sympathiser John A. Hobson was among the most prominent. He wrote extensively on the problems of the day, and on imperialism. His *The Problem of the Unemployed* (1896) tackles one of the major economic challenges of the time, and argues that the basic cause of unemployment was underconsumption, and its remedy some form of redistribution of income.[26] In an interesting chapter entitled 'Palliatives of unemployment', Hobson discusses various forms of labour colonies, ranging from penal colonies to colonies set up by boards of guardians, the large Salvation Army colony at Hadleigh, and other smaller schemes, for example, that of the Self-Help Emigration Society and the proposed schemes whereby county councils would set up farm training societies.[27] Although Hobson was right to fasten on underconsumption as one significant cause of unemployment, his practical suggestions for its relief hardly go beyond what was conventional at the time.

In his *The Social Problem: Life and Work* (1901), however, Hobson went a little more deeply into the ills affecting society. In chapter 2, 'Waste in work and life', he says that the 'largest and most palpable waste is that accumulation of industrial disorder known as "unemployment", while facing the unemployed in equal idleness were unemployed or under-employed masses of land and capital, mills, mines, etc'. Numbers of strong men were workless, yet the weaker women were 'increasingly driven to an excessive burden of wage work'.[28] Hobson then surveys some of the familiar features of the existing state of the working classes: conditions at work were often insanitary and dangerous, due to profit-seeking; the average town manual worker lived some fifteen years less than the average member of the well-to-do classes; there were a quarter of a million men aged 20–65 years in 1891 among the upper class of the unemployed without trade or profession; from the standpoint of healthy human life, the modern industrial town was a failure – in spite of sanitary improvements, mortality was nearly 20 per cent higher in towns than in rural areas; and lastly, 'the Social Question finds its directly moral significance in the growing sense of antagonism between classes and masses'.[29] In chapter 10, Hobson turns to 'humanitarian socialism', which for him simply means state ownership. After taking a side-swipe at the middle-class conscience – 'pity, sometimes ignorant and misguided sentimentality, plays an ever-growing part in the life of the educated classes' – he affirms that the problem of the insecurity of regular work can only be solved in one way, 'by an avowed adoption of the principle of public relief works'; and help to the young, the old, the sick, the injured, and the unemployed must continue as part of the public policy of civilised countries. He then refers to the 'provision of a social ambulance which shall take care of those wounded in the fray'.[30] This is an interesting use of the social ambulance metaphor used by Lloyd George subsequently in justifying his introduction of the National Health Insurance scheme in 1911. Perhaps Lloyd George had read his Hobson.

Chapter 11 of *The Social Problem*, entitled 'The problem of population', displays current anxieties about the physical and moral health of the nation:[31]

> Selection of the fittest, or at least, rejection of the unfittest, is essential to all progress in life and character. Any social organisation which checks the efficiency of such processes must of

necessity make for deterioration of the species. This is the gravest danger of our times ... the right to veto the production of bad lives is essential ... it is all important to society that propagation should only take place from sound stock.

To the modern reader, all this sounds somewhat alarming, and reminiscent of Hitlerian doctrines of Aryan supremacy, especially when Hobson goes on to argue that the population question is the question of how society is to secure the means of social progress by the elimination of the unfit. It is something of a relief to learn that the rejection of the unfit cannot take place after birth, and must therefore be directed to the prevention of unfit propagation; but Hobson does not explain how this can be achieved. The whole chapter is a good indication of the concerns of the time about national degeneration, and of the influence of the fashionable new 'science' of eugenics. We shall return to this subject in the next chapter.

As already indicated, the field of critical comment on society at the end of the nineteenth century is vast. So far we have selected for comment a political critic and activist, and a left-wing economist. Lastly, it is proposed to comment on the early writings of a distinguished journalist and later Liberal politician, Charles F.G. Masterman. Masterman had gained a brilliant double first at Cambridge in 1896, and regarded himself as a Christian Socialist. In 1900 he went to live in a slum tenement in Camberwell, and his first publication owed much to his knowledge of working-class life in South London. It was entitled *The Heart of the Empire* (1901), and was a volume of essays by different hands, edited by himself, to which he contributed a lengthy introductory essay. He begins by referring to the stupendous growth of cities, inhabited by the very rich and the very poor ('the broken classes'). In the 1880s there had been some hope of improvement with trade union strikes and demonstrations, the growth of socialism, the social surveys, the extension of elementary education, and so on, but all had been swamped by a wave of imperialism (a reference to the Boer War, of course); and so the 'condition of the people' problem was ceasing to trouble the public mind. He goes on to describe the 'fickle excitability' of the new city inhabitants, suggesting that there was now a new type of town dweller:[32]

stunted, narrow-chested, easily wearied; yet voluble, excitable, with little ballast, stamina, or endurance – seeking stimulus in drink, in betting, in any unaccustomed conflict at home or abroad ...

Yet these people can read – hence the new sensational press; but spiritual religion has decayed.

Throughout his essay, Masterman stresses the drabness, shabbiness, and sheer ugliness of London life, but at the same time he is careful to emphasise that not all Londoners were leading wretched lives. He points out that Charles Booth had shown that 200,000 of the poor in East London were 'neither ill-nourished nor ill-clad. Their lives are an unending struggle and lack comfort, but I do not know that they lack happiness.' Further, says Masterman, 'there is a vast amount of quiet family joy, of delight of parents in their children, of wives in their husbands'. And he admits that never in recent years, according to economists, has the English labourer been better off.[33]

So what is wrong? A great deal: packed in the midst of this peaceful and industrious population, there is the multitude of the criminal, the casual, the cadger, the chronically poor (who include the 'deserving poor'). Specifically, there is overcrowding (there are nearly a million said to be overcrowded in London), there is drinking ('habitual soaking'), long journeys to work, monotonous work, and lack of spiritual ideals.[34]

After surveying the strengths and weaknesses of the various denominations in London (Masterman was an Anglican, but this did not stop him from attacking the Church of England for being too conservative and under aristocratic domination), Masterman reaches his conclusion. Life may be tolerable, he thinks, or even happy in animal enjoyment and the alternation of rest and toil, but this can involve an enormous waste of human possibilities. He therefore sets out his case for reform:[35]

> Back to the land, from gigantic massed populations to healthier conditions of scattered industry; housing reform; temperance reform; a perfected system of national education; the elimination of the submerged tenth, the redemption of women's labour – all these are immediate necessaries – but these are all palliative of the fundamental malady – attempts in some degree to check the ravages of selfishness, indifference and isolation.

He concludes with a lengthy plea for spiritual regeneration – 'back to the Christ'.

There is very little in this article which was new at the time, and it is surprising that there is no reference to the rise of organised labour, government efforts to encourage public work schemes, the founding of new political parties, or even the continuing controversies over the nature of poverty and how far government aid should go in relieving it. On the other hand, Masterman does attempt to give a picture of working-class life as a whole, readily admitting that some sectors of the workers had fairly secure employment and led a moderately happy existence. What doubtless appalled Masterman in his tenement flat in Camberwell was the ugly, shabby, dirty nature of an inner-city working-class neighbourhood, very different from Cambridge and his home town, Tunbridge Wells (even today, modern Camberwell does not do much visually to lift the spirits). His remedies for the situation are scarcely novel, though reasonable enough, except for the call for a return to the land, which was hardly realistic. It was frequently heard at the time, of course, and was the result of the intense urbanisation which had occurred in the nineteenth century in spite of the perils of town life. Poor living and working conditions in the countryside had driven the more enterprising into the cities in search of something better, as we have seen.

So far this chapter has concentrated on the spread of socialism, the influence of New Unionism, the continued growth of craft unionism, and the founding of new political parties, together with some examples of the social criticism of the time. One important aspect of change of the period 1870 to 1900 and of newer attitudes has been hitherto neglected, and this is the changing role and status of women. It is a commonplace that in the early Victorian period, women's place was thought to be in the home, and women were often held to be inferior both physically and intellectually to men. As a consequence, the education of middle-class women was of a slight and genteel nature. From the mid-century on, significant change took place.[36] More rigorous secondary education for girls began with the opening of the North London Collegiate School in 1850, the first school of the Girls Public Day School Trust, under the formidable Miss Buss. In 1858 her famous opposite number, the equally impressive Miss Beale, became principal of Cheltenham Ladies College. After the reforms in the ancient universities of Oxford and Cambridge in the 1870s, new colleges were opened for women, hitherto barred from both universities: at Cambridge, Girton (1873) and Newnham (1880); at Oxford, Somerville and Lady Margaret Hall, both in 1879 (but at neither university were women admitted formally to degrees before the Great War). London University began life in the shape of University College in Gower Street in 1828, the University of London being officially established as an examining body in 1836. Meanwhile, Durham University had been founded in 1832. In 1880, London admitted its women students to degrees. University colleges, also with women students, were set up in Manchester, Birmingham, Liverpool, and Leeds, all becoming universities in their own right by 1904 (the University of Wales was founded in 1893, Sheffield in 1905, and Bristol in 1909). In this way, new avenues for advancement by women were opened up, although the educated middle-class woman who had been to university might still be regarded with some suspicion (not only by men) as a 'blue stocking'.

From the 1860s onwards, women began to become more prominent in public and professional life. Their champion in parliament was John Stuart Mill, who moved several unsuccessful motions for votes for women, and in 1869 published his essay, 'The subjection of women', which aimed 'to maintain the claim of women, whether in marriage or out of it, to perfect equality in all rights with the male sex', a landmark in the history of the campaign for women's rights. The 1870s saw the struggles of Josephine Butler for the repeal of the Contagious Diseases Acts of the 1860s; these acts permitted the establishment of brothels in garrison towns and the compulsory medical inspection of prostitutes. In the professions, Florence Nightingale had made nursing a respectable calling and one requiring proper training, Mary Carpenter has an honoured place in the history of reform schools, and Sophia Jex Blake became the first qualified doctor.

In 1882 the Married Women's Property Act at last established the right of married women to retain the ownership of their property instead of its passing to their husbands on marriage. Families were getting smaller, first among the middle classes, then in the working classes. Fertility fell from the 1870s, so that married women born in the 1880s had only half as many children to care for; in two generations the average number of children born to married women fell from around six to only a little over two.[37] Thus, the burden of bringing up a large family and all the household duties associated with numerous children was lessened by the end of the period. At the same time, women's civil rights were being widened: in 1869 single female ratepayers regained the vote lost in 1835; by 1900 there were over a million female voters for county, borough, and poor law elections. Women could be both voters and candidates on school boards and on parish councils in and after 1894.[38] In 1903 the Women's Social and Political Union was formed to campaign for the parliamentary vote. The suffragette movement had begun, soon to employ the argument of the 'broken pane'.

All these advances were of benefit ultimately to women of the working classes as well as middle-class women, and earlier in this book it was shown how women at work benefited from the regulation of working hours and conditions at their place of work. Whether industrialisation had actually increased the proportion of women employed outside the home is difficult if not impossible to ascertain,[39] but obviously enough, as the economy changed to an industrial basis, fewer women were engaged proportionately in agriculture and more and more in industry and the service trades. However, the decline of the small traditional domestic family workshop as in nailing in the Black Country helped to reduce male domination within the family. Its decline meant that fewer and fewer husbands, hitherto kings of their own little castles, were able to overwork their wives; and where a wife was able to obtain alternative employment locally in a factory or larger workshop, her hours were restricted and enforced by law. Moreover, it should be noted that the father's authority over his family in the domestic work situation was progressively weakened by visits from school attendance officers, NSPCC inspectors, health visitors from the local crèche, and the like. So working-class family life was exposed more and more to public scrutiny. Middle-class commentators such as Mrs Bosanquet, Miss Loane, and Lady Bell all noticed the increased refinement of working-class family life and the increasing disappearance of physical brawling, ascribing this principally to the beneficial effects of compulsory schooling on demeanour, attitudes, regular habits, punctuality, and self-control.[40]

Thus the decline of the small workshop, especially the domestic workshop, coupled with compulsory schooling and the growth of welfare services, brought about an improvement in the family life of working-class married women. Nevertheless, at the end of the nineteenth century, many women at work, whether married or single, were still subjected to long working hours and low pay. Hours were notoriously long in domestic service (the largest feminine occupational group), and also in retailing; while women were still being exploited in the sweated industries, such as domestic chainmaking, and paper box manufacture in the home (there was a House of Lords Select Committee on the Sweated Trades in 1888). Yet at the same time, newer avenues for occupational advancement were being opened up in the service industries as they expanded towards the end of the nineteenth century. This is particularly noticeable in office work, where the coming into use of the typewriter and the increasing demands for stenographers made more jobs available for women, whose native skills it was thought made them especially suitable for employment as shorthand typists. In 1914 about 20 per cent of clerical workers were women. Between 1861 and 1911, the number of women clerks quadrupled. Another sign of future developments was the growth of women's trade unionism: in 1886, women trade unionists numbered only 36,980. By 1892 the number had risen to 142,000, and by 1913, to 433,000, an increase of 300 per cent between the two dates.[41] A notable achievement of the movement was the successful women chainmakers' strike in Cradley Heath in the Black Country in 1910, supported by the redoubtable Mary MacArthur, leader of the National Federation of Women Workers, who afterwards became a sort of Black Country heroine.[42]

All in all, women's role in society showed considerable enhancement by 1900. With the qualifications just noted, conditions at work had become regulated and improved (though, for the majority of married women, 'work' still meant housework, cooking meals, and bringing up children, all arduous and challenging tasks, of course). But old stereotypes still lingered on, and indeed, had much life left in them. Pay was still unequal, men's higher pay in theory being supposed to be necessary to support a family; and in part, as further justification for this, women were still thought by many men to be inferior mentally and physically to themselves. Above all, women's place was still considered to be in the home. The employment of married women was still frowned upon. In 1911, the percentage of married women at work in England and Wales was only 13.7 per cent. The Census report of 1911 remarked of married women that 'The great bulk of women are fortunately, in this country, free at all ages to devote their attention to the care of their households.'[43] Attitudes of this kind were to persist throughout the inter-war period, and even into the late 1940s.

On the whole, it seems that significant changes in values and attitudes had taken place by the end of the century, though inevitably, the pace of change was uneven, as we have just seen. In many ways, however, society seemed to be on the move, shaking free from its old certainties and beliefs. This was so in one actual physical respect: if the working classes had taken to the roads in the 1880s in the new cycling craze, the wealthier classes had also done so in the new motor cars which were becoming increasingly available. Soon men would take to the air, and already H.G. Wells, a disciple of the great Darwinian and agnostic Thomas Huxley, was fascinating his many readers with *The Time Machine* (1895), *The War of the Worlds* (1898), *The First Men on the Moon* (1901), and *The War in the Air* (1908).[44] On the stage, the middle classes were being taught to laugh at themselves by Oscar Wilde and to question traditional thinking, and were being provoked to think by George Bernard Shaw in his *Arms and the Man* (1894) and

Candida (1897). In the literary field, there is a curious contrast between the early Rudyard Kipling (his *Barrack Room Ballads* came out in 1892) and the fashionable air of decadence and *fin-de-siècle* languor in the avant-garde *The Yellow Book* (1894–7), which contained illustrations by its youthful editor, Aubrey Beardsley, that were hardly for the prudish. Meanwhile, the works of the social investigators already mentioned were steadily coming before the public – Charles Booth's *London Survey* (1889–1903), William Booth's *In Darkest England* (1890), and the *Fabian Essays* (1889). Sidney and Beatrice Webb continued to publish their pioneer works of social history, *The History of Trade Unions* (1894) and *Industrial Democracy* (1897). Nor was it all middle-class reading: in addition to the new and respectable *Daily Mail* (1896) for the more serious-minded and newly literate working classes (according to Lord Salisbury, 'Written by office-boys for office-boys'), there was Robert Blatchford's popular weekly left-wing periodical, *The Clarion*. Blatchford also published an extremely popular work on socialism, *Merrie England*. It sold more than a million copies.[45]

What then was the moving force in all this activity, what doctrine could be applied to refashion industrial society into a new and shining version of its disreputable self? For many, the answer was not, as Masterman would have it, to go 'back to the Christ', but the secular doctrine of socialism in its widest sense. In its broad and general meaning, this could be interpreted to mean any extension of state power necessary to succour the needy and alleviate poverty. The power of the state had extended enormously both centrally and locally in the second half of the nineteenth century. It did not seem too unreasonable to use some part of the wealth and power of the new leviathan to remedy some of the deficiencies of industrial capitalism which were now being exposed. This kind of socialism was very different from Marxism, of course, with its belief in class struggle and the inevitability of revolution. Nor did it necessarily exclude religious belief. Indeed, it might be based fundamentally on the brotherhood of man. It is often said that the early Labour leaders owed much more to Methodism than they did to Marx.[46] Socialism in this very broad sense could be referred to in favourable terms by leading Liberal statesmen such as Sir William Harcourt, who made the famous remark, 'We are all socialists now.' The Conservative prime minister, Lord Salisbury, made some interesting observations on this subject in the House of Lords, on 19 May 1890, when drawing attention to the baleful results of industrialisation:[47]

Undoubtedly we have come upon an age of the world when the action of industrial causes, the great accumulation of population, and many other social and economic influences have produced great centres of misery, and have added terribly to the catalogue of evils to which flesh is heir. It is our duty to do all we can to find the remedies for those evils, and even if we are called Socialists in attempting to do it, we shall be reconciled if we can find those remedies, knowing that we are undertaking no new principle, that we are striking out no new path, but are pursuing the long and healthy tradition of English legislation.

This is a remarkable statement to come from a Conservative prime minister. It remains to be seen how far the Edwardians, and in particular the Liberal Party after its landslide victory in the general election of 1906, were able to remedy the evils of industrialism and population growth to which Salisbury alluded.

6 Edwardian England and the Liberal reforms

The first years of the twentieth century were scarcely a propitious time for social reform. In the autumn of 1899 the British found themselves at war in South Africa with the Boer republics of the Transvaal and the Orange Free State, and in the course of one week suffered three substantial defeats. After Christmas 1899 the tide turned, and by the summer of 1900 all major military operations were at an end, though the Boers fought on using guerrilla tactics until forced to sign the Peace of Vereeniging in May 1902. Meanwhile, the Conservative government of the time held a general election in October 1900, hoping to capitalise on winning the war in South Africa, a war which had divided the Liberal opposition into pro-Boers and anti-Boers. The Conservatives won this so-called 'khaki election' (the war was the first in which the British troops fought in khaki), but improved their majority by only three seats. The war certainly occupied public attention for more than two years, and as we have seen, Masterman argued with some justification in *The Heart of the Empire* that imperialism had replaced social reform as a central issue.

Nevertheless, social problems were to come to the fore once more, even while the Boer War was still on. In 1901 Benjamin Seebohm Rowntree, son of Joseph Rowntree, the Quaker cocoa and chocolate manufacturer, published a work entitled *Poverty: A Study of Town Life*. It was a study of poverty in the city of York, based upon the supposition that a minimum weekly income of 21/8 for a man, wife, and three children was necessary if poverty was to be avoided. Further, Rowntree distinguished between 'primary poverty', where wages were simply not enough to meet basic needs, and 'secondary poverty', where wages were spent unwisely (through extravagance or ignorance) in a way so as to result in poverty. As a proportion of the population of York, persons in primary poverty constituted 9.91 per cent (a figure reminiscent of the earlier concept of the 'submerged

Table 6.1 Causes of primary poverty in York, c.1900

Immediate causes	Total affected	% of all in primary poverty
Death of chief wage-earner	1,130	15.63
Illness or old age of chief wage-earner	370	5.11
Chief wage-earner out of work	167	2.31
Irregularity of work	205	2.83
Largeness of family (more than four children)	1,602	22.16
In regular work but at low wages	3,756	51.96

tenth'); while persons in secondary poverty amounted to 17.93 per cent – a total for both classes of the poor of 27.84 per cent, remarkably similar to Booth's 30.7 per cent for London.

Rowntree's approach was somewhat more sophisticated than Booth's, and his poverty line was drawn rather more generously than in the London study. Moreover, he introduced the new idea of the 'poverty cycle' (familiar enough to the poor themselves, of course), whereby poverty was first suffered by the individual when a child; he would then become more prosperous on starting work; only to become poor again when he married and started a family. A degree of prosperity would be regained when the children started work and left home, only to be lost once more when the worker became too old to work. As for primary poverty, Rowntree gave the causes as shown in Table 6.1.[1]

These figures pinpointed certain facts which were to be at the root of a number of the Liberal reforms some years later: the hardships caused by the wage-earner being sick, or out of work, or unable to work through old age (indeed, all of these causes of poverty have subsequently been tackled by welfare reforms throughout the twentieth century). Rowntree's survey was a striking vindication of Booth's recent finding for London. It could be objected, of course, that York, a small cathedral town, was very different from London. Yet York, too, had an important industrial sector, witness the extensive Rowntree works south of the city, and the railway works on the west, so that it was far from being merely an agricultural centre. Low wages were clearly a potent cause of poverty, and this in itself made it difficult to sustain traditional ideas that poverty was due mainly to laziness or to drink.[2]

Even before the Boer War was over, much disquiet was aroused by a statement from Sir Frederic Maurice that some 60 per cent of the recruits for the war in South Africa were unfit for military duties.

Once more the spectre of national degeneration manifested itself. So much anxiety was aroused that the Inter-Departmental Committee on National Deterioration was appointed in 1903, which found that the true figure was 34 per cent of would-be recruits had failed the army's minimum standards for height, weight, and eyesight. Of course, it seems likely that a minor war fought out not in Europe but thousands of miles away in Africa against amateur armies of Boer farmers was not likely to have attracted the flower of the nation's manhood. The incentive to join up was certainly not very strong for young men in regular employment, and the contrast with the rush to join the colours in the early months of the Great War in 1914 is very noticeable. Nevertheless, it is understandable that even the reduced figure of a third being unfit for service should have caused great concern at the time.

Meanwhile, the battle of words over the social problem continued unabated. On the right, Helen Bosanquet published two volumes of essays, *Rich and Poor* (1896) and *The Standard of Life and Other Studies* (1898). In the latter volume, she produced a not unsympathetic survey of working-class life, taking into account variations in supply and demand, and in prices, but excluding the *residuum* from her study of the standard of living: they were 'people we cannot help because they are without a standard to maintain ... they marry without passion of any kind'.[3] By this time, the Bosanquets were beginning to drop the terms, 'deserving' and 'undeserving' in favour of 'helpable' and 'unhelpable'. Presumably, the *residuum* as a whole were now considered 'unhelpable' – they were simply the dregs of society and considered to be beyond the pale. Throughout the 1898 book there are references to the two cardinal principles of the Charity Organisation Society: that self-help was all-important, and that if charitable aid was offered, it must be carefully organised. Thus Helen Bosanquet asserts, 'there is nothing to prevent an artisan from giving his son an education enabling him ultimately to enter the professions'[4] (however worthy an aspiration, surely unrealistic for most artisans); and 'the greatest blunder any philanthropist can make is to give money because wages are low – by doing so, he makes them lower still'.[5]

Themes of this kind were developed further by Bosanquet in another book published in 1902, *The Strength of the People: A Study in Social Economics*. This book really provides a further general statement of COS principles. Nothing should be done to sap personal independence and self-help. Old-age pensions, for example, would remove the need for working men to provide for the future, and diminish family responsibility for the aged. Free school meals (already being provided here and there in the poorest parts of London) would reduce parental responsibility for feeding their children. Simple giving of money to the poor must be avoided – it could not in itself bring happiness, and could do so 'only when the power to use it wisely is present'.[6] Bosanquet made the point (which was to become a favourite with her) that two families in the same tenement might have the same income, but in one household there is order and comfort, while in the other there is disorder and squalor. What counts most is character and determination. Naturally enough, this belief that money was of only limited importance to the poor was directly opposed to socialist thinking, and was attacked violently by a leading Fabian, George Bernard Shaw, in the preface to *Major Barbara*, his entertaining comment on the earnest endeavours of the Salvation Army:[7]

> The universal regard for money is the one hopeful fact in our civilisation, the one sound spot in our social conscience. Money is the most important thing in the world … The crying need of the nation is not for better morals, cheaper bread, temperance, liberty, culture, redemption of fallen sisters and erring brothers, nor the grace, love and fellowship of the Trinity, but simply for enough money.

This approach was hardly likely to appeal to Mrs Bosanquet, who opposed any idea of the minimum wage, or of the fixing of wage scales by parliament. In retrospect, of course, the beliefs of the Bosanquets, and of the COS as a whole, may seem in many respects extraordinarily reactionary and unsympathetic to the poor; not only that, some of their ideas seem positively unrealistic at the time – for example, how could the poor save enough to support themselves for any length of time in old age? Nevertheless, for many at the turn of the century the opinions and basic principles of the COS seemed reasonable enough, and they were to prove influential when the Poor Law Commission was appointed in 1905, as we shall see later.

On the left, the Fabians continued to propagate their views. In *Socialism in England* (1890), Sidney Webb provided a broad, general view of the development of socialism, in which he even includes the group of anarchists led by Kropotkin. He also spent some time on the topic of socialism in the churches, mentioning the Guild of St Matthew (founded by the Reverend Stewart D. Headlam) and the Christian Social Union (founded by Canon Scott Holland in 1889).

Perhaps the most famous passage in this book concerns the spread of municipal socialism. Webb portrays an 'Individualist Town Councillor' boasting about the extent of his council's local services – water supplies, roads, libraries, and so on – and then concluding with a triumphant flourish:[8]

> Socialism, sir – don't waste the time of a practical man by your fantastic absurdities. Self-help, sir, individual self-help, that's what made our city what it is.

Webb then refers to the way in which the Liberal Party has become permeated by socialist thinking:[9]

> The Liberal Party has now definitely discarded the Individualist Laissez-Faire upon which ... it was so largely founded, and with every approach towards democracy becomes more markedly Socialist in character.

This was simply wishful thinking, for the Newcastle Programme of 1891 showed few signs of being socialist in outlook, and when the Liberals returned to office in 1892, their short period of office was dominated by Gladstone's last desperate and doomed bid to secure Home Rule for Ireland (the House of Lords rejected his second Home Rule bill).

In 1902 Charles Masterman published his second book, *From the Abyss: Of its Inhabitants, by One of Them*. It was again a book of essays but this time all by his own hand. All the articles had been published before in the *Speaker* and the *Commonwealth*. They provide a striking but surprisingly muted account of life in Camberwell, where Masterman continued to live until his marriage in 1907. The title of the book might lead the reader to expect a graphic and perhaps harrowing account of life in the slums, of the kind portrayed in A. Morrison's 1896 fictional account, *A Child of the Jago* (the 'Jago' was a notorious slum area in East London). It was not so at all; Masterman actually emphasised that life in Camberwell was 'peaceful and contented' and (no doubt with intended irony), 'Life is very pleasant down in the Abyss. We desire no better country'; but his main theme was the mean and shabby environment, and the grossly overcrowded houses and great tenement blocks of the area into which the 'good-humoured, tired, contented populace' was crammed. The emphasis was really upon the poor quality of life in an inner-London, working-class suburb. No doubt the book helped to keep attention focused upon working-class living conditions, but Jack London's *People of the Abyss* (1903) probably did more to trouble the middle-class conscience. It was an account, highly impressionistic, of sweating practices in the East End of London as investigated by a brief visit of six weeks. Masterman's book is probably more accurate and thoughtful in its portrayal of life in South London, but Jack London's book has a more striking impact.

A more direct attack on what was considered by the author to be the maldistribution of national wealth was launched in L.G. Chiozza Money's *Riches and Poverty*, written in 1905, and running into three editions in 1906. According to this book, there was a massive contrast between the incomes of the rich and the rest of the nation: the 5 million enjoying annual incomes of £160 and upwards had an aggregate income of £825 million a year, whereas the 38 million with incomes with less than £160 yearly shared an aggregate income of £880 million.[10] Under the heading 'Riches, comfort and poverty', the national income was analysed as follows:[11]

Riches:	Incomes £700 p.a. and above	
	and their families 250,000 x 5 = 1,250,000	
	Income £580m.	
Comfort:	Incomes £160–£700 p.a.	
	and their families 750,000 x 5 = 3,750,000	
	Income £245m.	
Poverty:	Incomes less than £160 p.a.	
	and their families, 38m.	
	Income £880m.	

Thus, more than one-third of the entire income of the UK is enjoyed by less than one-thirtieth of its population. Further, out of the UK population of 43m., 38m. are poor.

These striking figures were rounded off at the end of the book by a forthright socialist conclusion:[12]

> To deal with causes we must strike at the Error of Distribution by gradually substituting public ownership for private ownership of the means of production.

How far the Conservative government of the time was influenced by the barrage of comment coming from both left and right is hard to judge. It was not all equally persuasive: Chiozza Money's figures, although impressive, were open to question. For example, not all who earned yearly less than £160 (the figure at which the wage-earner had to begin paying income tax) could fairly be called 'poor'. Some of the better paid in this category constituted the respectable working classes and lived lives of simple if not ample comfort. On the other hand, the Conservatives were well aware that there was a social problem – witness Lord Salisbury's remarks quoted at the end of the previous chapter – but it was not clear what, if any, legislation was required to set things right. In any case, at the beginning of the century, the Conservative government had its hands full with the Boer War, and when in 1902 Salisbury handed over to his nephew, Arthur Balfour, a crisis developed within the ranks of the Conservative Party. In 1903 Joseph Chamberlain resigned from the government in order to pursue his campaign for tariff reform, and henceforth the Conservative government was in some disarray, split over the issue of free trade versus tariff reform. It was a split gratefully seized upon by the Liberal opposition, themselves divided originally over the Boer War but now happy to unite over free trade, which remained a basic principle with them.

Arthur Balfour was a highly intelligent man, with intellectual tastes. He was not without sympathy for the poor, and he certainly was familiar with all the Fabian arguments; he enjoyed intellectual company, and had lunch with the Webbs from time to time.[13] Nevertheless, his first political duty obviously enough was to maintain unity within the government and within his party. He tried hard to reach a compromise with Chamberlain over tariff reform, and especially strove to ward off the threat of taxation of food imports, which was highly unpopular in the country. Perhaps it is not surprising that, given the political difficulties of the time, Balfour failed to provide any programme of social legislation to meet the growing demand for reform. Apart from the Education Act, 1902, already discussed, only two measures require comment here: the Unemployed Workmen Act, 1905, and the appointment of a royal commission on the poor laws, also in 1905.

As for the Unemployed Workmen Act, it followed efforts made to encourage public work schemes in London, where, on the suggestion of the Local Government Board, joint distress committees were formed on which local authorities, boards of guardians, and charitable bodies were to be represented. They could then exercise powers to set up relief schemes. The act simply allowed such committees to be set up nationally. They had powers to provide work, establish labour exchanges, and assist emigration of the unemployed. The committees proved to be not much more successful than those previously set up following the issue of the Chamberlain Circular in 1886. The other step taken by the administration was Balfour's announcement of a royal commission on the poor laws on 2 August 1905. There has been a good deal of discussion of the reasons why Balfour decided on this step – for example, Mrs Bosanquet claimed that it was in response to the COS demand for an enquiry – but at the time of his announcing the appointment, Balfour simply remarked that there had been no such enquiry since the great commission of 1832, which had effectively abolished the old poor law.[14] This is probably as good a reason as any for a large-scale investigation of a system which had undergone much modification and adaptation since the act of 1834. When the Liberals took office in December 1905, and resumed office after the general election of 1906, the commission had already begun to meet and collect evidence.

Before this, there had been significant developments in the affairs of the trade unions. In the previous chapter it was explained how the Labour Representative Committee was formed in 1900 to elect members of parliament whose task would be to support legislation in the interests of labour; and this was in response to a number of threatening legal decisions and actions by employers. In the 'khaki election' in October 1900, the LRC succeeded in getting two candidates elected – Keir Hardie at Merthyr Tydfil, and Richard Bell at Derby – but future prospects did not look very promising. Affiliations from trade unions came in only very slowly – in the first year they represented only 253,000 members, and after two years, still only 455,450. At this point, yet another case in the courts went against the trade unions, the Taff Vale Railway case, 1901. It was the result of a strike on the Taff Vale Railway in South Wales. The strike was quickly settled, but the railway company decided to sue the union for damages and costs. Hitherto it had been taken for granted that a trade union could not be sued for losses arising out of a strike. The House of Lords thought otherwise, and the Society of Railway Servants had to pay £23,000 in damages and a further £19,000 in costs, £42,000 in all. It looked as if the right to strike had been effectively challenged, since any strike in future might result in court action by the employer and severe financial loss by the union.

The effect of the Taff Vale decision was to galvanise the trade unions into action. Clearly it had become vital to strengthen labour representation in the House of Commons so as to reverse the Taff Vale verdict. In 1903 affiliations to the LRC shot up to 847,315. More than this, in the same year the LRC decided to impose a compulsory levy on the unions to pay for the support of LRC members in parliament. R.C.K. Ensor was an active Fabian journalist of the time. Describing these events over thirty years later in 1936 in his classic volume in the Oxford History of England, he observed that a sudden wind had filled the sails of the LRC and blew hard in its favour until the general election of January 1906.[15] Indeed it was so: if the Taff Vale Railway case at first seemed an ill wind, it ultimately proved of great advantage to the LRC, whose vessel otherwise seemed becalmed.

One other circumstance favourable to the LRC must be mentioned here. In 1903 the secretary of the LRC, Ramsay MacDonald, drew up a secret electoral pact with Herbert Gladstone, representing the Liberal Party, whereby it was agreed that in the next general election the Liberals would not oppose LRC candidates in about thirty constituencies. For their part, the LRC would support the next Liberal government. This would avoid splitting the left-wing vote, save Liberal election expenses, and give the LRC a better chance of success in constituencies where they had good support. The pact was kept secret so as not to alienate Liberals hostile to the LRC, or LRC supporters who were against any kind of Lib-Lab alliance.

Perhaps this pact would not have been so much to the advantage of the LRC had Balfour's government not failed to solve the problem presented by Chamberlain's tariff reform campaign. The Conservative Party was clearly divided over the issue, and many working-class voters were antagonised by Chamberlain's frank admission that the price of some foreign imported foodstuffs would go up if his plans were adopted; they were not reassured when he told them that the cuts in the duties on sugar, tea, and coffee would offset any new taxes, so that the worker would be better off than before. A famous Liberal poster in the general election campaign of January 1906 showed a large loaf and a small loaf. The reader was asked which would he choose, the Liberal big loaf or the Conservative small loaf. There was also another issue in the election which told against the Conservatives. This was the question of the permission which had been given by the government for Chinese labour to be imported into South Africa to help reopen the mines on the Rand where both local labour and white labour were in short supply. The Chinese were to be indentured for a number of years, and would be housed in special compounds which they could not leave without permission. Further, they would not have any right to settle in South Africa. In theory, they could bring their wives; in practice, when more than 27,000 Chinese had arrived, only two had brought their wives with them. An outcry immediately arose in England against what was soon termed 'Chinese slavery'. In particular, working men resented the use of Chinese labour instead of white labour (which would have been far more expensive), all to help the wealthy South African mineowners. Questions were also asked about the unmentionable vices which might be fostered in the vast, all-male compounds. So Chinese slavery (which in fact was opposed by Joseph Chamberlain) was much disliked by many working-class voters, and in some constituencies became an even bigger issue than tariff reform.[16] Another Liberal election poster simply showed a Chinese face without wording – the face was a sufficient reminder of Chinese labour.

In December 1905 Balfour resigned, handing over the reins of government to the Liberals. It was a tactical move: he hoped that as soon as they took office, the Liberals (who would be without a majority, of course) would show their internal divisions over Home Rule, and as a result might lose the general election which they would be obliged to hold. Balfour miscalculated badly. In the general election held in January 1906, tariff reform and Chinese slavery told strongly against the Conservatives. Trade unionists in particular were upset that although the Conservative government had appointed a royal commission to enquire into the position of the trade unions following the Taff Vale Railway case, no trade unionists were appointed to the commission, and it was accordingly boycotted by the trade union movement. Of course, in addition there were still Nonconformists who were aggrieved at the 'Church on the Rates' issue raised by Balfour's Education Act, and this added to the opposition to the Conservatives in the election. For all these and other reasons the Conservatives were heavily defeated: the Liberals secured 377 seats with an overall majority of 84, while the Conservatives were reduced to only 157 seats. Thus, it seems that the Conservatives were the victims of their own unpopular policies rather than being borne down by the appeal of the Liberals' electoral programme. In fact, the Liberals put their divisions over the Boer War behind them, happy to unite over the issue of free trade, and also happy to condemn Chinese slavery. It is a curious fact that what was to become the greatest reforming ministry of the early twentieth century entered office with no very clear commitments to welfare reform. True, vague references were made by individual candidates to the need for housing reform, or for old-age pensions, or even to the need for land reform, but there were no direct party undertakings in these matters. The Liberals were back in office after ten years in opposition, but it was not at all clear what policies they proposed to adopt. The one exception to this was that sometime in the future they would be obliged to honour their obligation to introduce Home Rule for Ireland. Yet even here the approach would be cautious, and step by step. Further, traditional Liberalism, with its belief in individual liberty, still looked askance at collectivism, even though younger Liberals, followers of New Liberalism, were much less opposed to state action to help the poor.

What in fact were the practical political possibilities facing the new government in January 1906? It is true that they had a massive majority, and that they had the support of the LRC members, now known as the Labour Party, together with the smaller group of the Lib-Labs (twenty-nine LRC candidates were elected, and they were joined by one other MP shortly after the election; the Lib-Labs numbered twenty-four). In theory, therefore, the Liberal government was free to introduce any programme of social reform they might choose, confident of being able to secure its passage through the House of Commons. Nor were they hampered by any specific promises made during the election campaign. Legislation on old-age pensions seemed likely – there had been a royal commission on the aged poor in 1895, together with the Rothschild Committee (1896) and the Chaplin Committee (1899) on old-age pensions; but the only real commitment was to Home Rule, and that was not under immediate consideration. The other possibility was some form of amendment to Balfour's Education Act, of a kind to satisfy Liberal Nonconformists, incensed at church schools (the vast majority being Church of England) receiving aid from the rates. With these exceptions, the government had a clear field before them in which to legislate.

On the other hand, in practice there were several positive restraints which might operate so as to restrict measures of reform. The first, and greatest, was the vast Conservative majority in the House of Lords. Although heavily defeated in the general election, the Tories could always rely on their majority in the Lords to delay or defeat any bill sent up to them. Further, it is clear that Balfour was quite willing to use this power to block any bill which the Conservatives thought unsuitable. Thus Birrell's bill to modify the 1902 Education Act was subsequently so amended in the Lords that the government withdrew it completely. In this way, since there was no limit to the Lords' power to amend or reject legislation, the Conservative Party held the whip hand – the Liberal Party might be in office, but the Conservatives were in power. Naturally enough, Balfour was not likely to use this power recklessly, for to do so would provoke political outrage; but the threat was there, it was exercised from time to time, and it was to lead to confrontation and a constitutional crisis over the 'people's budget' in 1909.

The other restraint on social reform was of a more predictable kind, perhaps – it was that it cost money. Old-age pensions provide a good example. A non-contributory scheme of the kind advocated by Booth was estimated to cost the government (and ultimately the taxpayer) up to £16 million. In the event, the plan finally adopted by the government cost just over £8 million, a sum which was still enough to scandalise some of the older statesmen of the time. Lord Rosebery, the former Liberal leader, thought that the cost would be ruinous and in his opinion 'so prodigal of expenditure that it was likely to undermine the whole fabric of the Empire'.[17] Moreover, the cost of the pensions scheme was under debate just when there was a public demand for the building of new dreadnought battleships for the navy to match the German naval building programme; and battleships were remarkably expensive, though vital to Britain's security. So even though Britain was an extremely wealthy country, government expenditure had to be watched. All in all, government action in theory was unfettered, but in practice it was subject to definite restraints.

How strong in fact was the demand for social reform in 1906? This is not easy to determine, and the concentrating by many Liberal candidates in the general election on Chinese slavery and tariff reform made for further difficulties (in some parts, such as the East End of London, Chinese slavery was a bigger issue than the more abstruse tariff reform). In other words, promises of social reform were not really regarded as immediate issues. On the other hand, there was a great groundswell of informed opinion on the shortcomings of the new industrial state – the findings of Charles Booth, William Booth, Rowntree, Chiozza Money, the propaganda of the Fabian Society, the writings of William Morris, the Webbs, Hobson, Hobhouse, Blatchford, the spread of Marxist ideas, the founding of new political parties, the concern at the physical degeneration of the nation – all testify to middle-class and educated working-class concern at the extent of poverty and unemployment. University settlements in the East End of London, the idea of labour colonies, and the increased emigration during the 1880s, when about 100,000 were emigrating annually,[18] all point in the same direction.

On the central issue of the relief of poverty, as we have seen, the arguments of the Webbs and the Bosanquets represent the two dominant schools of thought. First there was the Fabian belief in collectivism – the use of the power of the state to improve conditions. Then against this there was individualism – the need to let the individual exercise self-help and stand on his own two feet. The latter belief was very much that of the COS and was perhaps the more popular of the two (it certainly persists today and influences the views of those who attack the scroungers and workshy who allegedly batten on the Welfare State). It is significant that of the eighteen members appointed to the Poor Law Commission in 1905, six were members of the COS. This was because, in Professor McBrier's view, they represented the predominant thinking of the time – the 'common sense' point of view.[19] Yet in the other political direction, in Helen Bosanquet's opinion, there were another five socialists among the commissioners, such as George Lansbury and Beatrice Webb, though the remaining three named by Mrs Bosanquet were hardly strong socialists – indeed, William Booth had become a member of the Conservative and Unionist Party.[20]

What is of particular interest at this juncture is, what were the views of the Liberal Party as a whole on social reform at this time? It is an interesting and indeed perplexing question. The fact is that, as might be surmised from the absence of any agreed political platform, there was no coherent programme for reform. There were those on the right of the party who supported social reform on an *ad hoc* basis, prepared to remedy social abuses and weaknesses as they became exposed. On the left of the party, however, there was an ill-defined group of so-called New Liberals, certainly not socialists, but prepared to go further than their brethren in the use of state power to cure social ills. One of this second group was Charles Masterman, newly elected to parliament in 1906. What did he think should be the programme of the new Liberal government?

There is no difficulty in ascertaining his views on this. In a newspaper article in January 1906 he predicted that the 'condition of the people' problem would be the dominant theme in the politics of the coming years. Further, he declared that the prime minister (that is, Campbell-Bannerman) had promised social reform 'not in tiny or niggardly doses, but in measures not unworthy of a government possessing this magnificent majority'. He then proceeded to enumerate a lengthy list of aims: to repeople the deserted countryside of England; to lift the burden of taxation from its heavy pressure on the poorest of the people; to grapple with the disease of unemployment; to provide better houses and cheaper houses for the people; to bring more elements of health and beauty and physical wellbeing into the lives of the city population; to fight with all the weapons of an organised society the physical degeneration of the children of the slums; to ensure by careful and deliberate legislation a more just distribution of the national income, and a more adequate contribution of the wealthiest towards the expenses of government.[21]

It is an interesting and impressive list of reforms advocated by a young and ambitious MP who was to become a junior minister within two years, when he took office under John Burns, the minister for local government. It betrays his own special interests and knowledge: the romantic notion of back to the countryside; unemployment and housing; the physical state of city populations, and of slum children; and the need to redistribute income (no doubt Chiozza Money would have approved of this). Of course, it was all somewhat idealistic, and it is noticeable that he does not refer anywhere to foreign policy, relations with Germany, or even to the Gladstonian mission 'to pacify Ireland'. But there is no doubt that his aims and objectives were held by many on the left wing of his party; this is what New Liberalism was all about, and Masterman's views are indicative of the political possibilities in the Liberal New Dawn of 1906. After twenty years of mounting evidence that all was not well in Britain's industrial state, and that even though for the majority of the people there was a better standard of life, a substantial minority were still poor, and experiencing (as an earlier commentator had put it) 'a mean and grovelling mode of existence'. The Liberals now had the opportunity to right a number of social wrongs. We have now to consider what they really achieved before Armageddon in August 1914.

Perhaps the most notable of the Liberals' early reforms was the Trades Disputes Act, 1906. Early in 1906 a royal commission on trade unions published its report which recommended that trade unions should be given legal recognition as corporate bodies, that their funds should be protected, and that the right to picket should be confirmed. However, when the government introduced a bill to carry out these recommendations, it met opposition from the unions, which simply wanted a return to the legal immunity which they had thought existed before the Taff Vale decision; if the government bill went through, union members would be able to sue their own unions. The government therefore withdrew its measure, substituting for it a bill already drawn up and approved by the Parliamentary Committee of the TUC. The bill then became law as the 1906 Trades Disputes Act. It gave the remarkable privilege to the unions of immunity in tort – that is, unions could not be sued for civil damages arising out of a strike. The Conservative politician, Edward Carson, remarked that immunity in tort placed the unions in a similar position to the crown, which likewise could not be sued in tort: as he said, 'The king can do no wrong; neither can a trade union.' The act also redefined picketing, and confirmed that it was legal. Carson's comment on this was frank and to the point: 'I have always thought that the matter of peaceful picketing is a matter of absolute hypocrisy – peaceful persuasion is of no use to a trade union.'[22]

Other social reforms in the early years of the Liberal administration include the provision of school meals for needy children, and the medical inspection of school children. School meals were already being provided (either breakfast or dinners) in some of the poorest parts of London, but the Education (Provision of Meals) Act, 1906, permitted local authorities to raise a half-penny rate to pay for meals for necessitous children. There was to be no loss of the vote by parents accepting free meals. School authorities did not all immediately implement the act, and the quality of meals was often very poor, but the act was nevertheless a step in the right direction. School meals had been recommended by the Interdepartmental Committee on Physical Deterioration, 1904, which had also supported the idea of school medical inspections. Again, there were precedents for this: the London School Board had appointed its first medical officer of health for schools as early as 1891, while by 1905 there were eighty-five school medical officers, though mostly in urban areas, and mostly part time.[23] There was still some opposition to school medical inspections as infringing parents' personal rights, so Sir Robert Morant, permanent secretary to the Board of Education, quietly inserted a clause permitting it into the Education (Administrative Provisions) Act, 1907. Lastly, with reference to the welfare of children, in 1908 the important Children's Act was passed, a great codifying act covering a good deal of ground: *inter alia* it redefined the responsibilities of both poor law authorities and other local authorities for the care of children, set up juvenile courts and borstals, and abolished the imprisonment of children under the age of sixteen.[24]

However, it was not until 1908 that the subject of old-age pensions was tackled, and the Old Age Pensions Act was passed. Here again was a subject with a long history. As noted earlier in this chapter, there had been a royal commission on the aged poor in 1895, and two committees (in 1896 and 1899) on the subject; and the question remained controversial – would old-age pensions remove the incentive to save for old age? Further, if the scheme was to be non-contributory, how could the state afford to pay for it? By 1908, however, the friendly societies were less opposed to the idea of old-age pensions, since they were experiencing increased demands on their sick funds from elderly members. The COS was similarly less hostile than before, though they wanted a contributory scheme to encourage self-help. Then again, the TUC had been supporting the idea of pensions since 1896, while abroad, Germany and Denmark had been paying old-age pensions since 1891, and New Zealand had become the first country in the British Empire to do so. The Old Age Pensions Act, 1908, was steered through the Commons by the new chancellor of the exchequer, David Lloyd George, whose name became identified with the pension. The act provided a weekly pension of 5/– a week at the age of seventy, paid through the post office and not the Board of Guardians, so as to avoid the taint of poverty. The amount was kept deliberately small, so as to encourage savings (a nod in the direction of the COS: it also saved the government money). There was an astonishing list of conditions attached to payment – the claimant was not to have been in prison during the preceding ten years, was not to be foreign, not to have been guilty of 'habitual failure to work', and not to have been in receipt of poor relief at any time after 1 January 1908 (most of these requirements were soon dropped). Today the amount paid in 1908 seems pitifully small (an adult labourer of the time earned about a pound a week), and the qualifications for payment seem harsh and grudging. But the scheme was very popular, and it must be remembered that Charles Booth had calculated that 38.4 per cent of old people over sixty-five were receiving poor relief. Lloyd George commented on the numbers applying for pensions, and remarked that this showed:[25]

> a mass of poverty and destitution in the country which is too proud to wear the badge of pauperism and which declines to pin that badge to its children. They would rather suffer deprivation than do so …

The reference here, of course, was to the old practice of badging the poor, that is, requiring paupers to wear a badge to show they were receiving poor relief. In future, people in need of help would be able to avoid the stigma of having to seek poor relief, and could draw their 'Lord George' (he was often referred to by pensioners as 'Lord George') at the post office. In fact, 1908 proved to be the turning point in the history of Liberal welfare legislation. Up to then, as has been noted, the pace had been uneven, and the Liberals had lost several by-elections. A number of measures had been either amended and abandoned, or rejected outright in the House of Lords, such as Birrell's education bill, and a bill to abolish plural voting. The prime minister was a sick man, and was actually mortally ill with cancer. There was a clear need to revive electoral support. Lloyd George remarked to his brother, 'It is time we did something which appealed straight to the people – it will, I think, help to stop this electoral rot, and that is most necessary.'[26] In April 1908 Campbell-Bannerman retired and was replaced by Herbert Asquith, who had formerly been chancellor of the exchequer. That post was now taken by Lloyd George, with Winston Churchill moving to the Board of Trade. Lloyd George took over the pensions bill from Asquith, and when it became law it proved to be the first of a new series of important welfare reforms in which the problems of unemployment and sickness were faced directly. One element in this was the flying visit of five days to Germany made by Lloyd George in August 1908, where he had been greatly impressed by the German pension and insurance schemes.

In 1909 Churchill introduced and saw through parliament the Labour Exchanges Act, the detail of the bill owing much to a senior civil servant, William Beveridge. Churchill was an enthusiastic convert to the cause of the poor, of whose existence he had hitherto hardly been aware. The idea of labour exchanges was not new: they had been tried locally under the Unemployed Workmen Act, 1905. What was now proposed was a national scheme of such exchanges where the unemployed looking for work could register, and employers could notify job vacancies. The scheme began to function in 1910, under the direction of Beveridge, and registration was free and voluntary. Labour exchanges had some success, though regarded with suspicion by some working people, who regarded them as operating largely in the interests of employers seeking blackleg labour. Also in 1909 Churchill piloted through the Trade Boards Act (the Sweated Industries Act), which set up trade boards to fix minimum wages and maximum hours in sweated trades (many in the East End of London) such as tailoring, paper box making, lacemaking and chainmaking (this last industry being in the Black Country). Another act passed in 1909 affecting the working classes was the Town and Country Planning Act, which did little for town planning, but did give local authorities additional powers to inspect and repair poor quality housing. Little was done as yet to provide local authority housing, this still being regarded as more properly the sphere of private enterprise.

However, the major event in parliamentary affairs in 1909 was Lloyd George's famous 'people's budget'. Lloyd George had to raise an additional £16 million to pay for the cost of the new pension scheme and the building of eight new dreadnoughts. He did this by imposing seven new taxes in all, and putting up the duties on alcohol and tobacco. There was to be a new vehicle licensing duty and a tax on petrol. The new taxes included a 20 per cent tax on the unearned increment in the value of land when it changed hands, death duties were increased, and a surtax was designed to bring in an extra £3.5 million. Most of the new taxes were aimed directly at the wealthier classes, though of course, smokers and drinkers of all classes were affected by the increase in duty. The landowning classes found the proposal to tax profits made on the sale of land especially offensive as it involved a preliminary valuation of all landholdings. Although the House of Lords had not rejected a money bill for over 200 years, in November 1909 it withheld its assent pending a general election in which the judgement of the electorate could manifest itself. The election campaign which followed was marked by bitter attacks on the House of Lords and was characterised as a 'peers against the people' struggle. Lloyd George excelled himself in two famous speeches in Limehouse and in Newcastle. The Newcastle speech is still so striking that it deserves quoting yet again:[27]

> The question will be asked, should 500 men, ordinary men, chosen accidentally from among the unemployed, over-ride the judgement – the deliberate judgement – of millions of people who are engaged in the industry which makes the wealth of the country? ... Another question will be asked: who ordained that a few should have the land of Britain as a perquisite, who made 10,000 people owners of the soil, and the rest of us trespassers in the land of our birth?

The result of the general election in January 1910 was that the Liberals lost their massive majority (Liberals 275 seats, Unionists 273), but with the support of the 82 Irish nationalists and 40 Labour MPs, they still had a majority of 124 seats. The verdict of the country was thus narrowly in support of the budget, and the House of Lords passed it (a year or so late) on 28 April 1910. By then, a greater threat to the Lords had appeared in the shape of a parliament bill to restrict their powers.

The parliament bill provided a further period of extended controversy. By its terms, no finance bill (as defined by the speaker) could be delayed by the House of Lords for more than a month (this ensured that no budget however controversial could be held up as the 'people's budget' had been). Further, any other measure could not be delayed for more than two years, once it had been passed by the Commons in three successive sessions. Lastly, the life of parliament was shortened to five years instead of seven years. The details of the constitutional struggle resulting need not concern us here: suffice to say, the sudden death of Edward VII in May 1910 complicated matters further. To spare the new king, George V, from being drawn into political controversy, a constitutional conference was held in an attempt to find an agreed inter-party solution (Lloyd George displayed his well-known flexibility by actually proposing the formation of a coalition government). The conference broke down. Another general election was held in December 1910, the result leaving the main parties very much as before. At this point, Asquith revealed that the new king was prepared to create as many new Liberal peers as necessary to outvote the Conservative peers in the Lords. At this disclosure, the Conservative peers gave way and passed the parliament bill which became law in 1911 (but as some peers voted against the bill, thirty-seven Conservative peers were forced to vote for it in order to ensure its passage, while others abstained). Thus, the way was cleared not only for future budgets, but also for controversial measures, such as Home Rule – or so it seemed.

Meanwhile, in 1911 Lloyd George introduced a national insurance bill to insure all the working classes against ill health, and a proportion of them against unemployment. He had been greatly impressed by his visit to Germany in 1908, and his 1911 proposals were a natural sequel to his old-age pension reform. His health insurance scheme was brought forward at a time of increasing anxiety over the state of the nation's health and efficiency, when even the British Medical Association, hardly a radical organisation, produced a report which advocated the setting up of a public medical service for those not receiving poor law benefit. The scheme compulsorily insured all workers earning less than £160 a year, 4d a week being deducted from wages, while the employer contributed 3d, and the state 2d ('ninepence for fourpence', as Lloyd George put it). In return for this, the worker was paid 10/– a week when off sick, together with free medical care from his local practitioner, chosen from a panel of doctors joining the scheme. Dependants such as wives and children were not covered, and hospital treatment still had to be paid for, though there was free treatment for tuberculosis, and also a small maternity grant. The administration of the scheme was put into the hands of 'approved societies', that is, the existing friendly societies who had long experience in insuring their members against ill health, and the large and powerful insurance companies, also accustomed to giving cover in the form of life policies. At first, the friendly societies hoped to gain exemption for their members from the whole scheme, but Lloyd George could not allow this. He was more inclined to give in to the insurance companies, who had an army of 70,000 full-time door-to-door collectors, a weekly contact with working-class voters.[28] Lloyd George could not afford to antagonise the insurance companies, and indeed dropped his original scheme for widows' and orphans' pensions to bring the companies in.

The scheme was not without its critics. The Labour movement as a whole greatly disliked the compulsory deductions from wages which it was claimed by some opponents would deprive the working man of his beer and 'baccy'. Keir Hardie complained that it failed to get to the root of the problem of poverty, which was the capitalist system. He claimed that it was as if the government was declaring, 'We shall not uproot the causes of poverty, but will give you a porous plaster to cover the disease which poverty causes.' The Webbs disliked the scheme, too, largely because they opposed the contributory principle (in fact, it would have been impossible to finance the scheme on a non-contributory basis). There was some opposition from middle-class employers: the *Daily Mail* ran a campaign against middle-class ladies having to 'lick stamps' for their domestic servants. (Weekly contributions in the form of stamps had to be stuck onto employment cards. This campaign even extended to a mass meeting in the Albert Hall.) Altogether Lloyd George fought a remarkable battle to get the whole project through, and in spite of its undoubted merits, it remained unpopular for some time, mainly because of the compulsory deductions from wages. As for the medical profession, in spite of its initial doubts, it profited greatly from the fees payable for each panel patient, some doctors doubling their incomes, though careful to segregate the national insurance patients from their private patients.

The unemployment scheme was much smaller in scope, applying only to about 2.25 million workers in trades notoriously subject to periodic unemployment. The contributions were again compulsory, $2\frac{1}{2}$d each from employer and workman, and $1\frac{2}{3}$d from the state. The benefit payable was only 7/– per week, this being intended both to encourage saving, and to deter the workshy. The whole scheme was masterminded by Churchill, and is the most radical achievement of this stage of his career. He had been home secretary since February 1910, and left the Home Office to become first lord of the Admiralty in October 1911. His career as a social reformer was over. Though the scheme was limited in nature, it is worth noting at this point that it was to expand enormously between the wars as unemployment grew more severe, reaching 3 million or more in the early 1930s.

The 1911 National Insurance Act was the greatest achievement of the pre-war Liberal governments, and a very real advance in the fields

Table 6.2 Strikes and working days lost, 1907–14

Year	No. of strikes	Days lost
1907	585	2,150,000
1908	389	10,790,000
1909	422	2,690,000
1910	521	9,870,000
1911	872	10,160,000
1912	834	40,890,000
1913	1,459	9,800,000
1914	972	9,880,000

of ill health, poverty, and unemployment. Yet, as we have seen, it was not popular at the time, and it was passed at a time of increasing and unprecedented industrial strife. The number of strikes and working days lost reached extraordinary levels, as shown in Table 6.2.[29] From these figures it is apparent that the worst years were 1911 and 1912, with 1914 showing some levelling off. It would be tedious to list all the major strikes of this period, but in 1907 there was the threat of the first national railway strike; it led to government intervention, with Lloyd George persuading both sides to set up boards of conciliation. In 1908 the ASE came out in the north-east against wage cuts, but was forced back to work after seven months. In 1909 and 1910 the main cause of strikes was the varying interpretation of the Miners Eight Hour Day Act from coalfield to coalfield. A strike against new pay rates led to rioting and looting in Tonypandy in 1910. London police were drafted in, and also troops, and one miner was shot dead. In 1911 there were strikes in the Southampton, London, and Liverpool docks, while in August 1911 the national railway strike which had been threatened in 1907 actually took place. Lloyd George again negotiated with both sides and managed to have the strike called off after five days. Nevertheless, there was serious rioting and looting in Llanelly, two men were shot dead while attempting to stop a train driven by blacklegs, and five men were killed by an explosion in the freight (Keir Hardie published a famous pamphlet, *Killing no Murder: The Government and the Railway Strike*). In 1912 the miners struck for a minimum wage in their industry, and this led to the Minimum Wage Act, 1912 (the strike was ended by a negotiating committee of four ministers, led by Asquith). Also in 1912 there was another strike in the London docks, and in 1913 a lengthy and violent strike of transport workers in Dublin, led by Jim Larkin, a well-known syndicalist.

What were the causes of such an outbreak of strikes, so severe as to lead to a direct government intervention? One explanation propounded in a popular work by G. Dangerfield, *The Strange Death of Liberal England*,[30] is that there was increasing violence at home (the struggle over the parliament bill, actual violence in the House of Commons, and the threat of civil war in Ireland), together with an increasing threat of war in Europe. Only the coming of the Great War in August 1914, it is said, prevented a revolutionary explosion at home. This is entertaining fantasy: there is nothing to show a link between domestic and foreign affairs as suggested in this book, and certainly nothing to demonstrate the existence of a revolutionary situation at home before the war. Philip Snowden, afterwards chancellor of the exchequer in both inter-war Labour governments, summed up neatly the major causes of unrest in a passage written subsequently on this subject:[31]

> In 1910 – a year of record trade – wages remained practically stationary. The cost of living increased, and the working people's desires rightly grew. But with stationary wages, the real condition of the workers is one of diminishing power to satisfy desires. This is one of the causes of unrest in the Labour world. With the spread of education, with the display of wealth and luxury by the rich, it is certain that the workers will not be content.

Though the language is oddly stiff and formal, Snowden's major point is clear enough: real wages were falling. Though they had risen by well over 10 per cent between 1889 and 1900, from 1900 to 1910 there was a fall of nearly 10 per cent. Further, boom conditions after 1908 made for full employment, thus limiting the fear of unemployment. There is Snowden's other point, too, that the spread of education meant that the literate working classes could read about the great displays of wealth by the upper and middle classes – the Edwardian period was notoriously one of showy social occasions, and the increasing use of the rich man's new toy, the motor car (Ensor, the young journalist of the time with Fabian views, mentioned earlier, wrote in the 1930s about the hedonism and self-indulgence of the age).[32] So, thinking men and women of the working classes as well as middle-class intellectuals were becoming more and more concerned at the state of society.

There were several other causes of unrest as well. One was yet another legal decision which upset trade unionists. This was the judgement in the Osborne case, 1909. In this case a trade union member sued his trade union for paying part of his subscription to the Labour Party – the compulsory political levy. Osborne was a committed Liberal who objected to being forced to support a party which included socialists. He won his case, the TUC was prevented from subsidising Labour MPs, and a number of them were placed in financial difficulties as a result (this was eased when parliamentary salaries of £400 p.a. were paid for the first time in 1911). The TUC demanded legislation, but the Liberal government took no action for the time being.

Another cause of unrest was the somewhat tepid performance of the new Labour Party in the Commons. Keir Hardie was a charismatic figure, but not a good chairman of the Parliamentary Labour Party. Party discipline was slack, and trade union members were often absent from the House on union business. There was also some tension and mistrust between them and the socialist members. The party had a constitution, but lacked a clear political programme until 1918. As early as 1907, Ben Tillett produced a pamphlet challengingly entitled *Is the Parliamentary Labour Party a Failure?* In 1911 the ILP annual report for 1910 quoted Keir Hardie as saying, 'At the present time, the Labour Party has almost ceased to exist.' In 1914, Beatrice Webb wrote in her diary that the Labour members had lost confidence in themselves and each other: 'there is little leadership, but a good deal of anti-leadership'.[33] All the same, this criticism should not be taken too far: better leadership of the parliamentary party was provided when Ramsay MacDonald took over as chairman in 1911, with Arthur Henderson becoming secretary of the Labour Party itself. Membership of the House was maintained at a reasonable level of forty-two after the two general elections of 1910 in which their allies, the Liberals, had lost considerable number of seats. Outside parliament, support for the Labour Party was actually increasing. Although the Parliamentary Labour Party did not secure any outstanding legislative success before 1914 – the Trades Disputes Act, 1906, was their greatest achievement – they were of course in no position to defeat the government before 1910, and had no reason for trying to do so after 1910. As Henry Pelling has said in a famous observation, circumstances made the Labour Party the hand-maiden of Liberalism before 1914.[34]

However, in 1911 some members of the ILP joined with the SDF, which had withdrawn from supporting the LRC in 1901, to form a new party called the British Socialist Party (this led ultimately to the creation of the Communist Party of Great Britain in 1920). Another indication perhaps of dissatisfaction with the Labour Party was the spread of the new doctrine of syndicalism. This variety of socialism had origins in both the United States and in France (the French word for 'trade union' is *syndicat*), and it was based on the belief that each industry should have a single big union, which would run the industry for the benefit of the workers. When the time became favourable, the workers in each industry would seize control of the state. The idea therefore was for the working classes to gain power not through parliament, but through industrial power, employing the weapon of the general strike. Tom Mann became a strong believer in syndicalism when he returned from Australia in 1910. The movement had some support on the Clyde, and especially in South Wales, where a pamphlet published in Tonypandy was entitled *The Miners' Next Step*; the step was the creation of one massive union covering all the extractive industries, with 'one central objective', or so it was said.

The syndicalist movement gained only limited support in the trade union movement. Its only successes were the creation by Tom Mann in 1910 of the National Transport Workers Federation (it brought together dockers and seamen), and the merger of the Society of Railway Servants with the General Railway Workers Union to form the National Union of Railwaymen (NUR) in 1913. Even then, two small but important unions were still left outside the NUR – the Associated Society of Locomotive Engineers and Firemen (ASLEF) and the Railway Clerks Association. Formerly it was thought that the so-called Triple Alliance of trade unions in 1914 was a sign of the influence of syndicalism. The Triple Alliance was an agreement between the railwaymen, the miners, and the Transport Workers Federation for joint action should any member of the alliance go on strike, possibly leading to a national strike. However, more recent research has shown that it was really a practical plan for co-ordinating action and avoiding losses resulting from unilateral action. The details were not worked out till 1915, and when the alliance was put to the test in 1921, the railwaymen failed to respond, and the alliance collapsed.

This survey of Labour activity both inside and outside parliament shows that once the Labour Party had gained a foothold in parliament, the Labour movement tended to switch activity to the industrial field where it was facing the challenge of the fall in real wages. It remains to be seen now what other social reforms were achieved by the Liberal governments in the years after 1911 and before war broke out in August 1914. One reform was the direct result of the Osborne case. After some delay, the government passed the Trade Union Act, 1913. This provided that any union which wished to establish a political fund had to ballot their members. If a majority was obtained, two separate funds could then be set up, a political fund and a general fund. Any member not wishing to support the political fund could 'contract out' and all his subscription would go into the general fund. The trade unions disliked 'contracting out', though in practice it could operate in their favour, since many members who were not really supporters of the Labour Party might not bother to 'contract out'. Voting in individual unions seemed to show that there were plenty of Conservatives and Liberals among their members. For example, the miners voted 261,643 for a political fund, but 194,800 against, while the cotton weavers voted 98,158 for, and 75,893 against.

The great social reforms of the Liberal administration were undoubtedly the Pensions Act and the National Insurance Act, while the 'people's budget' of 1909 by its new scheme of taxation helped to increase the national revenues so as to pay for social reform. Other reforms included the Workmen's Compensation Act, 1906, which improved an earlier act so as to cover not only accidents at work but illness or disease resulting from work, and the Shops Act, 1911, which at last began to regulate the notoriously lengthy hours worked by shop assistants (though the act was much amended). There was one legislative field, however, in which the Liberals signally failed to achieve any success: votes for women. Women had gained the vote in local elections in 1894, and in 1907 became eligible to be county councillors, aldermen, and mayors. By now there was considerable support for some form of female franchise, and private members' bills on the subject passed their second reading in the Commons by comfortable majorities in 1908, 1909, 1910, and 1911. What was necessary was for the government to introduce a measure of its own. Unfortunately the cabinet was divided on the subject, and Asquith himself was hostile, arguing that there was no electoral mandate for it. In 1912 a bill for votes for women was defeated by the opposition of the Irish nationalists, who had hitherto supported similar proposals, but who now wanted a clear run for a Home Rule bill. In the following year, Asquith introduced the franchise and redistribution bill which would have added a further 2.5 million male voters to the electoral register, and at the same time promised to consider female suffrage amendments. This promise would have given votes to up to 10.5 million women. However, the speaker ruled that any such amendments would so change the bill as to make it necessary for it to be withdrawn and reframed. One last effort was made in 1913 when another private member's bill was introduced which would have given the vote to 6 or 7 million women. It was rejected by 269 votes to 221. Unionists voted by five to one against it, but by now many Liberals also voted against.[35]

The reason for this was the increasing violence of the suffragette campaign. This had been growing since 1908 when there was a split in the Women's Social and Political Union, led by the Pankhursts, and a new, more peaceful body, the Women's Freedom League, was set up by Mrs Despard. By 1912 there was a campaign of window smashing in the West End of London. By 1913 there were arson and bomb attacks on public and private property, including an arson attack on Lloyd George's new house at Walton on the Heath in Surrey. Christabel Pankhurst in particular provoked opposition to her cause by her allegations in *The Great Scourge* that three-quarters of all men suffered from venereal disease, and that only votes for women could be a cure for male immorality. Her slogan was 'Votes for women, chastity for men'.[36] By now there were personal assaults on ministers, acid poured on golf greens, the contents of pillar-boxes set alight, and so on; and although there had been abhorrence expressed at the forcible feeding of imprisoned suffragettes who went on hunger strike, the change in attitudes was indicated when the Cat and Mouse Act, 1913, was passed. Under this act, suffragettes could be released from prison and rearrested later if thought necessary. The act was carried by a large majority. By 1914 the very real violence and damage to property made further progress difficult to predict when war broke out on 4 August. It is possible to blame Asquith, of course, for failing to take a firm line on this subject, but the threat of violence in Ireland against Home Rule was growing steadily, and increasingly preoccupied him. Government action earlier on when public opinion was more favourable might have brought votes for women before the first instalment came in 1918, but a hardening of opinion against it was very evident in the last years or so of peace.

We may now attempt some kind of final assessment of the Liberal government's efforts to bind up the wounds of the industrial society which had grown up in the preceding century. That industrialisation had brought forth both gains and losses was generally acknowledged; and even among the most bigoted reactionaries, there were not many who subscribed to the views of Voltaire's Dr Pangloss, or would echo the opinions of Lord Braxfield on the outbreak of the French Revolution that the landed interest alone had a right to be represented in parliament, and that:[37]

> Two things must be attended to which require no proof. First, that the British Constitution is the best that ever was since the creation of the world; and, it is not possible to make it better.

Quite obviously, since the 1880s – or even earlier – it was clear that although the standard of living had risen, and compulsory education had come for the working classes, the great towns contained their own abominations; and among them were poverty, sickness, and unemployment.

How far then had the Liberal government's measures gone to solve these social problems? It is worth recalling that the Liberals did not enter government committed to any grand programme of social reform, and indeed their reforms for the first two years in office were by no means very striking. The leisurely pace at which they proceeded owed something perhaps to the prime minister being an elderly and increasingly sick man. There is also the point that foreign affairs – the Algeçiras crisis, the settlement in South Africa, and the Entente with Russia – all occupied a good deal of governmental time and attention. In fact, it is difficult to estimate how far the average Liberal MP regarded his government as committed to social reform: Masterman did, of course, but he was hardly an average Liberal MP. Only after the change of leadership at the top, in April 1908, with Lloyd George taking the Exchequer, and Churchill the Board of Trade, did the pace quicken. Thereafter a number of important measures were passed, in particular, the Pensions Act, the 'people's budget', and the National Insurance Act. The importance of the pensions scheme and of the National Insurance Act has already been stressed, while the budget set important precedents for the taxation of the upper classes, even though the land taxes were never fully implemented. Taken altogether, the Liberal social reforms were the greatest body of social legislation ever passed up to that time.

The other side of the coin, of course, was that the reforms were very limited in scope and obviously did not go very far to reduce poverty, unemployment, or sickness. They were a beginning, an important beginning, but not more than that, an attempt to reach out to the poorest – Churchill talked about spreading a net over the abyss, and about old-age pensions being a lifebelt. On the whole, they were seen as being based on fundamental Liberal tenets, for example, the need to encourage savings, and the employment of the insurance principle as a form of self-help. At the same time, some aspects of the reforms were examples of collectivism, or direct state intervention as in the non-contributory nature of old-age pensions, the compulsory deductions from wages for health and unemployment contributions, the fixing of miners' hours and wages, and the regulation of hours and wages in the sweated trades. This was certainly New Liberalism or progressivism, as opposed to old liberalism. It was not very different from the kind of state action advocated by socialists, though the Liberals were emphatic that it was not socialism. As Churchill put it in a speech in 1908:[38]

> Socialism wants to pull down wealth, Liberalism seeks to raise up poverty ... Socialism assails the maximum pre-eminence of the individual – Liberalism seeks to build up the maximum standard of the masses.

Charles Masterman, who was close to Churchill at this time, would have agreed with this, being a radical Liberal: he rejected socialism as leading to an 'ant state'. Of course, it is still possible to see the views of both Lloyd George and Churchill as not based on political principle at all, but as being purely pragmatic in nature – they were, after all, the two great outsiders of their time. Churchill had originally been a Conservative, and was at this time in his reforming Liberal mode, which he left behind him once he had moved to the Admiralty. Lloyd George was often accused of having no principles at all, and was quite prepared to propose a coalition with the Conservatives at the constitutional conference 1910, and later he headed such a coalition as prime minister from 1916 to 1922. Neither man therefore was exactly a prisoner of traditional nineteenth-century Liberal beliefs.

It is interesting to enquire into what further reforms each men had in mind at the time. Both seemed to think that their reforms were only a beginning. Making notes for a speech, Lloyd George jotted down the following points:[39]

> Insurance necessarily temporary expedient. At no distant date hope state will acknowledge full responsibility in the matter of making provision for sickness, breakdown, and unemployment.

As early as 1908 Churchill was considering proposals for welfare services, which included special state industries, a reformed poor law, railway amalgamation under state control (there were over 200 separate railway companies before 1914), and compulsory education to the age of seventeen. Of the budget of 1909, he said it was intended to fortify the homes of the people:[40]

> We ought to be able to set up ... an unbroken bridge or causeway, as it were, along which the whole body of the people may move with ... security and safety against hazards and misfortunes.

After Churchill had left the Home Office for the Admiralty in October 1911, Lloyd George was left as the leading reformer in the government. He planned next to begin a campaign for reform in the countryside, calling (as he put it) for the final dismantling of feudalism there. The land campaign was launched in October 1913 after repeated postponements due first to the outbreak of war in the Balkans in 1912, and then the Marconi scandal in 1913 in which Lloyd George himself was involved (he extricated himself with considerable skill from what today would be called a case of insider dealing in company shares). The campaign was an odd episode in the short time remaining before the outbreak of war. No doubt its origins lay in part in Lloyd George's antipathy to the landlord class in North Wales where he had grown up and first practised as a solicitor, often acting on behalf of tenant farmers against their landlords. The proposed campaign was a curious example of private enterprise by Lloyd George, and was not at first put forward as the official policy of the government. It envisaged better rural housing for labourers, minimum wages, rent controls for tenant farmers, the abolition of the game laws, and the setting up of a new ministry of land and natural resources. A parallel scheme for urban reform featuring slum clearance was launched in April 1914, and in June 1914 Asquith agreed to the principle of a minimum urban wage. Two months later, war broke out.

It is evident from all this that Lloyd George's inventiveness was not exhausted after the achievement of the National Insurance Act, which itself made necessary the creation of a vast new administrative machine under the National Insurance Commission. This body was chaired by Charles Masterman who was closely identified with the new insurance schemes, and who as financial secretary to the Treasury was subjected to a continual barrage of questions on the subject in the Commons. It is impossible to say, of course, how far the land campaign in both its rural and urban aspects would have gone had the Great War not brought it to an end. Even before then, public attention was being distracted, of course, by the Irish problem across the water and the suffragette agitation. Nevertheless, the steam had not entirely gone out of Asquith's government by the time war came, and there was even talk of land nationalisation. The Land Nationalisation Society actually claimed to have ninety-eight members in the House of Commons.

However, there was one area of possible reform left entirely untouched, and that was the poor law. When the commission appointed by Balfour concluded its investigations, the results were published in forty-seven volumes in all. Two reports were issued in 1909. The majority report was signed by the chairman and fourteen members, while the minority report was signed by Beatrice Webb, George Lansbury, Francis Chandler (a trade unionist and Manchester poor law guardian), and Francis Russell Wakefield (Dean of Norwich). The reports had a good deal in common: they both condemned the existing poor law system which lacked uniformity in granting relief, and also supplied services in education and health care already provided by local councils. Further, in some places the old mixed workhouses lingered on in which children and lunatics had still not been removed to other places of care. The differences between the reports lay in the new administrative machinery suggested as a replacement for the boards of guardians, which both reports wanted abolished. The majority report proposed that the powers of the guardians should be transferred to the county councils, which should then set up public assistance committees (PACs) made up of elected council members and co-opted members. In addition, there should be a Voluntary Aid Committee, consisting of local charity representatives. Only the really destitute would be cared for by the PACs. This system would clearly leave much responsibility for the care of the poor in the hands of voluntary agencies, always a primary objective of the COS. Its representatives made sure that its belief in the moral failure at the heart of much poverty was clearly expressed in their conclusion:[41]

> we feel strongly that the pauperism and distress we have described can never be successfully combatted by administration and expenditure. The causes of distress are not only economic and industrial: in their origin and character they are largely moral. Government by itself cannot correct or remove such influences.

As a matter of fact, the Webbs did not entirely disagree with this COS belief. Beatrice Webb herself thought that destitution had to be prevented and if necessary penalised as a public nuisance. In other words, extreme cases of poverty might result in punishment for the offender – a somewhat bizarre thought for present-day reformers. Where the minority report differed from the majority report was that it recommended the breakup entirely of the poor law. The powers of the guardians should not go to the proposed PACs, but to the appropriate existing committees of the county councils – children to the education committee, the sick and aged to the public health committee, and so on. As for the able-bodied unemployed, theirs was a national problem, and the national labour market should be in the hands of a minister responsible to parliament, who would be the minister for labour. This was intended to solve the problems of boards of guardians in impoverished areas such as Poplar in London, which had great difficulty in raising enough money from the poor rates to meet their heavy expenditure on the poor. There should also be labour exchanges, public works schemes, and penalties for the persistently idle.

Neither report was implemented before 1914, and it was not until 1929 that the majority report was adopted and the boards of guardians abolished. The reason why the government failed to take action is sometimes said to be the vigorous propaganda campaign waged by the Webbs in favour of the minority report. This certainly antagonised the minister for local government, John Burns, who personally disliked and feared the Webbs, and it also upset many boards of guardians. A private member's bill based on the minority report in 1910 did not pass even its second reading. In fact, the government had ample reasons for not proceeding: they already had plans for helping the unemployed and the sick outside the poor law system. Further, the commission was not unanimous in its recommendations, and reform of the poor law administration in any shape or form would have been both contentious and expensive. From the government's point of view, the whole subject was therefore best left alone until some more opportune time arose in the future.

Finally, it may be said that the Liberal administrations did well before 1914 to face directly some of the outstanding problems arising from industrialisation at the end of the nineteenth century. It is perhaps as well to remark here that not all the social ills of the time can be traced back directly to industrialisation: the problems of old age, for example, were due to increasing longevity, itself the consequence of some improvement in the standard of living; but considerations of this kind hardly qualify substantially the direct link between unemployment, bad housing, and poor health, and the driving force of industrial change. The social problems of the Edwardian period were stark and undeniable. The Liberal governments at least did something about them, particularly by way of old-age pensions and the National Insurance Act, which according to Dr Jones, secretary to the cabinet and one of the earliest of Lloyd George's biographers, was the greatest act of parliament ever passed. These two measures alone in time became a fundamental part of the Welfare State of the 1940s. Yet the 1911 act continued at first to be unpopular, and when it finally came into operation in July 1912 the papers were highly critical, and contained some remarkably condemnatory headlines.[42]

The period 1906 to 1914 saw the heyday of Liberalism, and indeed of New Liberalism and its efforts to right social injustices. The opportunity would not come again for the Liberal Party, and the last Liberal ministry of the twentieth century ended in May 1915, when Asquith formed a coalition government. New Liberalism had achieved much, but the basic issue of collectivism versus individualism had not been solved. In practice, as we have seen, there are plenty of examples of collectivism in the Liberal legislation, though the Liberals were much concerned to justify it by reference to insurance principles, and so on. The Labour Party produced few new ideas of their own, and indeed their voting support for the national insurance bill was obtained only by the promise of salaries for MPs. The Liberal reforms occupy an honoured place in most social history books covering the nineteenth and twentieth centuries, and rightly so, with all their admitted shortcomings. No government of the time could possibly have remedied all the adverse social consequences of industrialisation at a stroke, and this was to become painfully obvious with the onset of mass unemployment between the wars.

7 The Great War, 1914–18

The theme pursued in this book so far has been the results of industrialisation for this country, for good and for ill, up to 1914; and the last chapter in particular tried to show how the pre-war Liberal governments attempted to face directly some of the social evils which were so prominent a feature of urban, industrialised life. There were plans early in 1914 for further social reform as envisaged in Lloyd George's land reform campaign. These plans were abruptly abandoned at the outbreak of war on 4 August 1914. During the years of conflict which followed, some five million men were to serve in the army. A recent estimate is that 723,000 British soldiers were killed, or died, and millions were wounded and often permanently maimed or disfigured; 160,000 wives lost husbands and over 300,000 children lost their fathers.[1] In addition, some quarter of a million of Empire troops were killed. The Great War remains as a searing experience in the memories of the dwindling few alive today who actually experienced it, and haunts the minds of those who grew up in its shadow in the 1920s and stood with bowed heads for the Two Minutes' Silence, which in those days was observed every year at eleven o'clock on Armistice Day, 11 November. The war was an extraordinary time of national trauma. How far can its progress be linked with industrialisation? Was industrialisation actually speeded up by the war, or was the economy adversely affected by, for example, the interruption of trade? How far was the labour force affected by the war? Was any social reform possible under war conditions?

A basic preliminary point may be made here that only an advanced industrial state such as Britain could have stood the strain of four years of such intense conflict. The war was enormously expensive, not only in manpower, but also in financial terms; income tax was levied at 6/– in the pound in 1918 (up eight times since 1914), while three years after the war had ended the government was paying out

3.5 million war pensions.[2] The national economy was geared directly to war production. Following the shell shortage in early 1915, the Ministry of Munitions was set up with Lloyd George as minister in charge, and extraordinary quantities of munitions were turned out: the Ministry of Munitions headquarters staff alone numbered 25,000.[3] Added to the cost of munitions, of course, was the cost of paying, feeding, clothing, transporting, and hospitalisation of the troops, together with the expense of building the ships required to replace the heavy losses due to U-boat attacks, especially in the spring of 1917. The day-to-day costs of the war mounted remorselessly, and the government was forced to borrow abroad, so that by 1918 Britain was heavily in debt to the United States, with consequences to be noted in the next chapter. Over the whole period of the war, national expenditure went up six times. The national debt increased from £650 million in 1914 to £7,435 million in 1919.[4]

In more specific terms, the staple industries of iron and steel, coal mining, engineering, and shipbuilding were under the greatest pressure, for obvious reasons. Here the government faced a dilemma: on the one hand, the demand for manpower in the trenches was immense, but on the other hand, it was vital to maintain the flow of war production. As a result, many of the miners who joined up in the early stages of the war had to be recalled and returned to the mines. In spite of the remarkable flood of volunteers to the colours in 1914 and 1915, it became necessary to introduce conscription in May 1916, something utterly opposed by Liberal opinion in peacetime. By the end of the war, conscription applied to all males between the ages of eighteen and fifty-one, with exceptions for exceptional personal circumstances or conscientious objection to war service.

Inevitably the government was forced increasingly into collectivisation. First the railways were placed under government control, then later the South Wales coal mines, and afterwards the mining industry as a whole. By 1916 government controls extended to the export of chemicals (vital for the manufacture of explosives), to the supply of sandbags, to the purchase and distribution of sugar, and even to the purchase of quantities of wheat from abroad (though this was kept secret).[5]

Meanwhile, as early as 8 August 1916, the government acquired very extensive powers under the Defence of the Realm Act (DORA) (extended in 1915 and 1916), enabling it to issue regulations and to try offenders by court martial. Later in the war, in 1917, the government took on further powers with the introduction of a limited scheme of food rationing. By the end of the war, the government had direct control of 218 munition factories, and government regulations (often the product of the much-disliked DORA) were to be encountered on all sides. Collectivism was conceived to be wartime necessity, adopted on an *ad hoc* basis, and not intended to set precedents for the future. Nor did it, as will be seen in the following chapter.

If the exigencies of war forced government action in this way, similar change was inevitable in industry itself at the point of production. The enormous demand for munitions meant that it was vital to increase the numbers of workers in industry. This meant the introduction of dilution, that is, breaking down skilled operations whenever possible into a number of semi-skilled or unskilled jobs which could be undertaken by women. By March 1915 the engineering union (the AEU) had agreed to this by the Shells and Fuses Agreement. This was followed by a conference at the Treasury, and a further agreement, the Treasury Agreement, provided that trade unions engaged on war work would forgo the right to strike, and refer all disputes to arbitration. The Munitions of War Act, 1915, put much that had been agreed into statutory form: strikes and lock-outs in war industries were forbidden, arbitration became compulsory, profits were to be limited, trade union restrictions on output were suspended, and no worker was to leave a job in munitions without a leaving certificate of consent from his employer (a provision much disliked by the workers).

In this way the government secured substantial control over war production, but the necessity remained of securing an adequate supply of recruits to the front. As a means to this end, the National Register of all males and females between the ages of fifteen and sixty-five was compiled, based on a special census held in August 1915. As the information came in, the names of men of military age were noted carefully, and an asterisk placed against those in essential occupations. Some suspicion was aroused by the compilation of the register, since it was thought that it could possibly be a first step towards conscription; though the prime minister denied that this was so. The register was followed by a further attempt to increase recruitment, the Derby Scheme, whereby men were invited to attest their willingness to serve, if and when called upon to do so; there was also to be a scheme for exemptions, and single men were to be called up before married men. Unfortunately, in the White Paper published at the beginning of 1916, it was made known that only about half of the single men on the National Register had attested, and less than half the married men. Clearly, the blaze of enthusiasm which had characterised the first few months of war had died down, and this made conscription inevitable. As already noted, peacetime Liberal opinion was strongly against conscription as an infringement of personal liberty, and this view was still maintained in wartime by Liberal newspapers such as the *Daily News* and the *Manchester Guardian*; the TUC also strongly opposed it, as they feared it might be followed by industrial conscription. However, by May 1916 conscription had become law, and the way was open for compulsory call-up of men, and also for the employment of more women in the factories and elsewhere.[6] It was necessary, of course, to make provision for men in skilled and reserved occupations, but there was so much friction with the trade unions over this that by December 1916 the government allowed the issue of trade cards by the unions themselves which conferred exemption from service. This was a remarkable accession of authority by trade unions, who could therefore decide whether a man would go to the trenches or not. Dark stories are still told in the Black Country of the bribery which was the result of this concession by the government.

The demands made by the war on the national economy were extraordinary and indeed unprecedented. During the previous century, warfare had become increasingly mechanised, fire power had grown tremendously, and all the major continental powers had built up large conscript armies. This was particularly true of Germany where even the railway system had been constructed with strategic, military aims in mind. Hitherto, Britain had fought wars in Europe with small armies and generous subsidies to her allies, relying on her large navy for protection of her shores. In 1914, Britain's army was miniscule, intended mainly for fighting small-scale colonial wars. Hence the remarkable demands made by the Great War not only on the manpower needed to oppose the large enemy armies, but also on the munitions industry. By the spring of 1915 these demands were becoming painfully apparent. As we have seen, it was vital to obtain the support of the trade unions for the war effort in order to gain maximum war production. More than that, it was essential for the unions and the fledging Labour Party to be brought into the process of government. In May 1915, when Asquith formed a coalition government, a historic step was taken when members of the Labour Party entered government for the first time. Industrialisation had certainly been the parent of the modern trade union movement. Now, under the pressure of war, the offspring of the union movement, the Labour Party, founded only nine years previously, was actually given a share in governing the country.

As might be expected, only minor posts were offered, but nevertheless, it was a significant advance for the party. Arthur Henderson, the chairman of the party, became president of the Board of Education, and unofficial adviser on labour affairs. Two other Labour MPs were also honoured: William Bruce, a miner, gained an under-secretaryship, while G.H. Roberts, a printer, became a government whip.[7] As A.J.P. Taylor has remarked, Henderson's appointment 'was a portent: the industrial working class took a share of power, however slight, for the first time'.[8] Subsequently, in August 1916, Henderson became paymaster general, retaining his place in the cabinet. When Lloyd George became prime minister in December 1916, the coalition government was reconstructed, and a new inner war cabinet with only five members was set up. Henderson was promoted to this war cabinet as minister without portfolio. At the same time, John Hodge of the steel workers became minister of labour, George Barnes of the engineers became minister of pensions, while three other Labour MPs, Roberts, Bruce, and James Parker, were all offered minor posts.[9]

It would be wrong, however, to suppose that the Labour movement as a whole was fully in support of the war. Of the two wings of the movement – the trade unions and the Labour Party – the trade unions were more solidly in support, though determined to preserve their traditional privileges as far as possible, and when making concessions (for example, over dilution, and the right to strike) making it clear that it was for the duration of the war only. The Labour Party suffered more from ideological doubts: for some on the left, the war was a quarrel between imperialist powers in which innocent workers on both sides would be used as cannon-fodder. Certainly there were left-wingers who thought the war was the result of the pre-war treaty system, that it was unnecessary, and that it should be brought to an end as soon as possible. Ramsay MacDonald resigned as leader of the parliamentary party, and he, Philip Snowden, and other members of the left-wing ILP joined with a party of anti-war Liberals to form the Union of Democratic Control (UDC, September 1914). Their programme was for democratic control of foreign policy (i.e. no secret treaties), no annexations, an international organisation for peace, and disarmament.[10]

Nevertheless, the majority of the Labour Party supported Britain's participation in the war, though tension did manifest itself from time to time. This was especially to be seen following the revolution in Russia in March 1917. Lloyd George sent Henderson to Russia to promote good relations with Kerensky's government. When Henderson returned, he supported the idea of sending Labour Party delegates to an international socialist congress in Stockholm (Sweden was a neutral country, of course). It was expected that German socialists would be at the congress, the purpose of which was to discuss peace terms. The Labour Party backed Henderson, but the war cabinet did not. They kept Henderson waiting outside the cabinet room door (the famous 'doormat incident') before calling him in and reproving him. Henderson resigned, but was replaced by George Barnes of the AEU. The Labour Party remained part of the coalition government until the end of the war.

It is important to emphasise that although the Labour Party had its critics of the war, the split in the party was never very wide, and certainly did not amount to the creation of an outright opposition. After conscription had come in, such opposition was confined mostly to conscientious objectors, who numbered about 16,500.[11] MacDonald put the views of the UDC quite clearly: 'We condemn the policy which has produced the war, we do not obstruct the war effort, but our duty is to secure peace at the earliest possible moment.'[12] All the same, by the beginning of 1918, when it seemed that the war might at last be coming to an end, the Labour Party became increasingly interested in securing a just peace settlement, whatever had been the causes of the war. For this reason, in January 1918 the party published a Statement of War Aims, stressing the need for the settlement to be made on democratic lines. It had a good deal in common with President Wilson's Fourteen Points, which it anticipated, and it declared:[13]

> Whatever may have been the causes for which the war was begun, the fundamental purpose of the British Labour Movement in supporting the continuance of the struggle is that the world may henceforth be made safe for democracy.

More detailed proposals included setting up a league of nations and an organisation for settling international disputes; the international trusteeship of African colonies; and international action to solve economic problems such as the supply of raw materials.

This was followed in the same year by a new constitution for the Labour Party drawn up by Henderson and Sidney Webb. The idea was to increase support for the party by permitting individual membership of the local branches (previously membership had been obtained through membership of the affiliated trade unions or socialist societies). This would permit membership by individual middle-class supporters, including women who were about to obtain the parliamentary vote (there were to be four seats on the national executive reserved for women out of a total of twenty-three). Although the LRC had been set up originally 'to promote legislation in the cause of labour' – that is, without reference to any socialist aims – the 1918 constitution had as Clause Four a statement devised by Sidney Webb and intended to attract the support of the middle-class intellectual:[14]

> To secure for the producers by hand or by brain the full fruits of their industry, and the most equitable distribution thereof that may be possible, upon the basis of the common ownership of the means of production and the best possible system of popular administration and control of each industry and service.

There is no evidence to show that the majority of trade unionists were very interested in the nationalisation of the means of production. Their interest lay rather in obtaining a fair day's pay for a fair day's work, and some degree of job security. Nevertheless, Clause Four, with minor variations in wording, was to become a socialist shibboleth for years to come. Gaitskell tried, and failed, to have it removed from the constitution in 1959. His successor, Harold Wilson, remarked that tampering with Clause Four was like trying to remove the Book of Genesis from the Bible. It remained an article of faith for older members of the party, and in fact was printed on every membership card in the 1990s until at last removed by the vote of the membership under the New Labour leader, Tony Blair.

The work of re-establishing the Labour Party so that it might face the coming years of peace with confidence was completed by a new programme of reform published in June 1918 and entitled *Labour and the New Social Order*. This was to form the basis of party policy for many years to come. It proposed the establishment of a new national minimum for all – full employment, with a minimum wage, a minimum standard of working conditions, and a maximum working week of forty-eight hours; the democratic control of industry, that is, a form of nationalisation; a 'revolution in national finance' – meaning the subsidising of social services by heavy taxation of the rich, including a capital levy to pay off part of the costs of the war; and the surplus for the 'common good' – the use of the nation's wealth to expand popular education and the people's culture.[15]

Why should the last two years of war have seen such a flurry of activity on the part of the Labour Party? In the first place, the party's experience of government office, extending even to the inner or war cabinet, gave it an increased self-confidence and hope for a further instalment of political power (it might be remarked incidentally that the Liberal government at the beginning of the war had no particular need for Labour Party support; it was the support of the trade unions that was vital to the war effort, and the Labour Party as the political wing of the unions profited thereby). Then again, the Labour Party was acutely aware of the very serious split in the Liberal Party which occurred when Lloyd George replaced Asquith as prime minister in December 1916. Here was a golden opportunity for Labour Party advance. Further overthrow of the Czarist regime in Russia in 1917 gave great encouragement to supporters of democracy everywhere, and a belief in popular revolution which was to last for years to come before the bitter truth about Stalinism began to sink in (though to the credit of the Labour Party, repeated attempts by the Communist Party of Great Britain, founded 1920, to affiliate to the Labour Party, were rebuffed; the Communist Party's belief in the necessity for violent revolution was a major stumbling block).

However, it should be pointed out that in spite of Clause Four, as suggested earlier, there is little to support the idea that the Labour Party as a whole was becoming permeated by socialist thinking. Its solid support was still in the trade union movement which financed it. The trade unions had certainly grown more powerful during the war, as we shall see very shortly, but this did not make them more socialist. Rather, it made them more collectivist as a result of the state control of the economy during the war, but this is not the same thing as becoming socialist. Class loyalty was probably increased by the greater strength of the unions in the war years, but again this did not necessarily lead to socialist thinking. Labourism rather than socialism was really the major characteristic of the Labour Party in 1918, and at the heart of it was the determination to gain a fairer deal for labour in the fields of employment, housing, and education, rather than a major transformation of society as a whole and a massive redistribution of wealth.[16]

Certainly the trade union movement increased rapidly in size during the war years. Even before the war, its numbers had shot up when the National Insurance Act came into force in 1912, due to the need for working men and women to become members of a friendly society. Many of the larger unions were registered as friendly societies, and their membership improved as a result. Then during the war there was little unemployment to speak of, and the unions benefited still further. The figures are shown in Table 7.1.[17] It is noticeable that the numbers rise sharply during the last two years of war, and the greatest advance of the whole period was in 1919, the first year of peace, which happened to enjoy a brief post-war boom in trade.

Undoubtedly the growth of the trade union movement is one of the most striking social changes brought about by the Great War. The

Table 7.1 Trade union membership, 1912–20

	TU membership (m)	% increase
1912	3.416	8.8
1913	4.135	21.0
1914	4.145	–
1915	4.359	5.0
1916	4.644	6.5
1917	5.499	18.3
1918	6.533	18.5
1919	7.926	21.4
1920	8.348	5.3

war demanded munitions in unprecedented quantities: the British labour force supplied them. The trade unions prospered as a result, their co-operation in achieving the maximum output being crucial in providing sufficient ammunition and weapons for the Western Front. In the first year or so of war, the shortages were acute: there were not even enough uniforms to clothe the early volunteers, and they had to wear temporary uniforms made from Post Office blue serge which looked like prison clothing. The total stock of rifles was less than 800,000, half of them obsolete, and output was less than 2,000 a week. Hand-grenades in November 1914 were still limited in supply to forty a week, the 18-pounder field gun was in short supply, the production of high explosive was negligible, and there was an acute shortage of specialist signals and engineering equipment.[18] All these deficiencies were made good as the war ground on, of course, and by its end the British army was probably the best fighting force in the world. This could not have been achieved without the valiant efforts of the trade union movement which suspended much of its former practices in order to maximise production.

Sidney Webb wrote in detail on this subject in 1917, pointing out the reorganisation of work practices by employers which the actions of the unions had made possible:[19]

> During these fateful two years, the employers in practically all industries have to a greater or lesser degree –
> (i) Changed the process of manufacture, notably so to enable work formerly done by skilled craftsmen to be done by women or labourers;
> (ii) introduced new and additional machinery with the same object;

(iii)   engaged in work or processes formerly done by skilled craftsmen, boys, women, and unapprenticed men;

(iv)   increased the proportion of boys to men;

(v)   substituted piece work and bonus systems for time wages;

(vi)   increased the hours of labour, sometimes refusing any satisfactory addition for overtime, night duty, and Sunday work;

(vii)   speeded up production, getting rid of all customary understandings among the workers of what constituted a fair day's work;

(viii)   suppressed demarcation disputes and ignored all claims, whether to kinds of work or particular jobs, of particular unions, particular grades, particular sets of workmen, or a particular sex.

This is a remarkable list of sacrifices made by the unions, and no doubt glosses over some of the difficulties which had arisen in practice. Nevertheless, Webb went on to claim that a large section of British industry had learned from experience the benefits of large-scale production, of standardisation and long runs, of team work and specialisation, and not grudging the larger earnings brought by piecework effort. In fact, he claimed that war production was turning out more than twice the product per operative employed than before the war; while labour costs were considerably lower than under the old system.

Sidney Webb was hardly the man to indulge in foolish exaggeration, and much of what he described was no doubt true enough, but inevitably glitches appeared in the system from time to time. Although strikes were officially forbidden, they did break out; for example, in July 1915 the South Wales miners went on strike. The government took the loss of production so seriously that it intervened at once, the miners' demands were met, and work resumed after only five days. There were occasional rumblings of discontent on 'Red Clydeside', too, where syndicalism still had its supporters. In 1917, there was considerable industrial discontent following a hard winter when there were shortages of both fuel and food. In Rochdale, a strike in April spread by May to forty-eight towns, involving 200,000 men, resulting in a loss of 1.5 million working days.[20]

A further manifestation of industrial unrest was provided by the development of a national shop stewards' movement. Many unionists on the shop-floor thought that their union officials at the highest level were becoming increasingly remote from them, and that, for example, national wage agreements negotiated by union leaders took insufficient account of local conditions and problems. Shop stewards therefore assumed an increased importance as representatives of the rank-and-file trade union members. In some places they formed workers' committees, and these became the basis of a strongly left-wing national movement which held four national conferences in all. For a time, the shop stewards' movement looked like developing into a rival movement to the trade unions. It was strongest in the engineering industry, where resentment against dilution was understandably strong, and many of its leaders were syndicalist or Marxist in outlook. It owed much to shop-floor grievances, to the feeling that the employers, the government, and trade union leaders were all in league together against the ordinary worker. Although it had some influence during the war, it declined rapidly as a force thereafter.[21]

Aware as always of the need to maintain industrial peace, the government did all it could to avoid protracted disputes. Nationwide pay settlements were part of this strategy, and by the end of the war, national pay agreements existed for the railways, the mining industry, and in most sections of the transport system. A further attempt to avoid pay disputes came after the Whitley Committee in 1917 recommended joint committees of employers and unions (a precedent had been set, of course, by the wage boards set up in the previous century, together with those established under the Sweated Industries Act, 1909). These committees were duly appointed, and seventy-three in all were in existence by 1921. They did not achieve very much, but remain as an example of government wartime efforts to maintain good labour relations in industry. It is evident that the war had profound efforts on industry, its labour force, the trade unions, and the Labour Party. Some of these results were of a temporary nature, but others, especially those relating to the Labour movement, took lasting effect. The other great aspect of social change during the war was the changing role of women.

The most striking feature of this change was the much greater employment of women during the war, due to the serving of so many men in the armed forces. As early as spring 1915 Lloyd George realised that large numbers of women would have to be employed in industry, and one result of this was the agreement for dilution with the unions which has already been described. By the end of the war, 947,000 women were engaged in munitions work, some of it both unpleasant and dangerous. Working with high explosive could result in TNT poisoning which turned the skin yellow – women so affected were nicknamed 'canaries'. More than 300 women died as result of

TNT poisoning and of explosions.[22] The hours worked in munitions were very long: shifts were of twelve hours or more. A report on the health of munitions workers put this very strongly:[23]

> A day begins at 4 or even 3.30 a.m. for work at 6 a.m., followed by 14 hours in the factory, and another two and a half hours on the journey back may end at 10 or 10.30 p.m. in a home or lodging where the prevailing degree of overcrowding precludes all possibility of comfortable rest.

This may be to exaggerate, of course – certainly not all women workers spent five hours a day travelling to and from work – but undoubtedly the work itself was arduous. The compensation lay in the wages. A starting wage might be 30/– a week, and £2 a week by the end of the war; an assistant forewoman might make £3 a week or more. These figures were a great advance on the woman's average wage before the war of 11/7 a week, though it must be remembered that the cost of living rose during the war, especially during the last two years.[24]

Of course, women were employed in a number of occupations other than munitions. All in all, the number of women in full-time jobs during the war rose from 5.96 million in 1914 to 7.31 million in 1918. In metalworking, there was a rise from 170,000 to 894,000, in transport from 18,200 to 117,200 (women porters and bus conductresses became a familiar sight), in commerce from 505,200 to 934,500 (including a rise in banking from 1,500 to 37,600), and in national and local government from 262,000 to 460,000. On the other hand, employment in domestic service fell from 1,658,000 to 1,250,000.[25] The vast majority of these jobs represented a gain for women in real terms, and their pay rates edged up from about half that of men to about two-thirds. However, much of the employment was strictly for the duration: this was so especially in the munitions industry, and women doing a man's job gave it up automatically when he returned home from the forces.

Women's contribution to the war effort was widely praised, and it was clear that this had to be recognised by the granting at last of the vote (the pre-war suffragettes had been among the most enthusiastic supporters of the war). Some change in the franchise was in any case unavoidable. Not only were about a third of adult men still barred from voting, but many of those who did have the vote had lost their residential qualification for voting as a result of service in France and elsewhere. It was therefore increasingly urgent for the whole matter of the right to vote to be reviewed. As early as 1916 a Speaker's

Conference was held to consider the matter. In January 1917 it reported in favour of 'some measure of woman suffrage'. One immediate problem was to decide at what age women should be given the vote. They were in a majority in the nation, and to give votes to all women of twenty-one and over, would be to allow women voters to outnumber male voters. This was thought to be somehow wrong. Finally, it was agreed to give votes to all men of twenty-one and over, based on a residence qualification, and to all women of thirty and over, provided they or their husbands had the residential property qualifications for voting in local government elections. In February 1918 the Representation of the People Act was duly passed.

This act was followed in the next year by the Sex Disqualification (Removal) Act, which laid it down that 'no person should be disqualified by sex or marriage from the exercise of any public function or from being appointed to any civil or judicial office or post'. Women could now serve on juries or become magistrates for the first time. They could also become members of most professions, though they were still unable to become ministers in the Church of England or members of the Stock Exchange. For the first time, a woman MP appeared in the House of Commons in 1919. She was a Conservative, Lady Astor, born in Virginia in the United States. She was elected for Plymouth in succession to her husband who had been raised to the peerage. In fact, she was not the first woman elected to the House. This was Countess Markiewitcz (Constance Gore-Booth), a Sinn Feiner who with the rest of her party refused to take her seat. Lady Astor became a well-known figure in the House of Commons, though relatively few women followed her example in standing for parliament. However, Margaret Bondfield, a union official, who was a Labour MP in 1923–4, and again in 1926–31, became the first woman cabinet minister as the minister of labour, 1929–31.

The problem that arises at this point is how to assess the contribution made by the war to change in women's roles – moreover, to determine how far their roles did indeed change. For some women, obviously enough, the major change was to acquire the status of widowhood, and to face the struggle of bringing up a young family without a father. For the many who went into war work, for most of them for the time being there was an improved standard of living and more money to spend (middle-class wives complained of women munition workers wearing fur coats). Greater financial freedom could mean a greater feeling of independence. According to the *New Statesman* for 23 June 1917, working women were displaying a more critical spirit:[26]

> They appear more alert, more critical of the conditions under which they work, more ready to make a stand against injustice than their pre-war selves, or their proto-types. They have a keener appetite for experience and pleasure and a tendency quite new to their class to protest against 'wrongs' even before they become 'intolerable'.

This is as may be – it is typical of the *New Statesman* of the time – but as women workers were in great demand, especially after conscription, this probably encouraged speaking-up; and a factory inspector in his report for 1916 also commented on the 'new self-confidence engendered in women' by the new conditions of work.[27] A similar spirit of independence must have been encouraged in those serving as nurses away from home, or in the Women's Auxiliary Army Corps (40,850 in number), or even in the British Expeditionary Force (17,000 in all by August 1918), or in the Women's Land Army. Any kind of service away from home and freedom from parental supervision could promote the spirit of independence.

The difficulty is to determine how far this change in attitude continued after the war, given the fact that women left their wartime employment *en masse* as soon as the war ended. Working-class women had always worked before the war, of course, both before marriage and often after marriage once free from family commitments; they continued to do so during the war though often at better rates of pay and earning more than before. All this ended when, as Ivor Novello's wartime song, 'Keep the Home Fires Burning', had it, the boys came home. It is true that the grant of the vote was a national recognition of women's rights, but it meant little or nothing to the young working-class woman. What was left was the feeling of greater freedom experienced by older working-class women during the war, at a time when families were growing smaller (contraceptives were issued to the troops during the war as prophylactic devices). It is hard to believe that the greater social freedom for working-class women during the war vanished entirely in the ensuing post-war period.

The same can be said – and perhaps with more force – of middle-class women. They were more likely than their working-class sisters to go into nursing, office jobs such as secretarial work, banking, and the civil service. Here, too, having a job could give greater freedom, and the day of the chaperone was at last over. According to the *Daily Mail*, as early as September 1915, 'No woman is in greater demand than the shorthand typist', and the paper went on to describe the wartime business girl:[28]

The war-time business girl is to be seen any night dining out alone or with a friend in the moderately-priced restaurants of London. Formerly she would never have had her evening meal in town unless in the company of a male friend. But now with money and without men she is more and more beginning to dine out.

There is something a little fanciful in this – few shorthand typists actually stayed on in town to dine in a restaurant in London; they had their lunch in an ABC or Lyons teashop, or took sandwiches to the office – but the idea of middle-class women dining alone in the evening has more substance. For middle-class women who read the newspapers, the gaining of the vote had rather more significance, and so did the Sex Disqualification (Removal) Act which opened up fresh avenues to women already used to playing an active part in local affairs.

Once more there is the problem that a certain degree of bourgeois freedom had already been gained before the war. Middle-class women already moved freely in society, giving and attending dinners, going to the theatre, lectures, concerts, art galleries, and supporting numerous good causes (as readers of E.M. Forster will be aware). Women like Beatrice Webb, Helen Bosanquet, and the Pankhursts were subject to relatively few restrictions in their social life. Mrs Webb was an habitual smoker before the war, while the Bloomsbury group (which included the Stracheys, Virginia Woolf, J.M. Keynes, and the Bells) were extraordinarily free and easy in their drinking and smoking. To judge from Vanessa Bell's correspondence, her conversation was not lacking in four-letter words.[29] Of course, the Bloomsburies were a highly exceptional London group with what was then called a Bohemian outlook, literary, artistic, self-indulgent, and very comfortably well off. For most of them, the war was an inconvenience, though obviously a matter for concern, especially for the men once conscription was introduced since this required a decision whether to serve or not to serve. Nevertheless, their attitudes and behaviour set certain standards for a certain tiny sector of London society. It is hard to believe that their freedom to do as they liked was much affected by the war. It was already extensive.

Rather greater changes were experienced by those lower middle-class women who were employed in offices during the war. Feminine employment in secretarial work actually increased after 1918, and the general employment of women in offices, banks, the civil service, insurance, and local government became commonplace. Commerce and government were the major areas where the recruitment of men had been heaviest during the war, so that many women wartime substitutes stayed on when peace came. Hence, between the wars a large proportion of all office workers in the City of London and other great cities were women. Among the multitudes who made their way across London Bridge and into the City between eight and nine in the morning and flowed back again in the late afternoon, young women were prominent. One distinct change in their appearance since 1914 was apparent: many more now used lipstick and powder, and their skirts were much shorter. Among the men, bowler hats and trilbies had replaced the pre-war top-hat. The war had brought a noticeable change in attire, especially in the costumes of women.

Finally, it is possible to argue that since social freedoms had been advancing even before the war – witness the suffragette agitation – the war simply confirmed the importance of women's place in society and their right not only to vote but also to greater choice in careers, especially in the professions and in parliament. For many working-class women, however, the return of peacetime conditions simply meant a loss of the high wages earned in munitions. There may be some truth in this interpretation of events, but it would be unwise to place too much emphasis on it and to underestimate the liberating effect of the greater individual freedom gained by many. The need to be chaperoned in public had disappeared, women smoked more openly in public, visited public houses more freely, went out alone more often. All this was a positive gain, and the giving of the vote acknowledged the value of women's contribution to society. Thus the path was paved to the greater freedom of the 1920s including the absurdities of the 'flapper' (the contemporary slang term for the unconventional, lively young girl of the time) with her high heels, short skirt, permanent-waved hair, and long cigarette holder, adept at dancing the Charleston – scarcely a figure to be encountered in the pre-war period.

One great feature of the pre-war scene to which lengthy attention was paid in the previous chapter was social reform. This necessarily was absent for most of the war period, and it was simply not possible to continue with the reforms envisaged by Lloyd George in the last days of peace in 1914. Housing in particular was neglected, and the pre-war housing shortage grew worse, so much so that as early as 1915 it was thought necessary to peg house rents at 1914 levels by the Rent and Mortgage Interest (Rent Restriction) Act, 1915. By 1916, ideas of reconstruction after the war began to be discussed, and Asquith had already appointed a cabinet committee on the subject. In March 1917 this was reconstructed with the new prime minister, Lloyd George, as chairman. Later in the year, the new Ministry of Reconstruction was set up to consider how social and economic conditions could be improved after the war. The new ministry was headed by Dr Christopher Addison, and the main items under consideration were health, housing, education, and unemployment insurance. Of these, health was still of major concern: pre-war unease at the possibility of national degeneration had not gone away, and of the 2 million or so men examined under the Military Services Acts, 1916, only 36 per cent were placed in Grade I, that is, 'of full normal standard of health and strength'. According to the Medical Board's report:[30]

> of every nine men of military age in Great Britain, on the average, three were perfectly fit and healthy; two were on a definitely infirm plane of health and strength whether from some disability or some failure in development; three were incapable of undergoing more than a very moderate degree of physical exertion and could almost (in view of their age) be described with justice as physical wrecks; and the remaining man was a chronic invalid with a precarious hold on life.

There was an urgent need for the creation of a Ministry of Health which would unite under one authority all the various health services supplied by so many different agencies such as the local education authorities, the poor law guardians, the public health authorities, and the insurance commissions. The case for establishing such a new ministry, even in wartime, was put forward by Lord Rhonda, president of the Board of Local Government in 1917, but the new Ministry of Health was not set up till 1919, being in effect the result of a merging of the Board of Local Government with the insurance commissions.

Education fared somewhat better with the introduction of an education bill in August 1917, although in the earlier years of the war the state system of education appears to have suffered a number of setbacks. It has been claimed that government pre-war plans for an increase in the educational grant were dropped when war began, that there was much early leaving to work either on farms or in industry, that medical inspection in schools was cut, and that attendance at evening classes was seriously reduced.[31] In fact, though there was widespread early leaving during the war – a figure of 600,000 over three years was mentioned in the House of Commons in August 1917 – early leaving was common *before* the war. Although the school leaving age was fourteen, about half left between twelve and fourteen, sometimes to become half-timers, sometimes because they had reached the minimum educational standard to start work, and sometimes because they had made the minimum number of attendances.[32] As for medical inspection, although the number of children inspected was cut in 1916 by 28 per cent, the medical inspection service was well maintained in a number of areas and even developed. In the year 1917–18, about 70 per cent of the normal numbers were inspected; the physical condition of the children improved owing to the rise in the standard of living, while the numbers of school meals provided for needy children dropped from 422,401 for the year to March 1915 to 60,582 for the year ending March 1918.[33] As for staffing, there were shortages, of course, but women, some of whom had been compulsorily retired on marriage, came back into the classroom, so did retired male teachers, and even, occasionally, disabled ex-servicemen. It is important, therefore, not to exaggerate the difficulties in the schools during the war, and in Birmingham, for example, where the educational authority was the second largest in the country, early leaving does not seem to have been much of a problem, while the dental and medical services in this city positively improved.[34]

It would be unwise in view of this evidence to stress too heavily the decline in the state educational system during the war, and it is important to note that by 1916 a substantial interest in educational reform was developing.[35] This was to lead to Fisher's bill in 1917. In its first form, the bill aroused the opposition of the local educational authorities, and it had to be withdrawn, redrawn, and re-presented. It finally became law in 1918. The act contained a number of important reforms. In the first place, it laid it down that 'children and young persons shall not be debarred from receiving the benefits of any form of education by which they are capable of profiting through inability to pay fees'. A start was made on this by abolishing all fees in elementary schools, and local authorities were required to submit proposals for schemes covering all types of education in their areas. The school-leaving age was fixed at fourteen without exception, so that the half-time system was at last abolished. Government grants to local authorities were increased, and so were teachers' salaries. One new element in the act was to be the introduction of part-time continuation classes for those leaving school until they were eighteen.[36]

It has been suggested that the Fisher Education Act, 1918, merely operated as a measure to abolish the half-time system,[37] but its significance is greater than this. It is true that the rather grandiose schemes for compulsory part-time day education classes for fifteen-to-eighteen-year-olds were abandoned as a result of the national economy cuts (the 'Geddes axe') introduced in 1922. Such a system of post-school continuing education has failed to be implemented even yet. Nevertheless, the Fisher act was a worthy attempt to remedy some of the defects in the elementary school system; and it led to further demands by the Labour Party for secondary education for all, and not just for the few who were bright enough to obtain free schol- arship places in the county secondary schools established after the Education Act, 1902. Certain post-war social reforms may properly be ascribed to the effects of the war, of course, an obvious example being the housing acts; but of the reforms passed during the war itself, the Fisher act is the most outstanding. It is understandable that until the guns stopped firing, the demands for war production allowed only limited attention to be given to the need for post-war construction. It was also a tragedy, as will be seen in the next chapter, that the Great Depression of the inter-war period prevented the continuance of the reforms in prospect in 1914; and the ills attendant on industrialisa- tion such as unemployment, in particular, were not only not solved but were exacerbated by the loss of overseas trade.

Efforts have been made in previous chapters to give some indica- tion of contemporary attitudes and values. For the period of World War I, the nation was substantially united in the belief that the war had to be fought and won – the great rush of volunteers in the first twelve months is a sufficient testimony to this – and only in 1917 was there a certain amount of restlessness and complaint among the working classes at the high cost of foodstuffs.[38] As for political oppo- sition to the war, it was very limited; the Union of Democratic Control, which has already been mentioned, did not seek to impede the war effort, but merely advocated a negotiated peace as soon as possible, believing as it did that the war had somehow been caused by secret diplomacy and the pre-war alliance system. Once conscription was introduced, provision was made for those refusing military service to register as conscientious objectors (COs). They numbered 16,500 in all, of whom 1,298 refused all service, combatant or non-combat- ant; they were sent to prison, where about seventy of them died as a result of ill treatment. Most of the COs were Christians who took their religion seriously; others objected on high moral principle. 'Conchies' were much disliked and abused. Indeed, any men of military age and not in uniform might be awarded a white feather in the street as a sign of cowardice (it became necessary to distribute badges to men in reserved occupations and engaged in war work). Some, of course, were well connected, and better able to withstand public hostility. They included the philosopher Bertrand Russell (Lord Russell), the author Lytton Strachey, and the painter Duncan Grant, close friend of Vanessa Bell. (Grant accepted non-combatant duties as a farm labourer.) Apart therefore from the tiny numbers of UDC supporters and the COs, it is very difficult to find examples of any significant body of opponents of the war. Middle-class intellectuals wrote in favour of the war effort, convinced of the justice of the Allied cause, while a number of leading authors were engaged in providing propaganda for use in friendly and neutral countries, working under the direction of Charles Masterman in the secret Department of Information.[39]

Thus, there was a generally held belief that the war was fought in a good moral cause. It was not simply or solely a matter of restraining and defeating an aggressor power which before the war had taken up a belligerent stance in European affairs under the active leadership of Kaiser William II. There was also the fact that Germany had violated the neutrality of Belgium which had been guaranteed by all the European powers (including Britain) in 1839. How far Britain was obligated by the terms of the 1839 treaty to defend Belgium is not entirely clear, but the German invasion certainly strengthened the British case for declaring war. So the moral case was strong; it was a war (or so it was thought) to defeat German militarism, a war against a ferocious and brutal enemy. Propaganda against the 'German Hun' was strengthened after the German use of poison gas in 1915, and the increase in attacks from the air on Britain by Zeppelin and Gotha bombers. For some, the war also provided an opportunity, when it came to an end, to return to the old liberal values which had seemed in some danger in the unrest before the war. For others, it represented the chance for noble self-sacrifice, for giving one's life in defence of great, personal ideals – the 'great sacrifice', a notion sanctified in the wording of many war memorials after the war. A sombre reminder of this aspect of wartime attitudes is provided by an inscription in the entrance hall to the University of Birmingham's Great Hall, which was used in the Great War as an emergency hospital:[40]

> From August, 1914 to April, 1919 these buildings were used by the military authorities as the 1st Southern Hospital. Within these walls men died for their country. Let those who come after live in the same service.

Religious idealism, the idea of the Christian soldier, was strong, but there were also those who lost their faith among the horrors of trench warfare, and there was a marked increase in interest in spiritualism and in communication beyond the grave.

Towards the end of the war, there was a shift in emphasis to the need to preserve the binding nature of treaties, to foster democracy, and above all, perhaps, to set up some sort of international organisation to stop such an appalling conflict from breaking out again. This kind of thinking is clearly to be seen in the Labour Party's Statement of War Aims, and in President Wilson's Fourteen Points. This is understandable enough, as greater awareness spread of conditions on the Western Front, and of the military stalemate there in spite of major offensives costing many thousands of lives. Lofty ideals of honour, heroism, and self-sacrifice became muted. Sometimes this change is seen in the change in tone in the remarkable amount of poetry published in the war years – according to Catherine Reilly, some 2,225 poets were published in the war years[41] – a marked change from the idealism of Rupert Brook in 1914 to the doom-laden disillusion of Siegfried Sassoon and Wilfred Owen at the end of the war. This change is really more apparent than real: idealistic poems were written long after 1914, and in particular they revived noticeably after the Germans began their spring offensive in 1918.

However, it is undoubtedly true that war weariness became increasingly obvious towards the end of hostilities; but all the same, much of the war poetry became well known only after peace had been restored. John Bourne has pointed out that Owen was unknown and largely unread during the war, and likewise Sassoon was barely known and only marginally more widely read.[42] One might also add that the war poetry can hardly be held to reflect the feelings and attitudes of the average soldier, deeply moving as much of it is. Poets by definition are both imaginative and sensitive, and the war poets have had a profound effect in defining images of the Great War. Nevertheless, the cartoonist Bruce Bairnsfather deserves an honoured place as the creator of the average Tommy in his famous cartoon of a private soldier lighting his pipe with the caption, ''Arf a mo', Kaiser' – the British Tommy being that legendary character who slogged on philosophically in what C.E. Montague was later to call the 'life of mud, stench, and underground gloom'.[43] Only after the war, and especially after the post-war boom and general euphoria were over, did the dam burst, and disillusion and despair break forth, as will be seen in the next chapter.

Thus, the war had a profound effect upon the nation's thinking and feelings. This effect had its roots in the sufferings of the troops in France and elsewhere, and was hardly the ongoing consequence of industrialisation. Yet industrialism played its part in that it fell to industry to meet the enormous demands made on it by the war in the form of munitions and other war supplies. This in turn had two major social consequences – the increased influence of the trade unions and of the Labour Party, and the greater freedom won by women in both the social and political spheres. Thus, in this unplanned and perhaps unpredictable way, the Great War resulted in two massive changes operating through the machinery of an industry geared to wartime production. One other consequence of importance deserves comment and has already been touched upon: this is the concern for the health and condition of the working population. The poor physique of some of the British troops was commented on not only by the medical authorities, as we have seen, but also by the more robust Canadian and Australian troops in France. C.E. Montague wrote both defensively and bitterly on this subject in 1922:[44]

> Our men could only draw on such funds of nerve and physique, knowledge and skill, as we had put into the bank for them. Not they, but their rulers and 'betters' had lost their heads in the joy of making money fast out of steam, and so made half our nation slum dwellers.

So, in Montague's bleak and somewhat jaundiced view, industrialisation still had much to answer for, a prime cause of the stunted nature of many of the urban working classes.

From the viewpoint of the present generation, the most poignant images of the Great War are those based on photographs of men struggling in Flanders mud, columns of blinded soldiers being led away from the line in single file, men going over the top, tanks straddling trenches, and desolate landscapes full of blasted tree stumps and shell-holes – the Western Front in all its dreary horror. Survivors carried such memories to the grave. In the early post-war years they would know, of course, that trade unions had become of greater importance, that the Labour Party was more influential in politics, and that the status of women had somehow altered since the war. What very few could have realised was the extent of the great economic changes brought about by the war – changes in overseas trade which were to have profound effects on the great staple industries which were the backbone of the British economy, giving employment to millions. Industrialisation overseas, especially in the USA and in Japan, proceeded unchecked during the war, scooping up market after market. Textiles, coal, iron and steel, shipbuilding were all gravely affected, with dire social consequences in the inter-war period. Of course, overseas competition in all those industries was nothing new: the threat to Britain's economic supremacy was already known and acknowledged before the war. But the war provided a great opportunity for Britain's industrial rivals to surge ahead. The results of this further phase of world industrialisation will be examined in the next chapter. The British people had endured much, but they could hardly have anticipated the social strains which industry's failure to meet the threat of foreign competition would inflict upon them between the wars. During the war, unemployment had ceased to be a problem and had become minimal, so that poor law expenditure had reached remarkably low levels. Between the wars, the twin spectres of unemployment and of poverty were to rise again.

8   The inter-war years, 1918–39

Some indication was given at the end of the last chapter of the fate which awaited the British ex-serviceman in the twenty years of peace before war came again. As it happened, the war had given a temporary boost to the staple industries already challenged in overseas markets by 1914. Textiles, iron and steel, coal mining, shipbuilding, all were kept in full production during the war, and indeed for a year or so after the war. The post-war boom came to an end in 1920, but for a time it appeared that pre-war prosperity had returned. Old trade routes abroad reopened, while consumer goods in short supply during the war years suddenly appeared on the market again; the returning troops had their gratuities to spend. By the end of 1920, depression set in, and unemployment increased. In the mid-1920s, conditions began to improve, only to fade again following the Wall Street Crash in America in 1929, and the development of a world depression in trade. The result here was the so-called Great Depression of the early 1930s, when unemployment reached the three million mark. The 1930s as a whole were later to become in the popular imagination the 'wasted years', the 'low, dishonest decade', and even 'the devil's decade' (the last two expressions reflected the subsequent distaste for the failures in foreign policy of the time). Conditions improved after 1932, and rearmament from 1936 onwards stimulated economic recovery, but it was of a limited nature, and there was a minor slump in 1938. When war came in September 1939 there were still 1.25 million out of work.[1]

The basic causes of the depression in the staple industries are well established and have already been touched upon: the USA and Japan, in particular, were able to take advantage of Europe's being at war to gain new markets. But there was more to it than this: Britain's major industries were set in their ways and slow to equip themselves to meet the increased competition overseas. The cotton industry, for example, failed to change over to the ring-spinning used in other countries, and much of its machinery was ageing badly. Meanwhile, both Japan and India employed more modern machinery to increase their production of cotton textiles. The steel industry had over-invested in the open hearth process which proved to be not as cheap as the Bessemer converter. The coal industry was old fashioned in its techniques and organisation. There were more than 2,000 mines worked by more than 1,000 separate companies, transport was still primitive, and output below that of other countries. In addition, oil fuel was replacing coal in steamships. The overseas markets of the coal industry, which were of vital importance to its economic well-being, were shrinking – Italy taking more coal from Germany, while Germany was beginning to use more lignite as fuel, and reduce imports so as to reduce her debts. As the textile and iron and steel industries at home declined, so their demand for coal also diminished. The coal industry therefore faced reduced demand both at home and abroad. The shipbuilding industry at first built record numbers of ships to replace those lost in the war (2 million tons in 1920), but in 1933, a record low tonnage of ships was launched – 133,000 tons. Thus, Britain's major industries all suffered in varying degrees not only from the increased competition from abroad, but also from increasingly out-of-date machinery and methods.

The social consequences of this decline in the staple industries were dire. Their concentration into relatively limited geographical areas – Clydeside, South Wales, Lancashire, Yorkshire, the north-east, and Cumbria – meant that heavy unemployment became endemic in these areas for most of the inter-war period. These became known as the Depressed Areas, renamed Special Areas after 1934 (in deference to the feelings of the unfortunate workers in these regions). Much of the social distress of the inter-war years – the unemployment, the dole, the means test, the hunger marches – has its origins in these areas. This is where what Mowat calls 'the myth of the hungry thirties' grew up, with its public images of gaunt, shabbily dressed men and women loitering about on street corners without work. J.B. Priestley's *English Journey* (1934) has a striking description of Jarrow, the town famous for the march of its unemployed to London in 1936:[2]

> One out of two shops appeared to be permanently closed. Wherever we went, there were men hanging about, not scores of them, but hundreds and thousands of them. The whole town looked as if it had entered a perpetual penniless Black Sabbath. The men wore the drawn masks of prisoners of war.

On his visit to nearby Stockton-on-Tees, Priestley commented on the grass growing in Stockton shipyards, and observed that the real town was finished, like a theatre kept open merely for the sale of drinks in the bars and chocolates in the corridors.[3]

In fact, conditions such as these were not to be found all over Britain. On the contrary, industrial areas such as the West Midlands enjoyed a mild prosperity due to the development of the so-called 'new industries'. Some of these had begun to develop even before the war and they expanded significantly between the wars. They included the motor industry, the electrical industry, the aircraft industry, chemicals, rubber, food processing, rayon, and films.[4] Their principal market was the home market rather than markets overseas. They required semi-skilled or unskilled labour to work modern, electrically driven machinery; steam power was not required. Hence they could be located away from coalfields, and in fact anywhere, given a supply of electrical power, good communications, and plentiful local labour, preferably cheap female labour. The new industries grew and flourished in London and the home counties, and in the Midlands. The value of output of all these industries was about 6.5 per cent of all British industry in 1907; in 1930, it was 16.3 per cent. The motor car industry, for example, grew annually by about 10 per cent between 1923 and 1935. The national grid was constructed in the 1930s, and output of electricity doubled between 1931 and 1937. As the production of electric fires, cookers, irons, radios, and vacuum cleaners increased, domestic consumers of electricity increased elevenfold between 1920 and 1938.[5] There was a building boom in the 1930s – for example, 314,000 houses were built in 1934 (the housing industry will be considered later in this chapter). New houses built in the 1930s were supplied with electric lighting and power as a matter of course. All in all, for those living away from the Depressed Areas, the reduction in the cost of foodstuffs, and the consequent rise in real wages and the standard of living, resulted in a mild prosperity, very different from life in the older centres of industry.

Industrialisation in the third and fourth decades of the twentieth century therefore produced some strange contrasts in the mode of life of the British working classes. Those whose livelihood depended on the staple industries were faced with continued unemployment and a life on the dole, with often little prospect of alternative employment; many mining villages, especially in Durham and Northumberland, were single-industry villages, and when the pits closed there was no other form of employment available locally. In the more prosperous Midlands, London, and south-east England, jobs were much more plentiful in the new industries and the ever-growing service industries. Since unemployment in the traditional industries was on such an unprecedented scale, it weighed heavily on the public conscience, and has certainly helped to create public memories of the 1930s (in particular) as a period of gloom and despair. In fact, this can be quite misleading. For many of those in work, the 1930s were a time of improved prosperity, although darkened by worries about the international situation and the threat of war. We shall return to the problem of assessing just how widespread poverty really was later in this chapter. In the meanwhile, it is necessary to ask what the inter-war governments did about the social problems of the day: what about housing? What about public health? What was done to help the unemployed? And what other areas of social need were explored and remedies sought?

Housing and public health

It has already been noted that there was a mounting shortage of houses before the Great War, and that very little domestic building was undertaken during the war itself. By 1918 it was estimated that the housing shortage had risen to 600,000.[6] In Birmingham, for example, where the housing situation was actually better than in some other industrial cities, a pre-war survey showed that there were about 200,000 inhabitants still housed in 43,366 back-to-backs. There was no separate water supply in 42,020 houses, and 58,028 had no separate lavatories.[7] Lloyd George's slogan of 'Homes fit for heroes' therefore had simple and direct relevance for many soldiers coming home to be demobbed. Once the new Ministry of Health began operations (it was virtually the only consequence of the setting up of the Ministry of Reconstruction), a start could be made on the massive task of house building. Addison's Housing and Town Planning Act, 1919, was the first of a succession of housing acts in the immediate post-war period. The act gave subsidies both to local authorities and private builders, and under its terms about 213,000 houses were built (they were very costly houses, too: the government paid £800 for houses costing only £300 only a year later). In 1923 the new Conservative government passed another housing act, Chamberlain's Housing Act, 1923, which gave another subsidy to private builders: another 438,000 houses were built. In 1924, under the first Labour government, a further act – Wheatley's Housing Act – led to the building of an additional 520,000 houses (this act increased the subsidy to local authorities for building at controlled rents, and is generally reckoned to be the major social reform achieved by the short-lived Labour government of 1924). In the 1930s building continued, encouraged by the lower cost of building materials, especially in the Midlands, London, and the south-east. In Birmingham, for example, the Corporation built 51,681 houses, providing accommodation for some 200,000 occupants, while private enterprise built 59,744 houses – a total from both sectors of 111,425. It was estimated that by 1939, about a third of the population of the one million inhabitants of Birmingham lived in houses built since 1918. Only 18.8 per cent of the city's working classes still lived in the central slum area in 1938, compared with 27.6 per cent in 1921.[8]

Nationally in the years between the wars, local authorities built 1.1 million houses, while private builders built 400,000 houses with government subsidies, and 2.5 million houses without subsidy. All in all, about 4 million new houses were built – an impressive number. In addition, local authorities were given additional powers to demolish slum property, and the Housing Act, 1930, provided subsidies for this purpose. In 1933 the government planned to demolish more than a quarter of a million houses, which meant rehousing over a million people. Yet there was still much overcrowding, with wide regional and local variations. Thus in Scotland, 22.6 per cent of the working classes were overcrowded, but in England only 3.8 per cent; in Jarrow, the figure was 17.5 per cent, and in Oxford, 1.0 per cent.

If industrialisation had helped very largely to create the industrial towns of the nineteenth century, and thereby to create extensive urban problems, the inter-war period saw much effort given to solving those problems. Indeed, the housing policies of the time are perhaps the most successful of all the various social policies pursued by the inter-war governments. Of course, they were not able to get rid of all the slums. Moreover, those rehoused on the vast new housing estates did not always appreciate their new surroundings. Some disliked being parted from the friends and relatives where they used to live, others objected to the higher rents imposed on the new estates (many councils wanted only the better-paid as new tenants, so that the estate could get off to a good start; rent subsidies to unemployed tenants were not paid till later). Travelling to work was often more expensive from the new, outlying estates, and amenities were frequently too few: on Birmingham's largest estate, the Kingstanding Estate of up to 9,000 houses, there was only one church and one hall, while the ancient town of Shrewsbury, with a smaller population, had thirty churches, fifteen church halls and parish rooms, five other halls, and two public libraries.[9] Tenants also grumbled at the cost of furnishing more extensive accommodation, and even complained that the fresh air gave the children better appetites, and made them more expensive to feed. Nevertheless, the new council estates became a permanent feature of the inter-war townscape. They were usually well planned, and individual houses were either semi-detached, or in short terraces, with gardens, front and rear. For many tenants they must have seemed positively luxurious, with their own water supply, hot water from either a kitchen boiler or living-room back-of-fire boiler, and their own internal lavatory.

Better living accommodation undoubtedly played its part in improving the health of the nation between the wars. Both death rates and infant mortality rates went down. In the pre-war years 1911–14, the death rate averaged 13.9 per 1,000; in the years 1935–8 before World War II, it averaged 11.9. The infant mortality rate was 105 per 1,000 in 1910. In 1940, the first year of war, it had fallen drastically to 56; and deaths among children from tuberculosis, measles, diarrhoea, and bronchitis were markedly reduced. However, there were substantial variations in the statistics from one region to another. For example, in 1935 the infant mortality figure in the prosperous south-east was only 47, but in Wales it was 63, in Northumberland and Durham 76, and in Scotland 77. We shall return to the problem of interpreting mortality statistics later in the chapter.

As for health services between the wars, they were still somewhat sketchy. It is true that all workers earning less than £160 a year were compulsorily insured against ill health under the 1911 act, but this did not cover dependants such as wives and children. Allowances paid while away from work due to sickness were lower than allowances paid for unemployment. Further, benefits available were still very limited, and hospital treatment other than in poor law infirmaries had to be paid for. In voluntary hospitals, an official known as the almoner was in charge of collecting the fees due. The whole system running the health scheme was administered by so-called 'approved societies', that is, insurance companies and friendly societies, and it was not very efficient. Indeed, the Royal Commission on National Health Insurance, 1926, recommended reform, but without immediate result. In 1929 the Local Government Act transferred the local administration of the poor law from the boards of guardians to committees of the county councils, and at the same time permitted local authorities to take over the poor law infirmaries, in effect converting them to municipal hospitals. Relatively few authorities did so, so that in 1939 about half of all public hospital services were still provided by poor law infirmaries. The health system made available by the state therefore supplied a basic service through the free treatment given by the 'panel' doctors, but it was limited in scope (the major additional benefit was the specialised care of tuberculosis patients), and hospital treatment still had to be paid for in voluntary hospitals (those relying on public subscriptions).[10]

The other social service offered by the state and affecting the health of the nation was the old-age pension. In 1919 the pension was raised to 10/– a week, and in 1925 the pension scheme was merged with the health scheme. Contributions now had to be made, but the pension was to start at the age of sixty-five (without a means test), and then at seventy the former non-contributory scheme took over and paid the pension. A widow's and orphan's benefit was also included in the new arrangements – something intended by Lloyd George in pre-war days. Government spending on social services rose from £101 million in 1913 to £596 million in 1938, with a *per capita* rise from £2.2 in 1913 to £12.5 in 1938. In real terms, expenditure had increased by over three times.[11] Spending was criticised for being without any overall plan. Local government services, such as the provision of free milk and child welfare clinics, varied from one authority to another. Free meals were available in some schools, but only after detailed enquiries into family means. Private charities still made direct gifts of clothing to the poor, and newspapers such as the *Daily Mail* had a scheme for free boots for children.

Working conditions

The general health of the nation was also improved by a considerable reduction in the length of the working day, by improvements in working conditions, and by a rise in real wages. Just before the war in 1914, there had been a mounting demand for the eight-hour day, at a time when a sixty-hour week and a ten- or ten-and-a-half-hour day (including meal times) were common. In 1919 in the metal trades and engineering the working week was reduced from fifty-three or fifty-four hours to forty-seven hours. Nationally there was a striking decrease in hours in 1919 of a total of 40.6 million hours a week, hours being reduced for 6.3 million workers in all.[12] Thereafter, only minor variations took place, and both overtime and short-time working were common. However, overall the trend was downwards. In 1936 the Factory Act ended the legal maximum sixty-hour week (55.5 hours in textiles), and established forty-five hours as a new maximum for all women and young persons, with a daily maximum of nine hours. There was also a noticeable spreading of the five-day week. In the flourishing motor industry, hours tended to be shorter in the larger firms. Thus in 1935, in firms in this industry with more than ten workers (76.6 per cent of all firms), the average working week was forty-seven hours. Only 4.2 per cent of the larger firms worked more than forty-eight hours.[13] Holidays in the 1920s were still restricted to the six days a year specified in the Bank Holiday Acts, though these were sometimes extended by a day, and a week's holiday without pay was usual in the summer. By 1937, about four million workers were entitled under collective agreements to holidays with pay. In the following year, the Holidays with Pay Act, 1938, brought in about a million workers, so that by June 1939 about half the manual workers in the country were entitled to holidays with pay.

As for working conditions on the shop-floor, safety improved. The mortal accident rate was about nineteen per 100,000 employed in 1901–7; in 1928–34, it had dropped to an average of eleven to twelve. Obviously enough, much depended on the nature of the work. Foundry work was always heavy and exhausting, while power presses as used in the motor industry were well known to be dangerous. The Austin Motor Company at Longbridge, Birmingham, began a campaign to reduce the number of accidents in April 1929, and in less than three years achieved a reduction of 41 per cent in the accident rate.[14] Another famous Birmingham firm, Cadburys of Bourneville, in the 1930s employed three qualified dentists, a dental mechanic, and five dental nurses: up to the age of sixteen, workers were provided with free toothbrushes and tooth powder. Their medical department was staffed by a doctor and three nurses. Smaller firms lacked all such facilities, of course, and might not even know who was supposed to look after the first-aid box if a bandage was required. It was the larger firm which could provide canteens and rest rooms. Some of them as early as 1930 installed a loudspeaker system so as to relay radio programmes or records in the workshops – something which became very popular in the guise of 'Music While You Work' in World War II (this also allowed bets on which popular tune was played first in both morning and afternoon sessions).

It is often taken for granted that the size of the work unit increased between the wars, and that large numbers of workers were employed on assembly lines, conveyor belts, and automatic machinery in extensive workplaces. It is true that factories did get larger: the number of factories employing 501 to 1,000 workers in 1933 was 800; by 1936 the number was 1,016. Factories with over 1,000 workers also grew in numbers from 335 in 1933 to 519 in 1936.[15] But at the same time the number of small factories was still very considerable – in fact, they were still the majority. It must be kept in mind that the word 'factory'

Table 8.1 Factory sizes, 1937

Size of factory	% of total
1–25	76.9
26–50	8.9
51–100	6.2
101–250	5.1
251–500	1.8
501–1,000	0.7
1,000+	0.4

was by now applied to any workplace using power; and very few work-places between the wars were entirely without power. Consequently, the word 'factory' by the 1930s was very elastic in use. Small factories still constituted more than three-quarters of all factories in 1937, when their relative sizes were listed as shown in Table 8.1.[16]

How far work discipline intensified in factories between the wars is difficult to say. The term 'scientific management' was becoming fashionable, as was the idea of time-and-motion studies in America, something satirised by Charlie Chaplin in the factory sequence in *Modern Times*. The leading systems of scientific management were Taylorism and the Bedaux system, and both were introduced into this country from the United States. Understandably, such efforts to streamline and speed up production met with hostility among the work force; in Birmingham, the Trades Council called the Bedaux system 'an inhuman system', although, rather surprisingly, the TUC was not altogether opposed to it. At all events, Bedauxism spread only very slowly, and by 1939 there were about 250 firms utilising various forms of the system, mostly in the newer industries of food processing, light engineering, and chemicals; it was also to be found here and there in iron and steel, textiles, and hosiery. All in all, its adoption was not widespread, for mass production methods were still the exception rather than the rule. Certainly it seems reasonable to suppose that the benefits of shorter working hours and a safer working environment were not cancelled out by greater stress produced by scientific management throughout industry.[17]

Working-class education

As for state schooling, that other great example of state action brought about by industrialisation, no major changes are to be discerned in the state system of schools in the inter-war period. The major influence here, of course, was the Fisher Education Act, 1918, but the economy cuts in government spending of the time rendered it of only limited effect. It is true that the school leaving age was fixed by the act at fourteen without exceptions, but the number of exemptions allowed previously was only relatively small. The undertaking to put up the leaving age to fifteen was not acted upon until 1936, and then the operative date fixed upon was 1 September 1939; the imminence of war then made a postponement of the date inevitable. The one cheering development from the reformers' point of view was the increasing belief that secondary education for all pupils in separate buildings and establishments was essential. The Labour Party demanded this in a 1922 pamphlet entitled *Secondary Education for All*, which advocated free secondary education for all children up to the age of fifteen, and later to sixteen.

In fact, informed opinion was coming round more and more to this point of view. The Hadow Report of 1926 suggested that the term 'elementary education' was out of date, and should be discarded. In future, education up to the age of eleven should be called 'primary education', and the following stage from eleven onwards, 'secondary education'. Alongside the county secondary schools brought into being by the Balfour Education Act, 1902, there should be created new secondary schools ('modern schools') to cater for the less academically able. They should have a status equivalent to the existing county secondary schools (to be renamed 'secondary grammar schools'), but should not be inferior in status: 'It is not an inferior species, and it ought not to be hampered by conditions of accommodation and equipment inferior to the schools now described as secondary.' The school leaving age should also be increased to fifteen.

Thus was born the idea of the 'secondary modern school', which species of school actually came into existence after the Butler Education Act, 1944 (unfortunately, it never achieved the academic respectability which was naively hoped for). The economy cuts of 1931 put paid to any idea of progress in this direction. Nevertheless, some local authorities showed initiative in providing more secondary education in the inter-war years. In 1920, free places in county secondary schools were limited to 33 per cent; by 1931, this figure had risen to 47 per cent. Also in 1931, about 25 per cent of children of eleven years and above were in separate secondary schools; by 1938, the figure was 64 per cent. There was also a distinct rise in the secondary school population (see Table 8.2).[18] So the chance for the working-class child to receive an academic education and to go on to

Table 8.2 Secondary school population, 1913–37

Year	No. of sec. schs	No. of pupils in sec. schs
1913	1,027	187,647
1921	1,249	362,025
1937	1,397	482,676

university was improving, though the numbers who actually achieved this were still very small, mainly because of the expense involved.

Unemployment

To return to the subject of unemployment: although the majority of British workers were in work throughout the inter-war period, unemployment affected millions and became the greatest social issue of the day. As we have seen, unemployment had certainly caused concern before the Great War, but it was limited in the worst years to 5 or 6 per cent of the work force. Significantly, although the National Health Act, 1911, sought to insure the entire working population against ill health, unemployment was regarded by many as a transitory matter caused by variations in seasonable employment or other fluctuations in trade. Insurance against it was therefore confined to seven trades known to suffer in this way, covering only 2.25 million workers. Between the wars this approach proved quite misconceived: much of the unemployment was deeply structural, and rooted in the staple industries. Probably the worst year of all was 1932, with some recovery thereafter. In that year, the total out of work was nearly three million, 23 per cent, or nearly a quarter of the insured population. Since certain occupational groups were still not insured under the 1911 act, such as agricultural workers, domestic servants, and the self-employed, the true total has been estimated at 3.75 million.[19] There was some recovery in 1933 and 1934, but there were still over a million jobless in 1939.

Just how badly the major, traditional industries suffered unemployment can be seen in Table 8.3, showing unemployment percentages.[20] From 1935 onwards, rearmament on a modest scale gave a boost to the economy, and this is shown in the improved figures for 1938. Because of the severe nature of job losses in the staple industries, certain areas were particularly badly hit – the Depressed Areas. In the Bishop Auckland area in south-west Durham, 80 per cent of the men in the mining district of Tow Law were unemployed, and nearly

Table 8.3 Unemployment in major industries, 1932 and 1938 (%)

	1932	1938
Coal mining	41.2	22.0
Woollen and worsted	26.6	21.4
Cotton	31.3	27.7
Shipbuilding	59.5	21.4
Iron and steel	48.5	24.8

100 per cent in Sheldon. In London, the percentage unemployed in 1930 was only 9.8 per cent; and there were few obvious signs of unemployment in either central London or in the suburbs. In the north-east, the figure was 24.5 per cent, and in Wales 31.2 per cent. In both these areas, long-term unemployment was a particular problem. In West Auckland in 1935, only a hundred men out of a thousand had been employed in the preceding seven years. In Crook, 71 per cent of men had been out of work for over five years. In the Rhondda in South Wales, the figure was 45 per cent for men unemployed for more than five years.[21]

The government was therefore faced with unemployment on an altogether unprecedented scale. Initially, the government's weapons were confined to the meagre insurance scheme of 1911, and the poor law. However, it had been anticipated that there might be some temporary unemployment immediately after the war ended among ex-soldiers and ex-munitions workers, and so special non-contributory 'out-of-work donations' were made in 1919 to both these categories of workers. In 1920 the government was forced to extend unemployment insurance to most workers earning less than £250 a year. This put a great strain on the insurance scheme, which was supposed to be self-financing through the contributions paid in, and it had been designed in any case to deal only with the limited numbers thrown out of work by cyclical as opposed to structural unemployment. Once the out-of-work donations had been used up, the unemployed were in theory obliged to go to the workhouse for help. Since this was obviously undesirable, they were permitted to go on drawing benefits from contributions they might be expected to make in the future. This was known as 'uncovenanted benefit'; this was to disguise its true nature, of course, but the government wanted to retain the insurance principle.

Uncovenanted benefit continued to be available to insured workers when their entitlement ran out. Uninsured workers still had to seek relief from the poor law guardians. The first Labour government put up the basic weekly benefit from 15/– to 18/–, but otherwise left the insurance scheme unchanged. After 1924, uncovenanted benefit became known as 'extended benefit'. In 1925 the Blanesburgh Committee was appointed to investigate and report on the insurance scheme, and in 1927 it recommended that standard benefit and extended benefit should be merged and made available to anyone who had paid thirty weeks' contributions. Other workers with less than thirty weeks' contributions could draw an allowance called 'transitional benefit'. These somewhat complicated arrangements came into operation as a result of the Unemployment Act, 1927. In practice, they meant that transitional benefit was disguised poor law relief. It was paid not by the poor law authorities but at the labour exchange, like ordinary benefit. By 1928 the insurance fund was £28 million in debt.

Meanwhile, the poor law relief system itself was under great strain. Many out of work who were not eligible for insurance benefit (or whose rates of benefit were too low) were forced to apply for outdoor relief. At the end of 1918, there were only 281,000 on outdoor relief: by June 1922 the figure had risen to 1.24 million, and was over 1.5 million during the coal strike which continued after the General Strike in 1926. Some poor law local authorities actually went bankrupt. In 1929 the government abolished the boards of guardians, transferring their powers to special public assistance committees (PACs) of the county councils. In 1930 the second Labour government abolished the requirement that applicants should be 'genuinely seeking work', which made it easier to gain transitional benefit. Within two months, the numbers obtaining this form of benefit rose from 140,000 to 300,000.

This second Labour government faced a financial crisis in the autumn of 1931 when it appeared that the country was on the brink of national bankruptcy. Among the numerous financial cuts proposed was the proposal to cut the dole by 10 per cent. The cabinet split into two almost equal groups on this, and had to resign. The new, incoming so-called National Government (a coalition really dominated by Conservatives) reduced the dole from 17/– a week to 15/3, reduced ordinary benefit to a period of only twenty-six weeks, and gave authority for transitional benefit to the PACs, also making it subject to a means test. From 1931 to 1934, the worst years of the Great Depression, anyone unemployed for more than twenty-six weeks had to undergo a means test – that is, all subsidiary sources of income, savings, pensions, wages earned by children, were all taken into account in calculating benefit. The means test was deeply unpopular as a humiliating enquiry into the intimate details of family life: heads of families were bitter at being made to rely on handouts from their children, some of whom left home to escape an intolerable situation. Prized family possessions such as pianos might have to be sold before full benefit was granted. The means test was not completely abandoned in its original form till 1941.

At last, in 1934, after fifteen years of improvisation by the government in an attempt to adapt a scheme never intended to deal with mass unemployment, a new Unemployment Act was passed. This introduced a complete reorganisation of relief. In Part I, which dealt with the insurance scheme, the cuts of 1931 were restored, although benefit was to be paid for only the first twenty-six weeks as before. Occupational groups not covered by the original scheme were now brought in, including farm workers. About 14.5 million workers were covered by 1937. A new statutory committee was to run the new scheme, which was concerned primarily with short-term unemployment. Part II dealt with long-term unemployment, and gave help to all in need of it, whether still in benefit or not. The Unemployment Assistance Board (UAB) was established on a national scale, administering national standards of benefit (previously the amounts given varied from one PAC to another). This board took over from the PACs some 800,000 on transitional payments, and later, 200,000 on poor relief. Its funds came directly from the Treasury, not from any form of insurance fund. The means test continued, but in a revised, less harsh form.

When the UAB commenced operations in 1935 it soon became apparent that it was paying lower rates of benefit than many of the PACs had done. For a time, applicants could claim either rate of benefit; but after a couple of years, rates had become uniform nationally. The new scheme actually worked well, and accumulated a surplus. The UAB in its local office effectively replaced the PACs, whose functions had become minimal and confined largely to running the workhouses, which contained as before the children, the sick, and the aged. All other types of applicants were given outdoor relief. The workhouse itself was to be eventually abolished (in name, at least) in 1948. However, although the government had at last set up a more efficient system for the relief of the unemployed, there was very little positive action taken to cure unemployment.[22] Public works schemes had been tried before the war, of course, together with labour colonies, but the 1920s saw a remarkable and stubborn adherence to the idea of free trade and the belief that open market conditions would ultimately solve all problems. To this was coupled the notion that government expenditure should be severely restricted – hence the 'Geddes axe' cuts in public expenditure in 1922. It is true that the Unemployment Grants Committee spent £69.5 million in public works operated by local authorities, but in 1931, when unemployment was about 2.5 million, not more than 60,000 men were employed on such schemes. After 1931 this kind of help was suspended, even though Roosevelt's massive New Deal programmes were setting an example in the United States, spending millions of dollars in relief schemes. In 1934, when the Depressed Areas officially became Special Areas, some financial help was given to firms setting up in these areas. The best-known example of government assistance, perhaps, is provided by the North Atlantic Shipping Act, 1934, whereby government loans were made available up to £9.5 million. for building ships for the North Atlantic service. As a result of this act, work was restarted on the *Queen Mary*. The British Shipping (Assistance) Act, 1935, provided further subsidies for tramp shipping, and encouraged the building of new ships by government loans.

Thus, the governments of the inter-war period up to 1932 put their trust in the operation of free-market forces. The McKenna Duties of 1915 were retained in part after 1918, but they were repealed altogether by the first Labour government in 1924. Churchill as chancellor of the exchequer restored them in 1925, with some minor extensions later, but they were hardly a formidable barrier to imports and it was not until after the scare of 1931 that real tariff barriers were erected, first by the Abnormal Importations Act, 1931, then by the Import Duties Act, 1932, imposing a general duty of 10 per cent on almost all imports. Further duties were imposed by the Import Duties Advisory Committee between 1932 and 1935, resulting in a general tariff. In this way, free trade was at last dead and buried.

Why did the government of whatever political persuasion do so little to solve the problem of unemployment, beyond the protective legislation of the 1930s? The simplest answer, perhaps, is that old habits die hard, and nineteenth-century attitudes towards trade and industry persisted strongly. As we have seen, only with the coming of world depression in the early 1930s was free trade abandoned, while direct government support of industry on any substantial scale was still thought improper. Further, in the 1930s the difficulties arising from the coincidence of both structural and cyclical unemployment were formidable: in 1931, the possibility of national bankruptcy seemed for a time both real and imminent. Even going off the gold standard to help solve the problem seemed a dangerous enterprise (in fact, to the surprise of many, it had few adverse international repercussions). It is true that more advanced economic thinking was available in the New Liberal policies of the time, and Keynesian views on the importance of stimulating demand were gaining increased favour. On the other hand, Keynes' theories related more to cyclical unemployment than structural, and in any case his major work was not published in its full form till 1936. Even in the United States where massive sums of money were made available by the government under the New Deal, unemployment was still very heavy in 1939, and the tide turned only with the entry of the USA into the war in 1941. By hindsight, it is easy to criticise inter-war governments for unadventurous policies and for failing to do more to reduce unemployment. However, it is difficult to see how, in an age when it was still thought vital to balance the budget, the electorate could be persuaded that heavy government subsidies to industry, paid for by the taxpayer, were the best solution. All in all, it is at least understandable that governments were like Mr Micawber, waiting for something to turn up (it did eventually, in the shape of World War II). Later in the century, when unemployment, having almost vanished, had once more risen to over a million in 1975, the Conservative governments of the 1980s thought they had found the solution in the doctrines of monetarism. Far from declining, unemployment then climbed to over three million in three successive years, 1985, 1986, and 1987. Industrialisation has brought many benefits to this country, but unemployment has remained a deep-rooted problem.

To turn back to the inter-war years: life on the dole has been described so often in so many books that it is not proposed to discuss it in any detail here. It has already been pointed out that in general terms, and except in 1931 and 1932, it was largely confined to the Depressed Areas, where whole communities were blighted by long-term unemployment. Consequently, older generations in these areas retain bitter memories of life lived on the dole, nobody actually starving, but many going hungry, long empty days which had to be filled up somehow by visits to the library in winter where it was warm, listening to the wireless, an occasional visit to the cinema. In fact, it was these simple inexpensive pleasures which probably kept recruitment to extreme political parties, such as the Communist Party and Mosley's Fascist Party, to a minimum. Orwell summed up the reasons for this very well:[23]

> Of course, the post-war development of cheap luxuries has been a very fortunate thing for our rulers. It is quite likely that fish and chips, art-silk stockings, tinned salmon, cut-price chocolate (five

two-ounce bars for sixpence), the movies, the radio, strong tea, and the football pools have between them averted revolution.

Orwell went on to say that some thought all this was an astute manoeuvre by the governing classes to hold the unemployed down, but he personally didn't think that the governing class had that much intelligence.

The major contribution, in fact, made by the Communist Party to the cause of the unemployed seems to have been the organisation of so-called hunger marches, though the most famous of all marches, the Jarrow March of the Unemployed in 1936, was organised by the Labour Party. Otherwise, a number of marches were led by the National Unemployed Workers Movement, its leader being the well-known communist, Wal Hannington. All in all, the worst thing about unemployment for many was boredom and a sense of uselessness, a loss of personal dignity and resentment against not being allowed to work. Walter Greenwood has one of his characters express his sense of frustration in his famous novel *Love on the Dole* as follows:[24]

> What had he been able to do other than what had been done? The responsibility wasn't his. He'd worked all his life: had given all he had to give. Oh, why the devil couldn't they give him work? The cancer of impotence gnawed his vitals.

It must be remembered, too, that housewives in the areas stricken by unemployment had a hard time of it. They had to make meals with the minimum of resources, and be expert in patching up the family clothes and household linen. They had to soldier on, just as much as their husbands. They are too often the forgotten army of the Great Depression.

Poverty

How far did poverty actually increase between the wars?[25] It is self-evident that life was hard for the unemployed and their families. Although the dole kept them from starvation, the rate of benefit was kept low to discourage scroungers, so that malnutrition due to a poor diet was common enough. Many unemployed men suffered from depression, and in the slump year of 1932, an average of two unemployed men committed suicide for every day in the year; in the 1920s, from 1921 to 1931, suicides among men under twenty-five years of age rose by 60 per cent.[26] The worst health statistics were usually found in the poorest urban areas, and it has been suggested that some local health statistics were manipulated by health officials to conceal high infant mortality figures.[27] The actual extent of poverty in some surveys of the time may actually be concealed by averages struck over a wide area: thus, in a 1928 survey of poverty in London, the average of 9.1 per cent estimated to be in poverty conceals the fact that the figure for Poplar was 24 per cent, and for Bethnal Green 17.8 per cent (these were two notoriously poor districts). On the other hand, some families were better off on the dole than in work because unemployment benefit included allowances for dependants, unlike ordinary wages. It has even been calculated that in South Wales, one-third of the single men, and nearly half of the married men were better off on the dole than in their last job.[28] Then again, in the 1930s the fall in food prices benefited all, whether in work or not. It was one justification put forward for the proposed cut of 10 per cent in the dole which caused the split in the cabinet and the fall of the Labour government in 1931. For all these reasons it is difficult if not impossible to be specific about the extent of poverty in individual families where the principal breadwinner was on the dole. Much would depend on the number of children still at school, the skill of the housewife in managing the family economy, the earnings of older children still in work, the availability of part-time jobs locally (these would often be undisclosed to the PACs or UAB), and so on.[29]

Is it possible then to state in any positive terms whether there was more poverty between the wars than before 1914? In certain places where there was full, well-paid employment before the Great War, and heavy unemployment after, such as Jarrow, it seems safe to say that there was more poverty – more unemployment, poor nutritional and health standards, and so on. But against this must be set the rise in real wages of about 17 per cent per head, or allowing for the unemployed, by about 9 per cent.[30] Numerically, those outside the Depressed Areas, who were in employment for most of the period, far outnumbered both the short-term and long-term unemployed. An outstanding survey of poverty in York in 1936 was carried out by Seebohm Rowntree, who was thereby able to make a direct comparison with his 1899 survey (though his 1936 survey fixed a more generous poverty line than in 1899, and included a higher dietary requirement, and also provision for beer, tobacco, a wireless, and newspapers). The results were summarised as shown in Table 8.4.[31] Thus, Rowntree was able to state that 'we should probably not be very far wrong if we put the standard of living available to the workers in 1936 at about 30 per cent higher than it was in 1899'. As for the 17.7

Table 8.4 Poverty in York, 1899 and 1936 (as % of York population)

	1936	1899
Below poverty line	17.7	27.8
Primary poverty	3.9	9.9
Primary poverty (of the working classes)	6.8	15.8

per cent of the total population still in poverty, Rowntree considered the biggest single cause was that although the head of the family was in regular work, his wages were too low to support the family adequately (32.8 per cent); the next most important cause was that the head of the family was out of work (28.6 per cent); and the third biggest cause was old age (14.7 per cent).

Of course, York was not a typical city, not being either very depressed or especially prosperous, but similar studies in other cities showed comparable results. In Bristol, a prosperous city, only 10.7 per cent of working-class families were 'in poverty'. In Merseyside, a more depressed area, the equivalent figure for 1928–32 was 16 per cent, though adjustment to Rowntree's more generous poverty line hoisted this figure to 30 per cent. In London in 1928, only 9.1 per cent were in poverty. There was general agreement among the local surveys that unemployment and low wages were major causes of poverty (a fact which reinforced the growing demand for family allowances), other causes being old age and sickness. Even then, it was sometimes alleged that an unemployed man and his family in the 1930s were better off than the unskilled labourer in full-time work in 1913.[32] As for the physical health of the nation, in 1947 a report was issued on the 7.2 million men examined for military service between 8 June 1939 and December 1946, using the same criteria for grading as was used in the report on the men examined for service in 1917–18. The contrasts are remarkable: in the earlier report, only 36 per cent were put in Grade I; the corresponding figure for 1939–46 was 70 per cent. The figures for the latter period for Grade I recruits, age group by age group, are equally remarkable: for those under 21, 81 per cent were Grade I; 21–25 years, 71 per cent; 26–30 years, 62 per cent; and 31 and over, 43 per cent.[33]

The only findings of the time which went against the figures denoting improvement were published by Sir John Orr under the title *Food, Health and Income* in 1936. Using an American standard of nutritional needs, Orr reached the conclusion that of the six groups of the population examined, only the last two could afford an adequate diet; as much as half the nation appeared to be ill-fed. Both Orr's sample and his nutritional standard were attacked. His study was also based on a very small sample, and made no proper allowance for regional variations.[34] He afterwards admitted that the average consumption of food per head had increased in everything except flour between 1909–13 and 1934: in fruit by 88 per cent, vegetables by 64 per cent, butter and margarine by 50 per cent, eggs by 46 per cent, meat by 6 per cent, and potatoes by 1 per cent.[35] He subsequently lowered his claim to one-third. Local studies of malnutrition help to illustrate the difficulties involved in definition. In Birmingham, for example, in 1938 the proportion of the 43,507 children who were examined and classified as 'badly under-nourished' was 1.4 per cent; but if one officer's report was excluded, the figure fell to 0.5 per cent. Of those classified as being 'badly ill-nourished', 21.1 per cent were due to pathological causes, and 63.2 per cent to financial causes. In summing up, the Birmingham report reached the commonsense conclusion that the most powerful factors were shortage of food due to lack of means, and illness, past and present. The proportion of malnutrition in Birmingham's schools was about the same as in the school population as a whole. Children receiving school meals appeared to be healthy and well nourished. Cases of malnutrition were more numerous in the central wards of the city (the worst slum areas) (1.29 per cent) than on the city's new estates (0.27 per cent).[36] This, of course, is just what one would expect.

Indeed, a survey of nutritional standards carried out in the new Kingstanding Estate in Birmingham in 1939 confirms the importance of the number of children in the family in determining its standard of living. At this time, the area was enjoying virtually full employment, and overtime was being worked. A 5 per cent sample was questioned, 269 families out of about 5,300 households. Of all the families, 33 per cent had no children under 14, and a further 46 per cent had either one or two children – that is, 79 per cent had small families with two or less children under 14. Only 21 per cent, therefore, had three or more children under 14 – but these are the really significant families, for it is largely these larger families who are most noticeable in the table drawn up by the authors of the survey, showing the percentage of families unable to confirm to a 'standard of sufficiency'. This means families either on the borders of the minimum acceptable nutritional standard (using the British Medical Association minimum diet scale of 1933), or within five points above, or definitely below. Table 8.5 shows families on or below the minimum standard of sufficiency.[37] As for the entire population of the estate,

Table 8.5 Families on or below the minimum standard of sufficiency, Kingstanding Estate, Birmingham, 1939

	%
Families with 1 child under 14	13
2 children	45
3 children	65
4 children	85
5 children	96
6 (or more) children	96

31 per cent of families were under the sufficiency line, and some 60 per cent were on or below the borderline. This is not altogether dissimilar to a figure of 54.5 per cent in the Bristol social survey.

It is evident that the methodology employed in the Kingstanding survey is a little odd – why include families as below the sufficiency line who are 5 per cent *above* the minimum? And again, the nature of the diet chosen as a standard may be open to question, as well as the amount of family income considered available for food after deductions for rent, fares, fuel, lighting, clothing, and so on. Nevertheless, the point is made yet again that the size of the family is highly significant in determining nutritional standards (and is to be noted that the 33 per cent of families with no children at all do not even appear in the table). The report suggested that rehousing was not enough – there was the need identified by Beveridge in 1942 for Family Allowances, which were at last made available by the Family Allowances Act, 1945.

In the final analysis, it is hard to escape the conclusion that although pockets of intense poverty still existed in 1939, especially in the Special Areas, and although large families certainly had to struggle to make both ends meet, most working people experienced a rising standard of living, especially in the 1930s. Further, since the average rate of unemployment in the years 1921–39 was 14 per cent, then in theory an average 86 per cent were in work and having the advantage of that improved standard of living, subject to obvious necessary adjustment, since not all workers were insured against unemployment or without family commitments. Nevertheless, it seems safe to say that more than half the workers were better off. This is not to ignore, nor to disparage, the sufferings of the unemployed (especially the long-term unemployed), but it seems a realistic representation of the facts of the matter. Professor John Burnett has put the case here in moderate terms: 'The proportion of the very poor fell between the wars, and that of the moderately prosperous increased.' He then goes on to point out that the nature of poverty had changed, and that a 'new poor' of unemployed miners, shipyard workers, and cotton weavers had emerged – a new 'submerged tenth'. Nevertheless, he goes on, 'No-one could seriously doubt that the working classes on the eve of the Second World War were better fed, better clothed and better housed than their parents had been a generation earlier.'[38]

The trade unions and the General Strike

During the first two years of peace, a good deal of trouble was anticipated in labour relationships.[39] By the Restoration of Pre-war Practices Act, 1919, the trade practices suspended by the Munitions of War Acts were restored. In the brief post-war boom, when employment prospects were good, trade union membership increased still further to reach a record total of over eight million. Meanwhile, trade union militancy increased, and there was a number of serious strikes, including strikes by the police in London and in Liverpool, and a national railway strike in September 1919. In particular, trouble was expected in the coal industry, which was still under government control. In 1919 the miners threatened a national coal strike, demanding a 30 per cent rise in pay, a six-hour day, and the nationalisation of the industry.

Faced with the very real threat of serious industrial disruption, Lloyd George sought to defuse the situation by appointing a royal commission (headed by a High Court Judge), the Sankey Commission. The major issue at stake, of course, was nationalisation of the mining industry; a good case could be made out for it, given the antiquated nature of the industry and its need for recapitalisation on a grand scale – many pits were far too small and uneconomic to run, quite apart from the long history of labour relations within the industry. In the event, four final reports were issued by the commission in 1919, two recommending national ownership, two opposing it (actually, seven out of the thirteen members of the commission were in favour of nationalisation). Lloyd George had a good excuse for taking no further action (his Conservative colleagues in his coalition government would not have accepted nationalisation, of course), though the Mines Act, 1919, did give a seven-hour day, and also accepted the principle of the nationalisation of royalties. Lloyd George had staved off trouble, but had done little or nothing to meet the deep-seated grievances of the miners.

This is shown by the simple fact that in the next year, 1920, the miners came out on strike for increased pay, and were backed by their partners in the pre-war Triple Alliance, the railwaymen and other transport workers. The government hastily backed down, and authorised an increase in pay. Another sign of trade union militancy of the time was the *Jolly George* incident in 1920. This concerned a ship in the London docks bound for Poland. London dockers refused to load munitions onto the ship which were intended to be used by the Poles in their war against the newly established socialist Soviet Union. Undoubtedly there was considerable support in the ranks of the Labour movement for what was seen as the first, experimental workers' state (its excesses were not to be widely known until much later). Industrial capitalism had been overthrown at last and replaced by a much fairer system in which workers would receive a just reward for their labours – or so it was argued at the time. The early post-war years were therefore years with a sharper edge to class relationships, and with some expectation among militant workers of further changes in society. All things were possible, or so it seemed, now that Czarist tyranny had succumbed to socialism and the dictatorship of the proletariat.

This mood did not last very long, and trade union militancy began to die down as the post-war boom came to an end, and unemployment rose. In 1921, union membership fell to 6.6 million, and although days lost by strikes peaked in that year at 85.87 million, in 1922 the figure was down to 19.85 million days. In 1921 the government handed back the mines to the owners, who promptly cut wages. When the new rates were rejected by the miners, the threat of concerted action by the Triple Alliance again loomed up; but this time the railwaymen backed out at the last minute (Friday 15 April, known thereafter as 'Black Friday'), arguing that there was still room for negotiation. The miners therefore had to go on strike alone, but after two months went back to work, having gained nothing. The leader of the railway union, Jimmy Thomas, was reviled thereafter as 'Traitor Thomas' (this did not prevent him from holding office in both the inter-war Labour governments). Thereafter, as depression spread, trade union militancy was diminished. It should be noted, however, that the trade union movement made some limited progress in modernising itself by the merger of several of the biggest unions which gave additional bargaining strength. The Amalgamated Engineering Union was set up (on the basis of the old ASE) in 1921, the large Transport and General Workers Union was established in 1922, while in 1924 a third major union was formed, the Union of General and Municipal Workers. The TGWU had as its secretary the formidable Ernest Bevin, later to be foreign secretary in the post-war Labour government of 1945–50. In 1921 the old Parliamentary Committee of the Trades Union Congress was replaced by a more powerful General Council.

In 1925 the government decided to go back to the gold standard which had been given up for the time being during the war. There is little doubt today that in doing so, the government overvalued the pound. The result was to make exports dearer for our overseas customers, and in particular to put up the price of coal exports. The mine owners reacted to this as expected: they announced a cut in wages. The General Council of the TUC responded by calling a meeting of the transport unions, all of whom agreed to stop all transport of coal, if and when the miners went on strike. This looked like another attempt to revive the Triple Alliance, and if implemented this time, could have had very serious consequences for the economy. Of course, there was the possibility of very serious political consequences, too, if it led to a general strike. Stanley Baldwin, the Conservative prime minister, moved quickly and appointed a commission of enquiry, headed by a leading Liberal, Sir Herbert Samuel. This commission immediately awarded a temporary subsidy to the coal owners so as to avoid the threatened cut in wages (this gratified the mining unions, who named the day 'Red Friday').

Baldwin believed in reconciliation, and in reaching amicable agreements between capital and labour. Nevertheless, he took the threat of a general strike seriously enough to make secret preparations in case negotiations should fail. England and Wales were split up into ten regions, each with a cabinet minister in charge, local committees were set up, and volunteers were enrolled. The great need was likely to be for the transport of food and other necessities, so that a new body was appointed, the Organisation for the Maintenance of Supplies. The trade unions, and especially the General Council of the TUC, made very few preparations. In his excellent account of the General Strike, C.L. Mowat tells the story of how the general secretary of the Miners' Federation, the fiery communist, A.J. Cook, declared that for some time past his mother-in-law had been buying in an extra tin of salmon when she went shopping, whereupon Jimmy Thomas exclaimed, 'My God! A British revolution based on a tin of salmon!'[40] It did not sound much like the storming of the Winter Palace. All the same, it was clear that the miners would not give in. Cook gave warning of this:[41]

I am going to get a fund, if I can, that will buy grub, so that when the struggle comes, we shall have that grub distributed in the homes of our people. I don't care a hang for any government, or army or navy. They can come along with their bayonets. Bayonets don't cut coal. We have already beaten not only the employers, but the strongest government of modern times.

These are brave words, and it is true that the government could not use the army to mine coal, but the claim that both the employers and the government had been beaten was pure fantasy.

The report of the Samuel Commission was published in March 1926, but it pleased neither side. It recommended that the government subsidy to the owners should be ended, some reorganisation of the industry should be undertaken, the seven-hour shift retained, and wages cut, but on a national, not regional basis. The owners wanted the return of the eight-hour day, and district wage cuts. The miners rejected both cuts in pay and the longer day demanded by the owners – in Cook's well-known words, 'Not a penny off the pay, not a minute on the day.' Four-sided negotiations followed between the government, the industrial committee of the TUC General Council, the owners, and the miners. On 30 April, the owners took unilateral action and declared a lock-out; the government thereupon declared a state of emergency. Negotiations intensified over the next two days, with the General Council representing the miners. Then, on 2 May, Baldwin abruptly broke off talks, his grounds being that certain 'overt acts' had occurred – he claimed that notices had already been sent out for a general strike, and that the freedom of the press had been infringed when the printers on the *Daily Mail* had refused to set up an editorial claiming that a general strike was revolutionary in nature. The leaders of the General Council were taken aback by this sudden ending of negotiations. They retired for discussion, repudiated the actions of the *Daily Mail* printers, and returned to Downing Street, ready to resume discussions. They found the room in darkness, and were informed that the prime minister had retired to bed. The General Strike began on the following day, 3 May 1926, and lasted nine days.

To the simple question, 'What was the cause of the General Strike?', the obvious answer is, Baldwin's breaking off negotiations on 2 May. Clearly he had decided that talking had gone on long enough, and action was now necessary. It has often been argued that he was exhausted by the days of negotiation, and that he finally gave in to the more aggressive members of the cabinet, such as Birkenhead and

Churchill, who thought that the miners had to be taken on. Against this argument, it can be said that even if the talking had continued, the miners were stubborn and unyielding, and would never have given way, so that Baldwin was quite right to call an end to the talks when he did. In any case, it is quite clear that the causes of the strike went back a long way: there was a long history of hostility between masters and men in the coal industry, and the miners were bitterly disappointed at the failure to gain nationalisation in 1919. The whole industry was old-fashioned and badly in need of modernisation. Yet the owners were not prepared to spend money in bringing it up to date. If the miners were intransigent, so were the coalmine owners. G.L. Garvin, editor of the *Observer*, wrote on 28 April, 'The owners have been tactless and irritating to the last degree. No responsible body of men has ever seemed more lacking in the common touch ...'[42] This was the opinion of a Conservative, but was shared by other Conservatives such as Neville Chamberlain, who described the owners as 'not a prepossessing crowd', and by Lord Birkenhead, another member of the government, who was certainly not a friend of the miners. He wrote in words which have often been quoted:[43]

> it would be possible to say without exaggeration that the miners' leaders were the stupidest men in England if we had not had frequent occasion to meet the owners.

Political theorists on the left had always predicted that industrialisation, especially when it reaches the advanced state of what Marx called monopoly capitalism, would lead to a final clash between capital and labour, and indeed, to revolution. Moreover, for syndicalists, the general strike was to be *the* chosen weapon when the workers, by first paralysing the nation's economy, rose up and took over the means of production, distribution, and exchange. The British General Strike of 1926 was utterly unlike anything envisaged by the syndicalists. In the first place, the union leaders were prepared to continue negotiations on behalf of the miners, and were generally unwilling to call a general strike which would take them into dangerous and unknown territory; and in fact, they preferred the term 'national strike' to 'general strike' because of the known political connotations of the latter term. In the event, it was Baldwin who made the decision for them. Second, the unions throughout regarded the whole controversy as essentially an industrial, and not a political dispute. They claimed they were supporting their comrades in a dispute over wages, and one in which they considered the miners had an obviously just and legitimate cause. Politics did not enter into it. Unfortunately for them, Baldwin and the government took a different view. For the prime minister, it was a simple constitutional issue: who was to rule the country, a democratically elected government or the TUC? For Baldwin, the strike was an attempt to coerce the government into intervening on behalf of the miners; as such, it was 'a gross travesty of every democratic principle'. It had therefore to be resisted. Logic was on his side. Later in the century, both Edward Heath and Margaret Thatcher as Conservative prime ministers were to face similar challenges from the miners, but with different results. Heath called and lost a general election over the issue, but Thatcher emerged triumphant without finding it necessary to appeal to the country.

The story of the nine-day strike is soon told.[44] It was not, in fact, a 'general' strike – only certain key unions were called out in iron and steel, gas and electricity, building, printing, the press, and transport. The government's plans, laid in advance, worked well, and essential supplies were kept moving, often with the aid of middle-class volunteers, who drove trains, buses, trams, and lorries. Although the government failed to persuade the director of the British Broadcasting Company, John Reith, to permit them to use the new medium, the government published its own newsheet, the *British Gazette*, editor Winston Churchill.[45] The trade unions, for their part, had made virtually no preparations for the strike, but a series of local committees to supervise picketing and so on worked effectively enough. On the whole, the strike was good tempered, and Baldwin did all he could to keep it so, at the same time maintaining that the strike was, in his words, 'a challenge to parliament, and the road to anarchy and ruin'.[46] There were some outstanding instances of good relations between strikers and the police, in particular, football matches between them, but violence did break out at times, especially towards the end of the strike. In all, there were 3,149 prosecutions in England and Wales for breaches of the peace, and for incitement to sedition. This represented a far more limited scale of violence and disturbance than was usual during a general strike on the Continent. After a week or more had gone by and the government gave no sign of yielding, the TUC leaders were thankful to have the opportunity of opening talks with Sir Herbert Samuel, who had just returned from abroad. By 11 May a memorandum was drawn up which set out possible terms for a settlement, and this was accepted by the General Council of the TUC, although the miners refused to accept it. On this basis, the General Strike was called off on 12 May. Arthur Pugh, of the Iron and Steel Trades Federation, led a deputation of the General Council to the prime minister to announce their decision: 'We are here today, sir, to say that the general strike is to be terminated forthwith in order that negotiations may proceed …'[47]

It was a total defeat for the unions. It took most of the strikers by surprise, for the strike was still solid. When they returned to work on 13 May, many workers were immediately dismissed, and for a while it seemed that the strike might be resumed again. However, Baldwin issued a warning to employers not to victimise men who had been on strike. He then attempted to negotiate a new wages agreement, but his efforts were rejected by both sides. Meanwhile, the miners stayed out on strike. Within weeks the government gave up all attempts at reconciliation, and passed legislation suspending the seven-hour day, and encouraging the merger of mining companies. By the end of the year, the miners were forced back to work on the owners' terms. Mining families suffered great privations by staying on strike – there was no dole, of course, for men voluntarily absenting themselves from work. When they did go back, they had to submit to an eight-hour day, and to wage rates based on district agreements, not national. Some of the miners' leaders were blacklisted, and were never able to obtain employment in the coal industry again. The owners also had the additional satisfaction of seeing the government pass the Trades Disputes and Trade Union Act, 1927, which banned sympathetic strikes, changed 'contracting-out' under the 1913 act to 'contracting-in' (which reduced the Labour Party's income from the political levy by over a quarter), forbade civil servants to join trade unions, and redefined the law regarding legal picketing so as to make it more difficult. The Labour movement as a whole regarded this act as a spiteful piece of revenge directed against themselves, and the Labour government elected in 1945 lost no time in repealing it in 1946.

The General Strike remains perhaps the most significant event in the history of British trade unionism in the twentieth century. In essence, it was a very British type of general strike, on the whole conducted with very little violence, and certainly not intended to lead to an overthrowing of the government. Indeed, once the strike had commenced and it became clear that the government would not give way, the union leaders were only too glad to take advantage of the Samuel Memorandum and to call the strike off before matters got out of hand. The strength of working-class solidarity remained remarkable. The miners were very much an exclusive part of the working-class community, and very few in other working occupations in industrial areas remote from the coalfields had ever met a miner; yet they were prepared to come out on strike on their behalf – only two

Table 8.6 Trade union membership and working days lost, 1925–39

Year	TU membership (m)	Working days lost (m)
1925	5.51	7.94
1926	5.22	162.23
1927	4.92	1.17
1928	4.81	1.39
1929	4.86	8.20
1930	4.84	4.40
1931	4.62	6.98
1932	4.44	6.49
1933	4.39	1.07
1934	4.59	0.96
1935	4.87	1.96
1936	5.30	1.83
1937	5.84	3.41
1938	6.05	1.33
1939	6.30	1.36

unions refused to call out their members in support. How far the General Strike increased class divisions is open to question. Certainly there was a ready flow of middle-class volunteers to keep essential services going, and Oxford undergraduates offered their services in considerable numbers (though among the students, A.J.P. Taylor, the historian and public figure-to-be, drove a lorry on behalf of the strikers). Middle-class hostility to the strike was to be expected, of course, and here and there working-class supporters of the Conservative Party also opposed the strike. In his patriotic production *Cavalcade* (1931), Noel Coward has a working-class father threatening his son with punishment if he ever supports anything of the kind again. But on the whole, memories of the General Strike faded quite fast. The Labour Party itself was careful to leave the management of the strike to the General Council, and Ramsay MacDonald himself wrote afterwards that 'The General Strike is a weapon that cannot be wielded for industrial purposes. It is clumsy and ineffectual ...'[48]

As for the trade union movement, it had sustained a severe defeat, and this, combined with the effect of the Depression in the early 1930s, is reflected in the membership figures (see Table 8.6).[49] Thus, membership dropped in 1926, 1927, and 1928, and fell to only 4.39 million in 1933. But these were not especially great losses, and the figures improved in the late 1930s, reaching 6.30 million in 1939. The number of working days lost from strikes also noticeably improved from 1933 onwards. This may have been due to an increased reluctance to go on strike, but a better explanation is probably that there were fewer national, as opposed to merely local, strikes than before, and none after 1932. During the period 1919–25, the average loss of working days was 28 million, but between 1927 and 1939 it was only just over 3 million. During the 1930s the trade union leadership benefited from the moderate leadership of the TUC secretary, Walter Citrine (later, Sir Walter Citrine) and of Ernest Bevin, secretary of the Transport and General Workers Union, the largest union of the time.

The Labour Party in office

As for the Labour Party, as already noted, it had been carried forward during the Great War on the shoulders of the trade union movement, and in 1918 it had adopted a new constitution. In the 'coupon election' of 1918, it had separated itself from the Lloyd George coalition government, and stood as an independent party, increasing its numbers of seats from forty-two to fifty-nine, and its popular vote very substantially from 400,000 to 2,374,000.[50] However, the parliamentary party lost two leading members, Ramsay MacDonald and Philip Snowden, on account of their UDC support during the war (they were described as 'Red Flag representatives' by one journal). Rather surprisingly, Arthur Henderson, who had been a member of the wartime inner cabinet, also lost his seat, but all three returned to parliament subsequently. Labour gains in the general election had been helpful, but hardly dramatic: the real loser in the election campaign was the Liberal Party, which had split in December 1916. The greater part stayed with Lloyd George in the coalition; those who kept apart, led by Asquith, secured only twenty-six members. Henceforth, the Labour Party was seen increasingly as the major representative of radicalism. Between 1918 and 1922, Labour won fourteen by-elections. In the general election of 1922 which ended Lloyd George's coalition government, Labour won 142 seats as compared with the Liberals' 116, thus becoming the official opposition in the House of Commons. At this point it could fairly be claimed that the Labour Party was becoming much more a national party rather than a mere pressure group, for only about half of its seats were held by trade unionist MPs.

The Conservative victory in 1922 resulted in a new government led by Bonar Law, who after a short period in office retired owing to bad health. His successor was the Bewdley ironmaster and business man, Stanley Baldwin. After a further six months, Baldwin surprised his party by declaring that in his opinion, only protection of the home market could solve the problem of unemployment. This threw the Conservatives into disarray, while leaving both the Labour Party and the Liberals still firm supporters of free trade. In the general election which followed in December 1923, the Conservatives lost 88 seats, though retaining 258 seats in all. The Labour Party, on the other hand, improved its representation by winning 191 seats, the Liberals 158. The two free-trade parties could now outvote the Conservatives, who resigned office. Asquith then offered his support to Labour, the bigger of the two free-trade parties, should it wish to form a government. It was an opportunity not to be missed. In January 1924 Ramsay MacDonald formed the first, minority Labour government, which was to last just nine months.[51]

It was a remarkable outcome, and by no means an inevitable consequence of industrialisation. It is true that the unprecedented growth and change in the nature of industry from the late eighteenth century onwards might conceivably have led to some form of political democracy and the enfranchisement of the working classes; but there is no reason to suppose that the Liberal Party in the last quarter of the nineteenth century would not continue to represent working-class interests, and indeed did so in the last fine flourish of Liberalism in the pre-1914 reforms. It was not to be. The party founded as a sort of watchdog over the interests of labour in 1900 found itself holding the reins of government in 1924. It was an extraordinary outcome, something quite new in British parliamentary history. Well might King George V note gravely in his diary, 'Today, twenty-three years ago, dear Grandmama died. I wonder what she would have thought of a Labour government!'[52] J.R. Clynes, Lord Privy Seal in the government, wrote later in his *Memoirs*:[53]

> As we stood waiting for His Majesty, amid the gold and crimson of the Palace, I could not help marvelling at the strange turn of Fortune's wheel, which had brought MacDonald, the starveling clerk, Thomas, the engine driver, Henderson, the foundry labourer, and Clynes, the mill hand, to this pinnacle …

It is a well-known passage, and one worth quoting again, though it might be observed that however lowly their origins, by 1924 all were seasoned politicians, well used to parliamentary life; in particular, Ramsay MacDonald was a prominent speaker in the Commons before the war. He may have once been a starving clerk, but he was comfortably off, having married a wealthy woman, grand-niece of Lord Kelvin, in 1896; while Henderson, however lowly his birth, had been a member of the wartime inner cabinet, and had mixed in the highest political circles in the land. However, there is a good story to the effect that at a meeting held in Jimmy Thomas' house in Dulwich to decide on the membership of the cabinet, they found it necessary to send out for an almanac in order to be certain as to the number and nature of ministerial appointments which had to be made.[54]

The major point to make about the Labour government is that it proved to be perfectly competent in conducting the day-to-day business of government. It became clear that ministers from working-class backgrounds displayed as much ability in carrying out their duties as ministers from public schools.[55] Second, its approach in domestic affairs was free from doctrinaire preconceptions. There was no suggestion of a Clause Four programme of nationalisation (it was a minority government, of course, and nationalisation as a policy would have been completely unacceptable to their Liberal allies). Even the trade unions were kept at a distance: MacDonald was prepared to bring in troops to break a threatened strike in the docks. In financial affairs, Snowden, chancellor of the exchequer, pursued a policy of the utmost, conservative rectitude. He abolished the remains of the McKenna duties imposed during the war. The most important social reform was Wheatley's Housing Act, 1924 (mentioned previously in this chapter). In foreign affairs, Labour commitment to international peace was shown in MacDonald's successful chairing of the Dawes Committee conference which revised sums payable as reparations by Germany (MacDonald took on the post of foreign secretary as well as the premiership). He also proposed to grant diplomatic recognition to the Soviet Union, and to sign a trade treaty with the new socialist state, which included financial assistance.

The first Labour government came to a sudden and unexpected end when, after the summer recess, the Liberals chose to support the Conservatives and outvoted the government over a comparatively trivial matter, the Campbell case. J.R. Campbell, a communist, had been prosecuted for alleged sedition (he had appealed to troops not to carry out what he conceived to be wrongful political orders), but the charge was dropped for lack of evidence. The opposition then accused the attorney general of bias and favouritism, whereupon MacDonald announced he would treat the decision of the House as a vote of confidence. When the vote was lost, the government accordingly resigned. There was no need for MacDonald to have taken this stand, and it has been suggested that he was exhausted by the strain of office, and was happy to resign once the government had shown its general competence.

In the election which follows, the Conservatives improved their position, increasing their seats from 258 to 419. Labour seats dropped from 191 to 151, but the party increased their share of the popular vote from 30.7 per cent to 33.3 per cent. The Liberals fared disastrously, their numbers dropping sharply from 158 to 42. From now on, the Labour Party was to replace the Liberals as the second great political party of the state. This general election is remembered for one of the greatest pre-election scares in history. This was the Zinoviev Letter, a secret letter from Zinoviev, President of the Third Communist International in Moscow, to the British Communist Party. It contained instructions on how to spread communist ideas in Britain, in particular in the forces and in industry. Copies were obtained by the Foreign Office and by the *Daily Mail*, which published it on the Saturday preceding the polling day on the following Wednesday. MacDonald ordered that its authenticity be checked, but having done so, does not seem to have taken it very seriously, for he then set out on a lengthy electioneering campaign by motor car. How far the Zinoviev Letter had any effect in turning voters against Labour is difficult to say; a very recent release of government papers seems to show it was in fact genuine. The letter is written in the political jargon of the time, but it does have one or two telling references to British political attitudes, and to the need, for example, to counteract the British workman's willingness to compromise, and to expect to make political gains peacefully rather than by the correct method of revolution.

Baldwin resumed office, and led a somewhat lacklustre administration until another general election was due in 1929. Baldwin's major achievement was to have settled the General Strike successfully (though the 1927 act rubbed salt into the wounds). His election campaign in 1929 was uninspiring, characterised by a rather dull election slogan, 'Safety First'. The result was a loss of Conservative seats, the total dropping to 260, a gain of Labour seats (rising to 288), and a minor rise in Liberal seats to 59. Labour once again took office as a minority government, with Liberal support. Over the next two years the government's principal successes lay in foreign and Empire affairs, with support for the Young Plan (replacing the Dawes Plan for reparations), the London Naval Conference, 1930, the First Round Table Conference, 1930 (concerned with the governing of the Indian Empire), and the Statute of Westminster, 1931, which defined the new relationships between Britain, the Dominions, and the Empire; but home affairs were increasingly dominated by anxiety over unemployment.

It was Labour's misfortune to take office a few months before the Wall Street crash in America which occurred in October 1929. In the following year, unemployment which stood at 2 million in July, rose to 2.5 million by December. The government was forced to borrow heavily to supplement the unemployment fund. The one member of the ministry who advocated planning to reduce unemployment, Oswald Mosley, had his ideas rejected, and resigned. Jimmy Thomas, who was in charge of the problem, proved useless, and was moved to the Dominions Office, being replaced by MacDonald himself. By the spring of 1931, the Liberals were demanding an enquiry into the government's finances, and the May Committee was appointed in February 1931. Its report, published in July, estimated a deficit of £120 million by April 1932, and recommended new taxes of £24 million, plus economies of £96 million, including a 20 per cent cut in the dole. A financial crisis then developed: the cabinet were recalled from holiday, and met repeatedly, while credits were sought from both French and New York bankers. Progress was made in agreeing economies, but the final stumbling block was the proposed cut in the dole (narrowed down to 10 per cent). On this rock, the cabinet split on 23 August – eleven for the cut, nine against (these nine, according to A.J.P. Taylor, thereby acquired a political bread ticket for life). Ramsay MacDonald maintained there was no alternative to balancing the budget, cutting the dole, and remaining on the gold standard – an entirely conventional approach. He therefore resigned. It was the end of the second Labour government.

Worse was to follow for the Labour Party: MacDonald was then persuaded by the King, Baldwin, and Samuel to stay on as prime minister of a national (that is, coalition) government to pass the necessary reforms. Only three members of his previous cabinet stayed in the new government – Snowden, Thomas, and Sankey. Baldwin and Samuel then joined the government, which passed the cuts (including the cut in the dole). In September, the national government went off gold, something which MacDonald had earlier refused to consider. In October, the national government held a general election, and offered itself for re-election (the Labour Party bitterly opposed this). National candidates scored an overwhelming victory, winning 566 seats. Labour seats were reduced from 288 to a lowly 46. Ultimately, all the three Labour ministers who stuck with MacDonald either resigned or retired, while the Liberal supporters of the national government withdrew after the 1932 tariff reforms. Thus, MacDonald was left as prime minister of a virtually Conservative government until his retirement in 1935.

It was a most remarkable political disaster for the Labour Party, who have always regarded MacDonald as the villain of the piece – the traitor who sold out to the Conservatives, deserting his own comrades in a moment of crisis, then having the impertinence to stay in office as a so-called saviour of the nation: Attlee even called the events of 1931 'the greatest political betrayal in our annals'. MacDonald made things worse by his own evident liking for mixing with high society. Some accused him of deliberately planning the downfall of his government and the creation of a national government. Others put it all down to a bankers' plot (a 'bankers' ramp', it was called at the time) which had been contrived to get rid of the Labour government. Robert Skidelsky has pointed out that the cabinet as a whole believed that the nature of capitalism was the root cause of the crisis, and socialism was the ultimate answer, but they had no mandate from the electorate for any fundamental change in the economic system. All they could do was to maintain the existing system, at the same time protecting the unemployed as far as possible. When this tactic failed, they had no answer left, and simply collapsed in disarray.[56] At the heart of the controversy lie MacDonald's beliefs and motives: and it is clear from his diary that he did not think he was deserting his comrades – on the contrary, they were deserting him. On 1 September he wrote:[57]

> The desertion of colleagues and the flight of the Lab govt having grievous effect … what a destruction of all we have done. Had the Govt done its duty there would have been little interruption in that work. They ran away & left everything unprotected.

According to David Marquand, in an impressive biography of MacDonald, there was no question of his wanting to break away from his party – he did not, but he failed to consult it, and he did admit this. His motives were genuine enough; he really thought the country would be ruined if the cuts were not made and the gold standard not maintained – he considered that there was no practical radical alternative. But according to Marquand, he could have introduced tariff reform earlier on, and he would have been supported by Keynes; but he rejected Keynes' advice on 31 August. All in all, it was his economics which were to blame, not his motives, in Marquand's view. In the last analysis, however, his government had collapsed, and he cannot avoid his share of the blame for this.

Curiously enough, the Labour Party made a good electoral recovery five years later from the debacle of 1931; they gained 154 seats in the general election held in 1935, and in 1939 some even thought they might have made a good showing and actually won the next general election due in 1940. The coming of war in 1939 prevented that election from being held. By that time George Lansbury, who had retired as Labour Party leader in 1935, had been replaced by the quiet, middle-class C.R. Attlee, MP for Limehouse, whose background was Haileybury, Oxford University, and social work in the East End of London (at one time he was mayor of Stepney). The inter-war years had seen some extraordinary changes for the Labour Party. It had established itself as one of the two great national parties of the time, replacing the Liberal Party as the leading party of the working classes, a remarkable feat considering the difficulty of any third party achieving this in a fundamentally two-party system. It was the split in the Liberal Party which was a major factor in bringing this about, although other factors such as the extension of the franchise in 1918 also played a part. A proportion of the working classes still voted either Conservative or Liberal in 1929, but the fact remains that one of the two leading political parties at that time was pledged to reform the whole political and economic system in accordance with Clause Four of its constitution. The wrongs allegedly inflicted on the working classes by industrialisation would then be righted. However, this task would not be undertaken without the full democratic support of the electorate. It remains to be seen how far the long-term objectives of the Labour Party were to be achieved in the 1940s.

Leisure interests

Something has still to be said about leisure interests, and about contemporary comments on the progress of the nation. For most of the working classes, leisure interests became more varied and also more numerous as real wages increased and the working day was reduced. The working week for the vast majority still ended at midday on Saturday, leaving the rest of the weekend free. For the middle classes, leisure pursuits included time spent at the tennis club or golf club, or in the family motor car, which increasingly became a cherished middle-class or upper-class possession. For the upper classes, many of the pre-war routines went on as before; young women ('debutantes') were still presented at court, weekend house parties were common, and Royal Ascot and Henley were still great social occasions. All classes were affected by two technological advances. The first was broadcasting and the wireless. The British Broadcasting Company was established as a commercial venture, with a formidable managing director in the person of John Reith. In December 1926 the company was replaced by the British Broadcasting Corporation, set up by royal charter, committed to providing not only entertainment but also educative programmes. It had a monopoly in broadcasting throughout the inter-war period. BBC programmes were a mixture of plays and features (mostly very worthy, and some very dull), sports commentaries, Children's Hour, variety and comedy shows, news bulletins (at first in the evenings only, to avoid competition with the newspapers), and dance music in the late evening, relayed from the London hotels (though an official BBC dance band was formed later, led by Henry Hall, late of the Gleneagles Hotel). By 1939 the BBC had become a national institution. The earlier receivers were run on batteries and accumulators, and needed headphones. By the 1930s they could be run off the mains, and had built-in speakers. What had been called the 'wireless' was by now the 'radio', and had become a new and immensely popular form of home entertainment, which was to be found in the humblest home. By 1939 the number of radio licences issued had risen to nearly nine million, though many listened in without the formality of having purchased a licence. The first TV transmissions began in 1936, but their audience was very small and confined to the London area; and transmissions ended when war began.

The other great technological innovation was the talking film, the first being *The Jazz Singer*, featuring Al Jolson, shown in 1927. Cinema-going was already well established, of course, but the coming of the talkies meant an enormous increase in the popularity of film, with a great influx of American-made films, usually made in Hollywood – musicals (such as the Fred Astaire–Ginger Rogers films); westerns, comedies; dramas; gangster, prison, and war films; and Walt Disney cartoons. Most programmes consisted of a major film, a supporting film, a news reel (either the *Pathé Gazette*, or the *Gaumont British News*), together with some advertisements. All this was provided for less than a shilling in the cheapest seats (those nearest the screen or at an angle), and in warm and comfortable surroundings. Bigger cinemas might even have a Crompton organ which rose majestically from the depths in the intervals to play popular music. Thus there developed a new and extraordinary form of popular culture, with its own palaces of pleasure, its own film star gods and goddesses, and its own fanzines, such as the *Picturegoer*. Cinema attendances reached remarkable figures: by 1937, about 20 million went to the cinema weekly, and about a quarter of these went more than once a week (most cinemas changed their programmes midweek). The weekly visit to the cinema became an accepted feature of both working-class and middle-class life. Britain had a film industry of its own, but it was very small by comparison with the American industry in Hollywood, where most of the great film studios were located, together with the luxurious homes of the film stars themselves. Cinema-going was immensely popular with employed and unemployed alike. For those out of work, a few pence spent on a seat was an agreeable escape from the privations and boredom of life on the dole.

The principal other working-class leisure activity outside the home remained a visit to the pub, still the meeting place for the friendly society, and a place for dominoes, cards, and darts. Prosecutions for drunkenness fell between the wars, possibly the result of the wartime restrictions on hours which continued in peacetime. The other great working-class activity at weekends was attendance at football matches, where attendances at First Division matches were much greater than today. In 1923 King George V presented the FA Cup at Wembley; leading footballers such as Alex James and Dixie Dean became well known nationally, though they were still paid little more than skilled workman's wages. Cycling became increasingly popular among the working classes, as did speedway racing; and from 1926 onwards, there was greyhound racing in specially built, floodlit tracks, with bookmakers in attendance. Rambling and country walking (hiking) also became popular, the Youth Hostel Association being founded in 1930. Railway excursions were still available, though the railways now had to compete against trips laid on in charabancs or motor coaches. In the towns, trams had as competitors increasingly comfortable motor buses, and also a new form of electric tram, the trolley bus, which was not restricted to rails and was immensely quieter and faster. All in all, in spite of the bleakness of life on the dole, there was an unmistakable air of greater affluence in working-class life as a whole between the wars. Everywhere, both men and women seemed to be able to afford to smoke (the cheapest cigarettes were Wills' Woodbines, and Players' Weights, both ten for fourpence). Most men and women went to the cinema at least once a week, and more and more read a popular newspaper; the Labour *Daily Herald* had a readership of two million. The popular press ran great competitions among their readers to increase circulation, giving as prizes complete sets of Dickens and similar worthy gifts. Newspapers were important for the racing and football results, of course, and football pools had 10 million customers by 1938. The beer can had yet to make its appearance, and beer off the premises was usually drunk from bottles (though it could also be purchased in jugs from the Bottle and Jug

Department of public houses). Potato crisps had come onto the market by 1939, principally in the form of Smith's Crisps, with salt included in a twist of blue paper. In the Midlands and the north, some traditional leisure pursuits lingered on, such as the keeping of racing pigeons (the 'Fancy') and whippets, though many aspects of contemporary life today were already evident in the crowded cities and towns of the time – the traffic jams, with motor traffic now predominating over horse traffic, the multiple shops (every town had its Woolworths with the familiar red and gold frontage), the urban emptiness at weekends when the nation took its leisure and deserted the business areas. Saturday night was still the great night out, of course, at the cinema, pub, club, or dancehall (the best place for youths to meet girls). Mass entertainment was becoming even more commercialised, whether it was in the form of the cinema or professional sport, or even in providing for some sudden craze such as the yo-yo.

Contemporary attitudes

Finally, what did contemporary observers think of England between the wars? The tone of much that was to be published afterwards was set by Lytton Strachey's *Eminent Victorians* in 1918, a gently iconoclastic series of biographies of leading Victorians such as Thomas Arnold, Florence Nightingale, and General Gordon, all of whom were shown (in varying degrees) to have had feet of clay. Yet for the first two years of peace, during the period of boom conditions, public attention was focused rather on the peace negotiations, the punishment of Germany, and demobilisation. Only after 1920 as unemployment grew did concern begin to manifest itself, not only with the economic and social state of the nation, but with the conduct of the war and the apparent failure of the great sacrifices made to bring about a brave new world. This can be seen in two books published in 1922. The first is Charles Masterman's *England After War*, which was intended as a sequel to his *Condition of England* (1909). The mood of Masterman's 1922 book is sombre – *The Times* criticised the gloom of the first chapter which dwelt upon the unemployed figure of 2 million. The author was clearly impressed by the extent of industrial conflict immediately following the end of the war; although sympathetic to the working classes, he claimed that after a war in which all classes should have learned to understand each other, there remained 'a greater cleavage of class than has existed for half a century'. His last chapter, 'In after years', argues that material progress in England was assured, but there could be no happiness or tranquillity of the nation without spiritual regeneration.

The second significant publication in 1922 was C.E. Montague's *Disenchantment*. Here the title says it all: the war had been fought for all the right things, but little had been achieved – 'so we had failed – had won the fight, and lost the prize; the garland of the war was withered before it was gained'.[58] The book is highly critical of the army's higher command, and of aspects of the old regular army, the politicians, and the church militant. There is a particularly strong passage on the last subject – 'Watered by "war's red rain", one bishop tells us, virtue grows; a cannonade, he points out, is an "oratorio" – almost a form of worship.'[59] Unlike Masterman, who was really too old to serve, Montague, an ex-*Guardian* journalist, had dyed his hair, joined up, and fought in the trenches. In his view, the only hope for the future was 'to stand up for what was right, proper, and decent, and support the League of Nations, as must all ex-servicemen – the most determined peace party that ever existed in Britain'.[60]

These two books were followed towards the end of the 1920s by a number of works which sounded a strong anti-war note. In 1928 they included R.C. Sherriff's famous play about bravery and cowardice in the trenches, *Journey's End*, and Edmund Blunden's *Undertones of War*; in 1929 Richard Arlington published his bitter novel, *Death of a Hero*; E.M. Remarque, *All Quiet on the Western Front* (perhaps the most famous of all World War I novels) also appeared, and so did Robert Graves' *Goodbye to All That*. In 1930, there was Siegfried Sassoon's *Memoirs of an Infantry Officer*. By the 1930s, hatred of war, which had become a familiar theme in literary circles, had acquired a political edge. By now the view that Germany had been primarily responsible for the war had become a minority opinion. It was now often argued that the war had begun by mistake; or because of the arms race; or it was due to national grievances; or it had been caused by capitalism, especially by armament manufacturers.[61] It is extraordinary how quickly the view was forgotten that the Great War had been fought for honourable reasons against an aggressor seeking to dominate Europe. By the 1930s, the war was often referred to as 'futile'. Yet at the time it had seemed clear that it was imperative to defeat the threat of German hegemony. As for wars being caused by capitalism, this was very much a left-wing view, encouraged by the apparent achievements of the Soviet Union where the First Five-year Plan had begun in 1928. It was in the 1930s that the younger generation of poets – W.H. Auden, Stephen Spender, Louis MacNeice, and Cecil Day Lewis – all exhibited a kind of unconsidered, left-wing acceptance that capitalism was doomed and grinding to a halt, just as Marx had predicted – was not the massive extent of unemployment clear evidence of this? The future was therefore dark and unpredictable:[62]

> We're afraid in that case you'll have a fall.
> We've been watching you over the garden wall
> For hours.
> The sky is darkening like a stain
> Something is going to fall like rain
> And it won't be flowers.

This belief in the approaching demise of capitalist society acquired additional urgency with the outbreak of the Spanish Civil War in 1936, and true believers in socialism joined the International Brigade to defend the left-wing Spanish government against the fascist uprising led by General Franco (Auden published his verse-poem *Spain* in 1937). For many, to be young and intellectual meant being, as a matter of course, against the national government, and left-wing, if not actually a Communist Party member or sympathiser.

However, as well as stimulating political opposition, the rise of fascist dictators in Europe increased the fear of war and the likelihood of mass bombing from the air of British town and cities. This in turn increased pacifist emotions in Britain. In February 1933 the Oxford Union passed its celebrated motion against fighting for king and country, and in the East Fulham by-election, Labour gained the seat from the Conservatives on a platform of support for the League of Nations and rejection of rearmament. In 1934 the Peace Pledge Union was formed: by 1936, it had 100,000 members, all of whom pledged never to support or approve another war. The League of Nations peace ballot of 1934–5 produced a more equivocal result: 6.25 million voted to stop an aggressor if necessary by war, 2 million disagreed, and another 2 million did not answer. The left-wing of the Labour Party was strongly anti-capitalist and pro-pacifist in its outlook. Not until 1935, as we have just noted, was its pacifist leader George Lansbury replaced by C.R. Attlee. Even then, Attlee continued to oppose rearmament. In May, 1935 he spelt out the Labour policy quite precisely:[63]

> We stand for collective security through the League of Nations. We reject the use of force as an instrument of policy ... Our policy is not one of seeking security through rearmament but through disarmament.

All this helps to explain why the Munich settlement in September 1938 was greeted with such approval: there was a very widespread fear of war, dating back to the 1914–18 conflict, and reinforced by the fear of bombing, which had been increased by Baldwin's sombre prediction that 'the bomber will always get through'. The Labour Party stubbornly stood by its policy. Every year between the wars up to 1938 it voted against the military estimates. Only after Munich did it change this policy: it abstained, instead of voting against. Somehow, it was thought that collective security could be achieved without armaments.

It is hard to sum up informed opinion on the state of the industrial nation between the wars. First there was a very natural and understandable revulsion against war in the 1920s, then later the ideological belief that war was somehow the product of capitalism, the greatest threat to peace being the great dictators, who had manipulated 'big business' in their own interests. Throughout the 1930s there was the persistent and increasing fear of aerial bombing, and of the use of poison gas as a military weapon (it will be remembered that gas masks were distributed to the civilian population during the Munich crisis). At the same time, unemployment was endlessly debated, many social surveys undertaken, and one of the most striking works on the subject was published in 1937, George Orwell's *The Road to Wigan Pier*. Yet it was not all debate about war, economics, capitalism, and air raids. Especially in the 1930s, there were middle-class planning groups concerned with a variety of social and economic issues, such as Political and Economic Planning (PEP), set up in 1931, and the Next Five Years Group, established in 1934. At the same time, the middle classes went on borrowing their novels from Boot's Circulating Library – Evelyn Waugh found literary fame with *Decline and Fall* (1928), *Vile Bodies* (1930), and *Scoop* (1938), while J.B. Priestley published his immensely successful *The Good Companions* in 1929. P.G. Wodehouse developed a unique vein of humour with his stories of Jeeves and Bertie Wooster, while in the 1930s Graham Greene published a series of novels exploring the bleaker sides of human nature, the best known before the war probably being *Brighton Rock* (1938). Among other novelists of note, Virginia Woolf became established as one of the most innovative with her use of the 'stream of consciousness' technique: see her *Mrs Dalloway* (1925), *To the Lighthouse* (1927), and *The Waves* (1931). In the same experimental field, the work of James Joyce, perhaps the greatest novelist of the times (*Ulysses* (1922) and *Finnegan's Wake* (1939)), remains unique. In a different field, Agatha Christie was the queen of detective fiction writers between the wars, with such classic works as *The Murder of Roger Ackroyd* in 1926.

For the youngster growing up between the wars in the prosperous south-east and London area, the world presented a curious mixture of fascination and of fear. On the one hand, there was the appeal of non-stop novelty – radio entertainment was new, the cinema with its all-talking, all-singing, all-dancing Hollywood extravaganza was new. Motor cars were increasingly numerous, fascinating, splendid, and symbolic of the new age, shops were modern in display and advertising techniques and had their names in the new coloured (and sometimes flashing) neon lighting, new buildings were constructed of ferro-concrete with flat roofs and steel-framed windows – everywhere there were signs of change, things were becoming smarter, more modern, all against the background of ragtime, jazz, and dance music, the popular music of the young. American influences and catchphrases were everywhere, and also a certain degree of American triumphalism (everyone knew, especially in the 1920s, that the Americans had the biggest and tallest of everything, and were not slow to inform everyone of it – as one popular American song put it, 'I'll tell the cock-eyed world …'). On the other hand, and especially in the 1930s, there was an increasing awareness that in the Depressed Areas there was real poverty, not only unemployment, but also malnutrition, ill health, and wretched housing – poverty in the midst of plenty, in fact, the old charge against industrial capitalism. If industrialisation had brought a better standard of living to many, it was not to all, and especially not to the long-term unemployed. Moreover, something had obviously gone wrong with the post-war peace settlement, for it had somehow spawned the dictators, and the threat of another world war. So life in the 1930s provided both the excitement and appeal of change, novelty, and innovation, and an increasing fear of another war, this time not a war in the trenches but one in which destruction would rain down from the skies on the civilian population ('And it won't be flowers …'). In the 1930s, cinema audiences watched entranced as Fred Astaire and Ginger Rogers in *The Gay Divorcee* sang, 'There may be trouble ahead, but as long as there's music, and love, and romance, Let's face the music and dance …' Indeed, there was trouble ahead, and war came again on 3 September 1939.

9 War and the coming of the Welfare State

The war period, 1939–45

The outbreak of hostilities again in September 1939 brought a very different kind of war from that of World War I. In fact, after a period of relative inactivity in military terms (the 'phoney war', as the Americans called it), France was overwhelmed and the British army evacuated from Dunkirk in May 1940. The second phase of the war was characterised by the defeat of the German attempts to destroy the Royal Air Force in the Battle of Britain and the attacks of the German *Luftwaffe* on British cities and towns (the Blitz). There was also extensive fighting against first Italian then German troops in North Africa and later in Italy. During this period, Germany invaded Russia in June 1941, and Japan attacked the USA in December 1941 at Pearl Harbour. Germany thereupon declared war on the United States, thereby bringing Britain a very welcome ally. The third period of the war may be said to date from this point to D-Day, in June 1944, when a so-called Second Front was opened up with massed Allied landings in France. During this period, Britain suffered serious losses of territory in the Far East to Japan, including Burma. The fourth and last period of war lasted till VE Day (Victory in Europe Day) in May 1945, which was followed shortly afterwards by VJ Day (Victory over Japan Day), Japan having surrendered after the dropping of two atom bombs on the Japanese mainland on 6 and 9 August.

World War II resembled the Great War in that it placed enormous strains on the British economy, and on the industrial system. Indeed, it was even more financially ruinous than the first war, and left Britain virtually bankrupt by 1945, especially when the lend-lease arrangement with the USA for the supply of military equipment was abruptly terminated at the end of the war.[1] However, it is possible to distinguish a number of social aspects of the war which will be commented on in this chapter. These include conscription, the regulation of the work force, the role of civilians, their health and welfare, and a much more vigorous attempt to plan the future than was apparent in the first war.[2]

To start with conscription: this had been introduced even before war began, and was continued after the war from 1947 onwards in the form of National Service. Men were called up from the age of eighteen, and for the first time, in and after 1941, women were also conscripted. At first women had to be single to be liable for service, and between the ages of nineteen and twenty-four, but these ages were later adjusted to eighteen-and-a-half to fifty. Women also had a choice between service in the Auxiliary Teritorial Service (ATS), Women's Auxiliary Air Force (WAAF), and the Women's Royal Naval Service (WRNS), and in civil defence or essential civilian jobs. By 1945 there were nearly half a million women serving in the women's forces, and five million men in the men's forces. Conscientious objectors were again allowed to register, and 2,900 objectors were given complete exemption, and 40,000 given conditional exemption, being allowed to undertake non-combatant duties as medical orderlies, service in bomb disposal units, and the like. Some very distinguished refugees from Nazi rule found themselves enrolled for the time being in the Pioneer Corps. Military casualties were light at first, and in the first three years of war, more women and children were killed than soldiers. Increasingly, bomber crews suffered very heavy casualty rates, at least as high as those of officers in the trenches in World War I. All in all, about 370,000 were killed in the armed forces, and 35,000 in the merchant navy.

As for the civilian work force, maximum war production was essential as in the previous war, and hours grew longer in the factories, especially after Dunkirk. New ministries were created to supervise production – first the Ministry of Supply, then a new separate Ministry of Air Production in 1940, and then later on in February 1942, a Ministry of Production. As might be expected, the direction and control of labour was considered essential, and this was secured very largely by four orders: the Defence Regulation 58A (issued under the Emergency Powers (Defence) Act, 1940) gave wide powers of control to the minister of labour, Ernest Bevin, while under Order 1305, strikes and lock-outs were made illegal. Wages disputes were to go to a national arbitration tribunal (it had issued 816 adjudications by the end of the war). The Restriction on Engagement Order, 1940, allowed the engagement of labour only through an approved trade union or a labour exchange. The fourth order, the Essential Work

(General Provisions) Order, March 1941, controlled the employment of skilled labour. Once in a specified skilled job, a worker was not permitted to leave it, and his or her wages and working conditions were under government control. All civilians had to carry their identity cards at all times, and in fact it has been said that the British worker was subject to more regimentation and restriction than the typical German worker under Nazi rule.

It was of course vital to maintain good labour relations in industry, and a number of consultative bodies were set up for this purpose. Regional boards of industry were established in 1941, and in 1942 the National Production Advisory Council was appointed. Lower down the scale were joint production committees, with direct representation of the workers; about 3.5 million workers were represented on such councils by 1945. Wage levels were generally left to negotiation, but in 1940 the Central Agricultural Wages Board was set up to fix minimum wages for male agricultural workers, and in 1943 the Catering Wages Act led to the appointment of the Catering Wages Commission. In 1945 the various trades boards were given wider powers as wages boards. Working conditions improved in a number of ways: welfare officers had to be provided in factories employing more than 250 workers. The number of factory doctors and nurses went up: in 1939 there were only 35 full-time and 70 part-time factory doctors, and 1,500 factory nurses. By 1944 there were 181 full-time and 890 part-time factory doctors, and by 1943, there were 8,000 factory nurses. Half-hour programmes of popular music were broadcast twice a day with the title 'Music While You Work', and large factories had their dinner hours enlivened by live broadcast shows cheerfully entitled 'Workers' Playtime'.

Since war production was so important, co-operation between government and the trade unions was clearly essential, as indeed it had been in the previous war.[3] As noted earlier, the leader of the Transport and General Workers Union, Ernest Bevin, became the formidable minister of labour once the coalition government was formed in 1940. As unemployment fell during the course of the war (it stood at only 112,000 in June 1943), so trade union membership increased from 6.05 million in 1938 to 8.07 million in 1944. After dropping in 1945 to 7.87 million, it rose again in 1946 to an unprecedented 8.8 million. Striking was illegal, of course, but according to Pollard, strikes were short, small, and unofficial, with the exception of miners' strikes, some engineers' strikes in 1940, and a boilermakers' strike in 1944.[4] In the engineering and associated industries, 90 per cent of strikes in 1943 and 1944 lasted for less than a week, and prosecutions for striking were relatively rare: during the six years of war, there were only seventy-one in Scotland and thirty-eight in England and Wales. In 1944 there were only three prosecutions in the whole of England and Wales, and although the maximum fine was £25, a fine of £5 was more usual. The mining industry remained a problem. Output actually fell up to 1942, when there was something of a crisis in production, leading to the setting up of the Ministry of Fuel and Power. Things were little better by the end of the war, though some improvements had been made by then in production methods: coal cut by machinery had gone up from 61 per cent of output to 75 per cent, while the quantity of coal conveyed mechanically had also gone up from 58 per cent to 71 per cent.[5] Most of the difficulties in the coal industry centred on disputes with the owners over low piece-rates, though there were also problems of manpower, so that Bevin was actually forced towards the end of the war to introduce a very limited degree of conscription into the mines. The unfortunate conscripts were promptly nicknamed 'Bevin boys'.

Altogether industry responded very well to the strains imposed by the war. Inevitably, certain industries of great strategic importance were stimulated as a result – engineering, vehicle, and aircraft manufacture, the iron and steel industry, the chemical industry, and agriculture. Aircraft production, for example, rose from 2,800 aircraft in 1938 to more than 26,000 in 1943 and 1944. The production of machine tools in which Britain had hitherto been backwards, rose from 35,000 in 1939 to 100,000 in 1942. The urgent need for greater production of foodstuffs at home led to a great extension of arable cultivation from under 12 million acres to about 18 million acres.[6] In few cases, if any, was any attempt made to reconstruct or modernise industry so as to make it better equipped to face the post-war challenge of rival industrial nations; but this is understandable enough in view of the need to meet the urgent demands for war production. Such efforts had to await the return of peacetime conditions, for any attempts to reorganise industry in the desperate and dark days of the early 1940s would have seemed impractical, foolish, and shockingly utopian in the face of the immediate threat to national freedom.[7]

What were the principal results of the war on workers' health and wellbeing? For many citizens, the Blitz was an outstanding and shattering experience.[8] London suffered the worst: after a daylight raid on the London docks on 7 September 1940, costing 430 lives, London was subjected to continuous raids at night in the autumn of 1940. On 30 December 1940, a great fire-bomb attack on the City of London started 1,500 fires and wiped out a large part of Cripplegate, off London Wall. Meanwhile, Coventry was targeted in a raid lasting ten hours and costing 554 deaths with 865 seriously injured. Attacks were also made on the ports including Merseyside, Bristol, Southampton, Portsmouth, and Plymouth. The raids eased off in January and February 1941, but increased again in the spring, with London having its worst attack on 10 May 1941 (1,436 killed, 1,792 seriously injured). The next most seriously bombed city was probably Birmingham, which had 400 killed in a raid on 19 November 1940. Three days later, another 113 were killed in Birmingham; on 11 December, 263 were killed; and on 9 April 1941, the heaviest raid of all on the city resulted in a death toll of 1,121.

The German attack on Russia in June 1941 brought some relief in the bombing, by which time more than 2 million houses had been damaged, 60 per cent of these being in London. But in January 1944 raids began again, and London, Bristol, and South Wales were again raided. After D-Day, June 1944, bomber raids ceased altogether except for a new menace in London and the south-east – first, flying bombs (V1s or 'doodle-bugs'), then rockets (V2s). The flying bombs were eventually mastered by moving AA guns to the coast, attacking the bombs by aircraft in the air, and by strengthening the balloon barrage round London. As for the V2, there was no defence. They travelled faster than sound, and gave no warning of their approach. They killed 2,724 and badly injured more than 6,000. Capturing the launching sites was the only way of stopping them. The last V2 fell on Orpington in Kent on 27 March 1945.

On the whole, civilian morale stood up to the air raids and the V1s and V2s very well, though nerves were strained to the utmost. All in all, 3.75 million houses were damaged, deaths from bombing in 1940 and 1941 amounted to 43,000, and the total of such deaths for the whole war came to 60,000, with about 86,000 seriously injured and 151,000 suffering minor injuries. The working classes, of course, bore the brunt of the German attacks – air-raid wardens, heavy rescue squads, firemen, policemen, and ambulance workers, all were active in rescue work, assisted by volunteers such as fire-watchers, Home Guard units, the Women's Voluntary Service (always on hand with mugs of tea), and the Salvation Army. These rescue workers did not exclude the middle classes, of course, but many of the middle classes were able to evacuate themselves from the cities to safer areas in the nearby countryside. Not all of whatever class behaved heroically. In 1941, there were 4,585 cases of looting in London alone.

Not only did civilian morale remain high during the war, but health statistics actually improved during the first half of the 1940s. Infant mortality figures, for example, declined from 56 per 1,000 live births in England to 45 in 1944–5. One reason for improved national health, paradoxically enough, was the introduction of food rationing from 1940 onwards which ensured a fair distribution of essential foodstuffs. At the same time, cheap milk was provided for younger children and expectant mothers, who were also supplied with orange juice, cod-liver oil, vitamins, and extra eggs. Another reason for the improvement in the health of the nation was the virtual disappearance of unemployment after mid-1941. The result was that personal consumption was improved for the unskilled worker, whose standard of living rose to something approaching that of the pre-war, skilled worker. It is true that the cost of living rose by about 50 per cent by 1944, but longer hours of work, more overtime, and more piecework meant that real wages rose substantially, by over 81 per cent. Life on the Home Front therefore became rather more comfortable in terms of real income, and rents were fixed as early as 1939. At the same time, there was increasingly less and less to buy in the shops. By mid-1941, personal consumption was down by 14 per cent on pre-war spending, and less was being spent on everything except beer, tobacco, the cinema, and public transport. Further, although women's wage rates rose faster than those of men, they were still only half the rates paid to men.

How far the status of women actually improved during the war is not easy to assess.[9] One school of thought has it that the war brought a further instalment of social and economic freedom for women, accompanied by a greater sense of self-esteem and confidence. This, it is argued, is because women welcomed the wartime changes, and the chance to improve their lives. Substantial numbers of younger women were engaged in one form or another of national service during the war, and the desire for greater personal freedom can be seen in the simple fact that in 1931, only 10 per cent of married women were at work, whereas by 1951 this figure had increased to 21.74 per cent. Against this can be set the fact that of the women caught up by conscription, many had worked before the war, but (according to a survey conducted in October 1941) about a third did not want to do any war work. As for the contention that women's attitudes had changed, in fact in a 1943 survey only a third of women in employment said they wanted to go on working after the war. Admittedly, the figure given earlier on for the increase in married women at work after the war appears significant, but for the fact that the number at work had increased by 4 per cent already by 1939, so that the increase which did take place was on a pre-war rising trend. Lastly, although the marriage bar on employment was dropped in both the teaching profession and in the civil service, it was for reasons unconnected with women's war work. Many other employers removed the marriage bar, but this was simply on account of the shortage of labour. All in all, there is a superficial attraction in the idea that the war period proved a great liberating force for women, but it is difficult to provide substantial evidence to support the argument. However, of the half-million women who served in the forces, it seems fair to say that some would have shouldered new responsibilities as non-commissioned or commissioned officers, and this could have given them increased self-confidence and self-reliance on their return to civvy street; and of those who remained humble rankers, experience of life away from the constraints of family life could have brought an added maturity and self-knowledge. What seems undeniable is that it did not result in any beneficial legislation such as, for example, the introduction of votes for women at the end of World War I. The one measure introduced in 1944 to end all forms of sex discrimination – the Citizen (Blanket) bill – was sunk without a trace.

Leisure activities were naturally curtailed during the war by the bombing, and by restrictions on travel by both rail and road (petrol was rationed, of course).[10] Seaside holidays of the conventional kind became difficult as access to south-coast beaches was often prevented by barbed-wire defences and pill boxes, while some major seaside resorts such as Blackpool were virtually taken over by the RAF or army as training centres. Nevertheless, many peacetime leisure forms of entertainment continued, such as professional football and cricket, but on a greatly reduced scale, sometimes with scratch sides, while cinema-going reached new heights of popularity: weekly attendances were between 25 and 30 million, three-quarters of the entire adult population going weekly to the cinema. For the working man, the pub was still his club, generally packed full with service men (including gum-chewing American GIs from 1942 onwards), noisy, the atmosphere suffocatingly hot and thick with cigarette smoke, especially once the blackouts were up after dark. At home, the radio was the principal form of entertainment, supplying not only news bulletins (a vital form of information on how the war was going) and government announcements – the news readers now giving their names for easy identification – but also for light entertainment such as Tommy Handley in ITMA (*It's That Man Again*), *Hi Gang*, and *Variety Bandbox*. Tommy Handley died suddenly in 1945. A.J.P. Taylor has remarked that Handley deserved a place in Westminster Abbey; he did not get it. The radio was the best source of getting to know the popular dance music of the day, with one American swing band becoming a great favourite – Glen Miller and his Orchestra. Vera Lynn, the 'Forces Sweetheart', was the leading British singer, famous for two hits in particular, 'The White Cliffs of Dover' and 'We'll Meet Again'. Some of the hits of the day had alternative, unofficial words, sometimes of a grossly improper nature, devised by unknown lyricists, and sung in service circles. Thus the catchy number, 'Jealousy', popular in 1942, had the following unusually innocuous and would-be humorous words ('SOP' means 'Sleeping-Out Pass'):

> It was all over my SOP
> I cried over my SOP
> For he was a squadron leader in the RAF
> And I was a poor little innocent WAAF
> He gave all his kisses to me
> And now I'm a mother-to-be
> For he was my lover
> I daren't tell my mother
> Twas all over my SOP.

However, the government did a certain amount to encourage interest of a more refined kind in the fine arts. The Council for Education in Music and the Arts arranged tours by leading ballet companies such as the Sadlers Wells Ballet Company and the Marie Rambert Ballet, together with concerts of classical music, and exhibitions of the visual arts. Myra Hess, the distinguished pianist, gave a famous series of concerts in the National Gallery at the height of the Blitz. Veterans of the variety stage provided a lighter form of entertainment, such as Max Miller, who specialised in smutty innuendo which curiously enough, did not always go down well with the troops. Dancehalls providing cheap 'hops' were still very popular, and often crowded with service personnel. A new organisation was set up by the government especially to entertain the troops – the Entertainments National Services Association (ENSA). The entertainment provided by ENSA varied in quality (the initials ENSA were said to stand for 'Every Night Something Awful'), but in fact ENSA did good work in garrison theatres both at home and abroad. The tradition of providing light and relaxing shows for the troops dated back at least to World War I with its touring concert parties, such as the famous 'Roosters'. An added refinement in World War II was the organisation on some of the larger units of record programmes and comedy shows over the station's tannoy system. Another alternative to the station cinema often took the form of bingo sessions, more commonly known as 'tombola'.

As for the nation's system of state schools, it suffered considerable disorganisation due to the war.[11] First there was the evacuation of children and of mothers of small children from the cities at the beginning of the war. Most city schools were entirely closed at first, but then gradually reopened as bombing failed to materialise. By the end of 1939, about half of those originally evacuated (344,900 out of 764,000) had returned home. Meanwhile, many school buildings had surrendered rooms for use as air-raid warden posts and first-aid posts. A survey conducted in January 1940 showed that of 1.5 million elementary school children, only 47 per cent were attending school. Another 24 per cent were being taught at home in home teaching classes, while 27.9 per cent were not being taught at all. By March 1940 things had improved, but attendance was still poor in places – for example, although Birmingham had 74.5 per cent in attendance, Liverpool had only 24.4 per cent, and Manchester 23.6 per cent. At this point the government decided that all attendance might be made compulsory from the beginning of April. Within three months the bombing of cities began which had been feared from the beginning of the war, so that a new evacuation of children took place.

Thereafter what happened varied from city to city, but there was often great damage to schools inflicted by the raids. Birmingham is a good example: after the heavy raid there of 22 November 1940, the local inspector of schools, Mr F.T. Arnold, wrote to the Board of Education that 75 per cent of the schools were closed, the result of the water supply being cut off over two-thirds of the city:[12]

> About 40 schools have received heavy damage, most of them direct hits. About another 100 have received minor damage ... To sum up, the educational machine as it was functioning up to November 20th has been smashed beyond repair. An emergency machine will have to be created.

No doubt the local educational authority struggled through somehow, but both children and teachers suffered from loss of sleep, quite apart from the danger of physical injury or death. By September 1941, to add to the general strain, the shortage of teachers was being felt more and more as teachers were called up. According to Arnold, 'for the children who remain in the cities, it is all loss. Their environment is even more hellish than it was in peacetime.'[13] No doubt Arnold was feeling the strain when he wrote in such terms (his superiors to whom he reported were in the relative safety of Bournemouth), but it was an anxious and difficult time. Earlier in 1941, the chairman of Birmingham Education Committee claimed that about 40 per cent of the city's children were playing truant, though this figure remains unsubstantiated.

From the summer of 1941 onwards, things began to improve not only in Birmingham but also nationally. Raids were less intensive, attendances improved, nursery education was greatly expanded in order to free young mothers for war-work. By February 1942, 80 per cent of school children were receiving school milk daily in one-third pint bottles, and most children were being provided with (and paying for) school dinners. In September 1944 the school evacuation scheme was officially ended, just when the V1s and the V2s were beginning to attack London and the south-east. This caused a further wave of evacuation, with Birmingham, for example, becoming a reception area for 6,000 children.

Although the school system settled down after the worst months of air raids were over in 1941, great educational problems remained. It was completely impossible, of course, to do anything about the inter-war demand for secondary education for all. The shortage of teachers intensified after the Board of Education changed the age of exemption from call-up for teachers from thirty to thirty-five. Class sizes climbed steeply in the summer of 1944: Birmingham had 279 classes with more than fifty children in them (the recommended class size was forty). Liverpool had 496 classes with over fifty children. Books and paper were in short supply, teachers were more elderly, younger PE staff few and far between, school medical and dental services were reduced as a result of staffing shortages. Overall, it seems that pre-war standards must have been adversely affected by the war. It is often claimed that evacuated children benefited from their new experiences in the countryside, but their reactions were not always favourable to their new surroundings; they were as disadvantaged by teacher shortage and scarcity of books and paper as urban children, and by 1944 they were in any case a small minority. Of course, there were benefits accruing from the improvement in milk and meal services, from the increase in nursery education, and ultimately from the 1944 Education Act (to be considered later in this chapter); but children must have been adversely affected by declining standards, especially in the first three years of war. Army tests in 1946 of men who had spent their last three years at school in 1939–42 showed an all-round drop in academic standards, and a marked increase in educational backwardness and retardation;[14] In London, the average retardation was up to a year.[15] Above all, perhaps, it must be remembered that any child starting school in September 1939 would have spent two-thirds of his or her school career under wartime conditions, including (it could be) an actual absence from school for the first six or seven months of the war. Whatever long-term educational gains may be attributed to World War II in this country, in the short term it seems likely that the average boy or girl experienced a decline in educational standards.

However, whatever was happening in the schools, there was nevertheless a general feeling in the country after Dunkirk, followed by the Battle of Britain and the Blitz, that Britain was going to survive and emerge triumphant from the ordeal of all-out war. Whatever doubts may have been felt in private by members of the government, in public its policy was clear and unequivocal; as Churchill put it in his most famous speech, 'We shall never surrender.' Although there has been some questioning more recently of the extent of national unity in the early 1940s, it still seems clear that the nation was largely united, surprised (it might well be) that it had survived so far, and had actually beaten off the immediate threat of invasion. As a result of the self-confidence gained from this, there was an increasing discussion of the need for social reform once the war had ended. The state of some of the working-class children evacuated in 1939 and 1940 had shocked middle-class opinion. The system of food rationing, based on the idea of fair shares for all, reinforced the idea of providing a better deal through the social services for the underprivileged. Above all, the increasing extent of government control over all aspects of daily life made it seem natural that in peacetime the government should extend the existing social services, and in particular, make greater efforts to reduce the unemployment which had been such an ugly feature of the inter-war social scene. 'Planning' was in the air, especially after the Soviet Union had entered the war, a country well known for its socialist control of the economy and its five-year plans.

For all these reasons, the movement for social reform gained momentum from 1942 onwards, assisted no doubt by the fact that Churchill found it natural to concentrate on the military side of the war, leaving the Labour members of his cabinet to keep an eye on plans for social reform. Already J.M. Keynes was influencing government economic affairs, in particular the 1942 budget and the drawing up of the first manpower budget in December 1942. In education, the Board of Education issued plans for post-war reform known as the Green Book, while in May 1942, the Medical Planning Commission proposed that a national health service should be established. In

September 1942 another report – the Uthwatt Report – set out plans for post-war town planning. The Labour Party in the same year issued its own plans for reform under the title *The Old World and the New*.

Although the year 1942 was a somewhat gloomy year for Britain in military terms, at home it was a remarkable year for the planning of social reform. Moreover, the most famous and influential of all the proposals was published in December 1942. This was the Beveridge Report. William Beveridge had been a senior civil servant with a vast knowledge and experience of social problems dating back to the pre-war Liberal reforms; he had been the principal author of the Labour Exchanges Act, 1909, and was a committed Liberal. Later he became the director of the London School of Economics from 1919 to 1937, and then Master of University College, Oxford. His report begins by naming the principal threats to working-class life as the five 'giants': want, disease, ignorance, squalor, and illness. He then goes on to concentrate on want, which could be attacked by a system of social security. Social security is then defined as:[16]

> 300. The securing of an income to take the place of earnings when they are interrupted by unemployment, sickness, or accident, to provide for retirement through age, to provide against loss of support by the death of another person, and to meet exceptional expenditures, such as those connected with birth, death and marriage.

Beveridge continued by advancing three basic assumptions, without which he considered no satisfactory scheme of social security could be devised. These were:[17]

> 301.(a) Children's allowances, for children up to the age of 15, or if in full-time education, up to the age of 16.
>   (b) Comprehensive health and re-habilitation services for prevention and cure of disease and restoration of capacity to work, available to all members of the community.
>   (c) Maintenance of employment, that is to say, avoidance of mass unemployment.

According to Beveridge, inter-war surveys had shown that three-quarters to five-sixths of want was due to interruption or loss of earnings; the remaining quarter to a sixth was the result of the family being too large for the family income. So the two major needs for getting rid of want were more comprehensive social insurance, and family allowances (these would also help to get rid of the other giants, too). It was essential then to have a full range of allowances to cover all eventualities, including family allowances. This would give security from the cradle to the grave (a phrase subsequently much bandied about). A special ministry of social security would also be necessary to run the whole scheme.

The Beveridge Report made no very novel proposals, and in fact was quite a conservative document in its thinking. It actually began by praising the existing social services which it considered were excellent in many ways, but it then goes on to point out weaknesses, such as the different rates of benefit under the health and unemployment schemes, and the very limited maternity and funeral grants (the most obvious weakness in modern eyes would perhaps seem to be the failure to include the housewife and her children, or to provide a free hospital service). The main aim was to fill up gaps in the social services then available, and to do so on the basis of the Liberal contributory scheme brought in by the National Insurance Act, 1911. However, all adults were expected to contribute, whether employed or not, on the wartime principle of all participating and all sharing alike. Certainly the report had an enormous appeal for the public: 635,000 copies were sold, and in a public opinion poll, 86 per cent were in favour of implementing the report. The government supported the plan in principle – it was really a blueprint for a welfare state – but in private there were doubts about its costs and feasibility. The Labour Party as a whole supported it strongly, but some leading members had reservations: Ernest Bevin, for example, would have preferred a minimum wage policy to family allowances. The government was against putting the plan into effect during wartime, and Churchill talked vaguely of a five-year plan when peace returned. As for the civil service, Jose Harris has argued that both civil servants and some politicians were much less enthusiastic about the report than has been assumed. Many thought that the plan was an inconvenient luxury best left until after the end of the war.[18] Thane has also argued that the impetus for reform came less from the impact of Dunkirk than from the revival of political and industrial conflict in the latter part of the war, and from the consequent need to contain it. Even then, both Conservative and Labour ministers were reluctant to make binding commitments.[19] Harris may have a point, though Thane's view is more difficult to sustain, since the Beveridge Report was published more than two years before the end of the war, and well before any marked increase in industrial and political conflict.

In 1943 the Ministry of Reconstruction was set up, and a series of

White Papers on subjects contained in the Beveridge Report were issued – so many that Beveridge called it 'the White Paper chase'. In February 1944 a White Paper recommended the setting up of a national health service, while in May 1944 a White Paper on employment policy committed the government to keeping employment at a high and stable level after the war, making favourable references to Keynesian methods of achieving this. In September 1944 there was a White Paper on social insurance which accepted the main principles of the Beveridge Report. The subject of full employment was rather taken for granted in the report itself, so Beveridge himself addressed the subject in a book entitled *Full Employment in a Free Society*. It is understandable that the Churchill coalition government should have wished to delay implementing the Beveridge plan till after the war, in spite of its great popularity, but it was prepared to push forward with the major advance in education contained in the Education Act, 1944 (otherwise known as the Butler Act, named after the Conservative president of the Board of Education, R.A. Butler). It followed in the wake of two influential reports – the Hadow Report, 1926, which advocated secondary education for all to suit varying degrees of academic ability, and the Norwood Report, 1943, which divided children of secondary age into three groups, grammar, technical, and secondary modern (the last group having already been suggested by the Hadow Report).

The 1944 act first divided state educational provision into the three stages of primary, secondary, and further education. County colleges were to be set up to extend further education provision, with compulsory part-time education up to the age of eighteen (like the similar proposal in the Fisher Act, 1918, this was never implemented). All local authority schools were to be completely free, including the county grammar schools. The school leaving age was to go up to fifteen. Church schools were divided into voluntary aided schools (the governors meeting half the building costs, and appointing their own staff), and controlled schools (the local authority being wholly responsible for the buildings, and for appointing the staff). Religious education became the one compulsory subject, and a daily act of corporate worship was also made compulsory. There was to be a drastic reorganisation of local education authorities; 169 out of the 315 in England and Wales were to be abolished. The old Board of Education acquired enhanced status as the Ministry of Education, and Butler became the first minister of education.

The attempt to provide free secondary education for all was worthy and well intentioned, and many working-class children profited from it. The difficulty lay in the mode of selection made necessary for entry into secondary school. In theory, the three different types of secondary school were all to have 'parity of esteem', that is, all were to be of equal educational value, and the 11+ selection test was simply designed to select the most appropriate school for the candidate's abilities. The selection procedure usually included an intelligence test so that a bright working-class child of only moderate attainment might still win a place in the academic grammar school. Unfortunately the 11+ prognostic tests turned out to be unreliable (there was another transfer test at 13+, but it was not always used), and the secondary modern school was too often regarded as the destination of the non-academic grammar school 'failure'. The county grammar schools taught on traditional lines, took the GCE O- and A-level exams, and sent their highest-achieving pupils on to university. The secondary modern pupil took no public exams at all at first, and left school at fifteen. Although there were some good, purpose-built secondary modern schools, many in this class of school were housed in old senior school buildings, and their staffs were largely certificated but non-graduate teachers. Yet they catered for up to 80 per cent of the secondary school population: the proportion taken by the grammar schools varied from authority to authority, but averaged out at about 20 per cent (only a tiny proportion went to the numerically few technical schools, some of which had an entry age of thirteen, not eleven).[20]

The Butler Act was certainly a well-intentioned attempt to provide good quality secondary education for all from the age of eleven to fifteen; and the abolition of all fees was undoubtedly a step in the right direction. Unfortunately, although it was intended to give better opportunities to the working-class boy or girl from the underprivileged home, the act was fatally flawed by the selection procedures at the age of eleven, and by the nature of the secondary modern school. The attempt to achieve parity of esteem proved an idealistic failure. By the 1960s the idea of deliberately restricting the more academic form of education to only 20 per cent of the secondary school population, selected at 11+, was increasingly regarded as mistaken. It is not surprising that the comprehensive school concept began to take hold in the 1960s.[21]

One other important reform must be mentioned. It was passed by Churchill's caretaker government, formed when the Labour Party withdrew from the wartime coalition government. This was the Family Allowance Act, passed in June 1945, which gave a grant of 5/– per week for every child after the first, the allowance being paid direct to the mother. The act at last addressed the problem of a father's earning low wages, insufficient to support a large family – a well-known and generally acknowledged cause of poverty. This cause of poverty had been highlighted in the Beveridge Report, of course, though as noted previously, there were some in the Labour Party who thought that the better policy was to fix minimum wages.

In concluding this section of the chapter, what finally can be said in assessing the relevance of this war to the changing perception of industrialisation? The contrast with World War I is very marked: that war began with a burst of patriotic enthusiasm and the conviction that fighting the war was morally right. It ended in a sombre mood and the anguished conviction that such an appalling loss of life must never be allowed to happen again. True, the trade unions had gained in influence in the first war, and there was some improvement in the social status of women; but there was little determination in evidence to remedy the shortcomings of industrialisation, save perhaps in the provision of working-class housing, and the resolution of grievances in the mining industry. World War II was quite different: it began in a mood of some doubt and anxiety, but after Dunkirk this turned to something like euphoria as the British people showed (in the idiom of the day), 'they could take it'. Of course, the degree of social solidarity can be questioned, and has been questioned, but there is no denying that a mood of strong self-criticism developed, allied with a determination that the ills of industrial capitalism must be addressed. J.B. Priestley, the most popular novelist of the day, delivered a number of impressive and critical radio *Postscripts* after the Sunday evening Home Service News broadcasts. In the *Postscript* on 21 July 1940, Priestley ended as follows:[22]

> Now the war, because it demands a high collective effort, is compelling us to change not only our ordinary, social and economic habits, but also our habits of thought. We're actually changing over from the property point of view to the sense of community, which simply means that we realise we are all in the same boat. But, and this is the point, that boat can serve not only as our defence against Nazi aggression, but as an ark in which we can all finally land in a better world.

This broadcast in particular caused some concern in government circles, and certainly not all at the time would have agreed that the nation was in fact 'changing over from the property point of view', but Priestley's talks made a profound impression. According to

Graham Greene (himself a somewhat hostile literary critic of Priestley's novels), in the months after Dunkirk, Priestley became a leader second only to Churchill 'And he gave us what our other leaders have always failed to give us – an ideology'.[23]

It was not only a matter of planning for a better future, but also of getting rid of the old political reactionaries who had contributed to the disaster of appeasement. Written at the time of Dunkirk, a slim volume entitled *Guilty Men* and published by the left-wing publisher Victor Gollancz, bitterly attacked the men who had ruled Britain from 1931 to 1940 for their failure to re-arm adequately, thereby contributing to the evacuation of the British army from Dunkirk. From then on, the left had the moral advantage, which indeed they held throughout the rest of the war. The right could do little about it, and had perforce to accept the general demand for a better world after the war. Once Russia joined in, somewhat fanciful pictures were drawn of life under socialism in the USSR; there was a very appealing propaganda film in colour giving a glowing account of an ordinary day in the life of a worker-citizen in what was described as 'the socialist one-sixth of the world'. It attracted large audiences, while other pro-Soviet propaganda was equally popular. The mania for discussion spread in the army, where the Army Bureau of Current Affairs (ABCA) distributed an informative newsheet giving details of military developments and of plans for the future, such as the Beveridge Report. There were even compulsory weekly discussion groups in the army. News was also disseminated by forces' newspapers – such as *SEAC*, for the South East Asia Command. Discussion was encouraged by innumerable brains trusts, and here and there, forces' parliaments (for example, the Cairo Forces Parliament).[24] The educational branches in the services were also kept very busy in laying on courses for men and women as they neared demobilisation. This was under a scheme known as Educational and Vocational Training (EVT).

Exactly how far all this went in fuelling expectations for the future and indeed in changing political beliefs is an interesting question.[25] It can be asserted with some confidence, however, that many men and women expected something different, some improvement in the quality of life in the immediate, post-war world. From the point of view from which this book is written, this is one major difference between the social outcomes of the two world wars – the second war ended with far higher expectations; and the second half of this chapter will shortly examine how far these expectations were fulfilled.

We may now dispose of the ending of the war quite quickly. The end of hostilities against Germany was followed by a general election on

Table 9.1 Results of the 1945 general election

Party	Votes cast	% of vote	No. of seats
Labour	11,995,152	47.8	393
Conservative	9,988,306	39.8	213
Liberal	2,248,226	9.0	12
Communist	102,780	0.4	2
Commonwealth	110,634	0.4	1
Others	640,880	2.6	19

12 July 1945. Both Labour and Conservative parties promised social reform, including the carrying out of the Beveridge plan, though Labour was rather more enthusiastic in its support for the plan than the Conservatives. The Labour election manifesto *Let Us Face the Future* also offered a certain amount of nationalisation, mostly of public utilities, the one exception being the iron and steel industry. No doubt many voters found this acceptable enough at the time, being used to extensive wartime government controls. It is sometimes asserted that the service vote went solidly against the Conservatives at the polls: in fact, more than half the serving men and women failed to vote, in spite of all the work of ABCA and the discussion groups. The Conservatives did not lose heavily in the popular vote, but the Labour constituency organisation was in far better shape than that of the Conservatives, which was somewhat run-down, and Labour scored heavily (to their own surprise) in terms of seats. In fact, they did not expect to win. They gained 393 seats compared with the 213 won by the Conservatives, and 12 by the Liberals. Table 9.1 shows the full results.

The third Labour government which was then formed had for the first time a clear majority over all other parties. On 14 August, Japan surrendered to the Americans. The way was now clear for the people's party, formed originally in 1900 to promote legislation in the direct interest of labour, to do just that. When parliament reassembled, Labour MPs sang the 'Red Flag' (those who knew the words) in the House of Commons – not a very appropriate song, or one very indicative of their intentions; but it seemed a suitable thing to do. When Churchill entered the chamber, he drew cheers from the Labour benches as well as the Conservatives. He was still immensely popular, but belonged to the past, not to the future.

The creation of the Welfare State

It is not intended in the second half of this chapter to give a general account of the social history of the period immediately after the war, but rather to concentrate on the efforts made by the government to remedy the obvious failings of the industrial system as they had been demonstrated in the inter-war years. This meant implementing the Beveridge Report, and also carrying out the limited programme of nationalisation envisaged in the Labour election manifesto. It also meant putting into operation the Family Allowance Act and the Butler Education Act. Altogether Labour faced a formidable task in the early years of peace, at a time when the country was in dire financial straits and more heavily in debt than even at the end of the Great War. As Keynes said, 'We threw good housekeeping to the winds, but we saved ourselves, and helped to save the world.'[26] Keynes himself was sent off to the United States to negotiate a loan of £3.75 billion from the US government (this loan alone made it possible to begin to organise the Welfare State – a curious thought, given the American hostility to national health services).

It also made it possible to begin the programme of nationalisation set out in *Let Us Face the Future*.[27] These measures owed their existence to Clause Four of the 1918 Labour Party constitution which we have already noted was the brainchild of Sidney Webb. Clause Four was intended to appeal to the more intellectual members of the party, and was not of great consequence to rank-and-file trade unionists. A good number of the industries concerned were public utilities. Thus, the Bank of England Act, 1946, brought little change in the overall administration and day-to-day running of the bank – it was already largely under government control. Similar considerations apply to the Cable and Wireless Act, 1946 (nationalising all international lines), and to the Civil Aviation Act, 1946 (nationalising Imperial Airways). The Coal Nationalisation Act, 1946, was rather different from the other acts. Nationalisation had been a possibility ever since the days of the Sankey Commission, 1919, and by now, the principle was widely accepted, though the details were much disputed, and the compensation paid to the mineowners (£164.6 million) was criticised by the miners. The pits could now be reorganised and new machinery introduced. Unfortunately, although production increased, the nationalised industry got off to a slow start. Vesting Day came on 1 January 1947 in the middle of an extremely harsh winter when railway points froze, and it was impossible to transport the coal. Industry suffered badly, and unemployment soared up. Production targets were not reached till 1949, and in spite of rises in wages there were still many disputes with the management, and much absenteeism.

In the following year, further legislation included the Electricity Act, 1947, the Gas Act, 1947, and the Transport Act, 1947. The first two industries were public utilities, already run for the most part by local authorities, and their nationalisation excited little interest. However, the Transport Act was rather different: it nationalised the railways and canals, as was generally expected – the railways were badly in need of more investment and had themselves run a campaign before the war with the slogan 'Give the Railways a Fair Deal' – but the act also attempted to nationalise road transport (with certain exceptions for local, 'class C' licences). Since road transport was a profitable, going concern, this was bound to cause controversy which rumbled on for some time. This was also true of the last effort at nationalisation, the Iron and Steel Bill, 1949. The iron and steel industry had recovered well from the war, was in a flourishing condition, and was an industry in which (unlike the coal industry) labour relations were good – its workers were not strongly in favour of state ownership. Up to 1949, nationalisation had not aroused any especial enthusiasm (the one exception was coal) or any passionate defence. The case of iron and steel was different. The cabinet had decided on nationalisation of this industry only after long and difficult debate, and thought it very likely that the bill would be rejected by the House of Lords. They accordingly introduced a bill shortening the delaying powers of the Lords from two years to one. In fact, the steel bill became law under the old terms of the Parliament Act, 1911, but it was speedily attacked and virtually repealed by the Conservative government which replaced Labour in 1951.

What is one to make of Labour's efforts at nationalisation of industry? Did it have much effect in permitting the planning of the economy, of ironing out booms and slumps? It was very different, of course, from the full control of the economy practised by states beyond the Iron Curtain. Eighty per cent of industry was still in private hands. In only two of the industries concerned – road transport and iron and steel – was private enterprise seriously affected. In fact, Labour's plans for nationalisation proved to be half-hearted and ineffective – indeed, the Labour leaders had no detailed proposals for nationalisation ready when the time came. The best they could do was to turn to Herbert Morrison's plan for London Transport in 1933, which was to set up a public corporation. In this, remarkably, there was no provision for worker representation. It might be expected that the trade unions would have objected violently to this omission; but they wanted to retain their traditional rights of collective bargaining, and not to become managers themselves. So it turned out that nationalisation under the third Labour government was something of a damp squib. It certainly did not spring from any conviction of the urgent need to seize control of the economy as a whole, and to run it in the interests of the workers. It was not the most successful part of Labour's achievements in the post-war period.

To turn to welfare legislation:[28] as far as education is concerned, the main task here was to implement the Butler Act, and this was duly done, including the raising of the school leaving age in 1947 to fifteen. Fees were abolished in state grammar schools, new secondary modern schools were built, and emergency training schemes for teachers lasting one year were set up. The scheme for selection for secondary schools at eleven plus became firmly established. Although the wartime Fleming Report (1944) on the public schools had suggested that the provision of a limited number of free places at these schools might be made available for working-class boys, little was done to put this into effect. Most labour leaders thought the free local authority grammar school gave an excellent opportunity for working-class advancement, though recognising that it did not match the social prestige and influence given by a public school education. So the two systems of education, state and private, remained almost completely separate, and the public schools were left untouched. In fact, both then and today they remain too explosive an issue for any Labour government so far to tackle.

However, the great jewel in Labour's crown was the National Insurance Act, 1946, which put into effect the Beveridge plan. All were to be compulsorily insured against both sickness and unemployment, the old-age pension was raised, and the Ministry of National Insurance established. In the same year, the National Health Service Act provided for the setting up of a national health system which had already become feasible with the creation of a national organisation of hospitals during the war. Nevertheless, it took the courage and vision of the minister for health and housing, Aneurin Bevan, to propose the nationalisation of the existing system of voluntary and municipal hospitals and poor law infirmaries – something which was not even in the Labour Party's election manifesto. As with the 1911 insurance scheme, the great problem was how to persuade the medical profession to come into the scheme. Bevan showed a good deal of guile if not actual cunning in first securing the co-operation of the hospital consultants. They had often given their services free in the voluntary hospitals (which were run as charities). Henceforth the consultants were offered fees for their services, at the same time being permitted to run private practices, and even to have private pay-beds in national health hospitals. Bevan put it very simply and crudely: 'I stuffed their mouths with gold.'[29]

Having got the consultants on his side, Bevan then had a protracted struggle to win over the general practitioners, who thought that under the new scheme they would become mere salaried state officials; they also objected to losing the right to buy and sell practices, which was the usual way of setting up as a general practitioner. Eventually, and in the nick of time, just before the National Health Service was due to start in July 1948, the doctors capitulated, and accepted a scheme whereby they were paid a small salary, topped up by a much larger amount from capitation fees, calculated on the number of patients in the practice. An elaborate system of authorities was set up – regional hospital boards in charge of the voluntary and local authority hospitals; local executive councils for both doctors and dentists; and local government authorities, in charge of health services such as food inspection, sewage disposal, and home welfare services. There were also to be experimental health centres offering a range of services other then those already provided by the hospitals.

It was a great, and some would say, noble scheme, very typical of the 'fair shares for all', and 'all to contribute' spirit of the time; and it was certainly the greatest triumph of Aneurin Bevan's career, that stormy petrel of both the 1930s and the war period itself (his speeches before the war, accusing the government of being prepared to use military force against the workers, have to be read to be believed; and during the war, he was a persistent critic of Churchill, who on one occasion called him 'a squalid nuisance'). Yet this ex-miner from the Welsh valleys, a dedicated Marxist in his early days, was well read, and had a taste for the good things in life. Brendan Bracken, like Bevan himself one of the Beaverbrook circle, is supposed to have called Bevan to his face, 'You Bollinger Bolshevik, you ritzy Robespierre, you lounge-lizard Lenin ...'

The National Health Service remains a monument (though still the subject of vigorous debate) to this remarkable man. In addition to the 19 million previously insured, an additional 21 million were brought in. It cost much more than expected. Four million dental cases a year were anticipated; 8 million applied for treatment. The cost of providing spectacles was estimated at about £1 million; in the first year it cost £22 million. Even Bevan was taken aback at the early demands made on the service, and he may even have envisaged some form of prescription charge (although none was imposed before 1950). In 1949 he warned that demand could become excessive:[30]

> Now that we have got the National Health Service based on free prescriptions, I shudder to think of the cascade of medicine which is pouring down British throats at the present time. I wish I could believe that its efficiency was equal to the credulity with which it is being swallowed.

The welfare services were designed to give security from the cradle to the grave. Yet some unfortunates who still fell through the net, for whom social security benefits were either not available or insufficient. Up to 1948 such claimants would have to seek help from the poor law authorities – the public assistance committees of the county councils. In 1948, however, the National Assistance Act abolished the PACs, and transferred their powers to the new National Assistance Board, with local offices. Henceforth, those described as being 'in need' could seek help from this new authority.[31] It was not anticipated that there would be many in this category (in practice, this belief proved quite mistaken, due to the inadequacies of the allowances provided under the national insurance scheme). The only social service provided by local authorities after the abolition of the PACs was residential accommodation for the aged and infirm. It was said that Bevan wanted to call such accommodation 'Twilight Homes', but was persuaded to adopt a more tactful title.

As well as his responsibilities for the National Health Service, Bevan was also in charge of the house building programme. The Labour election manifesto had promised 'homes for the people', and it was clearly necessary to build private homes in as large numbers as possible, since there had been no domestic building during the war and much damage caused by bombing. The system used was the same as after the previous war – that is, local authorities built houses and let them. Waiting lists for such houses grew longer and longer as returning servicemen married and entered the lists. In London, larger empty houses were taken over by squatters. Some 157,000 prefabricated bungalows were erected as temporary accommodation and were well designed. They usually included a much-prized refrigerator, not usually found in working-class kitchens at the time. These prefabs were built between 1945 and 1950, and were expected to last up to twenty years; some are still in occupation.[32]

Bevan experienced considerable difficulty in his building programme. Building labour was scarce, materials often not available (such as timber), and there was a curious and cumbersome system by

Table 9.2 New houses completed, 1946–51

1946	55,400	1949	217,240
1947	139,690	1950	210,253
1948	227,616	1951	204,117

which the Ministry of Works supplied the basic building materials, the Ministry of Supply the fittings, while the local authorities supplied the labour. Hence there were bottlenecks and innumerable delays. Bevan himself admitted that there were stacks of bricks all over London, waiting to be used. In 1947, timber imports were cut by £10 million. In 1949 the pound was devalued, and local building rates were cut. Table 9.2 shows the numbers of new houses completed. Meanwhile, there were housing acts in 1946 and 1949 which extended local government powers to build, rent control acts in the same years, and the Town and Country Planning Act, 1947, which added further to local planning powers. Fourteen new towns were also planned.

Considering that in 1945 proposals for building 4 million houses were made, and that by 1951 only just over 1 million homes had been built; and that in 1951 there were still 750,000 more households than houses, then Bevan's housing record does not seem very distinguished. Some have put this down to Bevan's not being able to find enough time for the building programme – he himself remarked that he spent just five minutes a week on housing. More recently historians have revised the number of houses built, and have given greater emphasis to the difficulties he faced, especially in 1947 and 1949. In 1984, Professor K.O. Morgan suggested that after a slow start, the government record in housing constituted 'a competent overall performance, if not outstanding'.[33]

The extension of the welfare services and the establishment of the National Health Service were popular measures, no doubt, but they might have been less popular had the promise of full employment given in *Let Us Face the Future* not been fulfilled. The extent of unemployment clearly depended to a large extent on how the government managed the economy. Although the words 'socialist' and 'socialism' were constantly bandied about, the government's economic policy was far from traditional socialist policy based on state ownership of the means of production, distribution, and exchange. Although this figured in Clause Four, there was never the remotest chance of a full-scale takeover of industry, commerce, and the banks. The concept of socialism held by the Labour Party still remained obscure and hazy (Herbert Morrison got round the difficulty by simply defining 'socialism' as 'what the Labour Party does'). In concrete terms, the government believed in a managed economy, 'cheap money' (that is, low rates of interest), and an export drive. In other words, the Labour government took industrial capitalism as they found it, and tried to make it more efficient. In doing this, they had some success, though there were two economic crises, one in 1947 and the other in 1949. The first crisis arose in mid-July 1947, when the American loan had nearly run out, and unemployment was temporarily high, due to the exceptionally bad winter of 1946–7; exports were still only 17 per cent above pre-war levels. In October 1947 the chancellor of the exchequer, Hugh Dalton, resigned over a minor budget leak, and was replaced by the high-minded Sir Stafford Cripps. Cripps instituted a new regime of austerity: new targets were set for production and the reduction of imports, raw materials were reallocated, and the armed forces were reduced in number. A policy of voluntary wage restraint was introduced (it lasted three years). In September 1948 the government was made an outright gift of $1,263 million from the Marshall Aid to Europe programme.

The second crisis in the autumn of 1949 was due to a brief American recession, which led Cripps to devalue the pound by nearly 31 per cent, from $4.03 to $2.80. Further cuts were made in government expenditure, and prescription charges proposed in the National Health Service (but not imposed). The economy soon picked up again, exports were cheaper, and in 1950 were 75 per cent above pre-war prices. Unemployment remained very low: its rate was 2.5 per cent in 1946, 1.2 per cent in 1949, and only 1.8 per cent in October 1951 when the Labour government finally left office. Thus the manifesto promise of full employment was amply fulfilled, assisted no doubt by Britain's advantage in resuming pre-war trading routes with her industries virtually intact, while the rest of Europe was struggling to get on its feet again.

As for conditions at work in the immediate post-war years, the normal week in a large number of industries had settled down to forty-five hours, and nearly all the forty-five-hour-week factories worked a five-day week.[34] Henceforth the long weekend from Friday evening to Monday morning became an accepted feature of working-class life. The annual report of the chief inspector of factories for 1947 commented on this rather solemnly:

> Its popularity with the workpeople is great: the opportunities it gives to the women to shop on Saturday morning when all the best available foodstuffs are displayed in the shops, the freedom

of the men and boys to attend sports meetings, even at a distance, or to follow other spare-time occupations, and the long break each week, combine to make it the most valued advance of modern times.

Actual conditions on the shop-floor did not alter much: lighting was better with the introduction of fluorescent strip lighting. Machinery still caused accidents and even deaths. In 1946, there were 826 fatal accidents, 180 of them in the building industry; in 1950, there were 799 deaths, with a rather larger work force. Many accidents were of a traditional kind, arising from the failure to operate safety guards correctly, and women's hair still got caught up in moving machinery and overhead banding. The Factory Act, 1948, simply amended the 1937 act by extending the age limits for the medical examination of persons entering factory employment. It also included male workers in the regulations for providing seats, and issued extensive new building regulations. The number of factory canteens increased, though by 1948 there were still only 14,717 hot-meal canteens in a total of 243,369 factories and workshops.

The tight control over workers' movements in industry continued, while the Control of Engagements Order allowed new employment only through labour exchanges. The idea behind this directive was to direct workers into more essential employment. Although the order was in force for two-and-a-half years, only 29 were directed to new employment, while 688 were frozen in agriculture and mining. There was also the voluntary wages freeze, for three years from March 1948 onwards, for the most part loyally observed by the trade unions. Order 1305 was still in force, forbidding strikes and imposing compulsory arbitration, but pay awards went up in step with prices, which was generally acceptable. There were no lengthy national strikes, and days lost through strikes averaged about 2 million in the years 1945–50. Since unemployment was so limited, trade union membership grew from 7.84 million in 1945 to 9.24 million in 1950, representing 43 per cent of all workers. Needless to say, one of the first legislative actions of the government was to repeal the 1927 Trade Union Act. General strikes were again declared legal, 'contracting out' replaced 'contracting in', and civil servants could again join trade unions. All in all, industrial relations were remarkably peaceful in the period 1945–50, and were in marked contrast to the unrest which was a feature of the early years of peace after 1918.

Daily life in the late 1940s was not without its old pleasures – the radio, the cinema, the pub, the dancehall, and the pools – and most were profoundly thankful to be at peace again ('Cassandra' of the *Daily Mirror* had written with feeling of the lot of ordinary people in his 1941 pamphlet, *The English at War*, 'the Common People who fight, who slave, who drown, who are burnt, who are mutilated, and who are entombed and who bear the fierce unremitting yoke of pain and tears ...'[35]). Most men and women were greatly relieved that, to adapt Robert Graves' words, it was 'Goodbye to All That', at least; but the times were certainly austere. Rationing continued, and was even stricter than in wartime. Bread was rationed for the first time in 1946, and stayed on the ration for two years. Potatoes were also rationed. Shops were relatively empty, and goods on short supply were put on 'dockets'; for example, furniture, curtain material, and bedding were all rationed. It is no wonder that a black market developed in scarce goods which could be bought in pubs or from street traders who rapidly disappeared should a policeman come into sight. It was the age of the 'spiv'.[36] In the interests of economy, Cripps even suggested that water in the bath should be limited to a few inches. For a time, he became known as 'filthy Cripps'.

So for the working classes, even if life was austere, unemployment was reduced almost to vanishing point, social security had greatly improved, and the standard of living rose. Though the cost of living had nearly doubled since 1938, earnings increased by two-and-a-half times. Thus, real wages actually went up. Striking proof of the change in working-class standards of living in York was given by a survey in 1950 by B.S. Rowntree and G.R. Lavers.[37] According to their figures, in 1936 poverty affected 17.7 per cent of the working classes in York, whereas in 1950, the figure was only 2.8 per cent – a remarkable tribute to full employment and the social services. In 1936, one-third blamed their poverty on unemployment; no-one did so in 1950 – though 68 per cent of those who were still classified as 'poor' thought that their poverty in 1950 was due to old age. If in 1950 the small welfare allowance of 1936 had still been the amount payable, then the proportion of those suffering poverty in 1950 would have risen from 2.8 per cent to 22.0 per cent.

It seems therefore that the working classes at least were materially better off after the war than before. The same does not necessarily apply to the middle classes under Labour rule. Some of course profited from free grammar school education for their children (others paid school fees in private schools rather than take up places in secondary modern schools), but on the whole it was the middle classes who complained of the extent of government controls, and at petrol rationing, and at restrictions on buying foreign currency. Most new cars went for export (with exceptions for doctors and other essential users), and if somehow a home purchaser acquired a brand-new car, he had to promise not to sell it within the next two years. Undoubtedly, by 1950 middle-class Labour supporters were becoming increasingly restless.

This was demonstrated clearly enough when in February 1950 a general election was held in which Labour retained a bare majority of only five seats. By this time, the Labour government had little new to offer the electorate – indeed, this had been very largely true since 1948 and the setting up of the National Health Service. Proposals were brought forward after the election for further adventures in nationalisation, including the state ownership of cement and sugar, but they were never carried out (Tate & Lyle, the sugar manufacturers, conducted a vigorous counter-attack, featuring a lively lump of sugar, Mr Cube). Industrial relations worsened as the wage freeze was more and more disregarded – prosecutions were begun against strikers, and troops were brought in to shift meat in a strike at Smithfield, London's main meat market.

The government's financial situation took a turn for the worse with the outbreak of the Korean War in June 1950. Defence expenditure shot up, and the 1951 budget presented by Cripps' successor, Hugh Gaitskell, contained NHS charges for both teeth and spectacles. There were exemptions, of course, for old-age pensioners and others, but the NHS was no longer free to all. This led to the resignation of Nye Bevan, who had become minister of labour, not only because he thought the charges were wrong in principle, but also because he claimed that the additional military spending made necessary for Korea had been overestimated (he was probably right on both counts). From spring 1951 onwards, the government was in increasing trouble. Attlee, still prime minister, was forced to go into hospital with a duodenal ulcer. Cripps and Ernie Bevin had both died, and Herbert Morrison was proving to be a somewhat disappointing foreign secretary. A balance of payments crisis bedevilled the government's finances between July and September. The one bright spot was the Festival of Britain, a kind of celebration of British achievement, held on the South Bank in London, and accompanied by pleasure gardens and a funfair in Battersea Park nearby (the gardens drew over 8 million visitors). In October, another general election was held. Clearly, the Labour government was very short of new ideas, and the Conservatives came home with a clear majority of seventeen seats, on a very high poll of 82 per cent. Even then, Labour scored the highest popular vote. Table 9.3 shows the results.

Table 9.3 Results of the 1951 general election

Party	Votes cast	No. of seats
Conservatives	13,717,538	321
Labour	13,948,605	295
Liberal	730,556	6
Communist	31,640	0
Others	177,329	3

It remains to assess the significance of the achievements of the third Labour government, both in their immediate context, and in the perspective of the development of industrialisation.

There has never been any difficulty in finding fault with Labour's reforms, and many of them were flawed in one way or another. For example, it is customary to point out that the welfare reforms were not *sui generis*, but were based on an existing structure of insurance dating back originally to 1911. Thus, in 1965 Professor Titmuss suggested that Labour's welfare state was 'little more than an administrative tidying-up of social security provisions'[38] (this seems a remarkable understatement, considering that the nationally insured population under the previous scheme was more than doubled by Labour, and that the hospital system was nationalised). Labour's housing provision has also been attacked, and it certainly took time to achieve respectable figures. Then again, left-wing historians such as Ralph Milliband have always been critical of Labour's failure to introduce a really socialist state. The answer to this criticism has already been suggested, that even if a small minority within the party wanted complete nationalisation, the country as a whole was certainly not ready for it, and only minor measures of nationalisation were included in *Let Us Face the Future*. A more realistic and just criticism of the new welfare system is that the level of allowances failed to take account of the rise in prices, and were simply too low: by the end of 1950, 1.35 million were receiving weekly allowances from the National Assistance Board. Of these, 873,000 were 'in need' because their benefit was too low; three-quarters of these claimants (650,000) were old-age pensioners.[39] Such claimants were obliged to undergo the embarrassment of means testing.

Another critic, Professor Keith Robbins, has observed that Labour set about planning to avoid the 1930s, and that 'Obsessed by a vision of a socialist future, and dominated by memories of the past, Labour tended to by-pass the present.'[40] This seems another remarkable judgement. It is quite true that Labour planned to avoid repeating the 1930s, and for that reason supported the Beveridge plan: but it is difficult to see them as being obsessed by a vision of a socialist future – certainly it was not the vision of a command economy. Further, to suppose that they 'tended to by-pass the present' is equally remarkable in view of the mass of social legislation passed, quite apart from the grant of independence to India and Burma, the virtual creation of NATO by Ernie Bevin, the government's participation in the Berlin airlift, and so on.

In fact, Kenneth Morgan in his standard work on the third Labour government, published in 1984, emphasised that Labour's achievements were a mixture of reform and conservatism:[41]

> Labour's welfare state then, was a mosaic of reform and conservatism. Innovation in health and social insurance, partial change in housing, relative quiescence in education covered the spectrum of social policy.

His final summing-up is that it was without doubt the most effective of all Labour governments, and perhaps the most effective of any government since the 1832 Reform Act. Certainly the Conservative Party was forced to adopt new policies – R.H.S. Crossman remarked later that Churchill's 1951 government was 'only slightly to the right of Attlee's cabinet'. Consensus politics became commonplace and accepted for the next twenty years or so, often referred to as 'Butskellism', a combination of the name of the leading Conservative politician R.A. Butler and of the Labour leader, Hugh Gaitskell.

However, it is interesting to note that in a book published six years later in 1990, the tone of Morgan's comments on the Labour record is much darker. He now argues that they were never really a group of social radicals; they adhered to the Empire, many believing in white supremacy, mostly believing in capital punishment. They produced no institutional reform, their repeated attempts to reform local government failed, industrial relationships remained unchanged, the House of Lords was unreformed, and the public schools were left alone. We are even told that Empire Day was still observed in state schools every May with the same intensity as under the Raj.[42] Morgan goes on to declare that 'Great Britain after 1945 celebrated its own preserving revolution', as it had done in 1688.[43] Lastly, we are told that the Attlee legend is in general 'warm and reassuring', but 'to some degree, it was based on fortuitous and temporary factors'.[44] In the five pages or so devoted to a final summing-up of the Attlee administrations, the Welfare State is not mentioned as such.

This is certainly a change in emphasis, owing something perhaps to Keith Robbins. There is also some indication of the influence of Corelli Barnett's ideas when, earlier in the book, Morgan writes:[45]

> In pursuit of the New Jerusalem, Labour looked to the past, through the eyes of relatively conservative, conventional leaders. Perhaps Britain in July, 1945 was simply too exhausted to offer any alternative prospectus. Amid the very euphoria of victory in 1945, the nation offered not a triumph of the will but a suspicion of change and the paralysis of self-doubt.

This last sentence is particularly puzzling. The Labour election manifesto hardly exhibits any 'suspicion of change', or 'paralysis of self-doubt', nor does the heavy legislative programme of 1946, nor does Bevan's work as minister of health.

The fact of the matter appears to be that in 1945, the Labour Party offered a change of government in the form of politicians already familiar to the public for the past five years, a body of men not tainted by appeasement, who seemed to promise a much greater degree of social security and the ending of unemployment. As European markets opened up, the export drive increased, unemployment virtually came to an end, the Welfare State came into existence, and the standard of living went up, albeit slowly. On the whole, Labour's economic policy was successful, although owing a good deal initially to American support in 1945 and 1947. If its success was 'fortuitous' and due to 'temporary factors', many key developments in history are due to favourable factors. This does not diminish their importance and significance. What alternative policies existed in 1945 when Labour took office? Should the government, for example, have devoted itself to a wholesale reconstruction of industry, with an eye on the inevitable increase in industrial competition in the post-war world? If so, in which year, and in which parts of industry initially? What effect would this have had on the export drive? The whole idea of modifying or abandoning a successful all-out export drive (there were posters which warned 'Export or Die') together with the extension of welfare services promised in *Let Us Face the Future* is really quite fantastic.[46] Other European countries were also building welfare states at the time, and devoting even more of their gross national product to welfare than was Britain. Politics, we are endlessly told, is the art of the possible. It appears to the present writer that the reconstruction of industry and the abandoning of welfare reform were not even remote political possibilities in the first years of peace.

But how may the Labour reforms be assessed in the wider context of the social problems arising from industrialisation? The theme of this book has been the ways in which industrial change threw up social problems from the accession of Queen Victoria onwards, and of how far such problems were recognised as such, and ultimately solved. Of course, and it must be emphasised, substantial benefits also accrued from industrialisation, especially as the standard of living improved in the second half of the nineteenth century and after. But against those benefits must be placed in particular the need to take action to regulate labour conditions, to improve squalid living accommodation, and to alleviate the great mass of urban poverty revealed towards the end of the nineteenth century. Social evils of this kind constitute the outstanding legacies of the darker side of unrestrained capitalism. A good start was made in the second half of the nineteenth century on regulating labour conditions and on solving public health problems, while the last Liberal administrations (1906–15) attacked problems of ill health, unemployment, and old age in their programme of welfare legislation. Between the wars, sheer necessity forced governments to extend very greatly the scheme for unemployment support. It was then left to the third Labour government to plug the gaps in existing welfare schemes, to incorporate the hospitals into the National Health Service, and to promise an end to unemployment. This was their impressive achievement. If industrial capitalism had its strengths, it also had its weaknesses, in particular, fluctuations in the demand for labour, and its effects on the lives of working men and women. Social security from the cradle to the grave, and the banishment of unemployment were Labour's triumphant answers.

Of course, if this is thought to put too high a gloss on the matter, it must be acknowledged immediately that not all aspects of the Attlee government's achievements were entirely satisfactory: as noted earlier, welfare benefits were often too low, and there was still a housing problem in 1951. Then again, the cost of even a minor war commitment such as the Korean War was sufficient to bring in the first breech in the principle of free prescriptions under the National Health Service. Nevertheless, great advances in welfare provision had been made. Moreover, Butskellism and consensus politics emerged in the 1950s. Conservative governments made no effort to modify the advances, and it obviously seemed to the electorate that the Welfare State was as safe in Conservative hands as in Labour's. If Labour had hoped for the development of greater community spirit and action based on wartime solidarity, they were disappointed, for the voters kept the Conservatives in office and the Labour Party in opposition for thirteen years after 1951. The electorate cherished social security and full employment, but they were less impressed by the more idealist aspects of Labour's policies.[47]

Paul Addison has clearly expressed the view that industrial capitalism had at last taken action against its own weaknesses and shortcomings. In writing about the significance of the war period, he says:[48]

> At the end of the day, political change was translated into more jobs, better medical services, higher standards of social security, greater educational opportunity ... In a sense, the war years can be understood as a phase of genuine change in which a spirit of parsimony and caution gave way to a spirit of greater welfare and more confident management.

Later on in the same work, he puts it in a nutshell: 'The war hastened the introduction of a reformed style of capitalism.'[49] Just so.

Envoi

Sadly, the new confidence and hopefulness engendered by the post-war Labour reforms were not to last. After a period of full employment in the 1950s and 1960s, unemployment again passed the million mark in the mid-1970s. Thereafter it reached 1.79 million in 1980, 2.24 million in 1981, and 2.92 million in 1982. After this, it soared above 3 million in every year from 1983 to 1986, peaking at 3.289 million in 1986.[1] In spite of careful government revision and massaging of figures, the unemployment totals have still to fall below a million. Meanwhile, great arguments have raged over the continued viability of the Welfare State in its present form, and of ways in which it might be reshaped and reformed to meet current needs. One of the paradoxes of industrial capitalism is that while it can bring golden rewards to the successful, it can also bring hardship and misery to the less successful at the bottom of the heap. It is an odd thought that this is something which the *Select Committee on Manufacturers' Employment* was aware of as long ago as 1830; it was also something acknowledged fifteen years later in 1845 by Benjamin Disraeli in the subtitle of his novel *Sybil, or the Two Nations*. The 'Two Nations', of course, were the Rich and the Poor. For the following century and a half after this, many thought an answer could be found in some form of socialism, but the widespread collapse of socialist-inspired command economies in the 1990s seems to have wrecked idealist hopes of creating economic and political systems based on higher ethical principles than those of the market-place. At the moment, indeed, humankind seems to be stuck with some form of industrial capitalism, and it has yet to find long-term solutions to the social problems which it has created.

Notes

1 The Victorian inheritance

1 The causes and course of the Industrial Revolution have been endlessly discussed by historians for many years. For recent summaries of the current state of play, see the introductory surveys in Joel Mokyr (ed.), *The British Industrial Revolution: An Economic Perspective* (Boulder CO, Westview Press, 1993), and in Julian Hoppit and E.A. Wrigley (eds), *The Industrial Revolution in Britain, I* (Oxford, Blackwell, 1994).

2 Peter Mathias, *The First Industrial Nation* (London, Methuen, 2nd edn 1983), 29.

3 B.R. Mitchell, *British Historical Statistics* (Cambridge, Cambridge University Press, 1988), 102.

4 All the figures in this paragraph are taken from Mitchell, ibid., 470, 280, 247.

5 Eric Hopkins, *Birmingham: The First Manufacturing Town in the World 1760–1840* (London, Wiedenfeld and Nicolson, 1989), 34–5.

6 For a remarkable survey of the extent of hand technology, see R. Samuel, 'The workshop of the world: steam power and hand technology in Victorian Britain', *History Workshop*, 3 (1977), 6–72.

7 J.D. Chambers, *The Workshop of the World* (Oxford, Oxford University Press, 1961), 21–2.

8 N.F.R. Crafts, 'British economic growth, 1700–1831: a review of the evidence', *Economic History Review*, 2nd series, XXXVI:2, May (1981), 177–99.

9 *Report of the Select Committee on Manufacturers' Employment*, 1830.

10 E.H. Hunt, *British Labour History 1815–1914* (London, Wiedenfeld and Nicolson, 1981), 64.

11 See generally on the whole subject, D. Bythell, *The Handloom Weavers* (Cambridge, Cambridge University Press, 1969).

12 Eric Hopkins, *Childhood Transformed: Working-Class Children in Nineteenth Century England* (Manchester, Manchester University Press, 1994), 74–7.

13 For the earlier history of trade unionism, see Eric Hopkins, *Working-Class*

Self-Help in Nineteenth Century England (London, UCL Press, 1995), chapters 4 and 5.

14 Ibid., 106–8.

15 E.A. Wrigley and R.S. Schofield, *The Population History of England 1571–1871* (Cambridge, Cambridge University Press, 1981), and E.A. Wrigley, 'The growth of population in eighteenth century England: a conundrum resolved', *Past & Present*, 98 (1983), 121–50.

16 Mitchell, op. cit.

17 On the new poor law, see Hopkins, *Childhood Transformed*, chapter 6; M. E. Rose, *The English Poor Law 1790–1930* (Newton Abbott, David and Charles, 1971); J.R. Poynter, *Society and Pauperism: English Ideas on Poor Relief 1795–1834* (London, Routledge and Kegan Paul, 1969); G.W. Oxley, *Poor Relief in England and Wales 1601–1834* (Newton Abbott, David and Charles, 1974); Karel Williams, *From Pauperism to Poverty* (London, Routledge and Kegan Paul, 1981); M.A. Crowther, *The Workhouse System 1834–1939* (London, Batsford, 1981); Derek Fraser (ed.), *The New Poor Law in the Nineteenth Century* (London, Macmillan, 1976); M.E. Rose, *The Relief of Poverty 1834–1934* (London, Macmillan, 2nd edn 1986).

18 A.G. Gilbert, *Religion and Society in Industrial England: Church, Chapel and Social Change 1740–1914* (London, Longman, 1976).

19 R.F. Wearworth, *Methodism and the Struggle of the Working Classes 1850–1900* (Leicester, Backus, 1955).

20 Asa Briggs, *Victorian Cities* (Harmondsworth, Penguin, 1968), 90, 91.

21 Eric Hopkins, 'Birmingham during the Industrial Revolution: class conflict or class co-operation?', *Research in Social Movements, Conflict and Change*, 16 (1993), 117–37.

22 See also on class relationships, R.J. Morris, *Class and Class Consciousness in the Industrial Revolution 1780–1850* (London, Macmillan, 1979), and Alastair Reid, *Social Classes and Social Relationships in Britain 1850–1914* (London, Macmillan, 1992).

23 Owen was a great believer in self-sufficient communities made up of both middle-class and working-class settlers: see Hopkins, *Working-Class Self-Help*, 185–8.

24 See Hopkins, ibid, chapter 9, 'Before Rochdale', for the extent of the movement before 1844.

25 On factory reform generally, see B.L. Hutchings and A. Harrison, *A History of Factory Legislation* (London, Cass, 1926), J.T. Ward, *The Factory Movement* (London, Macmillan, 1962) and *The Factory System* (2 vols) (Newton Abbott, David and Charles, 1970).

26 Eric Hopkins, *A Social History of the English Working Classes 1815–1945* (London, Arnold, 1979), 90, 91.

27 Quoted in Hopkins, ibid., 56.

28 Iain Hampsher-Monk, *A History of Modern Political Thought* (Oxford, Oxford University Press, 1992), 548.

29 J. Bentham, *Fragment of Government* ([1776] Cambridge, Cambridge University Press, 1988), chapter I, section I.

30 Hopkins, *A Social History*, 72.

31 David Cecil, *Melbourne* (London, The Reprint Society, 1955), 150–1.

32 See Oliver MacDonagh, *A Pattern of Government Growth: The Passenger Acts and their Enforcement, 1800–1860* (London, MacGibbon and Kee, 1961) and *Early Victorian Government* (London, Wiedenfeld and Nicolson, 1977). One criticism which has been made is that in the education department, changes were rarely made on the initiative of civil servants: see Anne Digby and Peter Searby, *Children, School and Society in Nineteenth Century England* (London, Macmillan, 1981), 6, 8.

33 E.L. Woodward, *The Age of Reform 1815–1870* (Oxford, Clarendon Press, 1938), 429.

34 For the Oxford Movement, see Owen Chadwick, *The Victorian Church, Part II* (London, Black, 1970).

35 Professor Burn gives examples of this in his original and remarkable book, *The Age of Equipoise: A Study of the Mid-Victorian Generation* (London, Allen and Unwin, 1964). Professor K.T. Hoppen has recently characterised this book as 'marvellous' (see the bibliographical reference in his own work on the period, noted below).

36 For a recent and informative survey of mid-Victorian attitudes and their sometimes contradictory nature, see K.T. Hoppen, *The Mid-Victorian Generation 1846–1886* (Oxford, Oxford University Press, 1998), chapter 4, 'The nature of the state', especially 92–108.

37 W.H. Auden, *Some Poems* (London, Faber and Faber, 1940), 73.

2 The mid-century years

1 Mick Jenkins, *The General Strike of 1842* (London, Lawrence and Wishart, 1980), provides a valuable if arguably somewhat one-sided account. See also John Rule, *The Labouring Classes in Early Industrial England 1750–1850* (London, Longman, 1986), chapter 13.

2 *Worcestershire Chronicle*, 3 November 1841.

3 Ibid., 5 January 1842.

4 Ibid., 9 February 1842.

5 Ibid., 24 June 1842.

6 Ibid., 7 September 1842.

7 Ibid., 11 January 1843.

8 Ibid., 22 February 1843, 22 March 1843.

9 Ibid., 16 August 1843, 27 September 1843, 8 November 1843.

10 Ibid., 14 February 1844, 11 September 1844, 27 November 1844.

11 The population of Stourbridge increased by 26.8 per cent between 1831 and 1841, well above the national increase of 14.3 per cent for England and Wales: *Census Reports for England and Wales*, 1831, 1841.

12 P.H. Lindert and J.G. Williamson, 'English workers' living standards during the Industrial Revolution', *Economic History Review*, 36 (1983), 1–25; and see the further appraisal in N.F.R. Crafts and T.C. Mills, 'Trends

in real wages in Britain, 1750–1913', *Explorations in Economic History*, 31 (1994), 176–94.

13 For an excellent survey of the subject, see François Crouzet, *The Victorian Economy* (London, Methuen, 1982), 297–305.

14 Peter Mathias, *The First Industrial Nation* (London, Methuen, 2nd edn 1983), 224.

15 Roy Church, *The Great Victorian Boom 1850–1873* (London, Macmillan, 1975), 78.

16 Quoted in Eric Hopkins, *A Social History of the English Working Classes 1815–1945* (London, Arnold, 1979), 64.

17 The controversy over the social results of enclosures is conveniently reviewed in Michael Turner, *Enclosures in Britain 1750–1830* (London, Macmillan, 1984).

18 A personal observation, based on Black Country enumerator books for 1851. The standard authority on short-term labour migration still seems to be A. Redford, *Labour Migration in England 1800–1850* (Manchester, Manchester University Press, 2nd edn 1964).

19 In the 1830s, the percentage of people living in cellars in Manchester was 11.75 per cent, while in Liverpool it was 15.00 per cent. There were many Irish in both towns who were used to poor living quarters and found cellars acceptable: T.S. Ashton, *The Industrial Revolution* (Oxford, Oxford University Press, 1948), 160.

20 Richard Rodger, *Housing in Urban Britain 1780–1914* (London, Macmillan, 1989) provides a useful short guide to housing in the nineteenth century. For local studies, see Eric Hopkins, 'Working-class housing in the smaller industrial town in the nineteenth century: Stourbridge – a case study', *Midland History*, 3–4 (1978), 230–54, and 'Working-class housing in Birmingham during the Industrial Revolution', *International Review of Social History*, XXXI (1986), pt 1, 80–94.

21 *Chadwick's Report, 1842* (report on Preston).

22 H.J. Dyos and Michael Wolf (eds), *The Victorian City: Images and Realities* (London, Routledge and Kegan Paul, 1973), 367.

23 According to *Chadwick's Report*, life expectancy for labourers in Rutland was thirty-eight, and in Kendal, thirty-four. In contrast, in Bethnal Green it was sixteen, in Manchester seventeen, and in Liverpool, fifteen: quoted in Derek Fraser, *The Evolution of the British Welfare State* (Basingstoke, Macmillan, 2nd edn 1984), 261.

24 Eric Hopkins, *Birmingham: The First Manufacturing Town in the World 1760–1840* (London, Wiedenfeld and Nicolson, 1989), 130–1.

25 Ibid., 126, 127, 172.

26 F. Engels, *The Condition of the Working Class in England in 1844* ([1845] Harmondsworth, Penguin, 1987), 98.

27 Report on Stourbridge, *Health of Towns Commission, 2nd Report, 1845* (vol. 1).

28 George Thompson, *Prize Essay upon the Sanitary Condition of the Town of Stourbridge* (Stourbridge, 1848).

29 Hopkins, *Birmingham*, 68, 140-1.

30 B. Disraeli, *Sybil, or the Two Nations* ([1845] Oxford, Oxford University Press, 1975), 87.

31 *Chadwick's Report*, 1965 edn, 433.

32 Quoted in Hopkins, *A Social History*, 66.

33 Ibid.

34 *The Times*, leader, 1 August 1854.

35 S.E. Finer, *The Life and Times of Sir Edwin Chadwick* (London, Methuen, 1952), 320.

36 Ibid., 298.

37 Ibid., 300.

38 Henry Mayhew, *London Labour and the London Poor*, Vol. 1 ([1861] Firl, Caliban, 1980), 409.

39 *Observer: Stourbridge, Cradley Heath, Halesowen and District Chronicle*, 28 July 1866.

40 F.M.L. Thompson, *The Rise of Respectable Society* (London, Fontana, 1988), 181.

41 For the reduction of child labour, see Hopkins, *A Social History*, 54–62; his *Childhood Transformed: Working-Class Children in Nineteenth Century England* (Manchester, Manchester University Press, 1994), chapters 1, 2, and 3; and his 'The Victorians and child labour', *The Historian*, 48, Winter (1995), 10–14.

42 For the relationship between trade unionism and Chartism, see Eric Hopkins, *Working-Class Self-Help in Nineteenth Century England* (London, UCL Press, 1995), 112–15.

43 Trade unionism in the middle decades of the nineteenth century is surveyed and discussed in Hopkins, ibid., chapter 6.

44 Ibid.

45 Ibid., 125.

46 Anne Digby and Peter Searby, *Children, School and Society in Nineteenth Century England* (London, Macmillan, 1981), 5, 29.

47 Michael Sanderson, *Education, Economic Change and Society in England 1780–1870* (London, Macmillan, 2nd edn 1991), section I, 'Literacy and mass elementary education'.

48 W.B. Stephens, *Education, Literacy and Society 1830–70: The Geography of Diversity in Provincial England* (Manchester, Manchester University Press, 1987), 264–5.

49 *Census of Great Britain, 1851: Education, England & Wales, Report & Tables, 1854*, xxvi, xxxvi.

50 C. Birchenough, *History of Elementary Education in England and Wales* ([1914] London, University Tutorial Press, 2nd edn, 1932), 92.

51 *Minutes of the Committee of Council on Education*, 1863–4.

52 Eric Hopkins, 'Working-class attitudes to education in the Black Country in the mid-nineteenth century', *History of Education Society Bulletin*, 14, Autumn (1974), 41–5.

53 Quoted in Sanderson, op. cit., 19.

54 Eric Hopkins, 'Tremenheere's prize schemes in the mining districts, 1851–59', *History of Education Society Bulletin*, 15, Spring (1975), 24–37.

55 *Enquiry into the State of Popular Education*, 1866, Vol. 1, 243.

56 J. Hurt, *Education in Evolution* (London, Hart Davis, 1971), 208.

57 Quoted in Hopkins, *A Social History*, 75.

58 H.A. Taine, *Notes on England*, trans W.E. Rae (London, Strahan, 1874), 200–2.

59 R.A. Arnold, *History of the Cotton Famine* (London, Saunders, Otley and Co., 1864), 150–3.

60 Sidney and Beatrice Webb, *English Poor Law History*, Vol. I (London, Longmans Green, 1929), 217, 253.

61 *21st Annual Report of the Poor Law Board*, 1868–9, 87.

62 *Household Words*, 18 July 1850, 362–4.

63 Poor law apprenticeship and the subject of children and the poor law are surveyed in Hopkins, *Childhood Transformed*, chapter 6.

64 F.M.L. Thompson, op. cit., 355.

65 M. Blaug, 'The myth of the old poor law and the making of the new', *Journal of Economic History*, 23:2, June (1963), 151–84; and 'The poor law report re-examined', *Journal of Economic History*, 24, June (1964), 229–45; Thompson, ibid.

66 In some Worcestershire unions, it was at first thought necessary to apply the 'less eligibility' rule to children: Frank Crompton, *Workhouse Children* (Stroud, Sutton Publishing, 1997).

67 By 1870, the two leading affiliated friendly societies were the Manchester Unity of Oddfellows (membership 434,100) and the Ancient Order of Foresters (membership 361,735). In addition, there were innumerable small local societies: Hopkins, *Working-Class Self-Help*, 31.

68 Report by Edward Smith in *Twentieth Annual Report of the Poor Law Board*, 1867–8.

69 W.L. Burn, *The Age of Equipoise: A Study of the Mid-Victorian Generation* (London, Allen and Unwin, 1964).

70 Both quotations from Fraser, op. cit., 103.

71 For a good recent survey of Bentham's works, see Iain Hampsher-Monk, *A History of Modern Political Thought* (Oxford, Oxford University Press, 1992), chapter 7, 305–38.

72 John Stuart Mill, *On Liberty* ([1859] Bristol, Thoemmes Press, 1993).

73 Samuel Smiles, *Self-Help* ([1859] London, Murray, 1905), 1.

74 For the Christian Socialists, see E. Norman, *The Victorian Christian Socialists* (Cambridge, Cambridge University Press, 1987). Their attempts at producer co-operation are described briefly in Hopkins, *Working-Class Self-Help*, 206–8.

75 Quoted in Stefan Collini *et al.* (ed.), *Victorian Thinkers* (Oxford, Oxford University Press, 1993), which contains a very helpful account of Ruskin by George P. Landow.

76 Quoted in ibid., 235, in an essay by Stefan Collini.

77 Ibid., 291.

78 For a helpful sketch of events in both boroughs and counties, see K.T. Hoppen, *The Mid-Victorian Generation 1846–1886* (Oxford, Oxford University Press, 1998), 114–15.

79 Ibid., 115–16. See also T.A. Critchley, *A History of Police in England and Wales* (London, Constable, rev. edn 1987), and C. Emsley, *The English Police: A Political and Social History* (London, Longman, 1991). For a good general survey of the efforts of the police to maintain law and order in urban areas and of the public reaction to these efforts, see F.M.L. Thompson, op. cit., 286–7, 329–36.

3 After equipoise: urban problems, 1870–1900

1 *Royal Commission Report on the Depression of Trade and Industry*, Final Report, 1886, xxiii, x.

2 For good general discussions of the Great Depression, see Peter Mathias, *The First Industrial Nation* (London, Methuen, 2nd edn 1983), 361–93; François Crouzet, *The Victorian Economy* (London, Methuen, 1982), chapter 12; G.B. Saul, *The Myth of the Great Depression* (London, Macmillan, 2nd edn 1985); M.J. Wiener, *English Culture and the Decline of the Industrial Spirit* (Cambridge, Cambridge University Press, 1981).

3 See Derek Fraser, *The Evolution of the British Welfare State* (Basingstoke, Macmillan, 2nd edn 1984), 75–6.

4 *16th Annual Report of the Local Government Board, 1886–7*, Urban Sanitary District of Stourbridge (Local History Collection, Stourbridge Library).

5 Fraser, op. cit., 76; Asa Briggs, *Victorian Cities* (Harmondsworth, Penguin, 1968), 226–31.

6 R. Sims (Arthur Mearns), *The Bitter Cry of Outcast London* ([1883] Bath, Chivers, 1969).

7 *Royal Commission on Housing of the Working Classes*, First Report, 1885, 7.

8 *Royal Commission on Housing*, Second Report, 1885, 11.

9 *Royal Commission on Labour*, 1892, Fifth and Final Report, 1894, 247.

10 Eric Hopkins, *Childhood Transformed: Working-Class Children in Nineteenth Century England* (Manchester, Manchester University Press, 1994), 223. See also the general discussion in this work of part-timers and of out-of-school employment, 222–5.

11 Eric Hopkins, *Working-Class Self-Help in Nineteenth Century England* (London, UCL Press, 1995), 123.

12 Ibid., 124.

13 *Report of the Examiners*, 2 August 1867, gives the full details of both cases, which also appear in Hopkins, ibid., 129.

14 *Royal Commission on Trade Unions*, 1867, Fourth Report, 1867, 12, 13.

15 Ibid., see the Eleventh and Final Report, 9 March 1869, which ends with a
Note of Dissent III, followed by a long statement signed by Hughes and Harrison.

16 Peter Mathias, op. cit., 364.

17 See W. Hamish Fraser, *The Coming of the Mass Market 1850–1914* (London, Macmillan, 1981), and John Benson, *The Rise of Consumer Society in Britain 1880–1980* (London, Longman, 1994).

18 Figures taken from Hopkins, *Working-Class Self-Help*, 135–6.

19 *Stourbridge Observer*, 5 June 1880, 21 August 1880.

20 The output of pig iron in South Staffordshire dropped from a peak of 726,000 tons in 1871 to 341,000 tons in 1901: B.R. Mitchell and P. Deane, *Abstract of British Historical Statistics* (Cambridge, Cambridge University Press, 1962), 132; the number of puddling furnaces in the West Midlands was reduced from 21,000 in 1865 to 661 in 1913: W.K. Gale, *The Black Country Iron Industry* (London, Iron and Steel Institute, 1960), 116.

21 For a more detailed survey of pauper children in and outside the workhouse, see Hopkins, *Childhood Transformed*, 181–4.

22 Lionel Rose, *The Erosion of Childhood: Child Oppression in Britain, 1860–1918* (London, Routledge, 1991), 181.

23 A.M. McBrier, *An Edwardian Mixed Doubles* (Oxford, Clarendon Press, 1987), 182.

24 Ibid., 60, 104.

25 Ibid., 182.

26 Rosemary O'Day and David Englander, *Mr Charles Booth's Enquiry: Life and Labour of the People in London Reconsidered* (London, Rio Grande Hambledon, 1993), 187.

27 Ibid., 44, 47.

28 C. Booth, *Life and Labour of the People in London*, Vol. II (London, Macmillan, 1892), 20–1.

29 O'Day and Englander, op. cit., 81.

30 McBrier, op. cit., 88.

31 John Lawson and Harold Silver, *A Social History of Education in England* (London, Methuen, 1973), 316.

32 *Schoolmaster*, 17 December 1872.

33 John Hurt, *Elementary Schooling and the Working Classes 1860–1918* (London, Routledge and Kegan Paul, 1979), 71; Carl Chinn, 'Was separate schooling a means of class segregation in late Victorian and Edwardian Birmingham?', *Midland History*, XIII (1988), 95–112.

34 The origins and nature of the Balfour Education Act are well-trodden ground in most histories of working-class education: for a recent account, see Hopkins, *Childhood Transformed*, 242–4.

35 Jose Harris, *Private Lives, Public Spirit: Britain 1870–1914* (Harmondsworth, Penguin, 1994), 242. H.G. Wells, in particular, could write savagely on this subject. In his *Anticipations* (Leipzig, Tauchnitz, 1902), he wrote that the world state would 'check the procreation of base and servile types, of fear-driven and cowardly souls, bodies, and habits of men ... For a multitude of contemptible and silly creatures ... ugly, inefficient, born of unrestrained lusts, and increasing and multiplying through sheer incontinence and stupidity, the men of the New Republic will have little pity and less benevolence' (quoted in Michael Covin,

The Invisible Man: The Life and Liberties of H.G. Wells (London, Bloomsbury, 1993), 64).

36 Harris, op. cit., 242.

4 Industrial change and the countryside, 1830–1951

1 For general works on Victorian agriculture, see the following works by G.E. Mingay: *Rural Life in Victorian England* (London, Heinemann, 1977); *The Victorian Countryside*, Vols I and II (London, Routledge and Kegan Paul, 1981); *A Social History of the English Countryside* (London, Routledge, 1990); *Land and Society in England 1750–1980* (London, Longman, 1994). See also Pamela Horn, *Labouring Life in the Victorian Countryside* (Dublin, Gill and Macmillan, 1976) and *The Changing Countryside in Victorian and Edwardian England and Wales* (London, Athlone Press, 1984).

2 For the oft-told tale of the repeal of the corn laws, see Norman Gash, *Peel* (London, Longman, 1976).

3 François Crouzet, *The Victorian Economy* (London, Methuen, 1982), 66–8.

4 A. Redford, *Labour Migration in England 1800–1850* (Manchester, Manchester University Press, 2nd edn 1964).

5 *Census Report for 1851* (1852–3), cvii–cviii.

6 Crouzet, op. cit., 151.

7 E.J. Hobsbawm and F. Rude, *Captain Swing* (London, Lawrence and Wishart, 2nd edn 1973).

8 D.A. Armstrong, 'The countryside', in F.M.L. Thompson, *The Cambridge Social History of England, 1750–1950*, Vol. I (Cambridge, Cambridge University Press, 1990), 117–19.

9 Eric Hopkins, *Childhood Transformed: Working-Class Children in Nineteenth Century England* (Manchester, Manchester University Press, 1994), 11–17.

10 Mingay, *A Social History*, 188.

11 Crouzet, op. cit., 170.

12 Ibid., 173.

13 Mingay, *A Social History*, 171.

14 Ibid., 174.

15 Hopkins, op. cit., 270.

16 Ibid.

17 David Brooks, *The Age of Upheaval: Edwardian Politics 1899–1914* (Manchester, Manchester University Press, 1995), 18.

18 H. Rider Haggard, *Rural England*, Vol. II (London, Longmans Green, 1906), 545–6.

19 Mingay, *A Social History*, 184, 192.

20 John Burnett, *A Social History of Housing 1815–1940* (London, Methuen, 1978), 134, 135.

21 C.L. Mowat, *Britain Between the Wars 1918–1920* (London, Methuen, 1956), 251–4, 438–40.

22 For further details regarding the transfers of property at this time, see F.M.L. Thompson, *English Landed Society in the Nineteenth Century*

(London, Routledge, 1963), and David Cannadine, *The Decline and Fall of the British Aristocracy* (London, Pan, rev. edn 1992), chapter 3, 'The decline and disposal of territorial wealth'.

23 For other increases in crop acreages, see B.R. Mitchell, *British Historical Statistics* (Cambridge, Cambridge University Press, 1988), 188.

5 The challenge from the left

1 For Robert Owen and the early history of co-operation, see R.G. Garnett, *Co-operation and the Owenite Socialist Communities in Britain, 1825–45* (Manchester, Manchester University Press, 1972); and Eric Hopkins, *Working-Class Self-Help in Nineteenth Century England* (London, UCL Press, 1995), chapter 9, 'Before Rochdale'. See also W.H.G. Armytage, *Heavens Below: Utopian Experiments in England, 1560–1960* (London, Routledge and Kegan Paul, 1961).

2 Karl Marx and Friedrich Engels, *The Communist Manifesto* ([1848] Harmondsworth, Penguin, 1967), Introduction by A.J.P. Taylor, 48.

3 Quoted by Hopkins, *Working-Class Self-Help*, 140.

4 *Royal Commission on Labour*, 1891, Fifth and Final Report, 1894.

5 Quoted in Eric Hopkins, *A Social History of the English Working Classes 1815–1945* (London, Arnold, 1979), 161.

6 G.D.H. Cole and Raymond Postgate, *The Common People, 1746–1946* (London, Methuen, 2nd edn 1956), 430.

7 For a discussion of the nature of New Unionism, see H.A. Clegg, Alan Fox and A.F. Thompson, *A History of British Trade Unions Since 1889, Vol. I, 1889–1910* (Oxford, Oxford University Press, 1964), chapter 2.

8 The origins and nature of the new political bodies are examined in all the standard textbooks. See, for example, Henry Pelling, *A History of British Trade Unionism* (Harmondsworth, Penguin, 4th edn 1987), chapter 6, 'New unionism and new politics 1880–1900'.

9 B. Webb, *My Apprenticeship* (London, Longmans Green, 1926), 155.

10 Peter d'A. Jones, *The Christian Socialist Revival 1877–1914* (Princeton NJ, Princeton University Press, 1986), 164, 177, 186, 197, 223.

11 For biographies of Keir Hardie, see I. McLean, *Keir Hardie* (London, Allen Lane, 1975), K.O. Morgan, *Keir Hardie* (London, Wiedenfeld and Nicolson, 1975), and F. Reid, *Keir Hardie* (London, Croom Helm, 1978).

12 For a careful examination of the legal cases, see J.V. Orth, *Combination and Conspiracy: A Legal History of Trade Unionism 1721–1906* (Oxford, Oxford University Press, 1991).

13 See also Hopkins, *Working-Class Self-Help*, 151–2.

14 The standard basic account of the founding of the Labour Representation Committee and the Labour Party is given in Henry Pelling, *A Short History of the Labour Party* (New York, St. Martin's Press, 9th edn 1991).

15 Quoted in Hopkins, *Working-Class Self-Help*, 154.

16 See Hopkins, *A Social History*, 155.

17 Beatrice Webb, *Our Partnership*, ed. Barbara Drake and Margaret I. Cole (London, Longmans Green, 1948), 86, 97.

18 The Newcastle Programme, 1891, may seem an exception to this observation, but these proposed reforms included little directly relevant to purely social reform: see R.C.K. Ensor, *England 1870–1914* (Oxford, Oxford University Press, 1936), 207–8.

19 For trade union membership figures about 1900, see Hopkins, *Working-Class Self-Help*, 157–8.

20 Webb, *Our Partnership*, 83.

21 Peter Stansky, 'Morris', in S. Collini *et al.*, *Victorian Thinkers* (Oxford, Oxford University Press, 1993), 335.

22 Ibid., 384.

23 Ibid., 386.

24 Ibid., 383.

25 E.P. Thompson, *William Morris, Romantic to Revolutionary* (London, Lawrence and Wishart, 1955), 843; Ian Bradley, *William Morris and His World* (London, Thames and Hudson, 1978), 115.

26 John A. Hobson, *The Problem of the Unemployed* (London, Methuen, 2nd edn 1904), 98, 102.

27 Ibid., 131–43.

28 John A. Hobson, *The Social Problem: Life and Work* (London, Nisbets, 1901), 8, 9.

29 Ibid., 10–15.

30 Ibid., 197–204.

31 Ibid., 214–16.

32 Charles Masterman, *The Heart of the Empire* ([1901] Brighton, Harvester Press, 1973), 8.

33 Ibid., 17–19.

34 Ibid., 20–30.

35 Ibid., 49–50.

36 For the basic changes in the education of middle-class women, see J.W. Adamson, *English Education, 1780–1902* (Cambridge, Cambridge University Press, 1930); S.J. Curtis, *History of Education in England* (London, University Tutorial Press, 7th edn, 1967); and John Lawson and Harold Silver, *A Social History of Education in England* (London, Methuen, 1973).

37 Eric Hopkins, *Childhood Transformed: Working-Class Children in Nineteenth Century England* (Manchester, Manchester University Press, 1994), 265–6.

38 Jose Harris, *Private Lives, Public Spirit: Britain 1870–1914* (Harmondsworth, Penguin, 1994), 190, 191.

39 Elizabeth Roberts, *Women's Work, 1840–1940* (London, Macmillan, 1988), 21. See also Pat Hudson, *The Industrial Revolution* (London, Arnold, 1992), 226–36, for a very helpful survey of feminist studies relating to the social consequences of industrialisation.

40 Hopkins, *Childhood Transformed*, 286–7.

41 Roberts, op. cit., 62.

42 See S. Blackburn, 'Employers and social policy: Black Country chain-masters, the minimum wage campaign, and the Cradley Heath strike of 1910', *Midland History*, XII (1987), 85–102.

43 Quoted in Roberts, op. cit., 42.

44 Wells was also a great believer in (and practitioner of) free love, and his portrayal of the new, liberated woman in *Ann Veronica* (1909) provoked some scandal – another indication of changing attitudes.

45 Ian Ousby (ed.), *The Cambridge Paperback Guide to Literature in English* (Cambridge, Cambridge University Press, 1996) is a useful reference book for all the writers mentioned in this paragraph.

46 But in the last quarter of the nineteenth century, attendance at Methodist chapels declined after 1880, as did Anglican attendances. Even in the Roman Catholic Church, where congregations were noted for their discipline, attendances fell between 1851 and 1881, and the trend continued in London between 1886 and 1903: Hugh McLeod, *Religion and Society in England 1850–1914* (Basingstoke, Macmillan, 1996), 172–3. There were substantial Irish Roman Catholic communities in London, Glasgow, Liverpool, Manchester, and other urban areas, the result of Irish immigration, especially after the Potato Famine. Many Irish labourers found employment in railway construction in the 1840s and after. For a recent and very helpful survey of the late nineteenth-century decline in religious observance, see McLeod, op. cit., chapter 4, 'The religious crisis', 169–220.

47 Quoted in B.W. Clapp (ed.), *Documents in English Economic History: England Since 1760* (London, Bell, 1976), 435.

6 Edwardian England and the Liberal reforms

1 See Eric Hopkins, *A Social History of the English Working Classes 1815–1945* (London, Arnold, 1979), 144–5. For a useful extract from Rowntree's report, see Derek Fraser, *The Evolution of the British Welfare State* (Basingstoke, Macmillan, 2nd edn 1984), 272–4.

2 But even so, Helen Bosanquet argued that both London and York were special cases; Charles Booth's 30 per cent poverty sector probably included much avoidable secondary poverty, so that only 10 per cent were in real poverty – even then, this was probably exaggerated; she also argued that poverty lines were relatively meaningless since the same income might be spent frugally in one family and recklessly in another.

3 Mrs Bernard Bosanquet, *Rich and Poor: The Standard of Life and Other Studies* (London, Macmillan, 1898), 43.

4 Ibid., 11.

5 Ibid., 49.

6 Helen Bosanquet, *The Strength of the People: A Study in Social Economics* (London, Macmillan, 1902), 100.

7 Quoted in A. M. McBrier, *An Edwardian Mixed Doubles* (Oxford, Clarendon Press, 1987), 152.

8 Sidney Webb, *Socialism in England* (London, Swan Sonnenschien, 1890), 116–17.

9 Ibid., 122.

10 L.G. Chiozza Money, *Riches and Poverty* (London, Methuen, 3rd edn 1906), 39.

11 Ibid., 42, 43.

12 Ibid., 323.

13 For example, shortly before he resigned, Balfour lunched with the Webbs on 28 November 1905, afterwards accompanying Mrs Webb to a performance at the Royal Court Theatre of *Major Barbara*: McBrier, op. cit., 175.

14 Ibid., 176, 178.

15 R.C.K. Ensor, *England 1870–1914* (Oxford, Oxford University Press, 1936), 378.

16 There is an interesting account of the issue in Elie Halévy, *A History of the English People 1895–1905*, Book III (Harmondsworth, Penguin, 1940), 128–30.

17 Quoted in Hopkins, *A Social History*, 186.

18 Peter Clarke, *Hope and Glory: Britain 1900–1990* (Harmondsworth, Penguin, 1997), 17.

19 McBrier, op. cit., 194.

20 Ibid., 188–93.

21 Eric Hopkins, *Charles Masterman (1873–1927), Politician and Journalist: The Splendid Failure* (Lewiston, Queenston, Lampeter, The Edwin Mellen Press, 1999), 66. Masterman was not to modify these views to any marked degree in his later parliamentary career. His best-known book is *The Condition of England*, ed. J.T Boulton ([1909] London, Methuen, 1960), which adds little to the aims set out in 1906.

22 Eric Hopkins, *Working-Class Self-Help in Nineteenth Century England* (London, UCL Press, 1995), 163.

23 J.S. Hurt, *Elementary Schooling and the Working Classes 1860–1918* (London, Routledge and Kegan Paul, 1979), 132, 133, 128.

24 Eric Hopkins, *Childhood Transformed: Working-Class Children in Nineteenth Century England* (Manchester, Manchester University Press, 1994), 202, 203, 208, 247.

25 Hopkins, *Working-Class Self-Help*, 64.

26 Chris Wrigley, *Lloyd George* (Oxford, Blackwell, 1992), 44.

27 Hopkins, *Working-Class Self-Help*, 179.

28 For the standard account of the 1911 act, see B. Gilbert, *The Evolution of National Insurance in Great Britain* (London, Michael Joseph, 1966). Gilbert calls the insurance interest a 'gigantic industry', with over 30 million funeral benefit policies outstanding, and a total workforce of about 100,000.

29 Henry Pelling, *A History of British Trade Unionism* (Harmondsworth, Penguin, 4th edn 1987), 297–8.

30 G. Dangerfield, *The Strange Death of Liberal England* ([1937] London, Macgibbon and Kee, 1966).

31 Quoted in J.T. Ward and Hamish Fraser (eds), *Workers and Employers: Documents on Trade Unions and Industrial Relations in Britain Since the Eighteenth Century* (London, Macmillan, 1980).

32 Ensor, op. cit., 142, 305, 309–10.

33 Quoted in Hopkins, *A Social History*, 175.

34 Henry Pelling, *A Short History of the Labour Party* (New York, St. Martin's Press, 9th edn 1991), 30.

35 David Brooks, *The Age of Upheaval: Edwardian Politics 1899–1914* (Manchester, Manchester University Press, 1995), 151–5.

36 Ibid., 155.

37 Hopkins, *A Social History*, 33.

38 Ibid., 193.

39 Ibid., 192.

40 Ibid., 193.

41 Michael E. Rose, *The English Poor Law 1790–1930* (Newton Abbott, David and Charles, 1971), 272.

42 The *Weekly Dispatch* called the act 'a gigantic fraud'; the *Evening News* headline read, 'Insurance Act Confusion: National Chaos to come on July 15th', and later this paper called the act 'the most ridiculously hodg'd Act of our legislative history'. The *Daily Herald*, the Labour paper, reported that the act had been burned publically on Tower Hill. Even the *Observer*, which had previously supported the bill, turned against it: 'The principle is good. The bill – a bad bill.' See Hopkins, *Charles Masterman*, 121–2.

7 The Great War, 1914–18

1 J.M. Bourne, *Britain and the Great War 1914–1918* (London, Arnold, 1994), 1, 178.

2 Ibid., 205, 178.

3 Ibid., 17, 189.

4 Arthur Marwick, *The Deluge: British Society and the First World War* (Basingstoke, Macmillan Educational, 2nd edn 1991), 204.

5 Ibid., 199–202.

6 Ibid., 101–2, 116–30.

7 Henry Pelling, *A Short History of the Labour Party* (New York, St. Martin's Press, 9th edn 1991), 38.

8 A.J.P. Taylor, *English History 1914–1945* (Oxford, Clarendon Press, 1965), 31.

9 For other accounts of Labour entering the government in 1915, see H.A. Clegg, *A History of British Trade Unions Since 1889*, Vol. II ([1911–33] Oxford, Oxford University Press, 1985); K. Laybourn, *A History of British Trade Unionism, c.1770–1990* (Gloucester, Sutton, 1992); Henry Pelling, *A History of British Trade Unionism* (Harmondsworth, Penguin, 4th edn 1987).

10 Marwick, op. cit., 120.

11 Bourne, op. cit., 212–13.

12 For further information on the Union of Democratic Control, see M. Swartz, *The Union of Democratic Control in British Politics Since the First World War* (Oxford, Clarendon Press, 1971).

13 Eric Hopkins, *A Social History of the English Working Classes 1815–1945* (London, Arnold, 1979), 221.

14 Labour Party, *Seventeenth Annual Report* (1918), 140.

15 Pelling, *A Short History*, 44–5.

16 For an important discussion of the ideological outlook of the Labour Party at this time, see Ross McGibbin, *The Evolution of the Labour Party 1910–1924* (Oxford, Oxford University Press, 1974).

17 Pelling, *A History*, 298.

18 Bourne, op. cit., 158–9.

19 Sidney Webb, *The Restoration of Trade Union Conditions* (London, Nisbet, 1917), 33–9.

20 Bourne, op. cit., 209.

21 For a sympathetic account of the shop stewards' movement, see J. Hinton, *The First Shop Stewards Movement* (London, Allen and Unwin, 1973). For another approach, see I. McLean, *The Legend of Red Clydeside* (Edinburgh, J. Donald, 1983).

22 Bourne, op. cit., 183, 195.

23 Hopkins, *A Social History*, 216.

24 Ibid., 216.

25 Bourne, op. cit., 196, 197.

26 Marwick, op. cit., 134.

27 Ibid.

28 Ibid., 132.

29 See her letters to J.M. Keynes, 16 April 1914, and to David Garnett, 12 April 1915, quoted in Francis Spalding, *Duncan Grant* (London, Chatto and Windus, 1997), 153, 171.

30 Theo Barker and Michael Drake, *Population and Society in England 1870–1939* (London, Batsford, 1982), 129. The men had been examined between November 1917 and October 1918.

31 A. Marwick, *Britain in the Century of Total War* (Harmondsworth, Penguin, 1970), 64.

32 J.S. Hurt, *Elementary Schooling and the Working Classes 1860–1918* (London, Routledge and Kegan Paul, 1979), 188. On the other hand, Tawney thought most boys in London did not start work until they were fourteen: 'The economics of child labour', *Economic Journal* (1909), 517–53.

33 *Report of the Board of Education, 1917–18* (1919), 8.

34 Eric Hopkins, 'Working-class education in Birmingham during the First World War', in Roy Lowe (ed.), *Labour and Education: Some Early 20th Century Studies* (Swansea, History of Education Society, 1981).

35 *Report of the Board of Education, 1915–16* (1917), 1–2. See also Richard Titmuss, *Essays on the Welfare State* (London, Allen and Unwin, 1958), 357.

36 Derek Fraser, *The Evolution of the British Welfare State* (Basingstoke, Macmillan, 2nd edn 1984), 183.

37 Brian Simon, *Education and the Labour Movement* (London, Lawrence and Wishart, 1965), 357.
38 They resulted in a series of commissions of enquiry into industrial unrest in 1917. See Hopkins, *A Social History*, 214.
39 See Eric Hopkins, *Charles Masterman (1873–1927), Politician and Journalist: The Splendid Failure* (Lewiston, Queenston, Lampeter, The Edwin Mellen Press, 1991),151–9.
40 The inscription is still there, but rather high up on the wall. It seems unlikely that many students read it.
41 Bourne, op. cit., 26. Among the many anthologies of poetry of the Great War, see Brian Gardner (ed.), *Up the Line to Death* (London, Methuen, 1964), and D. Hibbert and John Onions (eds), *Poetry of the Great War* (Basingstoke, Macmillan, 1986).
42 Bourne, ibid.
43 C.E. Montague, *Disenchantment* (London, Chatto and Windus, 1922), 30.
44 Ibid., 116.

8 The inter-war years, 1918–39

1 For the economic history of the inter-war years, see Derek H. Aldcroft, *The Inter-War Economy in Britain 1918–1939* (London, Batsford, 1970), and S. Pollard, *The Development of the British Economy, 1914–1980* (London, Arnold, 3rd edn 1981). See also C.L. Mowat, *Britain Between the Wars 1918–1940* (London, Methuen, 1956). This is a remarkable book, and is still an outstanding authority on this period, covering political, economic, and social aspects of the period.
2 J.B.Priestley, *English Journey* ([1934] Harmondsworth, Penguin, 3rd edn, 1977), 296.
3 Ibid., 320–1.
4 For these industries, see Aldcroft, op. cit., 177–206.
5 Mowat, op. cit., 454–5.
6 The best guide initially here is John Burnett, *A Social History of Housing 1815–1985* (London, Methuen, 2nd edn 1986); see also S.D. Chapman (ed.), *The History of Working Class Housing* (Newton Abbot, David and Charles, 1971); J.N. Tarn, *Five Per Cent Philanthropy: An Account of Housing in Urban Areas Between 1840 and 1914* (Cambridge, Cambridge University Press, 1973); E. Gauldie, *Cruel Habitations: A History of Working Class Housing 1780–1918* (London, Allen and Unwin, 1974); A.S. Wohl, *The Eternal Slum: Housing and Social Policy in Victorian London* (London, Arnold, 1977); M.J. Daunton, *House and Home in the Victorian City: Working Class Housing 1850–1914* (London, Arnold, 1983); D. Fraser and A. Sutcliffe (eds), *The Pursuit of Urban History* (London, Arnold, 1983); R. Dennis, *English Industrial Cities of the Nineteenth Century* (Cambridge, Cambridge University Press, 1984).
7 *When We Build Again, A Study Based on Research Into Conditions of Living and Working in Birmingham* (Birmingham, Bournville Village Trust, 1941), 44.

8 Eric Hopkins, 'Working-class life in Birmingham between the wars, 1918–1939', *Midland History*, XV (1990), 129–50.

9 Ibid., 139.

10 See Derek Fraser, *The Evolution of the British Welfare State* (Basingstoke, Macmillan, 2nd edn, 1984), 198–201.

11 Aldcroft, op. cit., 371.

12 *Labour Gazette* (1919), 345–6; (1925), 116.

13 Ibid., 1937.

14 *Reports of Chief Inspector of Factories and Workshops* (1931), 26.

15 Eric Hopkins, *The Rise and Decline of the English Working Classes 1918–1990: A Social History* (London, Wiedenfeld and Nicolson, 1991), 18.

16 *Report of the Chief Inspector of Factories and Workshops* (1937).

17 See C.R. Littler, *The Development of the Labour Process in Capitalist Societies* (London, Heinemann Educational, 1982), 114, 142–3; and also H.A. Clegg, *A History of British Trade Unions Since 1889*, Vol. II (Oxford, Oxford University Press, 1985), 534.

18 S.J. Curtis, *History of Education in England* (London, University Tutorial Press, 7th edn 1967).

19 Youths aged 14–16 were brought in only in 1934, agricultural workers in 1936, and domestic servants in 1938: Mowat, op. cit., 495.

20 Aldcroft, op. cit., 147.

21 Mowat, op. cit., 481, 483. These figures occur at the beginning of an immensely informative chapter, 'The secret people and the social conscience; the condition of Britain in the thirties'.

22 For a general account of the unemployment benefit schemes of the time, see Derek Fraser, op. cit., 185–98; Pat Thane, *The Foundations of the Welfare State* (London, Longman, 1982), pt I, pt 6; Eric Hopkins, *A Social History of the English Working Classes 1815–1945* (London, Arnold, 1979), 229–32.

23 George Orwell, *The Road to Wigan Pier* ([1937] Harmondsworth, Penguin, 1962), 80–1.

24 W. Greenwood, *Love on the Dole* ([1933] Harmondsworth, Penguin, 1969), 247.

25 For a more recent left-wing view on this, see Keith Laybourn, *Britain on the Breadline* (Gloucester, Sutton, 1990), chapter II, 'Poverty and ill-health during the inter-war years', 41–67.

26 On this subject, see John Stevenson, *British Society 1914–45* (Harmondsworth, Penguin, 1984), 287.

27 Charles Webster, 'Healthy or hungry thirties?', *History Workshop*, Spring (1982), 110–29.

28 Mowat, op. cit., 484.

29 In this connection, see Margaret Mitchell, 'The effects of unemployment on the social condition of women and children in the 1930s', *History Workshop*, Spring (1985), 105–25.

30 Mowat, op. cit., 492.

31 B. Seebohm Rowntree, *Poverty and Progress: A Second Social Survey of York* (London, Longman, 1941), 32, 96–102, 156–160, 451.

32 Mowat, op. cit., 492.

33 Ibid., 513

34 Aldcroft, op. cit., 379.

35 Mowat, op. cit., 505.

36 Hopkins, 'Working-class life in Birmingham'.

37 Ibid.

38 John Burnett, *Plenty and Want* (London, Nelson, 1968), 319. He is quoted with approval by Aldcroft, op. cit., 385.

39 For a standard history of trade unionism between the wars, see Henry Pelling, *A History of British Trade Unionism* (Harmondsworth, Penguin, 4th edn 1987).

40 Mowat, op. cit., 296.

41 Ibid.

42 Ibid., 325.

43 Mowat, op. cit., 300.

44 One of the most helpful accounts remains that of C.L. Mowat. A.J.P. Taylor, *English History 1914–1945* (Oxford, Clarendon Press, 1965) has a relatively short account. See also C. Farman, *The General Strike* (London, Hart Davis, 1972), Margaret Morris, *The British General Strike, 1926* (London, Historical Association, 1973), R. Renshaw, *The General Strike* (London, Eyre Methuen, 1975), and G.A. Philips, *The General Strike* (London, Wiedenfeld and Nicolson, 1976). Baldwin's actions before, during, and after the strike are discussed in K. Middlemas and J. Barnes, *Baldwin* (London, Wiedenfeld and Nicolson, 1969), 378–443.

45 Baldwin always claimed this afterwards as a master-stroke, since it kept Churchill out of mischief where he could do no harm.

46 Quoted from the *British Gazette*, 6 May, in Mowat, op. cit., 319.

47 Mowat, ibid., 325.

48 Quoted in Hopkins, *A Social History*, 251.

49 Pelling, op. cit., 298–9.

50 This of course was in part due to the great extension of the franchise by the Representation of the People Act, 1918.

51 The basic work here is R.W. Lynam, *The First Labour Government* (London, Chapman and Hall, 1957).

52 Taylor, *English History*, 209, quoting Nicolson, *George V* (1952), 329.

53 Quoted in Mowat, op. cit., 173.

54 Ibid., 172.

55 But not all members of the government had working-class backgrounds. There were four members of the House of Lords, and three middle-class ex-Liberals – Trevelyan, Buxton, and Ponsonby – occupying ministerial posts.

56 R. Skidelsky, *Politicians and the Slump* (London, Macmillan, 1967).

57 Quoted in D. Marquand, *Ramsay MacDonald* (London, Cape, 1977).

58 C.E. Montague, *Disenchantment* (London, Chatto and Windus, 1922), 136.

59 Ibid., 160.

60 Ibid., 163.

61 Taylor, op. cit., 361–2.
62 W.H. Auden, *Some Poems* (London, Faber and Faber, 1940), 36. This extract is from a kind of play, *The Dog Beneath the Skin*, written in conjunction with Christopher Isherwood. In the early 1950s Auden expressed severe criticism of the play, saying that most of it was written by Isherwood.
63 Taylor, op. cit., 368, 393.

9 War and the coming of the Welfare State

1 £1,118 million had been raised by the sale of overseas investments. 'Invisible income' from overseas had been halved. Exports were little more than 30 per cent of pre-war figures. Government expenditure abroad was five times greater than before the war: A.J.P. Taylor, *English History 1914–1945* (Oxford, Clarendon Press, 1965), 599.
2 There are two excellent books in particular which cover the social history of World War II in Britain. They are: Angus Calder, *The People's War* (London, Granada, 1969), and Paul Addison, *The Road to 1945: British Politics, and the Second World War* (London, Cape, 1975).
3 On the history of the trade union movement during the war, Henry Pelling, *A History of British Trade Unionism* (Harmondsworth, Penguin, 4th edn 1987), is again a reliable guide.
4 Sydney Pollard, *The Development of the British Economy, 1914–1980* (London, Arnold, 3rd edn 1983), 143.
5 Ibid., 169.
6 For all these figures, see ibid., 164–9.
7 For criticisms of wartime governments for failure to reconstruct industry, see Corelli Barnett, *The Audit of War: The Illusion and the Reality of Great Britain as a Great Power* (London, Macmillan, 1986).
8 Space does not permit a full account here of the Blitz. For a good general survey, including casualty figures, see Calder, op. cit.
9 A survey of the arguments may be found in Harold D. Smith, 'The effect of the war on the status of women', in Harold L. Smith (ed.), *War and Social Change: British Society in the Second World War* (Manchester, Manchester University Press, 1986).
10 There are many accounts available of leisure interests in World War II. See, for example, J. Walvin, *Leisure and Society 1830–1950* (London, Longman, 1978), and Eric Hopkins, *The Rise and Decline of the English Working Classes 1918–1990: A Social History* (London, Wiedenfeld and Nicolson, 1991), 72–5.
11 The most comprehensive book on state education during World War II is P.H.J.H. Gosden, *Education in the Second World War* (London, Methuen, 1976). See also Calder, op. cit.; Arthur Marwick, *Britain in the Century of Total War* (Harmondsworth, Penguin, 1970); R.M. Titmuss, *Problems of Social Policy* (London, HMSO, 1950); Gerald Bernbaum, *Social Change and the Schools, 1918–1944* (London, Routledge and Kegan Paul, 1967). For a

specialist case study, see Eric Hopkins, 'Elementary education in Birmingham during the Second World War', *History of Education*, 18:3 (1989), 243–55.

12 Public Record Office, ED 134/143.
13 Ibid.
14 Titmuss, op. cit., 409.
15 Gosden, op. cit., 73–4.
16 *Report on Social Insurance and Allied Services* (1942), 120–2.
17 Ibid.
18 Jose Harris, 'Some aspects of social policy in Britain during the Second World War', in W.J. Mommsen (ed.), *The Emergence of the Welfare State in Britain and Germany* (London, Croom Helm, 1981), 247–62.
19 Pat Thane, *The Foundations of the Welfare State* (London, Longman, 1982), 264.
20 For a general account of educational progress during the war, see Gosden, op. cit., 431, 433. For a critical account of what happened in the Birmingham elementary schools, see Hopkins, 'Elementary education'.
21 In fact, the Labour Party was formally committed at the party's 1942 annual conference to the comprehensive school: Addison, op. cit., 277.
22 J.B. Priestley, *Postscripts* (London, Heinemann, 1940), 38.
23 Quoted by Addison, op. cit., 119.
24 A popular BBC Home Service programme was *The Brains Trust*, in which a team of experts led by Professor C.E.M. Joad of Birkbeck College, a well-known Fabian socialist, answered listeners' questions on a variety of subjects. Joad was an excellent expositor of ideas, but lost his employment with the BBC after his conviction for avoiding paying his fare on the London Underground.
25 See Steven Fielding, Peter Thompson and Nick Tiratsoo, *England Arise! The Labour Party and Popular Politics in the 1940s Britain* (Manchester, Manchester University Press, 1995).
26 Quoted in Hopkins, *The Rise and Decline*, 89.
27 There are many accounts available of the nationalisation policy of the Labour government. Among those I have consulted here are: Roger Eatwell, *The 1945–51 Labour Governments* (London, Batsford, 1979); K.O. Morgan, *Labour in Power 1945–51* (Oxford, Oxford University Press, 1984); Henry Pelling, *The Labour Governments 1945–1951* (London, Macmillan, 1984); Alan Sked and Chris Cook, *Post-War Britain: A Political History* (Harmondsworth, Penguin, 2nd edn 1984): K.O. Morgan, *The People's Peace: British History 1945–1989* (Oxford, Oxford University Press, 1990); Peter Clarke, *Hope and Glory: Britain 1900–1990* (Harmondsworth, Penguin, 1997).
28 Helpful books on the implementing of the Beveridge Report are: Maurice Bruce, *The Coming of the Welfare State* (London, Batsford, 1968), Derek Fraser, *The Evolution of the British Welfare State* (Basingstoke, Macmillan, 2nd edn 1984), and Pat Thane, op. cit.
29 Quoted in Fraser, ibid., 235.

30 Eric Hopkins, *The Rise and Decline*, 96, 98; Fraser, op. cit., 238.

31 In practice, claimants familiar with the clerical staff of the PACs found the same old faces on the other side of the counter in the offices of the new authority.

32 Prefabs are now regarded as buildings of historical interest. A specimen is to be found at the Avoncroft Museum of Buildings, Bromsgrove, Worcs.

33 Morgan, *Labour in Power*, 169.

34 Changes in industrial working conditions in these years may be traced in the *Annual Reports of the Chief Inspector of Factories*, and in the *Ministry of Labour Gazette*.

35 Quoted in Hopkins, *The Rise and Decline*, 80.

36 Defined in the *Concise Oxford Dictionary* (Oxford, Oxford University Press, 9th edn 1995) as 'a man often characterised by flashy dress, who makes a living by illicit or unscrupulous dealings'.

37 B.S. Rowntree and G.R. Lavers, *Poverty and the Welfare State* (London, Longmans Green, 1951).

38 Quoted in Hopkins, *The Rise and Decline*, 112.

39 Sidney Pollard, *The Development of the British Economy 1914–1990* (London, Arnold, 4th edn 1992), 222.

40 Keith Robbins, *The Eclipse of a Great Power: Modern Britain 1870–1975* (London, Longman, 1983), 20.

41 Morgan, *Labour in Power*, 179.

42 Morgan, *The People's Peace*, 107–9.

43 Ibid., 111.

44 Ibid., 109.

45 Ibid., 28.

46 The desirability of reconstructing industry rather than instituting welfare reform is expounded in Corelli Barnett, op. cit., and his views are critically assessed by Paul Addison in Peter Hennessey and Anthony Seldon (eds), *Ruling Performance: British Governments from Attlee to Thatcher* (Oxford, Oxford University Press, 1987), 19–24.

47 See the conclusions in Fielding, Thompson and Tiratsoo, op. cit., for a recent discussion of this point.

48 See Addison, *The Road to 1945*, 21.

49 Ibid., 276.

Envoi

1 For the unemployment of the 1980s, see Eric Hopkins, *The Rise and Decline of the English Working Classes 1918–1990: A Social History* (London, Wiedenfeld and Nicolson, 1991), 215–21ß

Select bibliography

A full bibliography for the social history of the period 1830–1951 would occupy many more pages than are available here. Instead, a select bibliography is presented which is intended to guide the reader in search of further information to some of the basic sources for the text.

Official publications and other primary sources

Advertiser for Brierley Hill, Stourbridge, Dudley, and Kidderminster, 1876–1914.
Board of Education, 1915–16, 1917–18: reports.
Census reports for England and Wales, 1831, 1841, 1851.
Chief Inspector of Factories and Workshops, 1918–39: reports.
Department of Education reports on Birmingham schools, 1939–45 , PRO ED 134/236.
Enquiry into the State of Popular Education, 1866: reports and evidence.
Health of Towns Commission, 1843: report.
Household Words, 1850.
Labour Gazette, 1919–39.
Labour Party Annual Report, 1918.
Minutes of the Committee of Council for Education, 1844–1900.
Observer: Stourbridge, Cradley Heath, Halesowen and District Chronicle, 1864–74.
Poor Law Board annual reports, 1847–71.
Report on Social Insurance and Allied Services (the Beveridge Report), 1942.
Royal Commission on Children's Employment, 1840: reports and evidence.
Royal Commission on Children's Employment, 1862: reports and evidence.
Royal Commission on Housing of the Working Classes, 1885: reports.
Royal Commission on Labour, 1891–4: reports.
Royal Commission on the Poor Laws, 1905–9: reports.
Royal Commission on Trade Unions, 1867: reports and evidence.
Royal Commission on the Working of the Factories and Workshops Acts, 1876: reports.
Sanitary Conditions of the Labouring Poor Enquiry, 1842: report.
Schoolmaster, 1872.
Select Committee on Combinations of Workmen, 1838: reports.

Select Committee on Manufacturers' Employment, 1830: report.
Tremenheere's Report on the Mining Districts of South Staffordshire, 1850.
Worcester Chronicle, 1841–4.

Books

Adamson, J.W., *English Education, 1780–1902*, Cambridge, Cambridge University Press, 1930.

Addison, Paul, *The Road to 1945: British Politics, and the Second World War*, London, Cape, 1975.

Aldcroft, Derek H., *The Inter-War Economy in Britain 1918–1939*, London, Batsford, 1970.

——, *The British Economy, Vol. I: The Years of Turmoil 1920–1951*, Brighton, Wheatsheaf, 1986.

Arlington, R., *Death of a Hero*, New York, Corrici Friede, 1929.

Armytage, W.H.G., *Heavens Below: Utopian Experiments in England, 1560–1960*, London, Routledge and Kegan Paul, 1961.

Arnold, R.A., *History of the Cotton Famine*, London, Saunders, Otley and Co., 1864.

Ashton, T.S., *The Industrial Revolution*, Oxford, Oxford University Press, 1948.

Ashworth, W., *An Economic History of England 1870–1939*, London, Methuen, 1960.

Auden, W. H., *Some Poems*, London, Faber and Faber, 1940.

Barker, Theo and Drake, Michael, *Population and Society in England 1870–1939*, London, Batsford, 1982.

Barnett, Corelli, *The Audit of War: The Illusion and the Reality of Great Britain as a Great Power*, London, Macmillan, 1986.

Baxter, G.R.W., *The Book of the Bastilles*, London, John Stephens, 1841.

Bédarida, F., *A Social History of England 1851–1990*, London, Routledge, 1991.

Benson, John, *The Working Class in Britain 1850–1939*, London, Longman, 1989.

——, *The Rise of Consumer Society in Britain 1880–1980*, London, Longman, 1994.

Bentham, J., *Fragment of Government*, [1776] Cambridge, Cambridge University Press, 1988.

Best, G., *Mid-Victorian Britain 1851–1875*, London, Panther, 1973.

Biagini, E.F. and Reid, A. (eds), *Currents of Radicalism: Popular Radicalism, Organised Labour and Party Politics in Britain 1850–1914*, Cambridge, Cambridge University Press, 1991.

Blunden, Edmund, *Undertones of War*, London, Cobden Sanderson, 1930.

Bonner, A., *British Cooperation*, Manchester, Cooperative Union, 1961.

Bosenquet, Helen, *Rich and Poor*, London, Macmillan, 1896.

——, *The Standard of Life and Other Studies*, London, Macmillan, 1898.

——, *The Strength of the People: A Study in Social Economics*, London, Macmillan, 1902.

——, *The Poverty Line*, London, Macmillan, 1903.

282 *Select bibliography*

Bourne, J.M., *Britain and the Great War 1914–1918*, London, Arnold, 1994.

Bradley, Ian, *William Morris and His World*, London, Thames and Hudson, 1978.

Briggs, Asa, *Victorian Cities*, Harmondsworth, Penguin, 1968.

Brooks, David, *The Age of Upheaval: Edwardian Politics 1899–1914*, Manchester, Manchester University Press, 1995.

Brown, H.P., *The Origins of Trade Union Power*, Oxford, Oxford University Press, 1983.

Brown, John, *A Memoir of Robert Blincoe*, [1832] Firl, Sussex, Caliban, 1977.

Brown, K.D., *The English Labour Movement 1700–1951*, Dublin, Gill and Macmillan, 1982.

—— (ed.), *The First Labour Party 1906–1914*, Beckenham, Croom Helm, 1985.

Bruce, Maurice, *The Coming of the Welfare State*, London, Batsford, 1968.

Burgess, K., *The Challenge of Labour: Shaping British Society 1850–1930*, London, Croom Helm, 1980.

Burn, W.L., *The Age of Equipoise: A Study of the Mid-Victorian Generation*, London, Allen and Unwin, 1964.

Burnett, John, *A Social History of Housing 1815–1970*, London, Methuen, 1978.

Bythell, D., *The Handloom Weavers*, Cambridge, Cambridge University Press, 1969.

Calder, Angus, *The People's War*, London, Granada, 1969.

Cecil, David, *Melbourne*, London, The Reprint Society, 1955.

Chadwick, Owen, *The Victorian Church*, London, Black, 1970.

Chambers, J.D., *The Workshop of the World*, Oxford, Oxford University Press, 1961.

Checkland, S.G. and Checkland, E.O.A. (eds), *The Poor Law Report of 1834*, Harmondsworth, Penguin, 1974.

Chiozza Money, L.G., *Riches and Poverty*, London, Methuen, 3rd edn 1906.

Church, Roy, *The Great Victorian Boom 1850–1873*, London, Macmillan, 1975.

Clapp, B.W. (ed.), *Documents in English Economic History: England Since 1760*, London, Bell, 1976.

Clarke, Peter, *Hope and Glory: Britain 1900–1990*, Harmondsworth, Penguin, 1997.

Clegg, H.A., *A History of British Trade Unions Since 1889*, Vol. II, Oxford, Oxford University Press, 1985.

Clegg, H.A., Fox, Alan and Thompson, A.F., *A History of British Trade Unions Since 1889, Vol. I, 1889–1910*, Oxford, Oxford University Press, 1964.

Cole, G.D.H. and Postgate, R., T*he Common People, 1746–1946*, London, Methuen, 2nd edn 1956.

Collini, Stefan, *et al. Victorian Thinkers*, Oxford, Oxford University Press, 1993.

Constantine, Stephen, *Unemployment in Britain Between the Wars*, London, Longman, 1980.

Covin, Michael, *The Invisible Man: The Life and Liberties of H.G. Wells*, London, Bloomsbury, 1993.

Critchley, T.A., *A History of Police in England and Wales*, London, Constable, rev. edn 1987.

Crompton, Frank, *Workhouse Children*, Stroud, Sutton Publishing, 1997.

Crouzet, François, *The Victorian Economy*, London, Methuen, 1982.

Crowther, Anne, *British Social Policy 1914–1939*, Basingstoke, Macmillan, 1988.

Crowther, M.A., *The Workhouse System 1834–1939*, London, Batsford, 1981.

Cunningham, Hugh, *Leisure in the Industrial Revolution c.1780–c.1880*, London, Croom Helm, 1980.

Curtis, S.J., *History of Education in England*, London, University Tutorial Press, 7th edn, 1967.

Dangerfield, G., *The Strange Death of Liberal England*, [1937] London, Macgibbon and Kee, 1966.

Daunton, M.J., *House and Home in the Victorian City: Working Class Housing 1850–1914*, London, Arnold, 1983.

Digby, Anne, *Pauper Palaces*, London, Routledge and Kegan Paul, 1978.

——, *The Poor Law in Nineteenth Century England and Wales*, London, Historical Association, 1982.

Digby, Anne, and Searby, Peter, *Children, School and Society in Nineteenth Century England*, London, Macmillan, 1981.

Dinwiddy, J.R., *Chartism*, London, Historical Association, 1987.

Disraeli, Benjamin, *Sybil, or the Two Nations*, [1845] Oxford, Oxford University Press, 1975.

Dyos, H.J. and Wolf, Michael (eds), *The Victorian City: Images and Realities*, London, Routledge and Kegan Paul, 1973.

Eatwell, Roger, *The 1945–51 Labour Governments*, London, Batsford, 1979.

Emsley, C., *The English Police: A Political and Social History*, London, Longman, 1991.

Engels, Frederick, *The Condition of the Working Class in England in 1844*, [1845] Harmondsworth, Penguin, 1987.

Ensor, R.C.K., *England 1870–1914*, Oxford, Oxford University Press, 1936.

Epstein, J. and Thompson, D. (eds), *The Chartist Experience*, London, Macmillan, 1982.

Farman, C., *The General Strike*, London, Hart Davis, 1972.

Fielding, Steven, Thompson, Peter and Tiratsoo, Nick, *England Arise! The Labour Party and Popular Politics in the 1940s Britain*, Manchester, Manchester University Press, 1995.

Finer, S.E., *The Life and Times of Sir Edwin Chadwick*, London, Methuen, 1952.

Floud, R. and McGloskey, D.N. (eds), *Economic History of Britain Since 1700*, Cambridge, Cambridge University Press, 2nd edn 1994.

Fox, A., *History and Heritage: The Social Origins of the British Industrial Relations System*, London, Allen and Unwin, 1985.

Fraser, Derek (ed.), *The New Poor Law in the Nineteenth Century*, London, Macmillan, 1976.

——, *The Evolution of the British Welfare State*, Basingstoke, Macmillan, 2nd edn 1984.

Fraser, W.H., *Trade Unions and Society: The Struggle for Acceptance 1850–1880*, London, Allen and Unwin, 1974.

——, *The Coming of the Mass Market 1850–1914*, London, Macmillan, 1981.

284 *Select bibliography*

Gale, W.K., *The Black Country Iron Industry*, London, Iron and Steel Institute, 1960.

Gardner, Brian (ed.), *Up the Line to Death*, London, Methuen, 1964.

Garnett, R.G., *Co-operation and the Owenite Socialist Communities in Britain, 1825–45*, Manchester, Manchester University Press, 1972.

Gash, Norman, *Peel*, London, Longman, 1976.

Gauldie, E., *Cruel Habitations: A History of Working Class Housing 1780–1918*, London, Allen and Unwin, 1974.

Gilbert, A.G., *Religion and Society in Industrial England: Church, Chapel and Social Change 1740–1914*, London, Longman, 1976.

Gilbert, B., *The Evolution of National Insurance in Great Britain*, London, Michael Joseph, 1966.

Glasier, John Bruce, *William Morris and the Early Days of the Socialist Movement*, [1921] Bristol, Thoemmes Press, 1994.

Gosden, P.H.J.H., *The Friendly Societies in England 1815–1875*, Manchester, Manchester University Press, 1961.

——, *Self Help*, London, Batsford, 1973.

——, *Education in the Second World War*, London, Methuen, 1976.

Graves, Robert, *Goodbye to All That*, London, Cape, 1929.

Greenwood, Walter, *Love on the Dole*, [1933] Harmondsworth, Penguin, 1969.

Haggard, H. Rider, *Rural England*, London, Longmans Green, 1906.

Halévy, Elie, *A History of the English People 1895–1905*, Harmondsworth, Penguin, 1940.

Hampsher-Monk, Iain, *A History of Modern Political Thought*, Oxford, Oxford University Press, 1992.

Harris, Jose, *Private Lives, Public Spirit: Britain 1870–1914*, Harmondsworth, Penguin, 1994.

Harrison, J.F.C., *The Early Victorians 1832–51*, London, Panther, 1971.

Hay, G.R., *The Origin of the Liberal Welfare Reforms 1906–14*, London, Macmillan, 1975.

Hennessey, Peter and Seldon, Anthony (eds), *Ruling Performance: British Governments from Attlee to Thatcher*, Oxford, Oxford University Press, 1987.

Hennock, E.P., *British Social Reform and German Precedents: The Case of Social Insurance 1880–1914*, Oxford, Oxford University Press, 1987.

Hibbert, D. and Onions, John (eds), *Poetry of the Great War*, Basingstoke, Macmillan, 1986.

Hinton, J., *The First Shop Stewards Movement*, London, Allen and Unwin, 1973.

Hobsbawm, E.J. and Rudé, F., *Captain Swing*, London, Lawrence and Wishart, 2nd edn 1973.

Hobson, J.A., *The Social Problem: Life and Work*, London, Nisbets, 1901.

——, *The Problem of the Unemployed*, London, Methuen, 2nd edn 1904.

Holyoake, G.J., *The History of Cooperation in England* (2 vols), London, T. Fischer Unwin, 1906.

Hopkins, Eric, *A Social History of the English Working Classes 1815–1945*, London, Arnold, 1979.

——, *Birmingham: The First Manufacturing Town in the World 1760–1840*, London, Wiedenfeld and Nicolson, 1989.

——, *The Rise and Decline of the English Working Classes 1918–1990: A Social History*, London, Wiedenfeld and Nicolson, 1991.

——, *Childhood Transformed: Working-Class Children in Nineteenth Century England*, Manchester, Manchester University Press, 1994.

——, *Working-Class Self-Help in Nineteenth Century England*, London, UCL Press, 1995.

——, *The Rise of the Industrial Town: Birmingham 1760–1840*, Stroud, Sutton Publishing, 1998.

——, *Charles Masterman (1873–1927), Politician and Journalist: The Splendid Failure*, Lewiston, Queenston, Lampeter, The Edwin Mellen Press, 1999.

Hoppen, K.T., *The Mid-Victorian Generation 1846–1886*, Oxford, Oxford University Press, 1998.

Hoppit, J. and Wrigley, E.A. (eds), *The Industrial Revolution in Britain, I*, Oxford, Blackwell, 1994.

Horn, Pamela, *Labouring Life in the Victorian Countryside*, Dublin, Gill and Macmillan, 1976.

——, *The Changing Countryside in Victorian and Edwardian England and Wales*, London, Athlone Press, 1984.

Houghton, Walter E., *The Victorian Frame of Mind 1830–1870*, London, Yale University Press, 1957.

Hunt, E.H., *British Labour History 1815–1914*, London, Wiedenfeld and Nicolson, 1981.

Hurt, John, *Education in Evolution*, London, Hart Davis, 1971.

——, *Elementary Schooling and the Working Classes 1860–1918*, London, Routledge and Kegan Paul, 1979.

Hutchings, B.L. and Harrison, A., *A History of Factory Legislation*, London, Cass, 1926.

Jenkins, Mick, *The General Strike of 1842*, London, Lawrence and Wishart, 1980.

Johnson, Paul, *Saving and Spending*, Oxford, Oxford University Press, 1985.

Jones, G.S., *Language of Class: Studies in English Working-Class History 1832–1982*, Cambridge, Cambridge University Press, 1983.

Jones, Peter d'A., *The Christian Socialist Revival 1877–1914*, Princeton NJ, Princeton University Press, 1986.

Lambert, R.J., *Sir John Simon 1816–1904*, London, Macgibbon and Kee, 1963.

Lawson, J. and Silver, H., *A Social History of Education in England*, London, Methuen, 1973.

Laybourn, K., *Britain on the Breadline*, Gloucester, Sutton, 1990.

——, *The Rising Sun of Socialism*, Gloucester, Sutton, 1991.

——, *A History of British Trade Unionism c.1770–1990*, Gloucester, Sutton, 1992.

Littler, C.R. *The Development of the Labour Process in Capitalist Societies*, London, Heinemann Educational, 1982.

Lovell, J., *British Trade Unions, 1873–1933*, London, Macmillan, 1977.

Lynam, R.W., *The First Labour Government*, London, Chapman and Hall, 1957.

MacDonagh, Oliver, *A Pattern of Government Growth: The Passenger Acts and their Enforcement, 1800–1860*, London, MacGibbon and Kee, 1961.

——, *Early Victorian Government*, London, Wiedenfeld and Nicolson, 1977.

Marquand, D., *Ramsay MacDonald*, London, Cape, 1977.

Marshall, J.D., *The Old Poor Law 1794–1834*, London, Macmillan, 2nd edn 1985.

Marwick, Arthur, *Britain in the Century of Total War*, Harmondsworth, Penguin, 1970.

——, *The Deluge: British Society and the First World War*, Basingstoke, Macmillan Educational, 2nd edn 1991.

Marx, K. and Engels, F., *The Communist Manifesto*, [1848] Harmondsworth, Penguin, 1967.

Masterman, Charles, *The Heart of the Empire*, [1901] Brighton, Harvester Press, 1973.

——, *From the Abyss: Of its Inhabitants, by One of Them*, [1902] London, Garland Publishing, 1980.

——, *The Condition of England*, [1909] ed. J.T. Boulton, London, Methuen, 1960.

Mather, F., *Chartism*, London, Historical Association, 1975.

Mathias, Peter, *The First Industrial Nation*, London, Methuen, 2nd edn 1983.

Mayhew, Henry, *London Labour and the London Poor*, [1861] Firl, Caliban, 1980.

McBrier, A.M., *An Edwardian Mixed Doubles*, Oxford, Clarendon Press, 1987.

McGibbin, Ross, *The Evolution of the Labour Party 1910–1924*, Oxford, Oxford University Press, 1974.

McLean, I., *Keir Hardie*, London, Allen Lane, 1975.

——, *The Legend of Red Clydeside*, Edinburgh, J. Donald, 1983.

McLeod, Hugh, *Religion and the Working Class in Nineteenth Century Britain*, London, Macmillan, 1984.

——, *Religion and Society in England 1850–1914*, Basingstoke, Macmillan, 1996.

Mill, J.S., *On Liberty*, [1859] Bristol, Thoemmes Press, 1993.

Milward, Alan S., *The Economic Effect of the World Wars on Britain*, London, Macmillan, 1970.

Mitchell, B.R., *British Historical Statistics*, Cambridge, Cambridge University Press, 1988.

Mitchell, B.R. and Deane, P., *Abstract of British Historical Statistics*, Cambridge, Cambridge University Press, 1962.

Mingay, G.E., *Rural Life in Victorian England*, London, Heinemann, 1977.

——, *The Victorian Countryside*, Vols I and II, London, Routledge and Kegan Paul, 1981.

——, *A Social History of the English Countryside*, London, Routledge, 1990.

——, *Land and Society in England 1750–1980*, London, Longman, 1994.

Mokyr, J. (ed.), *The British Industrial Revolution: An Economic Perspective*, Boulder CO, Westview Press, 1993.

Mommsen, W. (ed.), *The Emergence of the Welfare State in Britain and Germany*, London, Croom Helm, 1981.

Montague, C.E., *Disenchantment*, London, Chatto and Windus, 1922.

Morgan, K.O., *Keir Hardie*, London, Wiedenfeld and Nicolson, 1975.

——, *Labour in Power 1945–51*, Oxford, Oxford University Press, 1984.

——, *The People's Peace: British History 1945–1989*, Oxford, Oxford University Press, 1990.

Morris, Margaret, *The British General Strike, 1926*, London, Historical Association, 1973.

Morris, R.J., *Class and Class Consciousness in the Industrial Revolution 1780–1850*, London, Macmillan, 1979.

Mowat, C.L., *Britain Between the Wars 1918–1940*, London, Methuen, 1956.

——, *The Charity Organisation Society 1869–1913: Its Ideas and Work*, London, Methuen, 1961.

Musson, A., *British Trade Unions 1800–1875*, London, Macmillan, 1972.

—— (ed.), *Trade Unions and Social History*, London, Cass, 1974.

Nowell-Smith, S. (ed.), *Edwardian England 1901–1914*, Oxford, Oxford University Press, 1964.

O'Day, R. and Englander, D., *Mr Charles Booth's Enquiry: Life and Labour of the People in London Reconsidered*, London, Rio Grande Hambledon, 1993.

Orth, J.V., *Combination and Conspiracy: A Legal History of Trade Unionism 1721–1906*, Oxford, Oxford University Press, 1991.

Orwell, George, *The Road to Wigan Pier*, [1937] Harmondsworth, Penguin, 1962.

Ousby, Ian (ed.), *The Cambridge Paperback Guide to Literature in English*, Cambridge, Cambridge University Press, 1996.

Oxley, G.W., *Poor Relief in England and Wales 1601–1834*, Newton Abbot, David and Charles, 1974.

Payne, P.L., *British Entrepreneurship in the Nineteenth Century*, London, Macmillan, 2nd edn 1988.

Pelling, Henry, *The Labour Governments 1945–1951*, London, Macmillan, 1984.

——, *A History of British Trade Unionism*, Harmondsworth, Penguin, 4th edn 1987.

——, *A Short History of the Labour Party*, New York, St. Martin's Press, 9th edn 1991.

Philips, G.A., *The General Strike*, London, Wiedenfeld and Nicolson, 1976.

Pimlott, B. and Cook, C. (eds), *Trade Unions in British Politics*, London, Longman, 1982.

Pollard, S., *The Development of the British Economy, 1914–1980*, London, Arnold, 3rd edn 1983.

——, *The Development of the British Economy, 1914–1990*, London, Arnold, 4th edn 1992.

Poynter, J.R., *Society and Pauperism: English Ideas on Poor Relief 1795–1834*, London, Routledge and Kegan Paul, 1969.

Priestley, J.B., *English Journey*, [1934] Harmondsworth, Penguin, 3rd edn 1977.

——, *Postscripts*, London, Heinemann, 1940.

Razzell, P.E. and Wainwright, W.R., *The Victorian Working Class*, London, Cass, 1973.

Read, Donald, *Edwardian England*, London, Harrap, 1972.

Redford, A., *Labour Migration in England 1800–1850*, Manchester, Manchester University Press, 2nd edn 1964.

Reid, Alastair, J., *Social Classes and Social Relationships in Britain 1850–1914*, London, Macmillan, 1992.

Reid, F., *Keir Hardie*, London, Croom Helm, 1978.

Renshaw, R., *The General Strike*, London, Eyre Methuen, 1975.

Robbins, K., *The Eclipse of a Great Power: Modern Britain 1870–1975*, London, Longman, 1983.

Roberts, E., *Women's Work, 1840–1940*, London, Macmillan, 1988.

Rose, Lionel, *The Erosion of Childhood: Child Oppression in Britain, 1860–1918*, London, Routledge, 1991.

Rose, M.E., *The English Poor Law 1790–1930*, Newton Abbot, David and Charles, 1971.

——, *The Relief of Poverty 1834–1934*, London, Macmillan, 2nd edn 1986.

Rowntree, B. Seebohm, *Poverty: A Study of Town Life*, London, Macmillan, 1901.

——, *The Poverty Line, A Reply*, London, Macmillan, 1903.

——, *Poverty and Progress: A Second Social Survey of York*, London, Longman, 1941.

Royle, E., *Modern Britain: A Social Survey 1750–1985*, London, Edward Arnold, 1987.

Rule, J., *The Labouring Classes in Early Industrial England 1750–1850*, London, Longman, 1986.

—— (ed.), *British Trade Unionism 1750–1850: The Formative Years*, London, Longman, 1988.

Sanderson, Michael, *Education, Economic Change and Society in England 1780–1870*, London, Macmillan, 2nd edn 1991.

Sassoon, Siegfried, *Memoirs of an Infantry Officer*, London, Faber and Faber, 1930.

Saul, G.B., *The Myth of the Great Depression*, London, Macmillan, 2nd edn 1985.

Searl, G.R., *The Quest for National Efficiency: A Study in British Politics and Political Thought 1894–1914*, Oxford, Oxford University Press, 1971.

Sherriff, R.C., *Journey's End*, [1928] Harmondsworth, Penguin, 1983.

Simon, Brian, *Education and the Labour Movement*, London, Lawrence and Wishart, 1965.

Sims, R. (Mearns, Arthur), *The Bitter Cry of Outcast London*, [1883] Bath, Chivers, 1969.

Sked, Alan and Cook, Chris, *Post-War Britain: A Political History*, Harmondsworth, Penguin, 2nd edn 1984.

Skidelsky, R., *Politicians and the Slump*, London, Macmillan, 1967.

Smiles, Samuel, *Self-Help*, [1859] London, Murray, 1905.

Smith, F.B., *The People's Health 1830–1910*, London, Croom Helm, 1979.

Spalding, Francis, *Duncan Grant*, London, Chatto and Windus, 1997.

Stephens, W.B., *Education, Literacy and Society 1830–70: The Geography of Diversity in Provincial England*, Manchester, Manchester University Press, 1987.

Stevenson, John, *British Society 1914–45*, Harmondsworth, Penguin, 1984.

Strachey, Lytton, *Eminent Victorians*, London, Chatto and Windus, 1918.

Sturt, Mary, *The Education of the People*, London, Routledge and Kegan Paul, 1967.

Sutherland, Gillian, *Elementary Education in the Nineteenth Century*, London, Historical Association, 1971.

Swenarton, M., *Homes Fit for Heroes*, London, Heinemann Educational, 1981.

Symons, J., *The General Strike*, London, Cresset Press, 1957.

Taine, H.A., *Notes on England*, trans. W.E. Rae, London, Strahan, 1874.

Tarn, J.N., *Five Per Cent Philanthropy: An Account of Housing in Urban Areas Between 1840 and 1914*, Cambridge, Cambridge University Press, 1973.

Taylor, A.J.P., *English History 1914–1945*, Oxford, Clarendon Press, 1965.

Thane, Pat, *The Foundations of the Welfare State*, London, Longman, 1982.

Thomas, M.W., *The Early Factory Legislation*, Leigh-on-Sea, Thames Bank Publishing, 1958.

Thompson, D., *The Chartists*, Aldershot, Wildwood House, 1986.

Thompson, E.P., *William Morris, Romantic to Revolutionary*, London, Lawrence and Wishart, 1955.

——, *The Making of the English Working Class*, London, Gollancz, 1963.

Thompson, F.M.L., *The Rise of Respectable Society*, London, Fontana, 1988.

—— (ed.), *The Cambridge Social History of England 1750–1950*, Cambridge, Cambridge University Press, 1990.

Thompson, George, *Prize Essay upon the Sanitary Condition of the Town of Stourbridge*, Stourbridge, 1848.

Titmuss, R.M., *Problems of Social Policy*, London, HMSO, 1950.

——, *Essays on the Welfare State*, London, Allen and Unwin, 1958.

Tobias, J.J., *Crime and Industrial Society in the Nineteenth Century*, Harmondsworth, Penguin, 1972.

Tranter, N.L., *Population and Society, 1750–1940*, London, Longman, 1985.

Turner, Michael, *Enclosures in Britain, 1750–1830*, London, Macmillan, 1984.

Walton, John K., and Walvin, J. (eds), *Leisure in Britain 1780–1939*, Manchester, Manchester University Press, 1983.

Walvin, J., *Leisure and Society 1830–1950*, London, Longman, 1978.

Ward, J.T., *The Factory Movement*, London, Macmillan, 1962.

——, *The Factory System*, 2 vols, Newton Abbot, David and Charles, 1970.

Wardle, D., *English Popular Education 1780–1970*, Cambridge, Cambridge University Press, 1970.

Wearworth, R.F., *Methodism and the Struggle of the Working Classes 1850–1900*, Leicester, Backus, 1955.

Webb, B., *My Apprenticeship*, London, Longmans Green, 1926.

——, *Our Partnership*, ed. Barbara Drake and Margaret I. Cole, London, Longmans Green, 1948.

Webb, S., *The Restoration of Trade Union Conditions*, London, Nisbet, 1917.

Webb, S. and Webb, B., *The History of Trade Unionism*, London, Longmans Green, 1920.

——, *English Poor Law History*, London, Longmans Green, 1929.

Wells, H.G., *Anticipations*, Leipzig, Tauchnitz, 1902.

When We Build Again: A Study Based on Research into Conditions of Living and Working in Birmingham, Birmingham, Bourneville Village Trust, 1941.

Wiener, M.J., *English Culture and the Decline of the Industrial Spirit*, Cambridge, Cambridge University Press, 1981.

Williams, Karel, *From Pauperism to Poverty*, London, Routledge and Kegan Paul, 1981.

Wohl, A.S., *The Eternal Slum: Housing and Social Policy in Victorian London*, London, Arnold, 1977.

Wood, Robert, *The Population of Great Britain in the Nineteenth Century*, London, Macmillan, 1992.

Woodward, E.L., *The Age of Reform 1815–1870*, Oxford, Clarendon Press, 1938.

Wrigley, Chris, *Lloyd George*, Oxford, Blackwell, 1992.

Wrigley, E.A. and Schofield, R.S., *The Population History of England 1571–1871*, Cambridge, Cambridge University Press, 1981.

Articles

Armstrong, D.A., 'The countryside', in F.M.L. Thompson, *The Cambridge Social History of England, 1750–1950*, Vol. I, Cambridge, Cambridge University Press, 1990, 89–153.

Chinn, Carl, 'Was separate schooling a means of class segregation in late Victorian and Edwardian Birmingham?', *Midland History*, XIII (1988), 95–112.

Crafts, N.F.R., 'British economic growth, 1700–1831: a review of the evidence', *Economic History Review*, 2nd series, XXXVI:2, May (1983), 177–99.

Crafts, N.F.R. and Mills, T.C., 'Trends in real wages in Britain, 1750–1913', *Explorations in Economic History*, 31 (1994), 176–94.

Cunningham, Hugh, 'The employment and unemployment of children in England, c.1680–1851', *Past & Present*, 126, February (1990), 115–50.

Harris, Jose, 'Did British workers want the Welfare State? G.D.H. Cole's survey of 1942', in J. Winter (ed.), *The Working Class in Modern British History*, Cambridge, Cambridge University Press, 1983, 200–14.

——, 'Some aspects of social policy in Britain during the Second World War', in W.J. Mommsen (ed.), *The Emergence of the Welfare State in Britain and Germany*, London, Croom Helm, 1981, 247–62.

Hopkins, Eric, 'Tremenheere's prize schemes in the mining districts, 1851–59', *History of Education Society Bulletin*, 15, Spring (1975), 24–37.

——, 'Working-class housing in the smaller industrial town in the nineteenth century: Stourbridge – a case study', *Midland History*, 3–4 (1978), 230–54.

——, 'Working-class education in Birmingham during the First World War', in Roy Lowe (ed.), *Labour and Education: Some Early 20th Century Studies*,

Swansea, History of Education Society, 1981, 25–36.

——, 'Working hours and conditions during the Industrial Revolution: a reappraisal', *Economic History Review*, XXXV:1, February (1982), 52–66.

——, 'Working-class housing in Birmingham during the Industrial Revolution', *International Review of Social History*, XXXI (1986), Part I, 80–94.

——, 'Elementary education in Birmingham during the Second World War', *History of Education*, 18:3 (1989), 243–55.

——, 'Working-class life in Birmingham between the wars, 1918–1939', *Midland History*, XV (1990), 129–50.

——, 'Birmingham during the Industrial Revolution: class conflict or class cooperation?', *Research in Social Movements, Conflict and Change*, 16 (1993), 117–37.

——, 'The Victorians and child labour', *The Historian*, 48, Winter (1995), 10–14.

Leeson, R.A., 'Business as usual – craft union development 1834–51', *Bulletin of the Society for the Study of Labour History*, 49 (1984), 15–17.

Lindert, P.H. and Williamson, J.G., 'English workers' living standards during the Industrial Revolution', *Economic History Review*, 36 (1983), 1–25.

Mitchell, Margaret, 'The effects of unemployment on the social condition of women and children in the 1930s', *History Workshop*, Spring (1985), 105–25.

Oliver, W.H., 'The consolidated trades union of 1834', *Economic History Review*, 2nd series, XVII (1964–5), 77–95.

Orth, J.V., 'The legal status of English trade unions, 1799–1871', in A. Harding (ed.), *Law Making and Law Makers in British Society*, London, Royal Historical Society, 1980, 195–207.

Purvis, M., 'Cooperative retailing in England 1835–50: developments before Rochdale', *Northern History*, XXII (1986), 198–215.

Reid, Alastair, 'Intelligent artisans and aristocrats of labour: the essays of Thomas Wright', in Jay Winter (ed.) *The Working Class in Modern British History*, Cambridge, Cambridge University Press, 1983, 171–6.

Samuel, R., 'The workshop of the world: steam power and hand technology in Victorian Britain', *History Workshop*, 3 (1977), 6–72.

Smith, Harold D., 'The effect of the war on the status of women', in Harold L. Smith (ed.), *War and Social Change: British Society in the Second World War*, Manchester, Manchester University Press, 1986, 208–29.

Tawney, R.H., 'The economics of child labour', *Economic Journal* (1909), 517–53.

Thompson, E.P., 'Time, work discipline, and industrial capitalism', *Past & Present*, 38 (1967), 56–97.

Webster, Charles, 'Healthy or hungry thirties?', *History Workshop*, Spring (1982), 110–29.

Wrigley, E.A., 'The growth of population in eighteenth century England: a conundrum resolved', *Past & Present*, 98 (1983), 121–50.

Index

A Dream of John Ball 117
abolition of slavery 12
Abstract of Education Returns 43
accidents at work 189, 250
achievements of third Labour
  government 256–7
Acts of Parliament: Illegal Oaths
  Act, 1797 5; Combination Acts,
  1799, 1800 4; Factory Acts, 1816,
  1825, 1830, 1831 11; Sturge
  Bourne's Act, 1819 7; Reform
  Act, 1832 1, 5, 10, 12, 52, 254;
  Factory Act, 1833 4, 11, 36; Poor
  Law Amendment Act, 1834 8, 14,
  45, 87; Municipal Corporation
  Act, 1835 12, 15, 56; Merchant
  Shipping Act, 1835 48; County
  Police Act, 1839 56; Mines Act,
  1842 37; Factory Act, 1844 37;
  Factory Act, 1847 4, 37; Poor Law
  (Schools) Act, 1848 47; Public
  Health Act, 1848 34, 51;
  Nuisance Acts, 1848, 1855, 1860,
  1863 34; Disease Prevention Acts,
  1848, 1855 34; Factory Act, 1850
  37; Common Lodgings Acts,
  1851, 1853 34; Factory Act, 1853
  37; Friendly Societies Act, 1855
  67; Metropolitan Local Management Act, 1855 34; Bleach & Dye
  Works Act, 1860 37; Lace Act,
  1861 37; Public Works Act, 1863
  49, 70; Contagious Diseases Acts,
  1864, 1866, 1869 122; Factory
  Act, 1864 38; Sewer Utilisation
  Act, 1865 34; Sanitation Act,
  1866 34; Torren's Acts, 1866,
  1879 60; Reform Act, 1867 24,
  41, 53, 54; Factory Act, 1867 38;
  Workshop Act, 1867 38; Metro-
  politan Poor Act, 1867 48; Agri-
  cultural Gangs Act, 1867 90;
  Trade Union Funds Protection
  Act, 1869 67; Forster's Education
  Act, 1870 45, 77–8; Trade Union
  Act, 1871 67; Criminal Law
  Amendment Act, 1871 67;
  Factory Act, 1871 62; Secret
  Ballot Act, 1872 92; Public
  Health Act, 1872 58; Agricultural
  Children's Act, 1873 90; Public
  Health Act, 1875 59; Conspiracy
  & Protection of Property Act,
  1875 68; Employers & Workmen
  Act, 1875 68; Cross's Housing
  Act, 1875, 1879 60; Trade Union
  Act, 1876 68; Lord Sandon's Act,
  1876 78; Factory & Workshops
  Act, 1878 62; Married Women's
  Property Act, 1884 81, 122; Fran-
  chise Act, 1884 92; Technical
  Education Act, 1889 79; Housing
  of the Working Classes Act, 1890
  61; Prevention of Cruelty to Chil-
  dren Act, 1890 82; Salisbury's
  Education Act, 1891 79; Cruelty

to Children Act,1894 82; Factories & Workshops Act, 1901 63; Balfour's Education Act, 1902 80–1, 133, 136, 137, 177, 191; Unemployed Workmen Act, 1905 133–4, 143; Trades Disputes Act, 1906 140, 149; Education (Provision of Meals) Act, 1906 141; Workmen's Compensation Act, 1906 151; Small Holdings & Allotment Act, 1907 95; Education (Admin. Provisions) Act, 1907 141; Children's Act, 1908 141; Miners' Eight Hour Day Act, 1908 147; Old Age Pensions Act, 1908 141–2; Labour Exchanges Act, 1909 143, 236; Trade Boards Act, 1909 63, 143, 169; Town & Country Planning Act, 1909 95, 143; National Insurance Act, 1911 146–7, 157, 166, 192, 237; Shops Act, 1911 151; Parliament Act, 1911 144–5, 244; Minimum Wages Act, 1911 147; Trade Union Act, 1913 150–1; Cat & Mouse Act, 1913 152; Defence of the Realm Acts, 1914, 1915, 1916 160; Munitions of War Act, 1915 161, 203; Rent & Mortgage Interest Act, 1915 174; Military Service Acts, 1916, 1918 175; Corn Production Act, 1917 96; Representation of the People Act, 1918 170–1; Fisher's Education Act, 1918 176–7, 191, 238; Sex Disqualification (Removal) Act, 1919 171, 173; Mines Act, 1919 203; Addison's Housing Act, 1919 185; Restoration of Pre-War Practices Act, 1919 203; Agriculture Act, 1920 96; Chamberlain's Housing Act, 1923 185; Wheatley's Housing Act, 1924 185, 213; Unemployment Act, 1927 194; Trades Disputes & T.U. Act, 1927 209; Local Government Act, 1929 187; Housing Act, 1930 186; Abnormal Importations Act, 1931 196; Import Duties Act, 1932 196; Wheat Act, 1932 96; Unemployment Act, 1934 195; North Atlantic Shipping Act, 1934 196; British Shipping (Assistance) Act, 1935 196; Public Health Act, 1936 59; Factory Act, 1936 188; Livestock Industries Act, 1937 96; Holidays with Pay Act, 1938 189; Emergency Powers (Defence) Act, 1940 226; Catering Wages Act, 1943 227; Butler Education Act, 1944 191, 234, 238–9, 243; Family Allowances Act, 1945 202, 239–40, 243; Bank of England Act, 1946 243; Cable & Wireless Act, 1946 243; Civil Aviation Act, 1946 243; National Insurance Act, 1946 245; National Health Insurance Act, 1946 245; Coal Nationalisation Act, 1946 243; Housing Acts, 1946, 1949 248; Trade Union Act, 1946 209, 250; Electricity Act, 1947 244; Agriculture Act, 1947 98; Gas Act, 1947 244; Transport Act, 1947 244; Town & Country Planning Act, 1947 248; Factory Act, 1947 250; National Assistance Act, 1948 247

Addison, Dr Christopher 175
Addison, Paul 257
administrative momentum 16–17, 52
adoption of children 72
age of consent 81
agriculture 2, 81, 84–99; animal diseases 90; apprenticeship 90; arable farming 91, 98; ganging 90; housing 90, 92, 93, 94; marketing boards 96; output 91, 96–7, 98; wages 17, 92–3, 96; Wages Board 96; war production 96, 98, 22; wheat prices 91;

workers in 86–7, 92, 192, 195;
    workers' union 17, 68, 69, 92
air raids in World War I 178
air raids in World War II 228–9
Algeçiras crisis 153
All Quiet on the Western Front 221
Allen, William 41
alliance system 41
Amalgamated Engineers Union 204
Amalgamated Society of Engineers
    39, 40, 69, 109–10, 147
Amalgamated Society of Railway
    Servants 68, 110
American Civil War 41, 57
Andover workhouse 46
annual grant to education 42
Anti-Corn Law League 23, 85
Anglo-Catholicism 18–19
anti-poor law movement 8
Applegarth, Robert 65, 66
apprenticeship 10, 48
Apostle of Free Labour 109
approved societies 145, 187
Arch, Joseph 68, 92
Arlington, Richard 221
Arms and the Man 124
Army Bureau of Current Affairs 241
army educational tests 234–5
Arnold, F.T. 233
Arnold, Matthew 50, 55, 220
Arnott, James 28
Artisans, Labourers and General
    Dwellings Co. 60
Ashley, Lord 37
Aspects of the Social Problem 76
Ashton under Lyne 30
ASLEF 150
Asquith, Herbert 143, 145, 147, 151,
    152, 158, 162, 166, 174, 211, 212
Association Football 219
Astor, Lady 171
attics 26
Attlee, C.R. 216, 217, 222, 252
Attwood,Thomas 10, 53
Auden,W.H. 20, 221, 222
Austin Motor Company 189

Australian unions 104
Austria 57
Auxillary Territorial Service 226

back-to-back housing 26–7
Bacon Marketing Board 96
Barnsfather, Bruce 179
Baldwin, Stanley 97, 205, 206, 207,
    208, 209, 211, 214, 215, 222
Balfour, A.J. 133, 134, 135, 136,
    137, 155
Barnes, George 163, 164
Barnett, Canon 83
Barnett, Corelli 255
Barrack Room Ballads 125
Battle of Britain 225, 235
Beale, Miss 121
Beardsley, Aubrey 125
Beaverbrook, Lord 246
Bedeaux system 190
Bedfordshire 89
Beehive, The 40
Belgian neutrality 178
Bell, Richard 134
Bell, Vanessa 173
Bentham, Jeremy 13–14, 52
Benthamism 1, 13–14
Besant, Annie 103, 104, 106
Bessemer converter 57, 183
Bevan, Aneurin 245, 246, 247, 252,
    255
Beveridge Report 236–7, 238, 240,
    242, 243, 254
Beveridge, William 82, 143, 202,
    236, 238
Bevin, Ernie 205, 211, 226, 227,
    228, 237, 252
Birkenhead, Lord 206, 207
Birmingham 3, 10, 28, 29, 30, 41,
    60, 64, 78, 103, 176, 185, 186,
    189, 190, 201, 229, 233, 234
Birmingham Political Union 10
Birrell's education bill 137, 142
Bishop of Rochester 15
Bishop Auckland 192
Bitter Cry of Outcast London 60, 73

Black Country 10, 21, 38, 43, 63, 64, 69, 70, 123, 124, 143, 162
'Black Friday' 204
Blake, Sophia Jex 122
Blatchford, Robert 125
Blanesborough Committee 194
Blaug, Professor M. 49
Blitz, the 225, 228–9, 232, 235
Bloomsbury group 173
Blunden, Edmund 221
Board of Education 80, 141, 163, 233, 234, 235, 238
Boards of Guardians 47, 49, 59, 142, 156, 157, 193, 194
Boer War 93, 114, 119, 127, 133
Boer War recruits 128–9
Boiler Makers Society 66
Bondfield, Margaret 171
Bosanquet, Prof. B. 75, 76, 83, 107, 138
Bosanquet (née Dandy), Helen 75, 76, 83, 107, 123, 129–30, 134, 138, 139, 173
Booth, Charles 73, 75, 82, 120, 125, 138, 142
Booth, William 72, 74–5, 125, 139
Boulton & Watt engines 4, 25
Bourne, Dr John 179
Bracken, Brendan 246
Bradford 6, 108
Braxfield, Lord 152
brickmakers 89
Bright, John 23, 85, 86
Brighton Rock 223
Bristol 61, 200, 202, 229
Bristol University 122
British Broadcasting Company 208, 217
British Broadcasting Corporation 218
British Empire 114, 254
British & Foreign Schools Society 15
British Gazette 208
British Medical Association 145
British Socialist Society 149

British Sugar Corporation 96
Brook, Rupert 179
Bruce, William 163
Bryant & May Matchgirls Strike 103
Buckinghamshire 89
burial boards 35
Burn, Prof. W.L. 19, 50
Burnett, Prof. John 202–3
Burns, John 104, 140, 157
Burt, Thomas 67
Buss, Miss 121
Butler, Josephine 122
Butler, R.A. 238, 254

cabinet makers 39
Cadburys 189
Caird, Thomas 88
Campbell case 213
Camberwell 119, 121, 131
Cambridge University 121
Campbell-Bannerman 139, 143
Candida 125
Cardiff 66
Carlyle, Thomas 51, 54
Carpenter, Mary 122
Carson, Edward 140, 141
Case against Picketing 110
'Cassandra' 251
casualties in World War I 159
casualties in World War II 226
cattle diseases 90
Cavalcade 210
cellars 26
CEMA 232
Census Reports 124, 161
Central Agricultural Wages Board 227
Central Board of Health 28, 32–3
cess pools 27, 28
Chadwick, Edwin 14, 29, 31, 33, 34, 52
'chasing' 65
chainmakers 124
Chamberlain Circular 70–1,134
Chamberlain, Joseph 60, 70, 101, 133, 135, 136

Chamberlain, Neville 97, 207
Chambers, Prof. J.D. 25
Champion, H.H. 104
Chaplin, Charlie 72, 190
Charity commissioners 80
Charity Organisation Society 73, 82, 83, 107, 129, 134, 139, 141, 142, 156
charity schools 15
Charnock v. Court 109
chartism 1, 5, 18, 24, 39, 52–3, 54, 85, 100
Cheltenham Ladies College 121
Cheshire 87
Child of the Jago 131
child labour 11, 24, 62–3
children in agriculture 89–90, 92
Chinese Labour 135–6, 138
cholera 25, 28
Christian Socialists 53, 100, 101, 107, 117
Chivers Preservative Works 89
Christie, Agatha 224
Church of England 120
Church of England National Schools Society 45
Church, Prof. Roy 24
Church schools 42, 77, 78, 79–80, 238
'Church on the rates' 81, 136, 137
Churchill,Winston 94, 143, 146, 153, 154, 196, 207, 208, 235, 237, 241, 242, 246
cigarette smoking 173, 219
cinema going 197, 218–19
Citrine, Sir W. 211
Clarion, The 125
class conflict 9, 24, 118, 204, 210, 220
class war 100, 112, 125
Clause Four 165, 166, 213, 217, 243, 248
Clydeside 150, 168
Clynes, J.R. 212
coal mining 2, 57, 160, 183, 203, 204, 228

Cobbett, William 49
Cobden, Richard 23, 85, 86
Cockerton's Judgement 80
collectivism x, 83, 106, 137, 138, 153, 158, 160, 161, 166
Collison, William 109
commerce 170
Committee of Privy Council for Education 16, 42, 44
Communist Manifesto 54, 101
Communist Party of GB 105, 149, 166, 197, 198, 214
communitarianism 100
compulsory school attendance 78–9
Condition of England 220
Condition of the Working Class in England 18, 29
Congress of Trades Unions 67
conscientious objectors 160, 164, 177–8, 226
conscription 160, 161, 162, 164, 226
Conservative Party 133, 135, 136, 137, 242, 252, 254
'contracting-out' 151, 209, 250
Constitutional Conference 145, 154
Control of Engagements Order 250
Cook, A.J. 205, 206
co-operative movement 10, 52, 100
corn imports from America 90–1
corn laws 1, 84
cottage homes 71
cotton famine 41, 47, 49, 57, 70
cotton industry 2, 3, 4, 182–3
council schools 80
County Agricultural Committees 96
County Councils 79
county secondary schools 80, 81, 191, 238
'Coupon' Election 211
Coventry 229
Cowper-Temple clause 77
Crafts, Prof. N.F.R. 25
crèches 82
cricket 231
crime rates 56
Cripps, Sir Stafford 249, 251, 252

Cromwell's Letters and Speeches 54
Crook 193
Crossman, R.H.S. 254
Crown & Summit Budget 23
Culture and Anarchy 55
Cumbria 183
Curzon, Lord 97
cycling 124, 219

Daily Herald 219
Daily Mail 125, 146, 172, 188, 214
Dalton, Hugh 249
dairy farming 91
Dangerfield, G. 148
Darwin, Charles 50, 82
Das Kapital 54, 83, 101, 116
Dawes Committee Conference 213
Death of a Hero 221
death rates 28, 187
Decline and Fall 223
deep drainage 31, 33, 59, 62
Denmark 142
Democratic Federation 105
Department of Information 178
Department of Science & Art 79, 80
depressed areas 183, 184, 192, 197,
    199, 224
Despard, Mrs 152
Derby Scheme 161
'Devilsdust' 53
Devon 89
Dickens, Charles 48, 51
dilution 161, 169
direction of labour 250
disarmament 163, 222
Disenchantment 221
Disraeli, Benjamin 24, 41, 53, 54,
    60, 70, 86, 258
district schools 47
Docker's Tanner 103, 104
Dock, Wharf, Riverside & General
    Labourers Union 104
Doherty, John 4, 5
dole, the 183, 184, 194, 198, 209,
    215, 219
doormat incident 164

domestic employment 123, 170, 192
'Dover Beach' 50
dreadnaught battleships 138, 143
Dublin 6, 147
Duke of Bedford 93
Dunkirk 225, 235, 240, 241
Durham 184, 187
Durham University 121

earth closets *see* privies
East Fulham by-election 222
early school leaving 63, 175–6
Eastern counties 87
Economist, The 32
Edinburgh 60
educational retardation 234–5
Edward VII 145
eight-hour day 147, 188
electrical power 184
emigration to colonies 138
Eminent Victorians 220
Empire casualties in World War I
    159
Employers Federation of Engineer-
    ing Associations 109
Employers Parliamentary Council
    110
enclosure movement 87–8
Engels, F. 18, 29, 30, 53, 105
engineering 169
England after War 220
England for All 105
English at War, The 251
English Journey 183
ENSA 232
Ensor, R.C.K. 135, 148
Equality 55
equitable labour exchanges 10
Essay on Population 12–13
Essex 87, 89
eugenics 119
evacuation of schools 233, 234
evening classes 79
Educational & Vocational Training
    241
export controls 160

extended benefit 194

Fabian Essays 106, 112, 117, 125
Fabian Society 75, 105–7, 108, 111, 112
factories 2, 17, 250
factory inspectors 11, 38
factory reform 11–12, 17
factory welfare services 227
family allowances 200, 236, 237
family limitation 122, 172
family relationships 123
Farringdon St 111
Fels, Joseph 73
fertilisers 88
Festival of Britain 252
Fever Reports 28
Fielden, John 37
film industry 219
Finnegan's Wake 223
First Grant to Education 12, 15, 42
First Round Table Conference 214
First Men on the Moon 124
flappers 174
Fleming Report 245
flight from the land 87
flying bombs 229, 234
Food, Health and Income 200
food rationing 160, 230, 235, 251
football 219
football pools 219
Forster, W.E. 173
Fourteen Points 164, 179
France 57, 150, 225
Fraser, Rev. James 44
free school meals 141, 188
free trade 12, 23, 52, 85, 133, 195, 196, 212
French Revolution 10, 54
French Wars, 1793–1815 7, 13, 26
friendly societies 141, 145, 166
frozen meat imports 91
From the Abyss 131

Gaitskell, Hugh 165, 252, 254
Garden City Movement 95

Garvin, G.L. 207
Gaskell, Mrs E. 18
gas lighting 30
Gay Divorce, The 224
Geddes Axe 177, 196
George, David Lloyd 94, 142, 143, 145, 146, 147, 152, 153, 154, 155, 160, 163, 166, 169, 174, 175, 185, 188, 203, 211
General Council of the TUC 205, 206, 208, 210
general elections 136, 137, 144, 145, 149, 211, 212, 214, 215, 217, 241–2, 252, 252–3
General Federation of TUs 110
General Railway Workers Union 150
General Strike of 1842 21
General Strike, 1926 194, 206–10, 214
Germany 57, 142, 143, 178, 183, 220, 221, 225, 229, 241
Gilbert, A.G. 9
Gissing, George 82
Girls Public Day School Trust 121
Girton College 121
Gladstone, Herbert 135
Gladstone, W.E. 41, 70, 78, 83, 113, 116, 131
Glasgow 5, 6, 28, 60
gloving industry 89
gold, shortage of 58
Gold Standard 196–7, 205, 216
Goodbye to All That 221
Good Companions, The 223
Gordon, General 220
Graham, Sir J. 45
Grand General Union of Cotton Spinners 5
Grand National Consolidated TU 5
grammar schools 191, 239
Graves, Robert 221
Great Depression 57–8, 68–70, 81, 101, 177, 182–4, 194, 198
Great Exhibition 23, 51, 60
Great Famine 85

Great Scourge, The 152
Great War ix, 121, 129, 148, 155, 159–81
Green Book, The 235
Greene, Graham 223, 241
Greenwood, Walter 198
greyhound racing 219
Guilty Men 241

Hadleigh, Essex 72
Hadow Report 191, 238
Haggard, H. Rider 89, 94
Halifax 109
Halévy, Elie 8, 9
Hammond, Mr & Mrs J.L. 25
Handley, Tommy 231
handloom weavers 3, 4
Hannington,Wal 198
Harcourt, Sir W. 125
Hardie, Keir 102, 104, 105, 108, 111, 112, 113, 117, 134, 145, 149
Hard Times 18, 51
Harris, Jose 237
Harrison, Frederic 65, 66
Headlam, Stewart D., Rev. 130
Health of Towns Association 31
health of recruits 175, 180, 200
health services 123, 187, 236
Heart of the Empire, The 119, 127
Henderson, Arthur 149, 162, 163, 164, 211, 212
Heroes and Hero Worship 54
Hertfordshire 89
Hi Gang 231
higher grade schools 79, 80
highway boards 35
hiking 219
History of Trade Unions 125
Hobson, John H. 82, 83, 117–19
'Hodge' 92, 98–9
holidays 189
Holland, Scott, Canon 130
Holmes, James 110
home investment 58
Home Rule 70, 95, 113, 131, 137, 151, 152

Hornby v. Close 64, 66–7
hospitals, voluntary 48, 187, 188, 246
House of Lords 137, 142, 144, 145, 244, 254
house rents 174, 230
housing 26–7, 36, 59–62, 139, 143, 184, 185–7, 229, 240, 247–8, 253
housing by-laws 62
housing, rural 93, 155
Howell, George 68
Hudson, George 19
Hughes, Thomas 65, 66
Hull 109
hunger marches 183, 198
hungry forties 21
Huskisson, William 84, 85
Huxley, Thomas 50, 115, 124
Hyndman, H.M. 75, 82, 105

idealism in World War I 178
immigration into towns 17
imperialism 114, 119, 127
Import Duties Advisory Comittee 196
improvement commissioners 30, 35
income tax 159
Independent Labour Party 108, 109, 111, 149, 163
India 104, 183
individualism x, 12, 138, 158
Industrial Democracy 125
industrialisation ix, x, 1, 2, 7, 8, 9, 10, 17, 19, 21, 22, 23, 123, 125, 152, 157, 158, 159, 162, 180, 181, 184, 186, 190, 212, 217, 224, 240
Industrial Revolution ix, 2, 6, 23
industries, staple 2–3, 57, 160, 180, 182–3, 184, 192
industry in countryside 89
In Darkest England & the Way Out 72
infant mortality 187, 199, 229–30
insurance companies 145, 146
Interdepartmental Comittee on Physical Degeneration 129, 141
Ireland 85

Irish nationalists 144, 151
iron founders 3
iron industry 2–3, 57
Is the Parliamentary Labour Party a Failure? 149
Italy 183
ITMA 231

Japan 180, 183, 225, 242
Jazz Singer, The 218
Jarrow 183, 186, 198, 199
jerry builders 26
Joint Production Committees 227
Jolly George incident 204
Journey's End 221
Joyce, James 223
junta, the 41, 54, 66

Kay, James 28, 42
Keep the Home Fires Burning 172
Keynes, J.M. 197, 216, 235, 243
'Khaki' Election 127, 134
Killing No Murder 147
King George V 145, 212, 215, 219
Kingsley, Charles 53
Kingstanding estate 186, 201–2
Kipling, Rudyard 125
Korean War 252

Labour and the New Social Order 165
labour colonies 72–3, 95, 117
labour exchanges 134, 143, 157, 236
Labour governments 185, 186, 194, 196, 199, 205, 212–13, 214–15, 242–57
Labourism 166
Labour Party 105, 111, 137, 144, 149, 150, 162, 163, 164, 165, 166, 177, 180, 198, 209, 211, 212, 214, 215, 216, 217, 222, 223, 236, 237, 239, 242
Labour Representation Committee 111, 134, 135, 137, 149, 164
Labour Representation League 41
lace making, rural 89

Lady Margaret Hall 121
laissez-faire 16, 33, 51, 54
Laindon, Essex 73
Lancashire 4, 21, 40, 47, 87, 110
Lancet, The 48
Land Campaign 95, 155
Land Enquiry Committee 94
Land Problem 94
Land Nationalisation Society 155
land taxes 153
Land, The 94
Lansbury, George 72, 139, 156, 217, 222
Larkin, Jim 147
Larkrise to Candleford 92
Law, A. Bonar 211
law of conspiracy 4
leaving certificates 161
League of Nations 221, 222
League of Nations Peace Ballot 222
Leeds 28, 60
Leeds Mercury 32
Leeds University 122
leisure activities 231–3
Lend-Lease Agreement 225
Lenin 112
Less Eligibility rule 8, 46
Let Us Face the Future 242, 248, 253, 255
Lewis, C. Day 221
Liberalism 154
Liberals and the countryside 93–5
Liberal Party 110, 113–14, 126, 135, 136, 137, 139, 144, 151, 153, 166, 211, 212, 213, 214, 215, 217
Lib-Labs 101, 108, 110, 135, 137
Life & Labour of the People in London 73–5
Lindert & Williamson 2
Link, The 103
literacy 42, 43, 44
Liverpool 60, 147, 203, 233, 234
Liverpool, Lord 16
Liverpool University 122
livestock farming 91
living conditions *see* housing

Llanelly 147
local boards of health 35
Local Government Board 33, 46, 58
Loch, C. S. 73
lodgings 26
Lombroso, Cesare 82
London 10, 28, 32, 39, 40, 41, 47, 48, 60, 61, 64, 67, 70, 73–5, 78, 82, 102, 106, 111, 115, 120, 128, 143, 147, 152, 183, 184, 186, 193, 199, 200, 203, 204, 217, 228–9, 229, 247
London County Council 108
Londonderry, Lord 36
London Docks Strike 71, 103–4
London Gas Workers Union 68
London, Jack 132
London Manufacturers' Relief Fund 22
London Naval Conference 214
London School of Economics 107, 236
London School Board 78, 141
London Trades Council 41
London University 121
London Working Men's Association 5
looting 229
Love on the Dole 198
Lowe, Robert 44, 78
Lye 70
Lye Waste 29
Lynn, Vera 232
Lyons v. Wilkins 109

MacArthur, Mary 124
McBrier, Professor A.M. 139
MacDonald, Alexander 64, 67
MacDonald, James Ramsay 111, 135, 149, 163, 210, 211, 212, 213, 214, 215, 216
MacNeice, Louis 221
malnutrition 198, 201
Malthus, Thomas 12–13, 15, 52
Manchester 4, 9, 10, 28, 29, 46, 48, 66, 233

Manchester Guardian 162
Manchester Trades Council 67
Manchester University 122
Major Barbara 130
Mann, Tom 102, 103, 104, 107, 150
Manning, Cardinal 104
Mansion House Committee 104
Marconi Scandal 155
market gardening 91
Markiewitcz, Countess 171
Marquand, D. 216
married women at work 124
Marshall Aid 249
Marshall, Alfred 57
Marx, Eleanor 104
Marx, Karl 8, 53–4, 105, 222
Mary Barton 18
Masterman, Charles F.G. 95, 119–21, 125, 127, 131, 139, 153, 154, 155, 178, 220
Maurice, Frederick 53, 128
Mathias, Peter 2, 68–9
May Comittee 215
Mayhew, Henry 34, 75
McKenna duties 196, 213
means test 183, 188, 194–5
mechanisation 3
mechanised farm machinery 97, 98
medical officers of health 59
Medical Planning Commission 235
Melbourne, Lord 16
Memoirs of an Infantry Officer 221
Merrie England 125
Merseyside 200, 229
Merthyr Tydfil 50, 108
metalware 23–24, 170
methodism 8, 9, 125
Metropolitan Police 56
miasmas 31
midden heaps 27, 35
middle-class recreation 217
middle classes under Labour 251–2
Midlands 21, 46, 89, 184
Midland Iron & Steel Wages Board 40
migration to towns 26, 86, 87

Mill, James 15
Mill, John Stuart 16, 52, 122
Miller, Glen 232
Million Pound Fund 49
Millwall Docks 103
Milk Marketing Board 96
Miners Association of GB and
  Ireland 39
Miners' Next Step, The 150
Ministry of Fuel & Power 228
Ministry of Health 175, 185
Ministry of Munitions 160
Ministry of Production 226
Ministry of Reconstruction 175, 237
Ministry of Supply 226
Minority Report of R.C. on Labour,
  1891 102
model unionism 3 9–40
monarchy, position of 19
Money, L.G. Chiozza 132–3, 140
Montague, C.E. 179, 180, 221
Morant, Robert 141
Morgan, Prof. K.C. 248, 254
Morning Chronicle 33
Morpeth 67
Morpeth, Lord 32
Morris, William 105, 106, 115–17
Morrison, Herbert 224, 248, 252
mortality rates 28, 118
Mosley, Oswald 197, 215
motor cars 124, 184
Mowat, C.L. 183, 205
Mowbray 30
Mrs Dalloway 223
municipal socialism 112, 131
munitions 160, 161, 162, 167,
  169–70, 180
Murder of Roger Ackroyd, The 224
Music While You Work 189, 227

nailers 3, 22, 70
National Arbitration Tribunal 226
National Association for the Protec-
  tion of Labour 5
National Debt 160

national degeneration 82, 93, 95,
  118–19, 139, 175
National Education League 78
National Federation of Women
  Workers 124
National Free Labour Association
  109
National Government 194, 215
National Union of Gasworkers 103
National Health Service 246, 248,
  252
National Insurance benefit 247, 253
National Insurance Commission
  155
national insurance scheme 145–6
National Production Advisory
  Council 227
National Union of Ironworkers 69
National Union of Mineworkers 69
National Union of Railwaymen 150
National Register 161
National Service 226
National Transport Workers Associa-
  tion 150
nationalisation 203, 207, 213, 242,
  243, 244, 245, 252, 253
National Unemployed Workers
  Movement 198
Newcastle Programme 131
Newcastle speech 144
New Connection 19
New Deal 196, 197
New Industries 184
New Liberalism 137, 139, 140, 153,
  158, 197
Newman, John 18, 60
New Model Unionism 68, 71, 102,
  104
Newnham College 121
News From Nowhere 116
news reels 218
New Statesman 171–2
New Unionism 71, 101, 104, 111,
  112
New Zealand 142
Next Five Years Group 223

Nine Hours Day 68
Nightingale, Florence 122, 220
Norfolk 87
North and South 18
North London Collegiate School
121
Northumberland 87, 184, 187
Norwood Report 238
Nottingham Board of Arbitration
40
nursery education 234

Oastler, Richard 11
occupations 1
O'Connor, Feargus 39, 101
Odgers, George 64
office employment 123, 174
old age pensions 82, 137, 138, 188
Old World and the New, The 236
Oliver Twist 48
Operative Plumbers 69
Organisation For the Maintenance
of Supplies 205
Origin of Species 50
Orr, Sir John 200–1
Orwell, George 197–8, 223
Osborne Case 148–9
outdoor relief 8, 47, 49, 71, 194,195
out-of-work donations 193
overcrowding 27, 60–1, 120
Owen, Robert 5, 10, 100, 113
Owen, Wilfred 179
Oxford 186
Oxford Movement 18–19
Oxford Union 222

Pall Mall 70
Pall Mall Gazette 73
Pankhurst, Christabel 152
parliament bill 144–5
Parliamentary Committee of TUC
67, 68, 101, 104–5, 110, 140
parliamentary enclosures 25, 87–8
Parliamentary Labour Party 149,
211
parliamentary salaries 149, 158

part-time school attendance 63, 176
paternalism 10
patronage 16
payment by results 44, 77
Peabody Trust 60
Peace of Vereniging 127
Peace Pledge Union 222
peasant proprietorship 102
Peel, Sir Robert 23, 56, 85, 86
Peers v. the People 144
Pelling, Henry 149
People's Budget 96, 138, 143–4, 154
People of the Abyss 132
Perkin, Harold 9
Peterloo 9
'phoney war' 225
picketing 65–6, 141, 209
Pitt, William 15
Place, Francis 11
pleasure-pain principle 13
ploughing by steam 88
Plug Plot 21
poison gas 223
police forces 56
Political & Economic Planning 223
Poor Law apprenticeship 48
Poor Law Board, 1847 46, 48
Poor Law Commissioners 28
Poor Law infirmaries 48, 187
Poor Laws and Pauper Management
14
Poor Law, New 8, 14, 18, 45–9,
71–2, 133, 155–7, 181, 187, 193,
194, 195, 247
Poor Law, Old 1, 7
Poplar Board of Guardians 72, 157
population 1, 6, 7, 12, 17, 25
potato blight 85
Potter, George 40
poverty cycle 128
poverty, extent of 18, 72, 74, 102,
138, 153, 185, 198–203, 251
poverty, primary 127, 148
poverty, secondary 127, 128
Poverty, a Study of Town Life 127
prefabricated buildings 247

Pre-Raphaelites 115
prescription charges 252
Preston 5, 6, 27
prices 93, 170, 184, 199, 230, 251
Priestley, J.B. 183, 223, 240, 241
primitive methodism 19
Prince Albert 23
Principles of Political Economy 16
printers 39
privies 27, 28, 35
professional classes 53
Prize Essay ... Stourbridge, 1848 30, 34
Prize Scheme in the Mining Districts 44
Problem of the Unemployed 117
Proper Sphere of Government 52
protection *see* tariff reform
Prussia 57, 78
Public Assistance Committees 156, 194, 195, 199, 247
public health 58–9, 62
public houses 219
public relief works 15, 49, 70, 118, 195, 196
public schools 245, 254
Pugh, Arthur 208
puritanism 55

Queen Mary 196
Queenswood 10

radicalism 9–10
radio licences 218
railways 19, 57, 88–9, 147, 154, 160, 203, 219, 244
Railway Clerks Association 150
railway mania 19, 23
rattening 65
rearmament 182, 192
'Red Friday' 205
Red Republican 101
reform 1
Regional Boards of Industry 227
Registrar of Friendly Societies 66
Reith, John 208, 218
religious census 50

religious idealism 178
religious observance 8, 18, 50, 114
Remarque, R.M. 221
repeal of the corn laws 85–6
Report on Workhouse Dietries 49
Report on health of munition workers 170
Reports of Poor Law Commissions 28, 156–7
Report on the Sanitary Condition of the Labouring Population of GB 29
residuum, the 53, 62, 76, 82, 129
retail shops 58, 63, 82, 123
Rhondda, the 193
Ricardo, David 13, 15
Rich and Poor 129
Riches and Poverty 132–3
Road to Wigan Pier, The 223
Roberts, G.H. 163
Robbins, Prof. Keith 253, 255
Rochdale 168
Rochdale Pioneers 10, 52
Rockets (V2s) 229, 234
Rosebery, Lord 138
Rossetti, D.G. 115
Rowntree, B.S. 75, 82, 127, 199–200, 251
Royal Commissions: Poor Law, 1832 7; Children's Employment, 1840 36, 89–90; Health of Towns, 1843 29l; Newcastle, 1858 44, 77, 78; Children's Employment, 1862 37–8; Agriculture, 1867 90; Trade Unions, 1867 65; Sanitation, 1869 58; Labour Laws, 1874 68; Factories & Workshops, 1876 62; Richmond, 1879 91; Working Class Housing, 1885 61; Great Depression, 1886 57–8; Elementary Education, 1889 80; Labour, 1891 63, 102; Agricultural Depression, 1893 91; Bryce, 1894 80; Aged Poor, 1895 137; Trade Unions, 1902 136; Poor Laws, 1905 73, 130, 133, 134, 139,

155–7; Sankey, 1919 203, 243;
Samuel, 1926 205, 206
Rushkin, John 54
Russell, Lord John 17, 44
Russell, Bertrand 178
Russian Entente 153
Russian revolutions 163, 166

Sadler, Michael 37
St Monday 64
sale of landed estates 97
Salisbury, Lord 97, 125, 133
Salvation Army 72
Samuel, Sir Herbert 205, 208, 215
Samuel Memorandum 208
Sankey, Lord 215
sanitary districts 58–9
sanitary law 59
Sassoon, Siegfried 179, 221
Saturday half-day 217
sawgrinders 65
scattered homes 71
scavenging 27
school attendance 43, 44, 77, 79,
175–6, 233
school boards 77, 80, 81
school fees 43, 77, 79, 176, 238,
239, 245
school leaving age 79, 175, 176,
191, 238, 245
Schoolmaster, The 78
school meals 141, 176, 201, 234
school medical inspections 141, 176
schools, private 42
Scoop 223
Scotland 186, 187
Scottish Labour Party 108
Scraggs, Thomas 88
scythe, the 88
secondary education 80, 177, 191,
192, 234, 239
Secondary Education for All 191
Secondary Modern schools 191,
238, 239
sectionalism 40

Select Committees: Poor Law, 1815,
1824 7; Manufacturers' Employ-
ment,1830 3–4, 258; trade unions,
1838 6; Health of Towns, 1840
29; Poor Law, 1846 46; Sweating
System, 1888 63, 123; Rothschild,
1896 137; Chaplin, 1899 137;
Physical Deterioration, 1904 129,
141
self-help 12, 51
Self-Help Emigration Society 117
Senior, Nassau 11, 15
Shaftesbury, Lord 52
Shaw, George Bernard 105, 117,
124, 130
Shaxby, W. J. 110
Sheffield 39, 66, 71–2
Sheffield Outrages 64–6
Sheffield University 122
Sheldon 193
Shells & Fuses Agreement 161
shipbuilding 183
shipping federation 109
shop stewards movement 168–9
shortage of army equipment 167
shortage of teachers 176, 233, 234
shorthand typists 172
Shrewsbury 30–1, 186
Siemen's Open Hearth Process 57
Simon, Sir John 34–5, 52
Sims, George (Arthur Mearns) 60
size of works 189–90
Slaney, R.A. 29
slavery, abolition of 12
sliding scales 40–1, 84
slum clearance 155
slumps 3–4, 21–2, 57–8, 68–70, 101,
177, 182–4, 198
Skidelsky, Prof. R. 216
Smiles, Samuel 51
Smith, Adam 12, 15, 41
Smith, Southwood 25, 28, 31, 52
Snowden, Philip 148, 163, 211, 213,
215
social Darwinism 76, 83

Social Democratic Federation 75, 105, 108, 111, 116, 149
Socialism in England 130
socialism 76, 83, 100, 105, 106, 113, 125, 126, 131, 132, 154, 241, 248–9, 253, 258
Socialist League 105, 116–17
social security 236, 237
Social Statics 52
Society of Railway Servants 134, 150
Somerset 89
Somerville College 121
Southampton 147, 229
South Metropolitan Gas Co. 103
South Staffs coalfield 69
South Wales 87, 150, 168, 199, 229
Soviet Union 204, 213, 221, 235, 241
Spanish Civil War 222
Speaker's Conference 171
special areas 183, 196, 202
speedway racing 219
Speenhamland system 7, 48
Spencer, Herbert 52
Spender, Stephen 221
spiritualism 179
spivs 251
sports 64
Stafford 67
Staffordshire 5, 87
Stamford, Lord 22
Standard of Life, The 129
standard of living 19, 58, 68, 82, 153, 170, 176, 184, 199, 230, 251, 256
Stanley, H.M. 72
Statement of War Aims 164, 179
Statute of Westminster 214
Steam Engine Makers Society 39
steam power 3, 88, 89
steam shipping 86
steel 57
Stockton on Tees 184
Stourbridge 21–2, 29, 30, 34, 35, 59, 61–2, 69–70

Stourbridge Improvement Commissioners 35
Stourbridge Manufacturers' Relief Fund 22
Strachey, Lytton 178, 220
Strange Death of Liberal England 148
straw plaiting 89
strikes 41, 64, 147, 161, 168, 203, 204, 209, 210–11, 226, 227–8, 250
Subjection of Women 122
'submerged tenth' 82, 120, 127–8
Suffolk 87
suffragette movement 95, 122, 152, 170
Sunday schools 42
suicide rates 198
surplus value 116
sweated industries 62–3, 123
Swing Riots 88
Sybil, or The Two Nations 18, 30, 53, 258
syndicalism 149, 168, 169, 207

Taff Vale Railway Case 134, 135
Taine, Hippolyte 46
talkies 218
tariff reform 133, 136, 138, 216
Taylor, A.J.P. 163, 210, 215, 231
Taylorism 190
teacher training 42, 245
technical schools 239
television 218
Temperton v. Russell 109
tenement occupancy 26, 60
Ten Hour Day 36
textile industry 11, 23
Thane, Pat 237
The Reformers' Prayer 9
The Social Problem: Life & Work 118
The Strength of the People: A Study in Social Economics 129
Thomas, Jimmy 204, 205, 212, 213, 215
Thompson, E.P. 8, 117
Thompson, Prof. F.M.L. 36, 49
Thorne, Will 103

threshing machines 88
threshing by steam 88
Time Machine, The 124
Tillett, Ben 103, 107, 149
Times, The 9, 32–3, 220
Titmus, Prof. R. 253
To the Lighthouse 223
Tolpuddle Martyrs 5
Tonypandy 147, 150
Tow Law 192
tractors 97, 98
Tract XC 18
trade cards 162
trades councils 41, 105
trade combinations *see* trade unions
trade unions 4, 5, 6, 38–42, 64–9,
    71, 109, 162, 163, 166, 167, 180,
    203–11, 213, 240, 245
trade union membership 39, 40, 68,
    71, 114, 203, 204, 210, 227, 250
Trades Union Congress 102, 110,
    142, 149, 162
transitional benefit 194, 195
Transport & General Workers
    Union 204, 205, 211, 227
transportation 170
Treasury Agreement 161
Tremenheere, H.S. 44, 90
Triple Alliance 150, 204, 205
Trollope v. London Trades Federation
    109
True Sun 36
tuberculosis 145, 188
Tufnell, E.C. 47–8, 90
Tunbridge Wells 121
Two Minutes Silence 159
typhoid 18
typhus 18

U-boat attacks 96, 160
Ulysses 223
uncovenanted benefit 193
Undertones of War 221
unemployment 1, 18, 58, 69, 72, 76,
    82, 95, 117, 118, 138, 139, 146,
    153, 157, 158, 166, 177, 181, 182,
    184, 185, 192–8, 202, 212, 214,
    215, 220, 223, 227, 230, 235, 236,
    243, 249, 255, 258
Unemployment Assistance Board
    195, 199
Unemployment Grants Committee
    196
unemployment insurance 4, 146,
    192, 193, 194, 195, 245
Union of Democratic Control 163,
    164, 177, 178, 211
Union of General and Municipal
    Workers 204–5
United Factory Textile Workers
    Association 110
United States of America 150, 160,
    180, 197, 225, 243
University of Birmingham 122, 178
University of Wales 122
upper-class leisure interests 217
urban conditions 17, 18, 24–5, 75–6
urban mortality 28
urban transport 219
Uthwatt Report 236
utilitarianism 14

Variety Bandbox 231
Victorians, the ix, 1
Vile Bodies 223
Voluntary Aid Committees 156
voluntary services 156
votes for women 122, 151–2, 170–1

wage agreements, national 169
wage freeze 249, 250, 252
wages, real 64, 91, 101, 148, 184,
    199, 217, 230, 251
Wales 187, 193
Wallis, Graham 105
Wall Street Crash 182, 215
War Agricultural Committees 97
War in the Air 124
War of the Worlds 124
war pensions 160
Warwickshire 87
Water Babies 53

water closets 28
Waterlow's Improved Industrial
    Dwellings Co. 60
water power 3
water supply 7, 27
Waugh, Evelyn 223
Waves, The 223
Wealth of Nations 12
Webb, Beatrice 5, 39, 40, 41, 76, 82,
    83, 105, 107, 113, 115, 125, 133,
    138, 139, 146, 149, 156, 157, 173
Webb, Sidney 5, 39, 40, 41, 82, 83,
    105, 106, 107, 112, 125, 130, 131,
    133, 138, 146, 157, 167–8, 243
welfare state 157, 237, 243–57, 258
Wells, H.G. 82, 105, 124
West Auckland 193
West Ham 108
West Midlands 184
Westminster 61
Whitley committees 169
wheat prices 84, 86, 91, 96, 98
'whisky money' 79
'white paper chase' 238
widows' & orphans' pensions 146,
    188
Wilde, Oscar 124
Wilson, Harold 165
Wilson, Havelock 108
Windsor Castle 28
wireless broadcasting 197, 217
Wodehouse, P.G. 223
Wolverhampton 70
Women's Auxiliary Army Corps 172
Women's Auxiliary Air Force 226

Women's Freedom League 152
Women's Land Army 97, 172
Women, middle-class 172–4
women miners 36–7
Women's Royal Naval Service 226
Women's Social & Political Union
    122, 152
women's social roles 1 21–4, 171–4,
    230–1
women trade unionists 124
women's wages 170, 230
women's war-time jobs 169–70,
    230–1
Woolf, Virginia 223
woollen industry 3
Worcester 89
Worcestershire Chronicle 22
work discipline 190
Workers' Playtime 227
Workhouse Test 8, 46, 49
workhouse children 47
working conditions 62–4, 167–8,
    188–90, 227, 250
working-class recreation 218–20
working hours 188–9, 217, 249
workshops 3, 123

Yellow Book, The 125
York 75, 82, 127, 199–200, 251
Yorkshire 87
Young Plan 214
Youth Hostel Association 219

Zinoviev Letter 214